Arthur N. Wiens, Ph.D.
Department of Medical Psychology
University of Oregon Medical School
Portland 1, Oregon

6 75

EX
Libris

Arthur N. Wiens, Ph.D.

The
Dynamics
of
Interviewing

The Dynamics of Interviewing

THEORY, TECHNIQUE, AND CASES

Arthur N. Wiens, Ph.D.
Department of Medical Psychology
University of Oregon Medical School
Portland 1, Oregon

ROBERT L. KAHN

CHARLES F. CANNELL

Survey Research Center, University of Michigan

NEW YORK · JOHN WILEY & SONS, INC.

London

FIFTH PRINTING, APRIL, 1961

Copyright © 1957 by John Wiley & Sons, Inc.

All rights reserved. This book or any part thereof must not be reproduced in any form without the written permission of the publisher.

Library of Congress Catalog Card Number: 57-8890

Printed in the United States of America

Preface

One of the things which authors should do in a preface is specify the audience for which they are writing. For a book on interviewing, this is a difficult thing to do. There are many fields in which interviewing is either the major professional technique or an important auxiliary skill. Such fields include medicine, journalism, law, social work, and the research aspects of the social sciences. In addition, there are the applied areas of survey research and market research, and important segments of management and business administration. There is considerable agreement that good management depends to a large extent on the character and the amount of communication between supervisor and subordinate. Moreover, we are convinced that people already in these fields, as well as students preparing to enter them, are interested in learning to interview effectively or in improving their interviewing skills. We have therefore attempted to write about the theory and practice of interviewing in a way that will be meaningful for both students and practitioners in these diverse fields. What these people have in common, we believe, is a growing awareness that their professional success depends to a considerable extent on their ability to obtain information from others.

Our own interests in interviewing have developed from a number of sources. We are both psychologists—one of us with a background in social psychology, the other in clinical psychology. We have been

CONCORDIA UNIVERSITY LIBRARY
PORTLAND. OR 97211

involved for some years in the large-scale collection of social data by means of the interview, in the Federal Government and more recently at the Survey Research Center of the University of Michigan. Our experience and that of our colleagues in research, as well as in business and other professions, led us to feel that there was an unmet need for a book on the theory and techniques of the information-getting interview. With the results of recent research on the communications process, on interaction in small groups, and on the nature of the psychotherapeutic relationship, the possibility seemed to exist for analyzing the dynamics of the interview process.

There are, of course, many ways of looking at the interview. The most common approach implies that it is a sort of battle of wits between respondent and interviewer. The respondent has somewhere inside him information which the interviewer wants, and the interviewing techniques are designed to force, trick, or cajole the respondent into releasing the information. The literature on research into the interview process and the firsthand experience of interviewers indicate that this conception is misleading and inaccurate. Rather, the interview is an interaction between the interviewer and respondent in which both participants share.

As in most communications processes, we have in the interview two people, each trying to influence the other and each actively accepting or rejecting influence attempts. The end product of the interview is a result of this interaction. Therein lie the strengths and weaknesses of the interview as an information-getting technique. If the interaction is handled properly, the interview becomes a powerful technique, capable of developing accurate information and getting access to material otherwise unavailable. Improperly handled, the interaction becomes a serious source of bias, restricting or distorting the flow of communication. Therefore, we must learn to control the interaction between interviewer and respondent in order that the purposes of the interview can be achieved. This in turn requires that we have some insights into the dynamics of the interaction.

Broadly speaking, then, the thesis of this book is that in order to be a successful interviewer, a person must first know and understand these dynamics—the psychological forces at work in the interview. It is this understanding which provides a basis for acquiring and using insightfully the specific techniques of interviewing. Without such understanding, the acquisition of technique becomes superficial and of limited value.

Throughout the book, therefore, our emphasis has been on the principles and theory of interviewing as well as on technique. We have attempted to develop a theoretical statement of what the information-getting and information-giving process involves, to derive a set of criteria for what constitutes an adequate interview, and finally to present techniques to meet these criteria.

The book is organized in two parts. The first part includes two chapters on theory, Chapters 2 and 7; the other chapters are devoted to exposition of principles and techniques. The second part of the book is a series of transcripts of recorded interviews, with the authors' comments. These interviews, from medicine, business, and social work, are included to illustrate further the techniques discussed in Part I.

In looking for a theory and a set of principles to encompass the information-getting interview, we have benefited from the work of others in a variety of fields. We wish to acknowledge especially the contributions of Carl R. Rogers and the late Kurt Lewin, whose influence on the authors is apparent in many places throughout the book. We are indebted to Rogers and his students for their insightful descriptions of the psychological climate in which free communication thrives, and for their analyses of the therapeutic process, on which we have drawn for our analysis of interaction between interviewer and respondent. Rogers' development of the client-centered interview as a therapeutic technique and his concept of nondirectiveness are basic to our approach to informational interviewing, although the information-getting interview is neither nondirective nor client-centered in the psychotherapeutic sense.

The work of Lewin and his students has been most useful to us in understanding the motivational aspects of interviewing. The Lewinian concept of the psychological field, with the representation of motives as forces in that field, is especially important in our treatment of respondent motivation. We have made extensive use also of the work of Festinger and his colleagues on communication in small groups, adapting their research findings to the peculiarities of the two-person interview. We have relied on Krech and Crutchfield for their lucid exposition of the principles of motivation and perception.

In addition to these sources, we have been fortunate in having the assistance of several people whose broad knowledge of social science has contributed a great deal to this book. These include Daniel Katz, whose critical review of the entire manuscript was most helpful and stimulating; Dorwin Cartwright, who helped us work through a field theoretical approach to problems of respondent motivation; and David Riesman and his colleagues, who led us to think about the sociology of the interview as well as its psychological aspects.

Many people have been extremely cooperative in recording and making available to us interviews which they conducted as part of their professional work. We wish to thank specifically Dr. J. Richard Johnson, Dr. James Walker, and Donald Dobbin, of the Veterans' Administration Hospital in Ann Arbor; Robert Schwab, Preston Amerman, and Miss Ellen Brennen, of the Detroit Edison Company; Robert Hood, President of Ansul Chemical Company; Robert Rosema, Miss Catherine Mude, and Mrs. Helen Rutledge, of the Michigan Children's Institute. Equally important have been the many interviewers at the Survey Research Center, the U. S. Bureau of the Census, and the U. S. Department of Agriculture, from whose comments, experience, and interviews we have drawn in the writing of this book.

Much of the credit for what this book offers of readability or style must go to Mrs. Sylvia Eberhart, who edited the manuscript. Her contributions go far beyond this, however. Her penetrating criticism and her constructive ideas on content and organization are gratefully acknowledged.

The effort of producing a book is seldom restricted to its authors. Producing this one has meant that our families were called on to schedule their lives for many months around the requirements of writing. This they have done with understanding and generosity, for which we are deeply grateful.

When a book is written by people who are part of an organization, the writing inevitably makes demands upon their colleagues. We wish to thank Rensis Likert and Angus Campbell for their support, and Morris Axelrod and Floyd Mann, on whom the weight of extra work often fell. We are indebted also to Mrs. Barbara Karoly, Miss Sharon Summers, and Mrs. Elizabeth Goetzke, whose typing of the many revisions of this manuscript has been done with expertness and good will.

Finally, we wish to acknowledge the kind permission of the following authors and publishers to reprint material: *Adult Leadership*, the American Psychological Association, Dryden Press, Harper and Brothers, *Harvard Business Review*, Houghton Mifflin Company, the Institute for Religious and Social Studies, Wendell Johnson, Daniel Katz, McCann-Erickson Advertising Company, McGraw-Hill Book Company, Macmillan Company, Princeton University Press, Carl R. Rogers, Ronald Press Company, *Sociatry*, and the University of Illinois Press.

ROBERT L. KAHN
CHARLES F. CANNELL

Ann Arbor, Michigan
April 1957

Contents

    Inexperienced Applicants for a Clerical Job   302

12 A Supervisor-Subordinate Interview: A Production
    Bottleneck and an Office Feud   316

13 A Social-Work Interview: Family and Job
    Adjustments of a Discharged Psychiatric Patient   328

    Bibliography   353

    Index   361

part I

Introduction:
The Interview as Communication

One evening, shortly before this book was written, five men gathered in the living room of one of them to listen to some tape recordings. Three of the men were physicians, the other two the authors of this book. The doctors had in common the rather unusual fact that each had agreed at an earlier time to permit a tape recorder to be set up in his office for the purpose of recording his conversations and interviews with incoming patients. Over a period of weeks a number of doctor-patient interviews had been recorded, and now for the first time the doctors were to hear them played back.

From the outset they had shown considerable interest in the project. They recognized the importance of the interview in their work and appreciated the fact that interviewing techniques were part of their professional equipment. It had been agreed in the original arrangements with the doctors that at a later date they would have the opportunity to hear the recordings and to analyze and discuss them with the authors. It was clear even before the tape recorder was turned on that this was an experience that the doctors anticipated with high interest and with some little apprehension and good-natured self-consciousness.

In the first recorded medical interview, after the usual exchange of greetings between doctor and patient, the following material was heard:

3

DOCTOR: O.K. Now I want to take a history and I want symptoms primarily. I mean I don't want to know what diagnosis you have, I want to go more by symptoms. So what is the chief thing that's bothering you—at the present time?
PATIENT: I don't have any pains right now, I feel wonderful.
DOCTOR: Well, what trouble have you had in the near past?
PATIENT: Well, this summer I had days that I don't feel so good. Lots of days that I had to take it easy and kind of loaf around.
DOCTOR: Why did you have to take it easy? What has your main problem been?
PATIENT: I just felt—I really had no bad pain—I just—er—sort of feeling bad inside me for a long time. I felt—
DOCTOR: Didn't you have any pain *at all?*
PATIENT: I wouldn't really say it hurt, but it felt bad, like—
DOCTOR: *Where* did it feel bad?

As the above passage was played, the doctor who had conducted the interview became increasingly tense. At one point he seized the arms of his chair and burst out, "I'm not letting the poor guy tell me what's the matter with him!"

The first medical interview concluded, and with noticeable relief the doctor who had been the major actor in that script turned his attention to the second interview, conducted by one of his colleagues.

The following excerpt is taken from the second medical interview to which the group was then listening:

DOCTOR: How many cigarettes do you smoke?
PATIENT: Oh, this package I have had pretty near . . . golly, almost—
DOCTOR: About a pack a week, perhaps?
PATIENT: Yeah, I guess about that. I am a pipe smoker—I have cigarettes here, but I smoke a pipe, probably more than I ought to.
DOCTOR: A pipeful a day?
PATIENT: Well, yes.

                                   * * * * * *

DOCTOR: Have you had any operations?
PATIENT: No.
DOCTOR: How about your tonsils; have you had those out?
PATIENT: No.
DOCTOR: Have you had any injuries . . . falls or such like?
PATIENT: No.
DOCTOR: Sounds like you have been pretty healthy. Generally, you would say your health was pretty good?
PATIENT: Well, yes, I would say it was all right.

As the recorded tape continued to play, the second doctor began to show many of the same reactions previously displayed by his colleague. He listened intently, and obviously with some embarrassment, to the sound of his own voice and that of his patient, and finally said, "My gosh, I'm answering my own questions. I ask one, and then I don't let him alone." And then, a few minutes later, "Listen to that, will you? I really butchered that question. I gave him the answer."

By the time the evening was over, the two authors had noted a continuing succession of such comments as the following: "There I go with that medical terminology again. How could I expect that patient to understand that?" "I see *now* what she was trying to tell me. I just really wasn't listening to her." "That was a good lead he gave me. I should have followed it up and I missed it." "Why was I so short with that patient just then? I didn't mean to be, but it certainly shut him up, and I really wanted to hear more about that symptom." "That woman is scared to death to tell me what's bothering her. She has an awful lot of trouble getting the words out, and I certainly didn't do anything to help her."

Most of us, if confronted with a record of some of the extemporaneous dialogues in which we take part, would undoubtedly discover similar discrepancies between what we thought was happening and what was actually happening. What someone was trying to tell us would turn out to have differed from what we took in. What he made of our communication would appear on re-examination to have differed from what we intended to communicate. The doctors' experience demonstrates that even where the dialogue takes the deliberate form of an information-gathering interview, with the parties to it presumably bent upon a common purpose, the difficulties of communication persist.

OBSTRUCTIONS TO COMMUNICATION

Why is this? Why, in the words of an exasperated parent, a puzzled school teacher, or a harrassed executive, can't I ask a simple question and get a straightforward answer? We begin to learn the question-and-answer process very early in life. ("How old are you, Jimmie?" "Two and a half," Jimmie says obligingly.) We carry it on assiduously day in and day out and in an endless variety of contexts, asking and being asked, answering and being answered, taking in and giving out by means of the spoken word bits of information beyond counting. It seems a paradox that so common a process should be attended by problems—problems so complex, in fact, that for some years, at least since the advent of the large-scale interview survey, they have been the subject of considerable research and experimentation.

Problems of Motivation

Since we are all, by training and experience, communicators, why is an interview not a simple and efficiently performed interaction between an expert sender and an equally expert receiver of messages? There are several reasons. Some of them are related to the very fact that we are so experienced in communicating. One consequence of our sophistication about communication is that we have developed ways and habits of reacting to each other that are not *intended* to simplify or facilitate the process. They are designed in large part to help us protect ourselves against making some undesirable revelation or against putting ourselves in an unfavorable light. They are man's methods of defending himself against the possibility of being made to look ridiculous or inadequate. And in most cases we are not content merely to avoid looking inadequate, we want also to appear intelligent, thoughtful, or in possession of whatever other virtues are relevant to the situation from our point of view. We want to put our best foot forward.

Most of us recognize that all manner of forces are exerted upon us through communications from other people. We are urged to join a church or some other organization; we are exhorted to buy a book or smoke a particular kind of cigarette, or drink a certain beverage, or not to drink at all, and so forth. We recognize that communications from another person may be an attempt to force or beguile us in a direction in which we may not wish to go. Therefore, we are defensive in another way. The general result of this kind of defensiveness, too, is to mar communication with omissions and inaccuracies. These defects are purposeful and functional; they are our defenses against permitting ourselves to be influenced against our will.

Again, through long experience in being communicated with, we learn to anticipate what is going to be said, and therefore not to listen well, as the doctors discovered on the tape recordings. Thus we may respond not to what is being said but to our own thoughts. We may hear only what we expect to hear, basing our expectations on all sorts of cues—the speaker's voice or diction or mannerisms or dress, or something he said at another time, or what other people he seems to resemble have said. We may listen only for what fits into our purposes, leaving off as soon as we have classified the speaker, or made the check mark, or satisfied our wandering curiosity, or decided what we ourselves are going to say.

Thus we see that there are negative consequences to the expertness people build up in the communications area. Each man comes to recognize that he is communicated to for a variety of reasons. He learns that these reasons may forward or frustrate his own purposes. As a result, the person to whom a communication is addressed— whether it is a question or an answer—is very likely to spend some of his attention and energy on trying to evaluate it in terms of the possible motives of the sender or of its adaptability to his own needs, including his need to make a certain impression. Both parties to communication are coding or classifying. They are constantly evaluating, sorting, accepting, rejecting, and assimilating.

Rogers suggests that the tendency to evaluate constitutes the major problem in communications:

I should like to propose, as a hypothesis for consideration, that the major barrier to mutual interpersonal communication is our very natural tendency to judge, to evaluate, to approve (or disapprove) the statement of the other person or the other group. Let me illustrate my meaning with some very simple examples. Suppose someone, commenting on this discussion, makes the statement, "I don't like what that man said." What will you respond? Almost invariably your reply will be either approval or disapproval of the attitude expressed. Either you respond, "I didn't either; I thought it was terrible," or else you tend to reply, "Oh, I thought it was really good." In other words, your primary reaction is to evaluate it from *your* point of view, your own frame of reference.

Or take another example; suppose I say with some feeling, "I think the Republicans are behaving in ways that show a lot of good sound sense these days." What is the response that arises to your mind? The overwhelming likelihood is that it will be evaluative. In other words, you will find yourself agreeing, or disagreeing, or making some judgment about me, such as "He must be a conservative," or "He seems solid in his thinking." Or let us take another illustration from the international scene. Russia says vehemently, "The treaty with Japan is a war plot on the part of the United States." We rise as one person to say "That's a lie!"

This last illustration brings in another element connected with my hypothesis. Although the tendency to make evaluations is common in almost all interchange of language, it is very much heightened in those situations where feelings and emotions are deeply involved. So the stronger our feelings, the more likely it is that there will be no mutual element in the communication. There will be just two ideas, two feelings, two judgments, missing each other in psychological space.[1]

So far, we have refrained from differentiating between the interviewer and the respondent—that is, the two parties to the particular kind of communication we are concerned with. The reason is that both bring to the interview situation habits thrust on them by their

---

[1] Carl R. Rogers and F. J. Roethlisberger, "Barriers and Gateways to Communication," *Harvard Business Review*, 30, No. 4 (July–August 1952).

common experience with communication. The interviewer is likely to have developed the same tendency toward evaluative reactions that characterizes the respondent. He may be under many of the same motivational forces or pressures to express or conceal his own opinions, to convey a certain impression of himself, and so on. He, too, is likely to have the habits in listening that we have described, based on the tendency to evaluate. Evaluative behaviors on the part of the interviewer can be predicted either to inhibit communication by the respondent or to create forces toward inaccurate or distorted communication. Thus, if the respondent perceives the interviewer to be approving of an attitude he has expressed, we can predict that the respondent will be motivated to repeat or overemphasize that attitude, and to avoid expressing feelings that might be in conflict with it. Conversely, if the interviewer's behaviors convey negative evaluation to the respondent, we can predict that some form of defensive reaction will take place, whether this be simply a refusal to continue the communication process, or (more likely) a tendency to avoid further risk of disapproval by modifying or withholding certain kinds of information.

The resolution of this problem seems to lie in making the interview an experience which differs in certain basic respects from the more usual kind of communication situation. The interview must be a process in which the forces to distort or withhold communication have been eliminated or reduced as much as possible. And of course we must rely primarily upon the interviewer to bring this about. He is the agent who must bear major responsibility for the pattern of interaction that occurs. This is so not only because his is the initiative in the interview situation, but also because it is he, rather than the respondent, who is directly accessible to be taught new skills and ways of behaving. What we are demanding of the interviewer is that he learn a new and specialized way of behaving and interacting with another individual for the purpose of improving communication.

This means, first, that he must acquire additional insight into the interactions that make up the interview. He must understand more about the forces that motivate the respondent and that influence his own reactions to the respondent. And second, he must acquire the specific skills that enable him to put this knowledge to use. We shall try in this book to help him on his way toward both these goals.

Psychological Barriers

So far we have spoken only about such barriers to communication as lie between the interviewer and the respondent. If all of these barriers were removed, the respondent still could not tell us everything about himself that we are likely to want to know, even provided that he were willing to do so. The situation is much more complicated. There may be psychological barriers that lie between the respondent and the material we want him to bring forth, which limit communication regardless of how highly motivated the respondent may be and how well disposed toward the interviewer.

The simplest example of such a barrier is memory failure. The respondent cannot tell us something that he has forgotten. But memory failure may result not only in the absence of information but also in distortion, so that in all innocence the respondent gives misinformation. The phenomenon of memory is by no means simple. It is not as though all facts have a "half life" of some given period of time so that we can predict their gradual, regular recession into the vast store of unremembered experience. On the contrary, psychologists have made it clear that we remember and forget in a selective fashion, and that the patterns by which memory alters or discards the past are influenced by emotional factors.

Emotional forces may set up barriers between the respondent and the material we seek from him, even when it has to do not with the past but with the present. Rogers tells about a young man in training for military aviation who found himself unable to carry out the directions of his flight instructor. He was a talented young man, he knew what he was supposed to do, but some perversity prevented his doing it, at considerable risk to himself and the instructor. Nor could he explain why. He was on the point of being dismissed from the air corps, when the instructor referred him to a clinic in the hope that the stubborn problem could be diagnosed. During the therapeutic sessions that followed, it developed that the cadet was acting out with the flight instructor an unresolved conflict with his father. This is a kind of information we do not ordinarily expect a respondent to be able to uncover except in the special circumstances of psychiatric therapy.

We need not turn to such dramatic examples for evidence that the reasons for a person's actions frequently are inaccessible to him. If someone is asked why he bought a new car, he is likely to tell about its mechanical superiority, or about the shortcomings of his older car, or about the economics of trading in. He is much less likely to report a desire to compare favorably with his neighbor, who bought a new car first, because he may not have insight into this reason.

In short, there are obstructions to communication that manifest themselves not in the respondent's wish to withhold or distort information but in his psychological inability to produce it. In part, the interviewing skills that will be discussed later in this book can render considerable assistance to the respondent in recalling forgotten material and in gaining insight into unrecognized motives. For the most part, however, we consider such materials to be in the special province of the therapist and outside that of the information-getting interview. Nevertheless, we shall find ourselves considering in this book, at least briefly, some of the psychological mechanisms human beings unknowingly employ to conceal from themselves some aspects of reality. For if our quest for information by means of interviews is to be as profitable as possible, we must understand the limitations of the technique and direct our efforts accordingly.

Language Difficulties

Thus far we have considered two categories of problems in interviewing: first, those deriving from the respondent's lack of motivation to communicate accurately, and second, those based on psychological inability to communicate, either because of memory failure or because of unconscious repression or distortion. We should consider, in addition, a third source of difficulty in the interviewing process. This has to do with language.

Experts in linguistics and semantics are agreed, as Wendell Johnson puts it, that the "languages available to us are such that they tend to make for oversimplification and overgeneralization. Reality—that is, the sources of sensory stimulation—is, so far as we know, decidedly processlike, highly dynamic, ever changing. Our language on the other hand, is by comparison quite static and relatively inflexible."[2]

Or, as Katz puts it, "Formal language is symbolic in that its verbal or mathematical terms stand for aspects of reality beyond themselves. . . . Because of its symbolic nature, language is a poor substitute for the realities which it attempts to present. The real world is more complex, more colorful, more fluid, more multidimensional, than the pale words or oversimplified signs used to convey meaning."[3]

Our linguistic problems, however, are not limited in the interview to those that are inherent in the nature of language. It has been estimated that the average individual knows less than 10 per cent of the more than a half million words in the English language. Thus in our interview with a typical respondent, we must accept not only the limitations of language in general, but the specific limitations of his vocabulary. Nor do these kinds of language difficulties manifest

---

[2] "Speech and Personality," in *The Communication of Ideas,* Institute for Religious and Social Studies, New York, 1948.

[3] Daniel Katz, "Psychological Barriers to Communication," *Annals of the American Academy of Political and Social Science,* March 1947.

themselves only when the subject under discussion is technical or of esoteric content. We have only to ask, as every physician must, that a person describe the character of a pain or other physical symptom he is suffering, in order to become convinced quickly of the inadequacies of the common vocabulary to identify and differentiate even so common an experience. That the physician has a highly technical and specialized vocabulary which would permit *him* to describe the symptoms does not in the least help resolve our difficulty. It is the vocabulary of the respondent or, more properly, the shared vocabulary and experience of the respondent and interviewer, that defines the maximum content of communication in the interview.

Vocabulary differences exist between regions of the country, between socioeconomic strata, between occupational specialties, and even between age groups, as any parent can appreciate who has puzzled his way through to the insight that when his young son says "Cool, man!" he in fact means the same thing that Father, a generation before, would have referred to as "hot stuff." On the whole, we can predict that the fewer such characteristics as age, socioeconomic status, and education the interviewer and respondent have in common, the more serious will be the general problem of lack of shared experience and the special manifestation of lack of common language.

There are several approaches which may be taken to resolve these problems of language as they affect the interview. It is in the formulation of questions that the language limitations of the respondent can best be taken into account. Attempts to do so are usually more successful when they depend primarily on the vocabulary which is common to respondent and interviewer, however restricted that may be. Teaching new language to the respondent is difficult and risky, and attempts to assume the respondent's vocabulary are more often ridiculous than effective. The correct use of the respondent's colloquialisms may suggest to him that he and the interviewer have things in common and are "within range" for communication purposes, but the interviewer's basic skills and his genuine acceptance of the respondent are more important indications than language.

THE INTERVIEW DEFINED
Personal Communication

Acts of communication in which one person requests information and another supplies it are, of course, extremely common in all human experience. We carry on such interactions almost continuously with friends, family, business associates, and casual acquaintances. From this stream of communications we come to know increasingly well how various people feel, what they think, what they may do or attempt, how they characteristically approach problems, and the like. The more frequent our communications with an individual, the more fully informed we are likely to be about him and the more accurate we become in predicting and understanding his behavior. Thus we may know how a close friend voted in the last presidential election, whether or not he plans to buy a new car, whether he is currently happy or unhappy with his job, what the state of his health is, and something about the harmony of his domestic life. In the case of a casual acquaintance, we are likely to have had far less communication and we will be correspondingly less informed about his life and thinking. In general, what we know of a person depends upon the amount and the character of our past interaction and communication with him. The communications which we have with people whom we know well and see frequently are not only more numerous, but are likely also to be more frank and more personal than those with casual acquaintances.

We might think of our relationship with an individual as consisting of a whole stream of interactions over a period of time, consisting of communications of information, attempts at influence, sharing of perceptions, and so on. If we are asked how a close friend or a member of our family thinks on a particular topic, or whether he will enjoy a certain movie or consent to wear a tie of a certain pattern, we can answer these questions with confidence because of the stream of interaction on which we can base our judgment. What we do, in effect, is to think back over the vast number of our interactions and communications with this individual and select those that are relevant for answering the specific question at hand. John once said that he would never wear a tie with a bold figure; Susan has said repeatedly that she hates movies with sad endings. For casual acquaintances we would find it much more difficult to make similar judgments, and for near strangers we would find it almost impossible. In such relationships the informational basis for judgments has simply not been laid down in the frequency and character of previous interaction. Nevertheless, we find ourselves frequently in situations where it is important to have knowledge of various kinds about an individual with whom we have had little or no previous acquaintance, information that would ordinarily be amassed only over a period of time. The following hypothetical case will serve as an example.

Bill and Joe have been friends and fellow workers for the past seventeen years. They share adjoining offices, often lunch together, live within three blocks of each other, and spend a good deal of time together socially.

Bill knows nearly all there is to know about Joe, and vice versa. Bill knows the kind of movies that Joe enjoys, what kind of cars he likes, and why. He knows that Joe dislikes his boss Harvey very much, and that in the ten years in which he has worked under Harvey, Joe has never ceased to feel that Harvey got the promotion which Joe himself should have had.

Bill knows that Joe and his wife nearly broke up about six years ago, but that things have been going better for them more recently.

Bill knows that Joe had an uncle who died in a mental institution after about ten years' stay, and that Joe has done a great deal of reading on the subject of mental disorders since; that while he says he is convinced that mental disorders aren't inherited, he is quite concerned about the possibility that he or some other member of the family might at some time have a serious mental breakdown. Bill also knows that Joe's mother had a series of operations a few years ago to arrest the development of a cancerous condition, of which she finally died; that this troubles Joe considerably from time to time because he feels her ailment may have some hereditary characteristics.

Bill has known for a long time that Joe feels very unsure of himself when he is talking to clients of the firm, and really suffers if one of them questions his judgment about some account or business proposition. In fact, Bill has classified his friend Joe as having some strong fears that he is not as adequate to his job and his responsibilities as he ought to be.

Bill has been getting somewhat worried about Joe lately. Several weeks ago, while sitting in the office discussing business, Joe complained of a severe headache. Bill laughed at him and suggested that he shouldn't have had that last martini, but he noticed that Joe seemed not to be feeling well for the next day or two. He was quieter than usual, and once in a while Bill saw him rub his hand over his forehead. Then last Tuesday, when Bill reminded Joe of their usual bowling date, Joe said that he didn't think he would go, that he just didn't feel up to it. And this morning, when they were late for the bus, Joe suggested that they wait for the next bus rather than run to catch the usual one. This just isn't like Joe. Joe's never sick. He hasn't been to a doctor for the past five years, in fact not since the time he broke his arm. Bill also knows that Joe has a distrust of doctors and thinks they used poor judgment in his mother's case—that they operated unnecessarily and created more misery for his mother instead of helping her.

But this afternoon Joe comes into Bill's office with his shoulders drooping and his hand to his forehead and says, "Well, Bill, I'm afraid I'm just going to have to go to the doctor. My head is killing me again."

Professional Communication

If the physician is to be of assistance to Joe, he must know certain things about him—the nature and duration of his complaints, the circumstances of the onset, and whether emotional factors may be involved. Since this is Joe's first visit to this physician, there is no pattern of previous interactions from which the physician can select the relevant information. Neither can the doctor spare the time nor can the patient postpone the cure until an intimate relationship can be established and an extensive array of miscellaneous facts accumulated from the patient. Many of the things which Bill knows about Joe need not concern the doctor. For example, it is irrelevant for him that Joe and his wife nearly split up six years ago, or that he likes a particular kind of car or movie. Other factors are, however, very relevant. The physician will be able to make a more intelligent diagnosis if in addition to knowing the physical symptoms, he understands some of Joe's concerns about his family medical history, particularly his uncle's and his mother's medical problems. It will also be useful to the physician if he recognizes that Joe is not the kind of person who goes to a doctor at the first sign of illness, but that his distrust of specialists has made him wait until the pain is intense and he is considerably concerned about himself. Joe's distrust of doctors may be a factor affecting their relationship, and if the physician can gain some insight into this, he may be able to understand better Joe's abrupt manner and reluctant answers.

What the physician requires, therefore, is some technique by which he can obtain in a relatively short time the special items of information he needs in order to solve the medical problems the patient presents. He needs a technique that will permit him to obtain from Joe the kind of information Bill could cull from the interaction product of a long period of time. The doctor must establish a relationship with the new patient in which the pattern of interaction and communications will consist almost exclusively of material that is relevant for the special purpose under consideration. It is to establish such a pattern of interaction that the doctor must acquire a special set of interviewing techniques and become an interviewer.

Nor is the physician unique in these respects. The supervisor who interviews a subordinate in order to learn something of his work situation, or the social worker attempting to gain some initial insight into the problems a new client brings, is confronted with much the same kind of problem. In all these situations a communicative relationship must be established in which items irrelevant to the problem at hand are eliminated and the relevant information selected and communicated fully in a brief period of time. The relationships established under these circumstances are not brief imitations of friendship patterns. They have a quality of their own, depending on the role and skills of the interviewer, the kind of information required, and the characteristics of the respondent.

Perhaps the contrast between the interviewing relationship and a friendship pattern can be grasped more clearly with the help of the following visualizations. If we think of a friendship pattern as in-cluding a stream of communicative acts on a variety of subjects over a substantial period of time, we might represent it as shown in Figure 1. In this illustration each such act is represented by a dot, and those communications that are relevant for some special purpose or subject (in our example, for helping a physician reach a judgment about the health of a patient) are further designated by a circle. If we are asked a question regarding the health of a close friend, we can answer

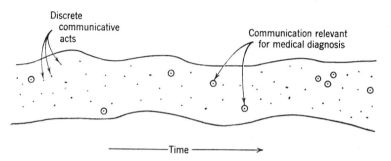

Figure 1. Schematic representation of communications from one friend to another over time.

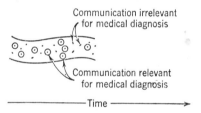

Figure 2. Schematic representation of communications from patient to doctor during a medical interview.

that question by drawing on this stream of past communications and selecting the relevant items.

The interviewer's problem is to bring about a much smaller stream of communications, consisting almost solely of the relevant items. The irrelevant topics must be avoided, and the relevant bits of in-formation must be communicated in rapid succession over a short space of time. Figure 2 is a schematic representation of the com-munications pattern which the interviewer is attempting to create. To the extent that the interviewer is not able to eliminate irrelevancies, the interviewing process becomes costly and inefficient. To the ex-tent that the interviewer fails to obtain full communication of the relevant items, the interview content becomes biased and the conclu-sions inaccurate.

Specific Definition

We can now attempt a more specific definition of the interview. We use the term interview to refer to a specialized pattern of verbal interaction—initiated for a specific purpose, and focused on some specific content area, with consequent elimination of extraneous material. Moreover, the interview is a pattern of interaction in which the role relationship of interviewer and respondent is highly specialized, its specific characteristics depending somewhat on the purpose and character of the interview.

Deductions and Applications

A number of deductions follow from this definition. First, it is clear that the interview makes certain demands upon the person who conducts it. He must possess special skills that enable him to achieve the required pattern of interaction. Furthermore, it is clear from the foregoing definition that interviewing is a very frequent occurrence and that it forms an important part of many business and professional activities. The importance and prominence of the interviewing function varies, of course, among professions. In some, interviewing is the major technique and the primary process around which the profession is practiced. For other professions or administrative functions, the interview is auxiliary to some more basic responsibility or activity. Let us consider some illustrations.

Some people are specifically designated as interviewers; we speak, for example, of personnel interviewers or public opinion interviewers. In such positions interviewing is the major function, and the people who fill such jobs are primarily interviewing technicians. Their training is specifically in the techniques of interviewing, and their vocational success depends primarily on their interviewing ability. A specialized literature has grown up regarding the techniques of particular use to practitioners in these areas.

We can discern another category of professions in which interviewing is a major technique although the professions have specialized content and subject matter apart from the interview. Persons practicing such professions are not thought of as interviewers, but rather each is identified according to the subject matter and primary purpose of his profession. In this category we might include (among others) psychiatrists, clinical psychologists, social workers, and journalists. These professions differ greatly in many characteristics, but they have in common the use of the interview as a major technique, although adapted to a highly specialized subject matter and content. The training of people for such professions is likely to include some attention to interviewing techniques, and the literature of such professions usually contains some material on interviewing.

In a third category of professions, interviewing is not a major basis of practice but is nevertheless an important auxiliary skill. It is likely that in these professions the need for special interviewing skills is less commonly recognized and techniques for interviewing are less frequently included in the formal training of candidates. Examples of such professions include medicine and law. In both these fields, some literature on interviewing is available and some training is offered; but on the whole, interviewing is given only minor attention.

Finally, we can point out some professions and business roles in which the interviewing function is practiced and yet goes virtually unrecognized. The supervisor, the administrator, the school teacher are not trained to interview, and they would not be likely to think of interviewing as one of the skills important for the accomplishment of their work. Nor is there for these professions a literature on the functions of interviewing and the skills required for it. Nevertheless, in these fields, and in others which have traditionally regarded interviewing with still less interest, there is a dawning conviction that communications skills are essential to successful practice, and that the specialized communications skills which we call interviewing have a considerable contribution to make.

The boss who complains that "no one ever tells me anything" is telling us that he has not learned how to take successfully the role of either interviewer or respondent with his peers and subordinates. The growing body of research findings which indicate relationships between such communications skills and the hard facts of turnover, absence, and industrial productivity provide important evidence of the contribution which good interviewing and communications practices can make. Among the most common complaints of industrial workers are the statements, "I don't know where I stand with my boss," or "My boss never asks me what I think." In part, of course, such statements may reflect a policy or administrative decision that employees are not to be informed or consulted. More frequently, however, the intention is quite the opposite, and the supervisor is laboring under the delusion that he is in satisfactory communication with his subordinates. Their dissatisfaction and his unawareness of it provide double evidence of his deficiencies as an interviewer.

The foregoing examples are drawn from business and professional situations, and it is with such formal interviewing situations that this book will be primarily concerned. But the basic skill of obtaining information from another individual with efficiency and tact is a requirement that falls on all of us in many aspects of our daily lives. It is likely that the experience of anyone who encounters human beings with problems—the minister, social worker, marriage counselor, school teacher, etc.—would confirm the fact that many of these problems are accompanied by difficulties of communication. In all our contacts with other people—as parents, friends, and business or professional colleagues—we require those skills which will facilitate communication. Some human problems have their origins in communication difficulties. Many more are aggravated by such difficulties or go unsolved for lack of communication skills.

The Information-Getting Interview

Earlier in this chapter we have referred to the type of interview in which we are interested as the information-getting interview. Moreover, the examples which we have used have been restricted to this type of interview, and have provided a partial definition of it. It may be useful at this time to make that definition explicit. Our use of the term information-getting interview is intended to include a broad range of material. We do not equate "information" with "fact-finding," but rather we think of this type of interview as concerned with attitudes, values, feelings, hopes, plans, and descriptions of self, in addition to more objective factual data. It is obvious, for example, that if an interviewer asks a respondent to state his age, his place of birth, or his income, this falls well within the boundaries of the information-getting process; but we include also in the information-getting category questions designed to learn the respondent's attitudes toward his supervisor, his own vocational plans, aspirations for his children, and his feelings regarding national or international issues. Further examples might include his relationships with family, colleagues, or friends.

It is clear from this range of material that the label "information-getting" does not restrict us to what is objective, superficial, or easy to verbalize; rather, this process includes attempts to get at partially formed attitudes and at private, seldom-verbalized feelings. The interviewer may even contribute, through his techniques and the relationship he establishes, to the respondent's ability to formulate and pull together his attitudes regarding the topic under discussion.

Nevertheless, there are limitations to the information-getting interview as we have defined it, and these limitations are also to be kept in mind. This interview is not designed to penetrate deeply into the personality structure of the respondent; it is not designed to bring forth material which has been kept at the unconscious level, and of which the respondent previously has been unaware. These are the business of the psychiatric interview and the techniques of psychotherapy. The information-getting interview does not partake of the psychotherapeutic character. It is not intended to change the respondent. Indeed, it is the absence of the intent to change which perhaps most sharply differentiates the information-getting interview from a variety of other kinds of interview situations.

The supervisor frequently engages in an interview with his subordinate in order to induce the latter to change, either by persuasion or command; the teacher may undertake a kind of Socratic interview with his pupil in order to bring about additional insight and learning on the part of the student; the conversation of a salesman with his client, of the political candidate with the voter, may be thought of as interview processes. All of these have in common that they are initiated by the interviewer for the purpose of exerting some influence, inducing some action or behavioral change on the part of the respondent. These objectives differ from the single objective of information-getting, and the techniques and interviewer-respondent relationships implied by these objectives differ also from the relationship between the information-getting interviewer and his respondent.

Admittedly, there are times when the line of demarcation among the various types of interviews is difficult to draw. The therapist frequently must play the role of information-getter before he can draw the diagnostic conclusions and attempt the therapeutic action which are his basic objectives. The supervisor frequently must conduct information-getting interviews in order to carry out the administrative actions which are his primary aim. To the extent that these various practitioners recognize the change in role and the corresponding changes in technique which are implied as they move from the process of information-getting to that of teaching, persuading, or disciplining, we would predict increased effectiveness. For them the rewards of improved interviewing skills should include a better informational base on which decisions can be made and a corresponding improvement in the quality and appropriateness of those decisions.

SUMMARY

For purposes of summing up our approach to the interview, let us assume that an interviewer—whether a social researcher, public opinion pollster, doctor, social worker, or supervisor—has introduced himself and his topic to the respondent of his choice and is about to initiate the interview itself. We will assume, furthermore, that the respondent is able to communicate regarding the topic of the interview, and that respondent and interviewer share enough language to permit easy communication. The task which remains for the interviewer is to elicit frank and complete answers from the respondent.

In attempting this task the interviewer faces a complex individual with a personality of his own, an individual who is already reacting to him, and with whom he must interact for the duration of the interview. The respondent may be trying to protect himself from attack, to present himself in a favorable light, to persuade the interviewer of his point of view, or to accomplish any number of purposes irrelevant to or in conflict with the interviewer's objectives. If the interviewer is to have any real success in getting accurate information, he needs an understanding of the dynamics of the interaction process which he has already begun and of which he is a part. He must be able to identify and in some degree control the psychological forces which are at work in the interview, both on the respondent and on himself. We will spend a good deal of time in this book in trying to devise a theory to help him understand these psychological forces, and in proposing methods to control them.

If we are to understand the process of interaction between interviewer and respondent, we cannot concern ourselves only with the mechanics of the interviewing process, nor can we be satisfied to study the interview as a series of discrete stimulus-response episodes. We must be concerned instead with the goals, attitudes, beliefs, and motives of the principals in the interview. We must be able to specify why, for example, a respondent gives, withholds, or distorts a specific piece of information. To be able to answer such questions, we must understand the forces which make up the psychological field of both interviewer and respondent. It is the writers' viewpoint that only as the interviewing practitioner has a thorough grasp of these psychological forces and their relevance is he able to make the most efficient use of the interview.

The practitioners of interviewing have known about problems of interaction for a long time, of course, and they have worked out empirically ways of getting around some of these problems. For example, it has been found that if you ask the respondent the date of his birth, the answer is likely to be more accurate than if you ask how old he is. If you want to know a person's income, it is more productive to give him some rough income categories from which to choose than to ask him to state the exact amount. Lawyers have found that if you ask a witness to confirm or deny the allegation of another witness, he is more likely to give you misinformation than if you ask him to tell you in his own words what he observed. These practices give us, at best, fragmentary information on the interaction problems of the interview; they do little to help us understand the relationship between interviewer and the respondent.

In recent years social science has begun to amass research findings about the process of communication between people. Social psychologists have conducted investigations on how people communicate with each other in small groups. Clinical psychologists have studied intensively the relationship between the therapist and the patient in the psychotherapeutic interview, in order to understand the nature of their interaction and to discover why such interactions sometimes help the patient to reorient himself. Other social scientists have been doing research directly on the data-collection interview, in an attempt to identify the sources of bias in the interview. The theorizing and research of these investigators have provided the basis for a more complete and satisfactory statement of the psychological forces at work in the information-getting interview.

From such a theoretical statement, and from the long experience of practitioners, the specific techniques of interviewing can be derived. It is the double task of developing specific theory and practical interviewing techniques that the writers have set themselves in this volume.

chapter 2

The Psychological Basis
of the Interview

The student of interviewing finds at hand a considerable literature of instructions and suggestions, but few attempts at describing what really goes on in an interview and in what general terms he can understand the interviewing process. Moreover, the lists of "dos and don'ts," though plentiful, are less than satisfying. They are for the most part unsystematic compilations of interviewing experience, derived from various situations over a long period of time. They are the folklore of interviewing, with the advantages and disadvantages characteristic of folklore. Based on experience, they have a good deal of pragmatic utility; practitioners who use them can point to a measure of success. But the miscellaneous rules of interviewing are not always consistent; they are not unified around any basic way of regarding the interview. Even more important, they do not help us understand the interaction between interviewer and respondent. They do not tell us *why* a specific practice makes for a successful interview, or in what context a practice is desirable or undesirable.

To the extent that a picture of the interview can be pieced together from such sources, it appears to have in the foreground a respondent who possesses some valuable opinion or item of information. Approaching him is an interviewer who wants an image or print of that opinion or information. The interviewer's task is to obtain this print efficiently, and to avoid marking it with his own opinions or knowledge in the process.

But this is a rather static, one-sided characterization of the interview. It may be convenient to think of the interviewer as doing no more than obtaining a fact or opinion which the respondent already has well in mind, but such a conception of the interview is not true to life. If one listens to recordings of interviews or has the experience of being a respondent or an interviewer, it is clear that the behavior of the respondent influences the interviewer and the interviewer's behavior is an influence on the respondent. The interview, in short, is an *interactional* process, and both interviewer and respondent contribute to the comunication that results.

In this chapter, we will examine the psychological basis of the interview, with special emphasis on the problem of respondent motivation. We want also to introduce the motivational and perceptual concepts on which we will depend throughout the book. Let us begin, then, with the problem of the respondent's motivation. Why does a respondent agree to or even seek out an interview? Why does he engage in and maintain the relationship that the interview requires? What behaviors on the part of the interviewer influence these decisions and the flow of communcations that follows them? What are some of the major barriers to communications between two people?

These kinds of questions are not specific to the interview, however. They raise the basic problem of how we are to understand human behavior, why people behave as they do in certain situations, and how their behavior can be influenced successfully. Few questions present a longer or more interesting history. The earliest scholars concerned themselves with the riddle of human motivation and behavior, and numerous theories have been offered as solutions. Nor has the interest in the rationale of human behavior been limited to the community of scholars. Practitioners in every field have long recognized that success or failure in their chosen endeavors depends to a considerable extent upon their ability to predict and to influence the actions of the individuals with whom they deal.

RATIONALITY AND EMOTION IN HUMAN BEHAVIOR

Some of the early efforts at providing a systematic explanation of human behavior were theological in origin. Questions of free will and predestination or of good and evil are not relevant to our present problem, but they remind us of an apparent duality in human motivation which has puzzled modern psychologists as well as the philosophers of the past. This duality has to do with what might be called the "rational" and the "emotional" components of behavior. The earlier explanation of some kinds of behavior as caused by demons did not add to scientific knowledge, but it did reflect the observation that an individual's behavior is sometimes unintelligible to his fellows.

"Rational" Behavior

Some later secular philosophies emphasized the rational components of behavior. The scientific enthusiasm of the eighteenth century led to the assertion that man was a rational being and that an individual's behavior could be understood largely as a sequence of situations in which he attempted to maximize his own well-being or self-interest. The concept of the economic man is an excellent example of this approach. Economic man went his income-maximizing way unhampered by uneconomic demands of family or by other personal relationships, uninfluenced by emotion—an abstraction both useful and misleading.

The strengths and weaknesses of this view of human behavior and motivation will become more apparent if we pose a common, contemporary problem and create a reasonable facsimile of the rational economic man to deal with that problem.

Mr. White has just come home from the office and parked his four-year-old sedan in the garage. As he and his wife discuss the affairs of the day, she remarks, "Bob, I've been thinking about that trip to Colorado we're planning this summer. Do you think we ought to get a new car?" "Well, Suzie," says Mr. White, "I really don't know. Let me think about that." After supper, he sits down in his chair, reaches for a pencil, and begins to work on this problem. His thoughts are somewhat as follows.

"Let's see, now. Our car is four years old and it's got about 32,000 miles on it. I wonder how much it will depreciate during the next twelve months." Mr. White reaches for the evening paper and begins to look through the used car ads. On the basis of his examination, he comes to the conclusion that his car is worth about $600 now, and that it will be worth perhaps $400 next year. Accordingly, he puts down on his work sheet, "Depreciation during the next year—$200." Continuing his estimate of the costs involved in keeping his old car, Mr. White moves to the item of "Repairs." He decides that the trip to Colorado will certainly call for a new set of tires, and estimates the cost of four tires at about $80. He recalls also that the old car, though still running satisfactorily, shows a colorful cloud of blue smoke when he starts it each morning and is beginning to use a quart of oil every week or so. He decides that a valve-and-ring job will have to be done in the course of the year and he allows $100 for it. Thinking over the possibility of other repairs, to be on the safe side, he includes $60 or $70 to take care of any repairs that may be heralded by the ominous and persistent hum that he hears in the rear axle, and allows an additional sum to have his brakes relined and overhauled.

All in all, Mr. White decides that it would be prudent to plan on spending about $300 to get the old car in proper condition for the coming year. By the time he had these repairs done, he tells himself, the car would be in good operating condition. Insurance represents another $100, and gas and oil add $250. The total comes to $850, and Mr. White considers this a realistic estimate of the costs involved in keeping his old car.

By comparison, Mr. White feels that a new car would require only negligible repairs or maintenance operations during the first year—probably no more than $25. It would be more economical on gas and oil, too; $200 for the year would be a good guess. On the other hand, he would want collision insurance on the new car, and that would bring his insurance bill up to perhaps $150. The big difference, however, would be in depreciation. The new car would drop about $700 in value during the first year. At this point, Mr. White has before him two columns of figures, which look something like this.

Total cost over next 12 months:

	Old Car	New Car
Repairs	$300	$ 25
Insurance	100	150
Depreciation	200	700
Gas, oil, grease	250	200
	$850	$1075

Cost of operating new car	$1075
Cost of operating old car	− 850
	$ 225

Thus, Mr. White comes to the conclusion that it will cost him $225 more during the year if he buys a new car than if he decides to keep his old one. He takes a deep breath, puts down his paper and pencil, and turns to his wife. "Suzie," he says, "the way I figure it, this isn't our year to buy a car. We'll save more than $200 by driving the old car another year. By then the old bus may be getting so expensive to run that it will pay us to buy a new one."

Mr. White's decision and the process by which he reached it conform to the rational model. He has a conscious economic goal—to provide dependable automotive transportation for himself and his family at the least possible cost. He considers carefully two alternative courses of action in terms of this goal, and makes a decision uninfluenced by extraneous factors. Surely this calculating, ratiocinative process conforms to some aspects of real-life behavior. Mr. White's motives are real enough and his decision seems plausible. Yet if we attempted to understand the behavior of all prospective new car buyers in Mr. White's terms, we would usually go wrong. Something is missing in such an approach. What is missing, of course, is emotionality and the place of emotion in human motivation.

This inadequacy is inherent in the concept of the rational man, and is revealed most clearly in the attempts of users of this concept to explain "irrational" behavior, behavior which appears contradictory to the individual's manifest and stated goals. Such behavior was explained on the grounds that it stemmed from inadequate information, that the individual was occasionally under misapprehension about the actions which would contribute to his self-interest. The process by which a man decided whether to buy this or that was a simple sifting and weighing of economic alternatives on a rational basis, and if his choice was economically "incorrect," it was only because he had his facts wrong. In such an explanation, the complexity of motive patterns, the conflicts among a person's various goals, are largely ignored. Most important of all, perhaps, emotional factors, unrecognized needs and drives, and interpersonal influences are omitted from the conceptual scheme of the rational man.

Emotional Aspects of Behavior

These theoretical problems and the one-sided character of the economical Mr. White become apparent when we witness a decision based on quite different kinds of motives. Take Mr. Brown, who is wrestling with the same problem that Mr. White handled with such dispatch.

Mr. Brown is sitting in his living room with the evening paper propped up in front of him, but he is not reading. He is thinking hard about a rather unpleasant subject. Joe Smith, one of the other men in the company for which Mr. Brown works, has just been promoted. Mr. Brown is trying to figure out just why Smith should have got that promotion instead of himself; try as he will, he is unable to see in Smith any superior qualifications for the job. As a matter of fact, Mr. Brown suspects from the way Smith has been living it up that this promotion may have come just in time to bail him out a bit. Smith lives in a neighborhood a cut above the Browns'. Smith's house is larger, his country club more exclusive. Only last week, Smith drove to work in a glittering new car that to Brown's envious eyes looked all of half a block long.

At this point in his irritated and rather aimless ruminations, Mr. Brown gives his newspaper a shake and turns his attention to it. Prominent on the page before him is an automobile advertisement. It shows an obviously prosperous, broadly smiling man happily piloting a large handsome automobile down an endless road. Above him is a cloudless blue sky, behind him, presumably, all the cares of a work-a-day world. Mr. Brown begins to read the text of the advertisement. "He's in good company . . . And he knows it!" Mr. Brown pauses to digest this headline and then reads on. "It doesn't really matter where he's heading, relaxed and assured at the wheel of his new Colossal. For a long time now he has actually been going in but one direction—up.

"And today, as a culminating achievement, he has joined fellowship with America's most select company of motorists . . . Men at the highest level of success, whose discerning judgment in their choice of motor cars parallels his own!

"He knows now a personal pride and satisfaction no other car ever gave him before. Everything about his Colossal tells him that . . . Its sleek and massive majesty of styling . . . Its immense reservoir of power and power-assisted control . . . The silent approbation of his peers."

Mr. Brown stops to consider involuntarily how enjoyable it would be to experience "the silent approbation of his peers" instead of their sympathy at his failure to obtain the promotion which Smith has just got. He pushes these thoughts aside and continues reading the copywriter's text.

"Yes, even the heads that turn his way as he passes by testify to the rightness of his choice and to the new excitement Colossal is creating in the field of highest quality cars.

"Could it be that *you* have waited long enough to enter the 'charmed circle' of Colossal ownership?"

With this question simmering in his fevered brain, Mr. Brown looks through the window at his own driveway, in which stands a mud-spattered, four-year-old sedan of nondescript color and modest make. He suddenly feels more than ready to enter "the charmed circle" of Colossal ownership. As a matter of fact, he has already embarked on a fantasy which places him at the wheel of such a new car. Its power is a thrill to him and he pictures the ease with which he pulls away from competing traffic at the stop light and takes command of the highway.

Mr. Brown considers also the pleasure such a car would give him when he began to receive "the silent approbation of his peers." The only recent experience he has had involving the reaction of a peer to the automobile he drives was a neighbor's remark a few days ago: "Brown, you're really getting your money's worth out of that old crate." Moreover, it would be a real pleasure to show Smith that, promotion or no promotion, John Brown is able to provide his family with the best. As a matter of fact, thinks Mr. Brown, it's more a question of the family than anything else. That old car really isn't safe, for one thing. And even if it were, it's unfair to expect the wife and kids to be making the neighborhood rounds in that beat-up thing. There are always some kids who are ready to make a point of these things—some grown-ups, too, for that matter. Mr. Brown pictures one or two of his wife's more feline bridge partners congratulating her on her frugality in continuing to drive the old Minuscule Six.

Taking it all in all, decides Mr. Brown, the new car would be a real pleasure for the whole family; it would show some of the men at the office and a few of the snobbish neighbors who's who; and when all's said and done, it would be good for business. With the sudden enthusiasm of a man who has just made an important decision, Mr. Brown tosses his paper aside and turns to his wife. "Abigail," he says, "it isn't safe or reasonable for us to drive that old car another month. We need a new one and we're going to get it."

Mr. Brown's behavior strikes us as not unrealistic, but how shall we understand it in the language of "rationality"? He has not even con-

sidered costs or the condition of his bank account. He seems instead
to be caught up in questions of prestige, competition with neighbors
and co-workers, vague gratifications from speed and power, and superficial rationalizations of what he owes his family. Some of these
factors Mr. Brown sees clearly enough; others he is less aware of,
although their influence on him may be no less great. To understand
Mr. Brown's behavior and the forces which motivated it requires a
point of view different from that which was adequate to understand
White's. A different approach to human behavior is required in order
to make these motives intelligible.

An approach which contrasts most sharply with the concept of the
rational man, and which has done most to illuminate the irrational,
emotional side of man's behavior, is psychoanalytic theory. Freud
and his colleagues, in attempting to understand the behavior of
neurotic patients, demonstrated the importance of the emotional components of human behavior, and the extent to which the behavior of
individuals in a given situation must be understood in terms of forces
which originated earlier in their lives. Moreover, Freudian psychology has taught us that many of the emotional forces which influence
a person's behavior are unrecognized by the individual himself. We
are aware of our motives in varying degree. Some of them are completely apparent to us; some we can recognize only partially or in distorted form. Still others we are entirely unaware of, even though
their effects may be extremely powerful. There are many colloquialisms which reflect some insight into this problem; for example,
such expressions as "I don't know why I did that," or "I don't know
why I feel this way, but—" or perhaps, "I don't know what got into
me."

Freudian theory explains that it is those needs which the individual
finds socially unacceptable that are repressed or distorted, and thus go
unrecognized. For our present discussion, there are two points which
are of cardinal importance: first, that such emotional needs are present
in all human beings; and second, that these needs demand gratification
--in other words, they act to motivate human behavior, whether or
not the individual recognizes the source of the motivation.

Behavior As Motivated by Both Rational and Emotional Forces

It is not our purpose to attempt a critical appraisal of psychoanalytic
theory, or any version of a more rationalistic approach to explaining
human behavior. Neither will we attempt to develop an integration
of such disparate theories. For present purposes, however, it is important to point out that human behavior contains both rational and

emotional components, that the motivating forces of a behavioral act may have rational and emotional sources. Moreover, the combined pattern of rational and emotional factors in motivation is characteristic not alone of the complex decisions and secret wishes that are the special business of the therapist. It is obvious that an interviewer who questions a respondent about the intimate details of his relationship with parents or spouse is likely to evoke marked emotional reactions. It is equally true, although less obvious, that an apparently simple and factual question such as "What is your age?" may encounter some of the same complexities. Normal behavior, even as manifested in relatively simple acts, is motivated by both emotional and rational considerations. A third example of car-buying, this time drawn to emphasize the duality of motivation, will illustrate the approach we will use throughout this book.

Mr. Adam is on the verge of deciding to buy a car. We won't try to guess at all the factors that might influence his decision, but we can quickly discern some that are very obvious. Pushing him toward buying is the fact that a neighbor, Mr. Bones, has just bought a car and the Bones children are excited and happy, whereas the Adam children, having had all the push buttons demonstrated to them, are piqued and a little whiny. Moreover, the Adam car may soon need a couple of new tires and a ring job. Its trade-in value is of course higher now than it will be next year, and Mr. Adam has in his head a figure representing the sum of tires plus repairs plus the loss in trade-in value if he keeps the car another year. And there suddenly comes into his head, too, a remark once made wearily by Mrs. Adam after she had had a day especially beset with parking problems, that power steering might be awfully nice to have.

All these forces push Mr. Adam in the direction of an automobile dealer's show room. Nor is he invulnerable to the prospective joys of owning and driving a brand-new car. Mr. Adam sometimes finds it intolerable to be passed on the highway or beaten at the traffic light by some young speed enthusiast. When his present car was new, he could take on any of them when he really wanted to, but now the old bus just isn't up to it. This doesn't bother Mrs. Adam, who never could understand the competitive aspects of her husband's driving, but it annoys Mr. Adam more than he will admit, even to himself.

For the moment, however, he remains rooted to his chair while opposite forces exert a restraining influence. No matter how he adds and re-adds the figures, it always turns out that the new car means the larger outlay of money. In three seconds Mr. Adam can think of six expensive items the family needs or desires that compete for that same money. For example, Mrs. Adam especially wants some new living room furniture; glancing about him, Mr. Adam is forced to admit to himself that there is merit in her request. The old furniture is beginning to look worn and shabby. The children don't care much one way or the other about the furniture, but they have been after Mr. Adam to build a recreation room in the basement. This would provide them with some much-needed play space and give room also for a Ping-pong table. Mr. Adam thinks that he himself could have a good deal of fun with the recreation room project, and besides it would give him a better place for his workbench and tools.

Moreover, the Adams' present car is less than four years old, and Mr. Adam remembers fondly the first car he and Mrs. Adam ever owned, which they got around in happily for the first eight years of their marriage. Thinking of that first car, Mr. Adam is reminded of the car belonging to the Duncans, the quiet, well-bred couple on the corner with the immaculately kept lawn. The Duncans' car must be seven or eight years old, but it's still as polished as the Boneses' new one and neat as a pin inside. Solid people, the Duncans. The Boneses are, after all, pretty brassy by comparison.

But it is only briefly that Mr. Adam contemplates with satisfaction the flaws of the Boneses' character. He and Mr. Bones drive each other's children to Sunday school on alternate Sundays, and Mr. Adam has no difficulty in foreseeing that on Mr. Bones's Sundays the Adam children will render the afternoon air intolerable with their complaints and cajolings about their old car. The fact is, Mr. Adam thinks irritably, holding a section of the Sunday paper open to a full-page automobile ad, both the Adam and the Bones children are spoiled brats. And yet, why shouldn't the Adam children expect their father to provide as well for them as Bones does for his family? After all, thinks Mr. Adam, my job is as good as Bones's; my professional position is as solid as his; my income must be comparable to his. Why should he have a better car than I?

THE PSYCHOLOGICAL FIELD

We leave Mr. Adam without learning how his dilemma is resolved, and instead, we consider his plight from a purely academic point of view. In analyzing Mr. Adam's situation, we will not be primarily interested in whether or not he buys a car, installs a new recreation room, or practices the virtues of thrift for a little longer; nor are we interested in the automotive market in general. Our interest in the Adam case will be to discover in it those processes and psychological principles that can help us understand all human behavior—verbal and nonverbal, simple and complex. What we will attempt to do, with Mr. Adam's situation as a starting point, will be to understand such basic processes as motivation and perception, memory and attitude formation. In this way we can define here those psychological concepts that will be used throughout the book in order to understand the interviewer-respondent relationship and the resulting content of the interview.

The general approach to human behavior which we will take is that developed by Kurt Lewin and his associates, commonly called *field theory*. According to this theory, any given behavior is the resultant of many forces within the individual—forces which often exert pressures in different directions, and which interact or conflict with each other. The pattern or constellation of such forces at any given time constitutes the "psychological field" of the individual, and his behavior as of that moment becomes understandable in terms of the properties of that field.[1]

Some aspects of Mr. Adam's psychological field are immediately apparent. There are a number of forces prodding him to "see a dealer today." These include a desire to please his wife and children by buying a car and the gnawing wish not to be outdone by his friend and neighbor Mr. Bones. No less strong than these is the purely personal pleasure which Mr. Adam would get from driving one of the gorgeous new jobs himself. In addition, he has persuaded himself that by buying a new car now he would avoid the cost of some expensive repairs required by the old one. If these were Mr. Adam's only goals, it is clear that the forces on him to appear in the dealer's showroom would be overwhelming and uncontested.

There are, however, a number of considerations which are prodding Mr. Adam away from the auto dealer. For example, he wishes to avoid the large expenditure a new car would require, partly in the hope of saving money and partly because of the competing needs (the recreation room and new furniture) which he has in mind. Moreover, his brief comparison of the Bones and Duncan families reminds him that there is a kind of moral value in keeping the old car. Solid people are thrifty and take care of their old things instead of rushing to buy new ones. Good parents do not overindulge their children. In addition, Mr. Adam feels a twinge of conscience over his own involuntary excitement about the possibility of owning a powerful new car. After all, a mature person doesn't have to prove himself by competing at traffic lights. We can probably visualize Mr. Adam's situation more clearly with the help of a pictorial or diagrammatic representation (Figure 3).

The first assumption underlying our representation of Mr. Adam's situation is that all behavior is caused; that is, people have reasons for the things they do, and their behavior becomes intelligible to us to the extent that we are able to understand those reasons and to visualize the situation as it looks to *them*. In other words, Mr. Adam's

---

[1] Our treatment of motivation and perception draws heavily on the following sources: David Krech and Richard S. Crutchfield, *Theory and Problems of Social Psychology*, McGraw-Hill, New York, 1948; Kurt Lewin, *A Dynamic Theory of Personality*, McGraw-Hill, New York, 1935; Kurt Lewin, *Principles of Topological Psychology*, McGraw-Hill, New York, 1936; Kurt Lewin, *Resolving Social Conflicts*, Harper and Brothers, New York, 1948; Kurt Lewin, *Field Theory in Social Science*, Harper and Brothers, New York, 1951; Theodore M. Newcomb, *Social Psychology*, Dryden Press, New York, 1950.

possible purchase of an automobile, like any other behavior in which
an individual engages, simple or complex, has for its immediate cause
some pattern of psychological factors or forces acting on him. Our
ability to understand, predict, or influence an individual's behavior
requires that we have insight into the goals, alternative choices, and
positive and negative forces as they appear to him. He will act not
on the basis of the objective situation, and even less perhaps on the
basis of the situation as it would look to other people. His actions
will depend upon the situation as he experiences it. Our understanding of him will therefore depend upon our ability to experience and
visualize the situation as he does.

This pattern of needs and goals, possible ways of attaining them,
forces urging their achievement or denial, is what Kurt Lewin has
called the psychological field of the individual. His theory is that

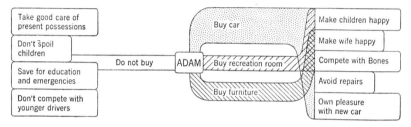

Figure 3. Mr. Adam's psychological field as he contemplates the purchase of a new car.

any specific act or behavior by a human being is immediately preceded by such a pattern of psychological forces and goals, and that
this pattern is the immediate cause which produces the behavior in
question.

Motives

This point of view does not imply, however, that an individual's
psychological field will consist of a single goal and a well-defined
path by which it may be attained. On the contrary, as in the case of
Mr. Adam, we see that he has some goals which would be met were
he to buy an automobile, but others which would be frustrated by the
same action. For instance, buying the car conflicts with his desire
for new furniture; it conflicts with his desire to save; it conflicts with
his desire to behave in accordance with a certain standard of values.
Many of the acts which we perform daily are the result of far
more complex motive patterns than this. They result from diverse
motivating forces, some of which urge the accomplishment of an act,
others its negation, and still others our withdrawal from the entire
situation.

Even an apparently simple kind of behavior is often motivated by more than a single force and is likely to serve more than one goal. Looking at the area in the extreme right-hand part of the diagram, we find that Mr. Adam wants several things, or that he has a number of goals. These include pleasing his children, pleasing his wife, competing successfully with neighbor Bones, avoiding high repair costs on his old car, and satisfying himself in other ways. Among Mr. Adam's many goals, these are especially relevant in the given situation. In the language of Lewin, these goals have a "positive valence" for Mr. Adam. As a result, he feels forces on him to achieve them; their achievement would satisfy certain needs or desires which he is experiencing. For example, pleasing his wife and children will satisfy Mr. Adam's need to see himself as an adequate husband and father. When such a broad need or desire as being a good father or a successful citizen is coupled to a specific goal such as pleasing the children or competing with one's neighbor, we call this combination of need and goal a *motive*. Thus, we can say that Mr. Adam is motivated to please his children or to compete with Bones.

The concept of *need* is used to refer to psychological phenomena at different levels of consciousness. There are, for example, needs of which the individual is well aware and which he understands. Thus, Mr. Adam recognizes that in a sense he *needs* to beat the sports car enthusiast at the stop light, and to compete successfully with Bones.

But such specific and recognized needs spring from deeper levels and reflect aspects of the personality which are likely to be unknown to the individual. Suppose, for example, that Mr. Adam's driving habits represent an effort to compensate for feelings of physical inadequacy, or that his need to outdo Bones in the automotive field reflects a sublimated wish to compete for Mrs. Bones's affections. The chances are that Mr. Adam would be either amused or outraged to hear these things, even if they were true. He would not recognize his own needs at this deeper emotional level.

For the most part, our concern as interviewers will be with needs which are closer to the conscious level. The deeper levels are not usually required for the information-getting function, nor are they available to the interviewer under ordinary circumstances.

There are a number of principles illustrated by this beginning analysis of Mr. Adam's situation:[2]

---

[2] The principles of motivation and perception as developed in this chapter do not represent a complete and integrated treatment of these topics. We have attempted only an exposition of those points that will be required for an understanding of the interview process. The reader who wishes to read more intensively is referred to the source material cited in the preceding footnote.

1. Human behavior is directed toward goals.
2. As the need or desire of an individual is linked to a specific goal which he sees as a means of satisfying the need, there are generated in him specific forces to move toward that goal.
3. This combination of need within the individual and perceived goal is what we shall call a *motive*.

Goals

The implication of these principles for interviewing is that in order to understand the behavior of interviewer and respondent, we must know the goals which are active for them at the time of the interview. Suppose, for example, that a personnel interviewer strolls into one section of a factory and asks for volunteers among the work force to discuss with him some of their on-the-job problems. Whether or not Bill Jones, a lathe hand in this section, volunteers to be a respondent will depend in part upon whether he has relevant goals, such as getting himself a new machine or a promotion or modifying his foreman's behavior. If we know that he feels the need to excel others in his work group, and is therefore motivated to get himself a new lathe, we have some of the information needed to predict whether or not he will volunteer for the interview. The remaining fact we need is whether Jones sees the interview as a way of achieving his goal of getting a new lathe. But this raises additional problems which we have yet to settle for Mr. Adam.

We left Mr. Adam with the goals of pleasing his wife, his children, and himself, and competing successfully with his neighbor. These goals are highly attractive to Mr. Adam, and as a result he feels strongly motivated to attain them. The problem which now confronts him is how can he attain them. In terms of Figure 3, how can he move from his present position to the goal area? What Mr. Adam is looking for is a course of action or a path which will represent a way of attaining his goals. But Mr. Adam perceives several paths by which one or more of his goals might be attained. They include buying the car, buying new furniture for the house, and fixing up a recreation room in the basement. If all these possible courses of action represent paths or ways of attaining Mr. Adam's goals, which one will he take?

The general answer to that question must be that Mr. Adam will follow the path which represents the maximum goal attainment as he sees it. If we can make the simplifying assumption that each of Mr. Adam's goals is of equal importance, then his problem becomes one of examining each path or course of action to determine how many of his goals it would lead him to. As the diagram indicates, buying a car would please all members of the Adam family, would compete successfully with the Boneses, and would avoid repair costs on the old automobile. Installing a new recreation room would please Mr. Adam and his children, and would, in a sense, represent successful competition with the Boneses. It would not, of course, avoid any repair costs in maintaining the old automobile, and it would not, according to Mr. Adam's thinking, give any particular pleasure to his wife. Buying the furniture appears to have the least favorable consequences for goal attainment, since it would not avoid repairs on the old car, satisfy Mr. Adam's own wishes, nor give any pleasure to his children. It would, however, make Mrs. Adam very happy and would be a successful device in the neighborhood competition.

In this further description of Mr. Adam's situation, several additional principles have been illustrated:

4. Behavior takes place only after an individual sees a path leading to a goal that he is motivated to attain.
5. There is often more than one path apparent to the individual that represents some degree of goal attainment for him.
6. Several paths available to the individual may differ in the extent to which they will satisfy his goals.
7. Which one of the several possible paths an individual selects will depend on the amount or degree of goal attainment that each appears to offer (see principle 6 above), and also upon the difficulties or barriers that the individual perceives in traversing a given path.

Some of the major points suggested by these principles can be illustrated in the following interview situation involving a social worker and a man who appears as a client. The client has come to the social agency in order to obtain money which he needs for immediate family expenses. In addition to obtaining financial help, he has the goals of getting psychological support and advice from the social worker, and at the same time maintaining his self-respect and the reputation of his family. Among the circumstances that have led to his family financial crisis is the fact that his wife is an alcoholic.

If in the course of the interview the social worker says, "Now, would you please describe your home situation for me," the client is faced with at least two well-defined alternatives. He may tell his story fully, including the fact of his wife's alcoholism. Or he may try to tell it in such a way as to conceal that fact. Which he will do will depend on what he sees as the paths to his goals. If he considers alcoholism a moral defect rather than an illness, he may feel that all respectable people view it in this way, including the social worker. He may therefore believe that all his goals will be blocked off if he reveals the whole truth—that is, that the social worker will not be sympathetic, that she will not assist him financially, that she will look down on him and his family. Even if he knows that more valuable advice and greater financial assistance may be forthcoming if he tells about the alcoholism, he may not do so because he believes the revelation will thwart his third goal of maintaining self-respect and family reputation. That he is wrong about the social worker's attitudes is, for the time being, irrelevant. He can act only on the basis of the situation *as he sees it.*

Perception

In this situation, as in the case of Mr. Adam and his problems, we have emphasized that the individual will act on the basis of the problem as he sees it, rather than in terms of its objective characteristics. This phraseology involves the concept of *perception.* By perception we refer to the process by which an object or external event becomes part of the internal life, the psychological field, of an individual. The way each of us sees the world or anything in it depends only in part upon external objective reality, and for the rest upon our individual needs, goals, motives, and past experiences. When Mr. Adam passes an automobile dealer's showroom on his way home from work and stops to glance at the shiny new cars inside, he is not viewing these automobiles as detached objects. He does not see the new model merely as an automobile having certain characteristics of style and performance. He sees it in relation to his own needs and goals; he sees it in terms of his wish to enhance the situation of the Adam family and get the best of neighbor Bones, and in terms of the demands which its acquisition might make on his pocketbook. By contrast, it is likely that Mr. Bones, already the leading contender in the neighborhood automobile sweepstakes, will pay relatively little attention to the new car. It is not relevant to Mr. Bones's current needs; he is likely to pass by the dealer's showroom with no more than a glance in the direction of the new model and perhaps the idle reflection that "They're slapping a lot more chrome on them this year."

The general principles of perception which we have just illustrated are as follows:

8. Perceptions are individual; that is, people see things differently, and what a person sees depends in part upon himself, his personality and his past experience.

9. Individual differences in perception can be understood largely in terms of the psychological field of the individual, and especially in terms of his needs and goals.

10. When we perceive an object or situation, we must somehow relate it to things already in our experience. Each new situation must be understood in terms of our past experience, even if in so doing we fail to apprehend the full complexity and meaning of a new situation. The process of perception involves the systematic modification and distortion of a situation, in ways which make it more understandable to us and more congruent with our experience and expectations.

The individuality of perception is a psychological fact, well within the experience of every survey interviewer. Such an interviewer knows, for example, that the way he is seen and treated by two respondents may be entirely different, even though his own appearance, approach, and introductory remarks are identical in the two cases. The wealthy owner of a suburban estate may see the interviewer as a person who is interested in selling him something or asking a favor of some sort. An industrial worker recently arrived in this country might perceive the same interviewer as an agent of the government who is checking up on him for some dire purpose.

Tension

Still another principle is illustrated by Mr. Adam's dilemma. We left him considering the relative merits of three purchases: a car, a recreation room, and some new furniture. If we look again at Figure 3, however, we find that these alternatives do not fully depict Mr. Adam's problem. On the left-hand side of the diagram are represented four additional goals which Mr. Adam recognizes—taking good care of his present possessions, bringing up his children properly (that is, not "spoiling" them), accumulating a fund of money for education and emergency, and being mature enough to avoid competing with younger drivers. These goals have in common the fact that they all imply not spending money at this time. The path to these goals is 180 degrees opposite in direction to the paths of car-buying, furniture-buying, and recreation-room installation. In effect, one set of goals dictates the expenditure of money, another set demands that money be saved.

As we have seen, the desirability of any goal is experienced by the individual as a force urging him toward its accomplishment. Mr. Adam is motivated to be a solid citizen, a thrifty person, and a good parent at the same time that he is motivated to please his wife and children and to compete with his neighbor. The complicating factor in the situation is that the forces urging him toward one set of goals inevitably urge him away from the accomplishment of the other. Thus, Mr. Adam is simultaneously experiencing the incompatible demands generated by two mutually exclusive sets of goals. This aspect of his situation is shown in Figure 4. An individual who is motivated

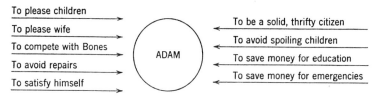

Figure 4. Opposing motive forces and resulting tension.

to the attainment of mutually conflicting goals experiences the opposite motive forces as *tension*, and he attempts in one way or another to take action which will resolve the tensions generated by these opposite forces. He may resolve them by moving in one direction or the other, or by escaping entirely from the tension-producing situation. The principle involved here might be summed up as follows:

11. Whenever a person's psychological field is such that motivating forces act on him in opposite directions, he experiences feelings of tension. Such feelings are unpleasant, and generate specific motivation to resolve the indecision and relieve the tension.

An application of this principle to interviewing can be cited from the field of personnel work. Suppose that a personnel interviewer, discussing with a job applicant his relevant experience, says, "Now, Mr. Jones, will you tell me just what your experience has been on the turret lathe?" This question may put the respondent in a situation where quite opposite motive forces are on him and where the resulting tensions are considerable. If he embellishes his experience on this machine, he may increase his chances of getting the job but reduce his chances of holding it. Elaborating his experience may lead his new employer to have unrealistic expectations of what he can do. If, on the other hand, he is conservative in his description of his experience, he runs the risk of making himself so much less attractive an applicant that he may never get the chance to try the job at all.

ATTITUDES, THE CONCEPT OF THE SELF, AND MEMORY

We have now attempted to understand Mr. Adam's situation and problems, and the possible solutions open to him, in terms of his motives, needs, and goals. We have dealt also with the concept of perception, emphasizing that Mr. Adam, like the rest of us, will behave according to the way he sees a situation rather than in terms of objective reality. We have found in the concept of the psychological field an organizing principle that permits us to handle these several terms simultaneously and to represent in a convenient way the relations among them. As we have suggested throughout this discussion, this kind of analysis will be useful to us in understanding the behavior of interviewers and respondents. Several additional terms and concepts will be of continuing use to us.

Attitudes

We saw that Mr. Adam in his car-buying dilemma wanted, among other things, to please his children. This implies that he has certain feelings toward his children, such as affection or indulgence, and that these feelings are not limited to the car-buying situation. They persist, and they are characteristic of this father's relation to his children in other situations as well. Furthermore, we saw that Mr. Adam's feelings toward his children influence or predispose him to act in certain ways. Again, in many situations we would expect to find Mr. Adam doing things which will be pleasing and rewarding to his children, and avoiding things which he thinks might give them displeasure. Such predispositions to behave in certain ways are what we will call *attitudes*.

An attitude can be defined as a combination of emotional and motivational factors connected with some object or person in the individual's world. An attitude may be properly thought of as characteristic of the individual and typically of substantial duration. Moreover, because of their motivational component, attitudes tend to generate forces on the individual to behave in certain ways. We can say, then, that Mr. Adam has an indulgent or generous or affectionate attitude toward his wife and children, and a competitive attitude toward neighbor Bones. In the same way we can characterize an interviewer-respondent relationship by saying that the respondent has an attitude of trust or skepticism toward the interviewer, and the interviewer may have attitudes of like or dislike, of prejudice or tolerance, toward the respondent. Such attitudes do much to influence the character of the interaction and the content of the interview.

The Concept of the Self

Some of the strongest needs which an individual experiences, and many of the goals toward which he strives with the greatest effort, have to do with the defense of the self. His behavior may become more intelligible if we consider his strivings not only in relation to his stated goals, but as attempts to increase feelings of self-esteem and self-regard. It may be, for example, that Mr. Adam's goals of pleasing his wife and children and competing with Bones are best understood as different ways of achieving self-enhancement. These several goals could be seen as reflections of the deeper level of increasing self-esteem. As Krech and Crutchfield point out, "The self is the most important structure in the psychological field, and it is likely, under normal conditions, to be one of the strongest structures. It has, therefore, a role of unparalleled significance in the determination of the organization of the field. The nature of the relationships of the self to other parts of the field—to other objects, to people, to groups, to social organizations—is of critical importance in understanding the individual's perception of a connection between various objects, individuals, and groups and himself."[3]

Everyday life is replete with examples of extremes of behavior which individuals will manifest in order to avoid placing themselves in situations in which they would feel threatened or inferior or ridiculous. Conformity in dress and speech, for example, can be explained in part as the effort of individuals to increase their feelings of security, their acceptance by others, and by these means their self-regard.

Since the need for self-esteem is so basic and since it underlies many of the specific goals toward which individuals strive, blockage of the gratification of that need will generate extreme tensions. Efforts to resolve such tensions may take a variety of forms, some apparently constructive and socially approved, others quite destructive in their results.

We can illustrate the foregoing points by drawing on the ubiquitous Adam family for an additional example. Mr. Adam's son, Abel, is about to begin his senior year in high school and wants very much to attend the state university when he has completed his high school training. However, Abel's grades for the preceding high school years are not distinguished, and it looks as if an academic record approaching perfection would be necessary in his terminal year, if he is to raise

---

[3] *Theory and Problems of Social Psychology*, p. 69.

his over-all scholastic average high enough to ensure admittance to the university. What is Abel to do? (1) He may attempt to solve his problem and attain his goals by sheer hard work, hoping by this intensification of effort to bring his grades to the necessary level. (2) He may find a substitute goal which retains most of the attractions of attendance at the state university and is considerably more attainable or realistic for him. Thus, he may decide to attend a business school or to make application at various colleges with less exacting entrance requirements. (3) He may attempt to find a new path or an alternate way of achieving his original goal. Thus, he may decide that he should resign himself to the fact that he cannot enter the university on the usual basis, but that he will have to prepare for entrance examinations. He may then turn his best efforts to preparing himself to pass the entrance examinations and in this way achieve the desired goal of acceptance at the university.

Defense Mechanisms

The three solutions to Abel's academic problems just mentioned have in common the fact that they are socially acceptable and objectively "constructive" ways of handling the problem. All three— the intensification of effort, the adoption of an adequate substitute goal, and the reorganization of the problem to ascertain a new path to the original goal—are modes of adjustment commonly found in everyday life. But Abel Adam's behavior in the face of this difficult problem may take less constructive forms. He may attempt to resolve the unbearable tensions of his scholastic situation by doing things which afford relief without actually solving the objective problem. Here again, we find that the various behaviors which Abel may follow have been well recognized by psychologists and have been described clinically and specifically labeled. Especially relevant here are the defense mechanisms of Freudian psychology.[4]

Abel may try to get out of his difficulties by escaping from the situation in a physical way. Dropping out of school would be the most obvious form of escape. Or he might attempt to achieve a psychological escape by remaining in school but manifesting no interest whatsoever in his studies and becoming increasingly remote from his

---

[4] The factors that lead a person to utilize one or another of the defense mechanisms and that determine which of them he uses are extremely complex. They are likely to have their roots in the early personality-forming experiences of the individual. As a result, the adult may show habitual reliance on a particular defense mechanism, even when the objective aspects of the situation do not appear tension-provoking and when more constructive solutions seem available.

teachers and classmates. Such behavior the psychologist would consider a well-defined example of *withdrawal.*

Abel may, however, behave in quite a different way. Within a short period of time his teachers may be talking to each other about the sudden changes in his behavior and asking such questions as "Whatever has come over that boy?" Abel at this point may be obtaining some apparently illogical release from his tensions by becoming something of a school bully, by being hostile and overbearing toward teachers and students. Such behavior would constitute another of the classical mechanisms of defense, *aggression.*

There is still a different way in which Abel might approach his problem. We all have strong needs to behave in ways that appear reasonable to ourselves and to the people whose opinions we value. We want to make it clear to them and to ourselves that our motives for doing things are proper and acceptable. Abel may make a strong attempt to convince himself and others that he is kept from attending the university by considerations which reflect only credit upon him. For example, he may be quite successful in persuading himself that he should not attend college because doing so would put an unreasonable financial burden upon his father. By looking for a job, Abel declares that he is really renouncing his own ambitions and potentialities in order to make a contribution to the family and ease his father's responsibilities. The process by which an individual comes to assign such plausible "reasons" for what he does, and comes as well to believe them himself, is known as *rationalization.*

Another defense mechanism closely related to rationalization in its dynamics is *projection.* Here again the individual acts in a way which is designed to make his behavior understandable and socially acceptable. In projection, however, the individual assigns to other persons or objects in his psychological field the characteristics or inadequacies which are in fact his own. Thus, if Abel were to insist that his failure to attain high grades was due to the incompetence of his teachers and the poor content of the high school curriculum, we might conclude that he was projecting.

Finally, there is a process which, although itself a mechanism of defense, can also be considered as basic to such defense mechanisms as rationalization and projection. This process, which Freud has stressed particularly, is called *repression.* By repression we mean "forgetting" an unsatisfied need, or pushing it down into the unconscious, so that the fact of its being unsatisfied is ordinarily inaccessible to the individual. The apparent purpose of the process of repression is, of course, to relieve him of tensions resulting from unsatisfied needs or unattainable goals. That certain needs are repressed, however, does not rob them of their power to influence the individual's behavior. They continue to generate forces in the individual's psychological field, even though he is no longer conscious of them. Thus, he may have needs of which he is unaware, and he may be strongly motivated by forces whose origins he does not recognize.

The fact that an individual may have needs and motives of which he is unconscious has particular importance for the process of interviewing, since no respondent can report directly aspects of his psychological life of which he is unaware. This poses a major problem in the design of interviews and in the techniques of interviewing. It means that when we ask an individual about his attitudes or motives, we must be prepared to find that he is unable to give us the actual basis for his thinking and behavior. We ask the individual to report all the phenomena in his psychological field, and he is able to report only those things of which he is conscious. Not only may he fail to report significant material, but he may, through such processes as rationalization and projection, give us misinformation. Considering again the example of car-buying: if we ask a man why he bought a new car, he is likely to answer in terms of certain of his needs. He may, like Mr. Adam, indicate that he wanted to please the family and that the condition of his old car left something to be desired. He may even show the insight into his own motives that Mr. Adam did in recognizing his desire to compete successfully with a neighbor. It is extremely unlikely, however, that the purchaser of a powerful new automobile would be able to tell an interviewer that the mere mastery of the powerful vehicle was rewarding psychologically because his physical weaknesses and inadequacies as a youth had developed in him strong needs to compensate.

Memory

Another psychological process of special importance in interviewing is memory. Often, we interview a respondent not to learn about his reactions at the moment, but to get information about a past experience. We ask the respondent to describe or reproduce for us a psychological field which he experienced at some earlier time. Such recall is in many ways even more difficult than obtaining insight into a current situation. We have discussed already the processes by which motives and goals that we are unable to handle consciously may be repressed or driven into the unconscious. By processes that are in many ways analogous, we tend in memory to modify, change, and distort past situations in order to make them fit more comfortably with other experience and with our image of ourselves.

Wallen[5] devised an ingenious experiment which provides a specific demonstration of the tendency to forget facts that conflict with one's self-image. He asked his experimental subjects to indicate which of forty personality traits they possessed and which they did not. At a later time the same list was given to the subjects, this time with a notation after each trait purporting to reflect the opinions of the subjects' friends as to whether or not the subjects possessed the trait. Still later, the subjects were asked to recall the friends' ratings. Subjects more often forgot ratings which conflicted with their own picture of themselves.

Edwards,[6] in order to test the dependence of memory on frame of reference, tested the ability of subjects to remember the content of a speech which included statements for and against the New Deal administration of Franklin D. Roosevelt. He found that subjects whose own attitudes toward the New Deal were favorable showed better recall of the favorable statements in the speech. Anti-New Deal subjects showed opposite results.

In work on consumer economics, the Survey Research Center has found that if we want to learn respondents' current incomes, the problems are mainly problems of motivation. Most people know at least approximately what their current income is; whether or not they will communicate this information depends on their willingness to do so. But if we want to know what their incomes were ten years ago, we have to enter much more difficult territory. However willing they may be to answer, many will have forgotten and many will "remember" so inaccurately that the information they offer is of severely restricted usefulness. It has been found that the inaccuracies seem to show a systematic pattern, and that the distortions are likely to be in the direction of putting the earlier situation in a more favorable light.

Memory, in short, is not a simple process by which the events of the present recede uniformly into the past. This kind of decay does occur, but it is modified by a number of other factors, including the meaningfulness of the initial experience, the degree to which it was "learned," and the interference of other experiences. In addition, as

---

[5] R. Wallen, "Ego Involvement as a Determinant of Selective Forgetting," *Journal of Abnormal and Social Psychology*, **37**, 20–39 (1942).

[6] A. L. Edwards, "Political Frames of Reference as a Factor Influencing Recognition," *Journal of Abnormal and Social Psychology*, **36**, 34–50 (1941).

we have seen, the way in which things are remembered depends upon their congruence with the individual's other experience and with his image of himself. Such factors determine whether or not we remember at all, and in what systematic ways our recollections differ from events as they actually occurred.

The implications of these facts for interviewing are profound. They mean that we must find techniques by which the respondent can be assisted in the difficult job of remembering, and still other techniques by which we may make inferences about things that will remain inevitably beyond his recall.

MOTIVATION WITHIN THE INTERVIEW

Let us turn now to an analysis of respondent motivation. The general point of view that we have taken regarding human behavior and the factors that motivate it must be adapted specifically to the interview. Moreover, we cannot be satisfied with treating each interview as a unique case, and studying each respondent as a totally new problem in motivation. In practical interviewing situations, we cannot work through for each respondent the kind of analysis with which we favored the Adam family. We must look instead for some general motivational principles that will facilitate the understanding of the interview process and provide a basis for teaching the essential skills of the interviewer.

Extrinsic Motivation

Recent work in communications within small groups has resulted in findings which appear relevant to our understanding of communication between an interviewer and a respondent. These findings can be summarized as follows. One of the motives for communicating is the desire to influence, in some manner, the person to whom the communication is addressed. That is, a person will communicate in a given situation if he believes that such communication will bring about a change or an action that he considers desirable.[7]

The interviewer may be perceived as a person who can bring about change himself, or he may be seen as an agent who can make some indirect contribution to a desired change. A clinical psychologist, a social worker, or a physician is likely to be seen by the patient or client as a direct agent of change. The respondent feels that he is communicating his symptoms or his problems to a person who has special skills and abilities which are to be put at his disposal. An

[7] Leon Festinger, et al., *Theory and Experiment in Social Communication,* Institute for Social Research, University of Michigan, Ann Arbor, 1950.

example of a less direct relation between interviewer and the goal of a respondent is provided by the typical market-research survey. The respondent realizes that the interviewer can render him no direct service, but may believe nevertheless that by expressing preference for a specific kind of packaging or for some change in a product, he will be contributing to the improvement of the product in terms of his own wishes and needs. The interviewer is not the direct agent of change, but he carries the message to that agent. There is a good deal of anecdotal evidence for the importance of this aspect of respondent motivation. It was common during World War II, for example, when frequent surveys were being conducted on government programs, for a respondent to preface his answer with, "You tell those people in Washington that . . . "

This type of extrinsic motivation can be developed only if the following relations are apparent to the respondent: (1) the relevance of the interview content to a change which he desires—the respondent will not spontaneously perceive every research project to be related to his goals and interests, and the researcher often must demonstrate this relationship; (2) the role of the interviewer in bringing about change, or as the representative of an agency which is able to bring about change.

Intrinsic Motivation

Investigations in the field of psychotherapy have identified a second major source of motivation in the interview. This motivation depends more directly upon the personal relationship between the interviewer and the respondent, and can be defined as follows. An individual is motivated to communicate with another when he receives gratification from the communication process and the personal relationship of which it is a part. Such motivation sometimes occurs because the interview offers the respondent an opportunity to talk about topics in which he is interested but which usually do not obtain adequate opportunity of expression. This does not imply that the respondent in an informational interview ordinarily obtains the cathartic release that we associate with the psychiatric interview. It means simply that he obtains satisfaction from talking with a receptive, understanding person about something in which he is interested and involved.

Interviewers are often surprised to encounter this intrinsic motivation in an interview in which the possibility (or desirability) of a therapeutic type of relationship appears remote. Experience shows, however, that if the information-getting interview is conducted properly, this intrinsic motivation is usually present. The relationship between interviewer and respondent in such interviews resembles the counseling relationship in many respects.

Recently the Survey Research Center sent mail questionnaires to respondents who had been interviewed on national surveys, to find out their reactions to the surveys. A high proportion of the respondents reacted in terms of feelings about the interviewer and the process of the interview rather than to the survey as such. It appears from reading the comments that what impressed itself on respondents was not the subject of the interview or the questions that were asked, but the relationships they established with the interviewers.

Counselors and therapists have found that one of their primary functions is to motivate and assist the patient to communicate material that is disturbing him. They have therefore attempted to understand and specify the circumstances that encourage such communication. Rogers[8] identifies four qualities as characteristic of the productive counseling atmosphere. Three of the four are relevant to the research interview. The first is "warmth and responsiveness" on the part of the counselor, which "expresses itself in a genuine interest in the client and an acceptance of him as a person." The second quality is described as "permissiveness in regard to expression of feeling. By the counselor's acceptance of his statements, by the complete lack of any moralistic or judgmental attitude, by the understanding attitude which pervades the counseling interview, the client comes to recognize that all feelings and attitudes may be expressed. No attitude is too aggressive, no feeling too guilty or shameful, to bring into the relationship." A third characteristic of the productive counseling relationship is "freedom from any type of pressure or coercion. The skillful counselor refrains from intruding his own wishes, his own reactions or biases, into the therapeutic situation."

Applying these criteria to the information-getting interview, we may conclude that a basic condition for optimum communication is that the respondent perceive the interviewer as one who is likely to understand and accept him and what he has to say. The interviewer must be perceived as "within range"—that is, he must be seen as a person to whom the respondent's statements and experience will not be foreign or offensive. This does not mean that the respondent needs to see the interviewer as similar to himself, but he must view the interviewer as capable of understanding his point of view, and of doing so without rejecting him. This perception will depend far more on the interviewer's attitudes and the relation he establishes

[8] Carl R. Rogers, *Counseling and Psychotherapy*, Houghton Mifflin, Boston, 1942, pp. 87–89.

than on such external factors as dress or appearance, although these may provide some initial cues for the respondent.

Conformance to Social Norms

There is a third source of motivation to communicate to an interviewer, which is quite distinct from either the instrumental or intrinsic kinds of motives already discussed. This motivation stems from certain social norms, and would vary among different groups in the population. There are ways of behaving toward a person that are thought of as "right" in our culture, and others that are "wrong," or at least inappropriate. Such norms become goals for the individual respondent; he feels that he should behave in certain ways and, other things being equal, he "wants" to do so. Among such social norms, which we find many people have accepted are the homely virtues of treating a stranger courteously, behaving hospitably toward a visitor, answering when spoken to, telling the truth, and conforming to the reasonable requests of persons in authority. The respondent whose image of himself includes such norms comes to an interview with an attitude that provides an initial motivational assist for the interviewer. It is not likely that these motives are sufficiently strong to sustain a long or difficult interview, but they at least give the interviewer an opportunity to tap the more important motive sources already described. They imply also that, other things being equal, a respondent will prefer to answer rather than to remain silent, and to tell the truth rather than to fabricate. In casual situations, where the demands of the interview are modest and the potential threat at a minimum, these norms may generate sufficient motivation to meet the interview objectives entirely.

Forces Inhibiting Communication

Unfortunately, a number of factors may inhibit communication or distort the content of the information given by the respondent. For example, the respondent may not accept the goal which the interviewer describes as the purpose of the interview. Thus, the goal of providing the Federal Government with information on income distribution may not appear worthwhile to some survey respondents about to be questioned regarding their own finances and economic situation. Even more frequently, the respondent may possess goals that are in conflict with the purpose of the interview. In an industrial plant, for example, a worker may be wholly sympathetic to the notion that employee opinions should be solicited, and he may be hopeful that frank expressions will result in improved working conditions. He may also think, however, that his expression of critical opinions may be dangerous and may make him liable to retaliation from his supervisor. He may even be convinced that loss of work or loss of promotion could follow an expression of harsh criticism. Such an attitude may not result in a refusal, but it will limit the content areas within which the worker will talk freely. He might discuss physical working conditions and wage policy quite frankly but be extremely guarded and reticent when discussing aspects of his job that might involve criticism of his immediate superiors.

Just as a respondent may refuse to communicate or may distort his communication because he rejects the goals of the interview process, he may also refuse or restrict communication because the personal relationship with the interviewer is unpleasant or lacks positive value. This kind of respondent reaction may occur as a result of a stereotyped judgment which he makes of the interviewer. If the respondent perceives a gap of education or an economic difference between himself and the interviewer, he may decide that the interviewer is incapable of understanding his family circumstances or of empathizing in any way with his predicament. A similar problem in communication may arise if the respondent sees himself as deviant within the content area of the interview. For example, a respondent holding radical political views might perceive the interviewer as differing so greatly from himself that tolerance for his point of view is unlikely. When a respondent concludes that the interviewer is outside the possible range of communication, the possibility of a complete and valid interview is remote.[9]

Respondent Motivation in Specific Kinds of Interviews

Survey Interview. An example will serve to illustrate the factors which motivate and inhibit respondent communication, and the interviewer's role in facilitating it. Consider the housewife whose doorbell has just been rung by an interviewer for the Midwestern University Research Center. When the interviewer has introduced himself as representing the Midwestern Research Center and has asked Mrs. Jones to give an interview about her plans for consumer purchases, he has set up for her a well-structured situation. She must choose between two roles, respondent or nonrespondent. What are the forces at work in Mrs. Jones's psychological field that will determine the choice she makes?

---

[9] Charles F. Cannell and Robert L. Kahn, "Collection of Data by Interviewing," in *Research Methods in the Behavioral Sciences,* Festinger and Katz (ed.), Dryden Press, New York, 1953, pp. 336–339.

Among the forces that urge her in the direction of accepting the respondent role may be the prospect of relief from the boredom of housework, the possibility of an interesting interruption to a lonely morning, the satisfaction of curiosity as to what the interview process is like, and a feeling that common politeness requires her to accede to a courteous request. In addition, the mention of the word "research" and the interviewer's reference to university sponsorship awaken some feeling of obligation to support research and institutions of higher learning.

But a considerable array of other forces is likely to urge the opposite course of action, and move her in the direction of becoming a nonrespondent. Such forces might include fear of inviting a stranger into her home, the neglect of household duties that would be forced on her by a lengthy interview, suspicion that the purpose may not really be that which the interviewer described, and an admonition from her husband to give no information whatsoever to strangers. The conflict in which Mrs. Jones finds herself can be visualized with the help of a diagram (Figure 5).

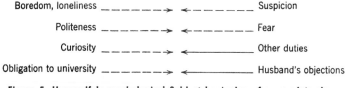

Figure 5. Housewife's psychological field at beginning of survey interview.

We cannot predict merely from this enumeration of opposing forces whether she will choose to become a respondent or a nonrespondent. This prediction can be made only if we know the relative strength of each of the forces involved. In the early moments of the interview, the interviewer attempts to get some indication of the forces that will determine the housewife's decision and of the relative strength of these forces. She may facilitate this process by verbalizing the conflict she is experiencing. Thus, she may say, "I'm afraid I won't have time to grant an interview, because I have to get a cake in the oven," or "I would like to cooperate with Midwestern University, but my husband has asked me not to give out information about the family."

The interviewer then will attempt to influence a favorable decision. This he may do by eliminating or reducing the strength of those forces that tend to move the housewife in the direction of nonresponse, or by increasing the number or strength of those forces that tend to move her toward taking the respondent role. He may show credentials that clearly identify him as a member of the Midwestern Research Center, promise that the interview will not exceed a half-hour, and point out the guarantees of anonymity. He may go on to explain that the interview is being conducted for an agency of the Federal Government, and that knowledge of consumer plans and expectations is of great importance for policy and administrative decisions.

We can show in a second diagram the restructured psychological field of the housewife following this interaction (Figure 6).

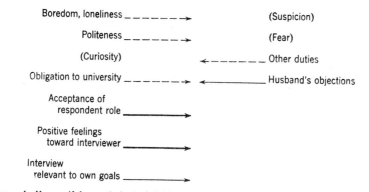

Figure 6. Housewife's psychological field restructured following interviewer's introduction.

The interviewer has succeeded in persuading the housewife to take the respondent role. Note that the opposing forces of suspicion and fear have been removed from the respondent's psychological field, or at least reduced to insignificance by the interviewer's successful introduction of himself, his organization, and the purposes of the study. Moreover, new positive forces are present, reflecting favorable feelings on the respondent's part for the interview and for the purposes of the research. In addition, we can consider as a positive force the commitment involved in the respondent's acceptance of his role. The respondent's positive feelings for the interviewer, for the purpose of the research, and for the respondent role result in a clear preponderance of forces to communicate. The competition of other duties has been temporarily diminished by the respondent's decision to enter into the interview. Only her recollection of her husband's warning against the interview process remains unchanged as a force of opposition. It remains for the interviewer to maintain and strengthen this favorable balance of motive forces throughout the interview, reducing or counteracting any negative forces which develop.

Medical Interview. As a second example of the psychological forces involved in the decision to become a respondent or nonrespondent, consider the case of a patient who has gone to a physician's office. The patient's initial attitudes toward the interview are likely to be better defined than those of the housewife in the previous example. The role of patient is one in which the individual has had previous experience. He understands what is expected of him; he knows that it involves his accepting the function of respondent in a medical interview. The major force tending to move the patient in the direction of accepting this respondent role stems from his perception that by doing so he will get relief from the pain and anxiety of illness. An additional force tending to move the patient in this direction derives from the position of the physician as an authority figure—a person who is to be obeyed, whose requests for information must not go unanswered.

Perhaps the major force against the patient's communicating freely in the medical interview is fear—fear that by indicating the nature of his symptoms he may bring about a threatening diagnosis or a painful course of therapy. Suppose that our patient is proving a poor respondent for just this reason. There are a number of ways in which the physician may restructure the patient's psychological field so as to facilitate the medical interview. One of the most important is to give reassurance. The doctor may convey this reassurance in subtle and covert ways—by his calmness and lack of shock or emotion at the patient's initial story, by his bearing of competence and knowledge. He shows interest in the patient's statements and accepts them as serious and meaningful. Or the doctor may find it necessary and justifiable to offer reassurance in more overt terms. This he can do by telling the patient that his symptoms are familiar and that there are powerful therapeutic resources at hand. The dangers of over-optimism and false reassurance are great, of course, and the physician must decide how far he can go in this direction without becoming unrealistic or untruthful.

There are other means which the doctor may use to encourage communication. He may remind the patient that he needs information to assist the process of diagnosis and cure, or even that withholding information would handicap their common goal of achieving a cure as rapidly and painlessly as possible. There is another aspect to the patient-doctor relationship that acts to bring them closer together and to facilitate such communication. The patient typically reacts to illness as an enemy, something to be fought; it is "me versus my illness." If the doctor makes clear his own involvement in the battle, he becomes an ally, or even a champion who takes over the patient's cause and much of his responsibility. Communication in these circumstances becomes easier, and the interview proceeds successfully.

Journalistic Interview. Other kinds of interviews present psychological problems basically similar to those of the research and medical interview. Suppose a journalist has requested an interview of a politician. The psychological field of our public servant may include such positive forces as his desire for "good" publicity, his need to be liked by many people and especially the press. On the other hand, the politician may tend to shrink from or refuse the interview because of the possibility that the journalist might be hostile and misrepresent his virtues to the voters. Whether or not the politician decides to become a respondent and grant the interview depends primarily upon the relation among these kinds of positive and negative forces. The journalist's success will therefore depend upon his assessment and manipulation of them.

Supervisory Interview. As a final example, let us consider the case of an employee who is suddenly invited to an interview with his immediate superior. The possibility of his refusing is remote indeed, because of the power relationship involved. However, the employee may accede to the interview only because of this requirement to follow the wishes of his superior. At the same time, the negative forces that lead the employee to want to refuse the interview may be numerous and powerful. These could include, for example, fear of disciplinary action or a wish to avoid criticism. Although there is small possibility of his refusing outright to be a respondent, the kind of respondent he becomes, the way in which he plays the respondent role, and the fullness and validity of his responses will depend in very great measure upon the established relation between him and his supervisor, and upon the kinds of forces which we have described in other interviewer-respondent situations.

Instability of Respondent Motivation during the Interview

Once the respondent has agreed to be interviewed, a specific relationship has been initiated between him and the interviewer, and mutual expectations are in process of being established. Some of the most important of these expectations have to do with the respondent role—the notions of interviewer and respondent as to the behaviors which are appropriate for a person who has agreed to be interviewed and the obligations which he has assumed. The primary obligation, of course, is the answering of questions; a respondent is one who responds. Barring questions which appear to be threatening or otherwise inappropriate, the respondent, in agreeing to carry on an interview, expects to answer queries, and the interviewer expects that his questions will be answered. However, the problems of how fully such questions will be answered, and with what validity and accuracy, is by no means solved by the initial decision to accept the respondent role. The solution to these problems lies in a successful pattern of interaction, which is in large degree controlled by the interviewer.

The respondent's agreement to the initiation of the interview, and the early interaction of questions and answers, typically produce a considerable stabilization of the forces in his psychological field. Moreover, this stability is one in which the predominant forces are in the direction of continuing respondent communication.

This highly favorable array of forces to communicate, while characteristic of an interview once the respondent has accepted his role, is not completely stable, however. The maintenance of positive forces is not assured, but depends upon the skill of the interviewer and the nature of his questions. There is always the possibility of a sudden increase in opposing forces. Perhaps the factor most frequently responsible for such a shift is the introduction of new material, or a new kind of question.

Figures 7 and 8 illustrate the psychological forces characteristic of two later moments in the interview on consumer purchases already described. Let us suppose that our research interviewer has just asked the following question of Mrs. Jones: "Are you planning to buy a new car?" Since the respondent has been told that this is a survey on consumer purchases, the question is accepted as legitimate and the balance of forces in the interview is positive, as illustrated in Figure 7. In comparison with Figure 6, we see the effects of successful interviewing in the strengthened acceptance of the respondent role by Mrs. Jones and more positive feelings toward the interviewer.

Somewhat later, however, he asks: "What was your income during the past year?" Such a question may well produce a less favorable array of forces in the respondent's psychological field. Plans to purchase a car were seen as appropriate to the interview topic, and not threatening to discuss. But the income question may arouse again the fear and doubts which characterized the earliest phases of the interview. The respondent may be concerned that giving information about income might somehow disadvantage the family with business associates, neighbors, or even the Bureau of Internal Revenue. Moreover, there may be social norms against the respondent's communicating family income. In many circles this topic is avoided as a matter of courtesy. The introduction of such emotionally loaded material may reactivate for the housewife respondent the forces of suspicion and the fear of the husband's reaction, which were dormant when more neutral material was being discussed. Concurrent with these increases in negative forces are losses in the respondent's acceptance of her role and in positive feelings toward the interviewer. The interview appears less congruent with the respondent's goals.

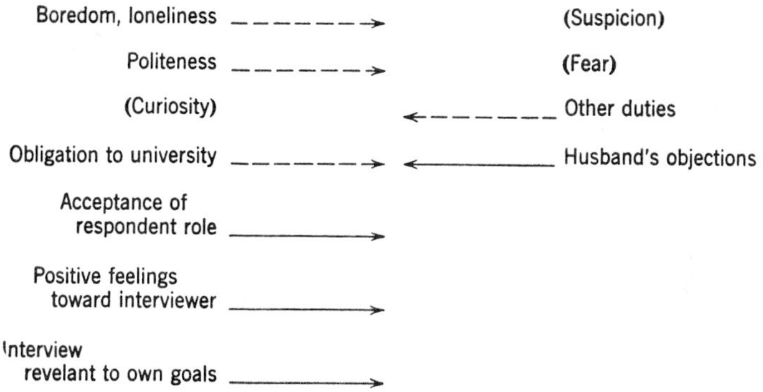

Boredom, loneliness _ _ _ _ _ _ ➤   (Suspicion)

Politeness _ _ _ _ _ _ ➤   (Fear)

(Curiosity)   ◄_ _ _ _ _ _ Other duties

Obligation to university _ _ _ _ _ _ ➤ ◄_____ Husband's objections

Acceptance of
respondent role _____ ➤

Positive feelings
toward interviewer _____ ➤

Interview
revelant to own goals _____ ➤

Figure 7. Housewife's psychological field following question: Are you planning to buy a new car?

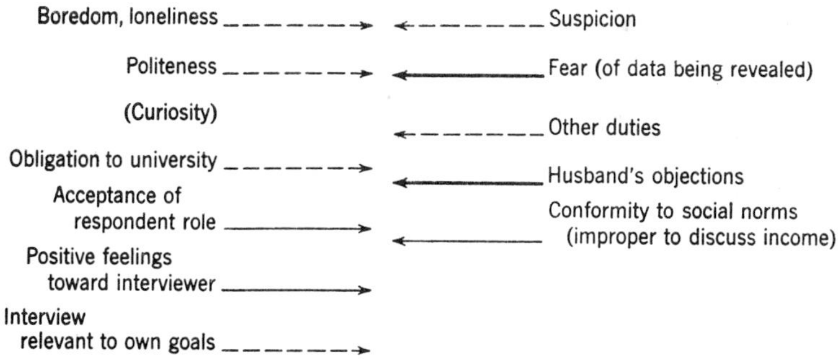

Boredom, loneliness _ _ _ _ _ _ ➤   ◄_ _ _ _ _ _ Suspicion

Politeness _ _ _ _ _ _ ➤   ◄_____ Fear (of data being revealed)

(Curiosity)   ◄_ _ _ _ _ _ Other duties

Obligation to university _ _ _ _ _ _ ➤   ◄_____ Husband's objections

Acceptance of
respondent role _____ ➤   Conformity to social norms
                          ◄_____   (improper to discuss income)
Positive feelings
toward interviewer _____ ➤

Interview
relevant to own goals _ _ _ _ _ _ ➤

Figure 8. Housewife's psychological field following question: What was your income during the past year?

There is ample corroboration from interviewers' reports and survey records for this sort of instability in motivation to communicate. Interviewers report that the introduction of a question on income will frequently result in hesitancy or temporary interruption of communication by the respondent. The respondent may bring the interview to a halt with a question of his own as to why such information is being asked, or he may challenge the introduction of the income question with a statement that it is not relevant to the purposes of the interview as previously stated.

The statistics with respect to nonresponse bear out these reports by interviewers. In the Survey Research Center's economic studies, for example, a typical refusal rate is approximately 6 per cent; that is, 6 per cent of the people approached for interview refuse initially to accept the respondent role. Among people who agree to be interviewed, however, an additional 2 per cent refuse to answer the question on income and savings. Nor is the income question unique in this respect; rather, it is typical of reactions to material which the respondent finds relatively threatening. The introduction of such topics will frequently evoke resisting forces too powerful for the respondent's motivation to communicate. When this occurs, the interviewer must restore the favorable balance of forces or accept the respondent's refusal to continue.

To restore the balance the interviewer can work with either of the major motivational sources—the contribution of the interview to the goals of the respondent, and the direct gratification that the respondent derives from the interview as an interpersonal experience. The respondent has agreed to the interview in the first place because he perceived its purposes to be consistent with or directly supportive of his own goals. If the interviewer can convince the respondent of the relevance of the offending question to the ultimate goals of the interview, the respondent will see the question in a new frame of reference and will find it acceptable. Needless to say, this may require patient explanation, reiterating and enlarging upon the discussion which led to the respondent's initial acceptance of his role. In our previous example, the interviewer might explain that the patterns of spending and saving and the attitudes of people on economic affairs become understandable and useful for policy decisions only insofar as these data can be analyzed separately for each income group.

An alternative or complementary approach to the problem might be based more directly on the personal relationship established between interviewer and respondent. The interviewer might postpone the offensive question until a later time in the interview, on the assumption that the interpersonal bonds are being steadily strengthened, and that they will sustain such a question best when they have approached their maximum. This is analogous to the frequent experience of the therapist, who avoids pressing a threatening question, well knowing that in later interviews the patient will feel sufficiently secure in their relationship so that he will be able to discuss freely material he now is unwilling to communicate.

Let us consider a further example of fluctuations in respondent motivation, this time from a medical interview. Assume that a prospective patient has overcome the negative forces of fear, anxiety, and the costs of medical care sufficiently to go to the doctor. He has appeared in the doctor's office and begun the interview process. A possible question on the part of the doctor after the amenities have been gotten over might be: "How long have you been feeling bad?" At this point the forces motivating the patient to prompt and full response are the needs for help, reassurance, and relief from pain, which were major factors in leading him to the physician's office in the first place. In addition, there are the forces represented by the patient's acceptance of his role and the realization that it involves his providing information to the doctor. The negative forces opposing communication are in abeyance at this point.

As in the case of the research interview, the introduction of new material by the interviewer (physician) can immediately bring new negative forces into play or arouse the old ones. Suppose, for example, that the physician asks, "Have you been carefully following the diet I gave you?" As a result of this question, the psychological field of the patient may undergo a considerable alteration, especially if he has been no more diligent than most of us in following the physician's suggested diet. Probably the major effect of such a question is to introduce several kinds of forces opposing prompt and full response. Such forces might include embarrassment at the prospect of admitting that the physician's advice has not been followed. There might also be fear of rejection, or exclusion from the needed assistance that the physician can offer, or some other punishment for having failed to follow his admonitions. At the same time, it is probable that at least one additional force in the direction of motivating communication is developed. This motivating force would be the respondent's recognition that falsifying an answer or failing to communicate at this point might block accurate diagnosis and therapy, and in that way complicate all the problems that led him to consult the physician in the first place.

As in the previous example from survey research, the problem of the physician-interviewer at this point is to increase the forces on the patient to communicate, or to decrease the forces against communication. The doctor might do the first by reminding the patient that the question is relevant to the future course of treatment, that the medical evaluation of his present condition and the prescription for the future will be based in part on what his intake of food has been. This explanation would encourage a frank response by stressing its importance in terms of the patient's own goals.

Alternatively, the doctor might concentrate on reducing the forces opposing communication.   This he might do by reassuring the patient that failure to follow his diet is a common fault, one not unexpected and well tolerated by the physician.   He might make it clear that the character and closeness of the patient-doctor relationship will not be influenced by the patient's success or failure in following the diet.

It is perhaps unnecessary to work through in similar detail examples from other fields.   In most cases the constellations of forces and the basic points to be made are similar to the patterns already described.

INTERVIEWER-RESPONDENT INTERACTION

The treatment of respondent motivation thus far has involved several simplifying assumptions.   First, we have talked about the psychological field of the respondent as of a particular instant.   It is convenient to do this, treating the respondent's psychological life as if it were made up of an infinite number of snapshots or glass slides from which we could select those that represented the set of forces operating at any particular moment.   It is much more realistic, however, to think of the respondent's psychological field as a dynamic process, always developing, always in a state of change.   The psychological field of an individual is more analogous to a moving picture than to a collection of lantern slides.   In attempting to reproduce the psychological field of the respondent as of a given moment in the interview, we have, in effect, stopped the motion picture projector and concentrated upon a single frame in the film.

The second simplification which we have made in discussing respondent motivation is that we have thus far limited ourselves almost entirely to the psychological field of the respondent.   Actually, the psychological field of the respondent must be thought of as developing throughout the process of the interview, and the interviewer must be thought of as the major influence on the respondent's psychological field during the interview.

Finally, influence between the interviewer and the respondent is by no means a one-way process.   The relation is reciprocal, with the psychological fields of both interviewer and respondent constantly in process of modification because of cues each receives from the other. Most students of interviewing recognize that the motivation of the respondent depends to a considerable extent upon interviewer characteristics and behavior.   It is less frequently recognized, however, that the interviewer's behavior depends in part upon the respondent— what he says and does, even how he looks.   In short, the end product of the interview depends not only on how the respondent approaches his role, but also upon the way in which the interviewer assumes his role, and upon the interaction or reciprocal-influence process which they jointly create. These aspects of the interview process must be considered in greater detail. In doing so, we will be elaborating and setting in broader context the foregoing discussion of respondent motivation.

The Danger of Bias in Interaction

If the interview is a product of interaction, what becomes of the conveniently simple notion that the ideal interview is something that springs from the soul of the respondent to the notebook of the interviewer without encountering any contaminating influences en route? And what becomes of the corollary notion that any vestige of interviewer influence in the interview process constitutes bias and must be avoided at all costs? The answer to these questions is that they represent a concept of the interview and the respondent and interviewer roles that is rejected by the interactional analysis we have just made. That concept places primary emphasis on the interviewer's negative function, that of not influencing what the respondent says. What we propose to emphasize in the interviewer's role is the importance of controlling and directing the process of interaction between himself and his respondent in such a way that the basic objectives of the interview are met. As we have already pointed out in discussing the basic functions of the interviewer, this requires that he play an active role in maximizing the fullness and completeness of respondent communication, and that he play a role also in focusing the content of the communication on the objectives of the interview.

Bias as an Unplanned, Unwanted Influence

From this frame of reference, interviewer bias becomes the intrusion of *unwanted* or *unplanned* interviewer influence in the interview process. A biased interview contains the results of kinds of interaction between interviewer and respondent that were not planned for and may well have been unrecognized. This concept of bias can perhaps be made more clear if we think of the interviewer as rewarding and punishing certain respondent behavior. The interviewer consistently rewards full and complete response, rewards responses focused on the objectives of the interview, and tends to discourage communications irrelevant to those objectives. Interviewer bias occurs when the rewarding and discouraging activities of the interviewer are not limited to these areas. For example, the interviewer may reward or punish certain attitudes or expressed values on the part of the respondent, thus motivating the respondent to a distortion of his own feelings.

Suppose that an interviewer is talking to a respondent about participation in foreign affairs, and the respondent says, "Well, I don't really know whether it is a good idea for us to get too involved in foreign affairs or not—sometimes I think probably we shouldn't," and the interviewer replies, "Yes, I feel the same way myself." It is safe to predict that this interviewer, if he behaves consistently in this fashion, will find a larger proportion of isolationist attitudes and tendencies among his respondents than will some of his colleagues.

Suppose that a physician asks a patient whether or not she experiences a certain kind of pain. The patient replies, "Well, not really, I guess, Doctor," and the doctor then says, "Well, I'm certainly relieved to hear that." By such a response the doctor has not only made it more difficult for the patient to answer but has complicated the problem of obtaining any valid response from the patient with respect to symptoms.

The major point can be summed up with a statement that if the basic purpose of the interview is to determine the attitudes, perceptions, or facts that a respondent has in his possession, the interviewer can and must be active with respect to motivating fullness of response and with respect to directing the communication to the objectives of the interview, but the interviewer must make it clear to the respondent that any point of view which he expresses on the relevant topics, any degree of enthusiasm or hostility, is equally acceptable. In this context, interviewer bias is the result of the interviewer's inadvertently communicating to the respondent the idea that certain attitudes or certain points of view on the relevant questions in the interview are particularly desirable or acceptable.

We have been talking about bias as the result of unwanted interaction between interviewer and respondent, initiated by some overt behavior of the interviewer. In fact, unwanted interaction and resulting bias may occur from much more subtle cues, many of which may be beyond the control of the interviewer and may function without any apparent behavior on his part. The supervisor who is unsuccessful in interviewing a subordinate because of his authority position provides an example of an unwanted interaction process that may occur without any verbal communication from the interviewer.

There is often a great deal of such nonverbal communication, and such cues are especially important in the earliest stages of the interview process, when the respondent is attempting to position himself and the interviewer. When a white interviewer drives into the yard of a Negro sharecropper whom he is planning to interview, he has influenced his prospective respondent even before he gets out of the car. The interviewer is perceived as a person who must enjoy certain prestige and respect simply because of his skin color. This social distance is likely to be increased if the interviewer is dressed as a white-collar worker and appears to be relatively prosperous. Out of such perceptions, motivating forces are generated, and the probability of biased results in this case is extremely high.

THE CONCEPT OF ROLE IN THE INTERVIEW

Despite the interactional character of the interview process, we will find it convenient at various times to concentrate separately on the situations and problems of either interviewer or respondent. In doing so we will temporarily put the person in question at the center of the interview process, so to speak, and think of all other factors in the interview situation as they affect him or as they are affected by him. The concept of *role* will be useful to us in this kind of analysis.

This concept is familiar enough in everyday speech, and it has rapidly been acquiring importance in the literature and theory of social psychology. By role we mean a particular position in an organization or society or group. For example, we might speak of the role of manager of a business, or the role of union organizer, or in the family circle we might speak of the role of father. It is clear that the same person occupies many roles in the various aspects of his life. One person may occupy the role of father and husband in the family, the role of lawyer in a corporation, and the role of president of a parent-teacher association in still another social structure. For each of these roles there are duties and obligations, certain ways of behaving which others expect. By and large these are accepted by the individual himself when he is "in role."

There are, of course, variations among individuals in the way in which they carry out the same role. Such individual variations and elaborations are observable in every case. For any role, however, there are certain behaviors that an individual must perform and certain others that are taboo for him. These can be thought of as constituting the *role prescriptions*. They are the aspects of the role which are compulsory for any individual occupying it. Other behaviors are optional and depend upon attributes of the person occupying the role. The combination of these prescribed behaviors and the individual elaborations we can conveniently think of as *role behavior*. (It is interesting to note that the behaviors prescribed for an individual in one role may be not prescribed or may even be taboo for the same individual in another role. A man who can get down on his hands and knees and build houses of blocks in his role as a father would be considered a candidate for mental therapy if he attempted the same activity in his role of manager of a business.)

The Interviewer Role

Let us now consider the role of the interviewer in somewhat greater detail. As for any role, the behavior of the interviewer is determined in part by the expectations of others. The doctor is prevented from visiting his patients in overalls or sport clothes, largely because of their expectations regarding the appearance and demeanor of a physician. Other aspects of his role he learned in more formal ways during his years in medical school. Similarly, the research interviewer approaching a respondent is likely to be guided largely by the specific teaching and rehearsal which he has had during training. In other words, the research organization is likely to have defined the interviewer role and to have set, in no uncertain terms, the prescribed behavior for a person in that role.

We have said that each person has not one but many roles to fill. In some cases, the multiple roles a person plays are disadvantageous to him as far as the interviewing function is concerned. A supervisor who wishes to act as an interviewer in ascertaining facts from an employee may be severely handicapped by the fact that he also plays the role of supervisor, of rewarder and punisher, and that it is therefore extremely difficult for the employee to accept him in the role of interviewer alone. The communication process, in other words, is likely to be affected by roles and role relations which the supervisor would like to exclude from the interview.

For purposes of convenience, we can distinguish two major aspects of the interviewer role. The first of these involves his function in maximizing the forces to communicate. At the same time, of course, he is attempting to reduce or eliminate the negative forces, the barriers to communication. It is this aspect of the interviewer role which has been our primary concern thus far. The specific skills required for this function will be elaborated in our discussion of interviewing techniques (Chapter 8).

The second major function of the interviewer is measurement, which requires him to direct and control the communication process to specific objectives.[10] The interviewer is aware of the basic reasons

---

[10] The measurement aspects of the interview involve question formulation and questionnaire construction, as well as the control of the interaction with respondents. These subjects are dealt with more intensively in Chapters 5, 6, and 7.

for which data are being collected, although the respondent may not share this information fully. The research interviewer comes equipped with a substantial list of specific research objectives to which the interview should conform; the physician is guided by his specialized knowledge of symptoms and diseases, and so on. Through the careful formulation of major questions and the use of supplementary probe questions, the interviewer ensures that the flow of communication which he has motivated is directed to specific objectives. It is the ability of the interviewer to so direct the communication that produces a valid interview—that is, an interview which measures the things it purports to measure.

A major part of this function of the interviewer is teaching the respondent what his role involves. The extent to which this is necessary in an interview varies a great deal, of course. If a physician is speaking to an experienced patient who is known to him, the amount of teaching required is likely to be small. On the other hand, a reporter interviewing a person who is naive about journalistic practice, or a lawyer interviewing a client seeking legal advice for the first time, is likely to have a substantial job of teaching to do. The teaching process is likely to be extensive also in the case of the research interviewer approaching a new respondent.

In all these cases, however, the means by which the teaching of the respondent role is accomplished are similar. The interviewer tells the respondent, directly and approvingly, when he has answered a question completely; he also lets the respondent know, tactfully but definitely, when he has not fulfilled the requirements of his role. Many of the cues which the interviewer uses to teach the respondent his role are considerably more subtle, of course. The respondent is taught, as the interview continues, to anticipate certain behavior from the interviewer, depending on the kind of response which the respondent makes.

During the course of the interview, the interviewer's main way of indicating that a response is inadequate is by probing or asking additional questions that urge the respondent to reply more fully. Similarly, the interviewer's means of discouraging an irrelevant response or digression on the part of the respondent are likely to be no more harsh than a comment that "this topic is interesting but perhaps we should get back to one of the specific objectives of the interview" (which the interviewer will specify). The interviewer's means of rewarding full and adequate responses may be even more subtle, consisting of no more than an encouraging nod of the head or a murmur of understanding. As the interview progresses, the encouraging and discouraging behavior on the part of the interviewer begins to assume a pattern intelligible to the respondent. Accordingly, the respondent, consciously or unconsciously, tends to behave in a way which he anticipates will meet with the interviewer's approval.

The interviewer is a major influence in the interview, not merely a device to start the process of communication or record the data. If the interviewer plays an important and continuing role during the interview process, it follows that the end product of that process is joint—that is, the interview is primarily a product of the interaction between interviewer and respondent. As such, its characteristics depend upon the individual behavior of the interviewer and of the respondent, but even more importantly upon the relationship between the two and the interaction between the two during the period of the interview.

SUMMARY

In this chapter on the theory of the interview, we have emphasized the interview as an interactional process. Consistent with this approach, we have insisted on the importance of both interviewer and respondent as partners in the process, and have argued that the interview itself, as the product of their interaction, depends on both of them. A considerable part of the chapter was devoted to an analysis of respondent motivation and the factors that influence it. With regard to the interviewer, two major functions were identified, a motivating and a measurement function. Our approach to understanding the interviewer role in subsequent chapters of the book will be built around these two basic functions, motivation and measurement.

In Chapter 3 we will continue the emphasis on motivating the respondent and will consider in detail the techniques by which adequate motivation can be generated in the interview. In subsequent chapters our emphasis will shift to the measurement aspect of interviewing. Chapters 4, 5, and 6, deal with the ways in which an interview can be focused on the objectives which have been set for it. Chapters 7 and 8 deal with the problem of unwanted or inappropriate influences in the interview process, that is, with the problem of interviewer bias.

chapter **3**

Techniques for Motivating the Respondent

MOTIVATION LEVEL AND DEMANDS ON THE RESPONDENT

In Chapter 2 we considered various motivational patterns and how they applied to the interview. The purpose of this chapter is to illustrate and discuss various techniques by which the interviewer develops and maintains the respondent's motivation. The motivation level necessary and the motive source that is relevant depend upon several factors: the amount of respondent resistance, the degree of personal threat which the interview topic represents to the respondent, the demands the interview makes upon the respondent's time and energy, and so forth.

Consider the following examples, all of them involving Mrs. Johnston, who in the course of several weeks is asked to be a respondent in different types of interviews.

As Mrs. Johnston is walking along Main Street one morning, a pleasant young man stops her.

INTERVIEWER: Good morning, madam, I'm from the Acme Poll. Would you mind telling me—do you think it is or is not proper for women to wear shorts for shopping downtown?
MRS. JOHNSTON: No, I don't think they should.
INTERVIEWER: Thank you.

The interviewer turns to the next approaching pedestrian, and Mrs. Johnston continues on her way.

In the example of the polling interview, few demands are made of Mrs. Johnston. It is very simple to be a respondent in such an interview; in fact, it is probably easier to be a respondent than to refuse to answer. The entire interview is a single question on an amusing, nonthreatening topic. Little in the way of motivating techniques is required, and common politeness is sufficient to motivate her to answer the question.

One evening several days later, the doorbell of the Johnstons' home rings, and when Mrs. Johnston opens the door she sees a woman with a large notebook.

CALLER: Good evening. Are you the lady of the house?
MRS. JOHNSTON: Yes, I am.
CALLER: I'm taking the school census. Here is my identification.
MRS. JOHNSTON: Oh yes, I remember reading in the paper the other night that the school census was being taken again. Won't you come in?
CALLER: Thank you. (Enters.) Do you have any children?
MRS. JOHNSTON: Yes, we have two. William is ten and Freddie is three.
CALLER: Let me get that down. (Writes down the information.) And that's all the children living here?
MRS. JOHNSTON: Yes, just the two.
CALLER: Is William in school now?
MRS. JOHNSTON: Yes, in the fifth grade.
CALLER: Well, I guess that's all I need. Thank you.

The census taker needed to say something more about the purpose of the interview than did the poll interviewer. Responses to her questions required more participation from the respondent than did the poll question. But a simple introductory statement was sufficient to give the interview its structure. Mrs. Johnston knew about the school census. She knew it was an official inquiry to determine the need for school facilities and teachers for the coming year, purposes she readily approved of. She also knew, from past experience, what questions were likely to be asked.

The short introduction used by the census taker did very little to establish anything in the way of interpersonal relationship between interviewer and respondent. This minimal personal relationship was adequate, however, because the interviewer was making minimum demands on the respondent. The information to be communicated was neutral, the possibilities of threat to the respondent were absent or remote, and the demands on the respondent's time were likely to be limited to a few minutes. In fact, not only is this minimum interviewer-respondent relationship adequate for such an interview, but more elaborate attempts at developing respondent involvement and affective feeling for the interviewer might be seen as unnecessary and inappropriate.

One afternoon several weeks later, Mrs. Johnston is reading on her front porch when a young man comes up the walk. He is carrying a portfolio under his arm, and Mrs. Johnston thinks, "Oh dear, here comes one of those book salesmen. I hate to be rude to him, but I wish he wouldn't bother me."

By now the young man has come up on the porch and says, "Good afternoon. I'm Ted Green from the Midwest University Research Unit. We are doing a study to discover how many people in the country have had some illness during the year, what kind of medical treatment they receive, and how they finance their medical treatment. We have been asked to do this study by the United States Public Health Service. They feel that if they can find out this information, they may be able to develop better health plans to meet public needs."

Mrs. Johnston is irritated at having her rest and her reading disturbed, although she is also interested in and curious about what the young man has said. Just how this information is going to help anyone, and especially how it will help her, is not clear. It also isn't clear why she was selected to answer the questions. Is there something fishy here? What's more, it occurs to her at once that the interview may take some time and may require her to work hard to recall the family illnesses; perhaps she will even have to look up some records to find out how much she paid the doctor when her younger son was ill. Even more important, perhaps, is the possibility that such an interview will make demands of a psychological or emotional sort. She sees the danger that she might be asked to discuss intimate matters of family arrangements and details of illnesses about which she has feelings of secretiveness or social embarrassment.

As a result, the interviewer-respondent relationship necessary to obtain such information will be of a quite different, more intense nature than in the previous examples. Moreover, Mr. Green is a stranger, whose purpose has no evident relation to any of Mrs. Johnston's goals. Mr. Green therefore has even more of a job of motivating to do. He will have to give the respondent a more detailed and more powerful statement of the ways in which the interview will contribute to the achievement of her goals. In addition, he must provide her with a considerable measure of security in the communication of facts about which she feels threatened or embarrassed. This the interviewer will have to do not by explicit assurances, but by demonstrating to the respondent that he is a person who can understand and accept such information without criticism, condemnation, or ridicule. These interviewer tasks are formidable and cannot be achieved merely by an introductory statement, however skillful. The respondent attitudes required for an interview of this kind must be developed in the course of interaction between interviewer and respondent.

The fourth interview is still more difficult.

Toward the middle of the school semester, Mrs. Johnston gets a phone call from Miss Kingsley, the teacher of the older Johnston boy. Miss Kingsley asks her if she can come to school next Tuesday at 4 P.M. to talk about the boy's progress. Mrs. Johnston rather dreads the interview, because she realizes that Bill has been something of a problem in school and she is quite concerned about what the teacher will have to say. But of course she goes to see Miss Kingsley at the time agreed upon. After greetings have been exchanged, Miss Kingsley moves to the point.

MISS KINGSLEY: Thank you for coming to talk with me, Mrs. Johnston. As you know, I've been somewhat concerned about William, and things don't seem to be getting any better. He is a nice boy most of the time, but sometimes he picks on the other children, particularly the smaller ones, and he sometimes gets quite belligerent in class.

MRS. JOHNSTON: Well, I've been worried about Bill for some time. I certainly hope something can be done for him.

MISS KINGSLEY: That's why I asked you to come in today. I thought if we could talk this over, I might be able to help. I thought that if I could find out something about how the boy gets along at home, it may help me to understand him at school. Perhaps if we can talk about how your boy gets along at home, with you and Mr. Johnston and your younger son, it will help us to understand him better.

What has the teacher demanded of the mother as a respondent? First of all, she has demanded a great deal in the way of time and effort on the parent's part. The topic is clearly a complex one, and the prospect is at least for a long interview, quite possibly a series of interviews. The goal of this interview is relatively clear for the respondent, and the motivation of facilitating her child's adjustment can be assumed to be strong. At the same time, this motive source is by no means sufficient for the interview task, because the interview demands much more of the respondent than a simple investment of time and effort. The respondent is required to reveal information which may be extremely ego-threatening, since it deals with difficulties and problems in the relationship between child and parents, and may involve problems of defensiveness, of guilt feelings, of unwillingness to reveal family secrets to a relative stranger.

The degree of threat and conflict represented by the communication of such information is more extreme than that posed in our previous examples. Yet Miss Kingsley's position gives her some advantages over the other interviewers. She is known to Mrs. Johnston; as William's teacher she has a "right" to privileged information that bears on her professional responsibilities, and the purpose of the interview is very important to Mrs. Johnston. She and Miss Kingsley, each for her own reasons, share the goal of improving William's adjustment in the classroom.

Mrs. Johnston will therefore accept the role of respondent initially, but her acceptance will be tentative; and whether she will enter fully into the role will depend upon the teacher's success in reinforcing her motivation to do so. The relationship the teacher must establish is one that will give Mrs. Johnston confidence in the teacher's warmth and understanding, and in the teacher's ability to accept and use sympathetically and constructively the information which she receives.

From these four examples we get some notion of the wide range of demands which interviews make of respondents. Interviews differ in the amount of time which they require, in the effort of recall which must be made, and in the threats and fears which they generate and must overcome. These and similar factors define the psychological and intellectual weight of the task with which the respondent is confronted—the total demand which the interview makes of him.

We can think of interviews ranked along a continuum of respondent demand, with the single-question poll interview at one end and the intense, deeply personal interview at the other. The four interview experiences of Mrs. Johnston represent points of increasing demand on this continuum. Moreover, there is a parallel between this continuum and another one which represents the range of respondent motivation. The greater the total demand on the respondent, the greater must be the level of motivation required to meet this demand and achieve a successful interview. The interviewer must assess for each interview what it requires of the respondent. This, in turn, will tell him the motivation level necessary for adequate communication.

We also note that in the examples various levels of motivation are present even before the interview begins. Mrs. Johnston was sufficiently motivated to talk with the school census taker because she understood the purpose and the usefulness of the census and also because the demand it made on her was slight. She was ambivalent about her interview with the teacher—that is, somewhat but not sufficiently motivated for it. And she was quite unmotivated to respond to a stranger about the family's illnesses. So we see that the distance that must be traveled along the motivational continuum depends on where the respondent stands at the outset as well as on the level we want him ultimately to reach.

DEVELOPMENT OF INTRINSIC MOTIVATION

The Psychological Environment of the Interview

We saw that only a minimal relationship between respondent and interviewer was needed to satisfy the motivational requirements of the school-census interview. A much closer one was needed for the two interviews that followed it. When we talk about the interviewer-respondent relationship, we are not referring to a temporal phase of the interview but to its total psychological climate. This is continually in the process of development and modification.

The more intensive relationships in the information-getting interview have some of the same characteristics as the relationship developed in the psychotherapeutic interview. We can think of the therapeutic interview as representing the upper extreme on the demand continuum. It explores the most difficult territory. It makes maximum demands of the respondent. As a result it also makes maximum demands upon the skills of the interviewer. Although the purposes of the therapist are very different from those of the information-seeking interviewer and lead into more difficult territory, we can learn much from his kind of interview about how effective interviewer-respondent relationships can be achieved.

What is this relationship between therapist and client? What are its components? What techniques are used to establish and maintain the relationship? Perhaps the easiest way to illustrate therapeutic techniques is to compare them with other interactional techniques with which we are more familiar.

For example, a twelve-year-old boy makes the following statement: "My old man does lots of things to make it tough for me. He's always picking on me and scolding me."

Suppose that this statement is made to his close friend of similar age. His friend is likely to respond: "Yeah, mine does too," or "Gee, that's tough," or "Why don't you keep out of his way and ask your mother things?"

If we analyze these comments, we see that they consist of statements of the listener's own situation, expressions of sympathy, and a suggested remedy. These interactions are typical of a friendship relationship. At a more sophisticated level, this interaction pattern is duplicated in adult social interactions. Suppose one person makes a statement that the Republican party is the only salvation for the country's economic needs. His listener may agree and amplify the position. He may disagree and state an opposing position. Or he may discuss the implications of the remark.

If our twelve-year-old makes the remark about his father to his schoolteacher, he is likely to have to listen to one of the following types of rejoinders: "I'm sure your father is doing what is right for you," or "Well, maybe your father is tired and you do too many things to annoy him," or "Oh, Tommy, you're mistaken. Your father wouldn't do that," or "Why don't you try to be a better boy at home?"

The main themes of these rejoinders are that they defend the father and put the blame on the boy. They accept the social norm that parents are always right, and if there is trouble, the boy is wrong.

All of the examples so far have one characteristic in common—they evaluate or pass judgment on the speaker's statement and, by implication, on the speaker himself. The direction which the evaluation takes depends upon the role of the person making the evaluation. It is to a large extent through many interactions of this sort that the relationship between individuals is determined. We expect our friends to interact with us in certain ways; typically, friendship reactions are understanding, supporting, helping. The teacher's remarks are also evaluative, but the content is different. They are characterized by moralizing, judging the speaker, rejecting his statements, and supporting the father as an authority figure. These remarks are typical of an authority relationship.

These evaluative remarks obviously have different effects on the speaker. He will be freer to discuss his personal situations and problems with his friends. Authority figures are unlikely to be the recipients of information that may result in negative evaluation.

Now suppose that the twelve-year-old makes the same statement to a psychologist or psychiatrist during a therapeutic interview. How will the therapist respond? Typical responses are: "You feel he doesn't really understand you," or "This is hard on you," or "You feel that's not right."

Contrasting these rejoinders with those of the friend or teacher, we notice that they make no evaluation, either negative or positive. The therapist neither agrees nor disagrees. The second important difference is that they neither suggest remedies nor tell about how the therapist feels. Instead, they focus attention on the statement and on the speaker's own attitude or frame of mind. The effect of this type of statement is likely to be supportive; it does not reject the speaker, it does not sympathize or condone, but it does imply an understanding and appreciation of the speaker's feelings and reactions.

Such a relationship, then, differs from both the friendship pattern and the authority pattern. The teacher's answers tended to make Tommy defensive, to give him feelings of being somehow wrong and rejected, and to discourage calm thinking and free communication on his part. The friend's comments offered support, which the teacher's lacked, but it was the biased support of a fellow victim, more likely to lead to an exchange of exaggerated paternal atrocities than to a genuine resolution of the problem in Tommy's own mind. If Tommy has doubts about himself as well as his father, if he wonders whether he is as good a boy as he should be, and whether he does not sometimes earn his father's displeasure, expressions of these self-doubts are as surely cut off by the too prompt partisanship of his friend as by the critical evaluation of his teacher. The nonevaluative support of the therapist is much more likely to result in Tommy's feeling free to express his own thoughts and emotions and encouraged to work them through more fully.

Psychiatrists and clinical psychologists recognize that the success of therapeutic interviews is based largely on the type of relationship they establish with the patient. The interpersonal relationship is directly derived from the interactions that occur in the interview. Because the relationship is so crucial, therapists have devoted much thought and research to investigating its components. The statements of therapists will be useful here to help clarify some of the elements illustrated in the brief example just given.

Some Characteristics of a Clinical Relationship

Shoben describes the relationship between the patient and the psychotherapist as "friendliness, warmth, and a comfortable emotional closeness."[1] The therapist is genuinely interested in his patient as a person, not as an object to be dissected and coldly studied. This implies a second characteristic, permissiveness. The therapist gives the patient full freedom to discuss any topic he chooses. The relationship also has an affective side: regardless of what his patient talks about, the therapist maintains an attitude of calmness and understanding. He remains unshocked and unruffled, even in the face of attack, but he evinces a genuine concern for what each item discussed means in terms of the patient's comfort and welfare.

> Warmth and permissiveness so described, shade into a third aspect of the therapeutic relationship, its "safety." The therapist is non-judgmental and non-commendatory in his reaction; he never rejects his patient because of the behavior he reports or the attitudes and affects he verbalizes. This is sometimes spoken of as "acceptance," a term which is a little troublesome because of its connotations of approval.

[1] Edward Joseph Shoben, Jr., "Some Observations on Psychotherapy and the Learning Process," in *Psychotherapy, Theory and Research,* O. Hobart Mowrer (ed.), Ronald Press Company, New York, 1953.

Fourth, the therapist seems to be constantly attempting to clarify his own understanding of the patient and to communicate that understanding within the therapeutic context. It is as if the therapist constantly kept before himself the question, "What is this person trying to tell me and how can I make it clear to him that I understand not only intellectually but in an emphatic sense?"[2]

Fiedler conducted a study in which he asked several therapists to describe the ideal relationship between patient and therapist. The following statements were reported most frequently as describing the ideal therapeutic relationship:

1. The therapist is able to participate completely in the patient's feelings.
2. The therapist's comments are always in line with what the patient is trying to convey.
3. The therapist is well able to understand a patient's feelings.
4. The therapist really tries to understand the patient's feelings.
5. The therapist always follows the patient's line of thought.
6. The therapist's tone of voice conveys the complete ability to share the patient's feelings.
7. The therapist sees the patient as a co-worker on a common problem.
8. The therapist treats the patient as an equal.[3]

Because the relationship between therapist and patient develops slowly over a long period, it is diffcult to observe it without studying the progress of an entire interview or series of interviews. Nevertheless, it may be useful to examine an excerpt from a recorded clinical interview to see how the therapist handles the interactions.

The respondent is Paul, a college student, who comes to a psychological clinic to talk about his poor academic standing. This is an excerpt from the counselor's second interview with this client:[4]

STUDENT: I haven't written to my parents about this at all. In the past they haven't been of any help to me in this respect, and if I can keep it away from them as much as possible, I'll do so. But there's a slight matter of grades to explain, and they're not good, and I don't know how I'm going to explain without telling them about this. [Meaning his upset emotional condition which, he has said, accounts for his problems.] Would you advise me to tell them about it?
COUNSELOR: Suppose you tell me a little more what you had thought about it.

This statement by the counselor sets the relationship as being something other than one of friendship or authoritative. The counselor

---

[2] *Ibid.*

[3] Fred E. Fiedler, "Quantitative Studies on the Role of the Therapists' Feelings Toward Their Patients," in *Psychotherapy, Theory and Research*, O. Hobart Mowrer (ed.), Ronald Press Company, New York, 1953.

[4] This example is taken from Carl R. Rogers, *Counseling and Psychotherapy*, Houghton Mifflin, Boston, 1942, pp. 135–136.

avoids advice, and he also avoids any critical or judgmental remarks. His remark is "neutral," since it merely suggests that the student verbalize his problem more fully. The example continues:

STUDENT: Well, I think I'm compelled to, because—(Pause.)
COUNSELOR: It's a situation you've really got to face.

The counselor's statement demonstrates a frequently used technique in psychotherapy. Analyzing the statement, we see that it consists of a succinct summary of the attitude which the student has expressed in the two previous statements. This summary serves two purposes. First, it focuses attention on the attitudinal content of the statements, which is in fact the objective of the interview. Secondly, it demonstrates that the student's statements have been understood, that is, communication is taking place and has been accepted uncritically. The student continues:

STUDENT: Yes, there's no use getting around it, even if they can't take it the way they should, because I've already flunked my gym course. I just haven't come. I've just been negligent about it. Now, they'll know that you can't flunk in gym without being negligent about it. They'll ask why.
COUNSELOR: It will be fairly hard for you to tell them.

This statement is similar to the previous one in that it summarizes the attitude which the student has been expressing.

STUDENT: Yes. Oh, I don't know if they're going to sort of condemn me. I think so, because that's what they've done in the past. They've said, "It's your fault. You don't have enough will power, you're not interested." That's the experience I've had in the past. I've been sort of telling them that I improved in this respect. I was—I was all right the first quarter. Well, I wasn't entirely all right, but I just got worse. (Pause.)
COUNSELOR: You feel that they'll be unsympathetic and they'll condemn you for your failures.

Let us leave the example at this point and imagine that we can question the student on his perception of the interview and how he feels about his relationship with the counselor. He might well describe his feelings as follows: "Well, first, this seems to be a person who is friendly and warm. He really seems to be interested in me and my problem, and what is more, his comments indicate that he has a sympathetic understanding of how my problem affects me—how I feel about it. He doesn't try to argue with me, advise me, or threaten me. On the other hand, he doesn't agree with me as my friends would do."

To put this in terms that Shoben uses, the client perceives the relationship to be safe, permissive, and warm. As a result, he is likely to feel freer to discuss more personal or "touchy" problems. Let's see how the interview develops from here:

STUDENT: Well, my—I'm pretty sure my father will. My mother might not. He hasn't been—he doesn't experience these things; he just doesn't know what it's like. "Lack of ambition" is what he'd say. (Pause.)
COUNSELOR: You feel that he could never understand you?
STUDENT: No, I don't think he is—capable of that, because I don't get along with him, don't at all!
COUNSELOR: You dislike him a good deal?
STUDENT: Yes, I—I did feel bitter toward him for a while and I've gone out of that stage, and now I don't feel bitter against him but I—I'm sort of ashamed. I think that that's it more than anything else, an experience of shame that he is my father. (Pause.)
COUNSELOR: You feel he isn't much good.
STUDENT: Well, he's putting me through school but (few unintelligible words) . . . I'm sorry to say that, but that's my opinion about it. I think he had a lot to do in forming it, too.
COUNSELOR: This has been something on which you have felt pretty deeply for a long while.
STUDENT: I have. (Long pause.)

In this section we see how the pattern of interaction enables the student to verbalize strongly antisocial statements about his father. Notice the calm, unperturbed reaction of the counselor to these strong statements. He maintains a permissive, accepting atmosphere. He helps the student to further expression of feeling by his adept summaries of the attitudes the student is expressing.

This brief excerpt from a counseling interview and the statements of Shoben and Fiedler are sufficient to give us some idea of the techniques used to establish and maintain the relationship in the therapeutic interview. The example also gives some idea of the effectiveness of the technique in motivating communication, particularly of highly emotional material.

Clinical Techniques in Information-Getting Interviews

The interviews in Part II of this book provide a demonstration of techniques used to develop and maintain a relationship with the respondent. In examining them, one can see the similarity to these psychotherapeutic techniques. In the information-getting interview, also, they serve to motivate the respondent to communicate and provide an atmosphere in which the respondent is free to bring out "real" information and feelings without need to defend them. The ideal relationship between an information-getting interviewer and a respondent has some of the characteristics of that described by Shoben and Fiedler as the ideal patient-therapist relationship.

A few examples will help to demonstrate how some of these quasi-therapeutic techniques are useful in developing a relationship in the information-getting interview.

An Adoption Interview. The first example is from an interview between a social worker in an adoption agency and a woman who wishes to adopt a child. The general purpose of the interview is to assess the woman's suitability as an adoptive parent. At this point in the interview, the social worker is attempting to gauge the importance of adoption to this woman, and to learn something of her depth of feeling about children.

INTERVIEWER: Have you had any medical advice about your difficulty in having children?
RESPONDENT: Oh, yes. I've been to three or four doctors about it at different times. Finally, I decided to see Dr. —— at University Hospital. He's the biggest man on this kind of thing, and he gave me all the tests. Then he said that there was no question about it; I could never have any children of my own. (Pause.) We had always wanted a big family . . .
INTERVIEWER: That made his diagnosis difficult to take.
RESPONDENT: Yes, it did; it did. (Pause.) I was somewhat prepared, of course. I had tried not to get my hopes up. But after he told me for sure, I was . . . disappointed. I had already expected as much when I went to see him, really. I just had to be sure.
INTERVIEWER: And now you know where you stand.
RESPONDENT: Yes, and that helps. It *was* real hard at first, but now I don't feel so bad, especially if we can adopt a baby.
INTERVIEWER: This would help things a lot, eh?
RESPONDENT: Oh, yes. It will make a lot of difference.
INTERVIEWER: Adopting a baby is very important for you, then?
RESPONDENT: It is the most important thing in my life; it would give me something to live for.

So far as the interviewer's techniques are concerned, this excerpt might well have come from a therapeutic interview. The interviewer's initial question brings forth a good deal of factual material, and the implication that the diagnosis was extremely disappointing. This implication, conveyed by the respondent's pause and her statement that she had wanted a large family, the interviewer accepts and verbalizes for the respondent. The effect of this summarization of the respondent's attitude lets the respondent know that her feelings are getting across and are understood and accepted. As a result, she is encouraged to make explicit the emotions which she previously implied. This she does ("Yes, it did; it did."), and then goes on to explain her need to *know,* to resolve an ambiguous situation, even if the resolution is negative. The interviewer's answer ("And now you know where you stand.") is almost entirely reflective, telling the respondent that she is understood and encouraging her to continue. The interviewer's last question illustrates another use of the reflective question. She echoes the respondent's meaning almost exactly, again letting the respondent know that the message is getting across and giving her a chance to hear what she is saying. The respondent's reaction is to amplify and deepen her previous statement.

Throughout this excerpt, the interviewer demonstrates her understanding of what the respondent is saying and her acceptance of respondent attitudes. The result is the motivation of additional communication. As in the clinical interview, this kind of interaction helps the respondent by providing a safe, permissive atmosphere and demonstrating the sympathetic understanding of the interviewer.

A Survey Interview. The next example also focuses on attitudes, but in a less personal, less emotional area. It is from a survey interview taken in the home of the respondent.

INTERVIEWER: Do you feel that group medical plans are a good thing or a bad thing?
RESPONDENT: Well, I suppose they aren't either all good or all bad.
INTERVIEWER: Somewhere in between, eh?
RESPONDENT: Yeah, there's something to be said on both sides.
INTERVIEWER: Tell me more about how you see it.
RESPONDENT: Well, I think perhaps a person who is poor is surer of better medical care under a plan like that, but the person ought to be able to select the doctor he wants. I guess in general I'd favor the group plan because it would help the poorer people who need it most.

The objective in this exchange is to determine the respondent's attitudes toward prepaid group health plans, which have been defined earlier in the interview. After the initial question in this area, the interviewer formulates two supplementary questions that serve the dual purpose of maintaining the relationship and motivating the respondent to define more fully his position on the topic. The interviewer attempts this first by means of a simple reflection of the respondent's statement ("Somewhere in between, eh?"). This accepts the respondent's ambivalence, and avoids the negative reaction which might have been generated by insisting that he declare himself on one side or the other of this controversial question. It does not, however, produce much more useful information than the initial question; the respondent's second answer ("something to be said on both sides") does not really amplify his original statement. The interviewer then attempts, with greater success, a direct bid for more information ("Tell me more about how you see it"). This expression of interest, coming after the preceding acceptance of ambivalence, works well. The respondent explains the good and bad aspects of the medical plan as he sees it, and goes on to resolve the dilemma for himself and the interviewer by stating a definite opinion and the basis for it.

Here is an instance where a single-question polling approach would probably have resulted in a classification of "undecided" or "pro-con." Even a brief interaction, however, was enough to demonstrate the interviewer's acceptance and interest, and to encourage the respondent to attempt a further exposition of his own attitudes. It is entirely possible that the resulting formulation represented an additional step in his own thinking, as well as a further communication to the interviewer.

A Legal Interview. The third example is different in that the subject matter of the interview is not attitudes but factual information. The example is from an interview between a lawyer and his client. The purpose of the interview is to determine some facts about the case prior to trial.

LAWYER: Mr. Jones, you told me over the phone that you wanted to talk about a possible action against your landlord.

MR. JONES: As I told you over the phone, my wife broke a bone in her ankle by falling on the front steps.

LAWYER: I see. How did it happen?

MR. JONES: The top step has a board broken in it. I told the landlord about it six months ago, and he said he'd have it fixed. Of course, you can't believe half of what he tells you!

LAWYER: And did he have it fixed?

MR. JONES: No, he never did a thing about that step, and I told him sooner or later somebody would be walking on crutches because of it.

LAWYER: Do you think your wife's fall was entirely the landlord's fault, then?

MR. JONES: I certainly do.

LAWYER: Is there anything else which could have been a factor in her accident?

MR. JONES: Absolutely not! There was nothing left on the step. She's a careful woman, and I want to sue!

Here the lawyer, while being permissive, focuses his summary statements on facts, not attitudes. For the objective of this interview, how the respondent feels is irrelevant. What is relevant are the facts of the situation, which the lawyer must get at through the respondent. The lawyer's interviewing problem is to develop a satisfactory relationship with his client, and at the same time focus the interview on the objective aspects of the client's battle with his landlord. Since the client is brimming with emotion on this topic, the lawyer's task is not easy.

He begins by stating the topic of the interview which is about to take place, as he understands it. The respondent agrees, and describes his wife's injury, on which he wishes to base his suit. The attorney acknowledges these facts, and asks for additional information about the accident. The respondent answers with a combination of facts and affect; he begins to describe the cause of the accident, but ends with a hostile burst against the landlord. The attorney's next question ("And did he have it fixed?") focuses on the factual part of the response, encouraging communication to meet this objective. This succeeds in eliciting two other facts—the landlord's failure to get the step fixed and the tenant's warning of its dangerousness.

The lawyer, wanting to ascertain other possible causes for the accident, moves into this sensitive area with a broad question which at once indicates his understanding and acceptance of the respondent's strong feelings and also bids for additional information ("Do you think that your wife's fall was entirely the landlord's fault, then?"). This is only partly successful; the respondent expresses his strong feelings ("I certainly do!"), but gives no further information. The interviewer must therefore ask directly about the possibility of other causes, hoping that the previous expression of emotionality, and his acceptance of it, make the direct question feasible. As the last response in this excerpt shows, the direct question, even at this point in the interview, produces as much indignation as factual material.

Summary. These examples illustrate the similarity between the techniques of the counselor and those of the information-getting interviewer. From them and from our earlier discussion of the clinical interview, we can make the following generalizations about the type of relationship which is often desirable in the information-getting interview.

(1) The interviewer must create and maintain an atmosphere in which the respondent feels that he is fully understood and in which he is safe to communicate fully without fear of being judged or criticized.

(2) Such a relationship frees the respondent for further communications, in which he does not need to be on the defensive.

(3) As the interviewer focuses attention on the content of the communication, the respondent is encouraged to consider the topic more deeply and to explore more fully and frankly his own position.

(4) This type of interaction also keeps the communication sharply focused on the topic in which the interviewer is interested.

DEVELOPMENT OF EXTRINSIC MOTIVATION

The Interview and the Goals of the Respondent

While the first three of the preceding generalizations derive from therapeutic techniques, the fourth is perhaps less relevant to therapy than to information-seeking. Unlike the therapist, the information-getting interviewer is primarily interested not in the respondent but in his own specific objectives, which may lie far outside. The problem he is working on is his, not the respondent's. This means that he asks questions on specific matters and cannot use communication from the respondent about other matters. The therapist also has objectives and directs the interview, but his objectives are such that nearly anything the patient reports about himself may be relevant. Because the interviewer wants information of only certain kinds, he has little interest in assisting the respondent to gain insight into himself, except as this may help to obtain the information he needs. He must keep the interview concentrated upon topics he has chosen in advance.

As a result, the respondent may see no connection between the interview, or some parts of it, and any of his own goals. It then falls upon the interviewer to establish this connection at the very outset. In the examples given earlier in the chapter we noted how the character of the interviewer's preliminary statements varied with the topics and with respondents. In some cases the interview was so well structured that the interviewer needed to say very little. For others a long statement was necessary.

There are certain things the respondent needs to know about almost every interview. (Exceptions to this occur only where the demands are so minimal, as in the early example of the single poll question, that virtually no respondent motivation is necessary.) In some cases the interviewer will feel or will have evidence that the respondent knows these things, whereas in others it is necessary to talk about them. If the respondent is to perceive some goal for himself in the interview and thus be motivated to participate in it, it is important that he clearly understands:

(1) The purposes of the interview. It is especially important that those purposes of the interview that may relate to the respondent's own goals and values be apparent to him.

(2) The ways in which information he contributes is to be used. For example, if the respondent's statements are to be confidential, this

must be known. If they are to be made available to other persons or incorporated in a publication of some sort, the respondent should know these facts.

(3) In a general way, what will be expected of him in the course of the interview. This means that he should have some idea of the length of the interview, of whether or not any degree of expertness is required of him, whether he is to report factual information or to communicate his own attitudes and feelings, and the like.

Though it is necessary in all interview situations for the respondent to have these factors clearly in mind in the early stages of the interview, the extent to which the interviewer must explain them will vary a great deal. In some kinds of interviews, the general structure and the respondent's understanding of it are well established at the moment when the interview begins. This is true, for example, in the typical case-history interview between patient and doctor. Here the patient approaches the situation with a fairly clear idea of the purpose of the interview, what is expected of him as a patient, what to expect of the interviewer-physician, and how the information he gives will be used. The other extreme may be represented by the public-opinion interview, in which the householder answers his door to find himself confronted by a stranger who offers as the only immediate clue to the purpose of the visit a portfolio or a notebook clutched in one hand. For purposes of illustration, therefore, the public-opinion interview is particularly appropriate, since it puts the full burden of the introduction on the interviewer.

When the public-opinion interviewer first faces a respondent, he finds that the relationship has some structure even before a word is spoken. On the one hand, the respondent will be polite enough to let him talk; on the other hand, certain barriers exist and must be overcome. The respondent may see the interviewer as a salesman, or he may think that the interviewer is a "spy" for a bill collecting agency or for the Bureau of Internal Revenue, a disguised book sales-man, or a burglar "casing" the house for a robbery. These perceptions must be neutralized by the interviewer's early statements. In some cases the respondent must be reassured about the anonymous or confidential nature of the interview. This calls for a convincing explanation by the interviewer of the purpose of the study and the method by which the person was selected as a respondent.

The positive motivation of the respondent's goals frequently comes from a careful statement of the purpose of the interview. The interviewer tries to sense the respondent's wishes or goals with respect to the interview process and, having appraised these, to explain to the respondent how the interview relates to them. An interviewer working on a study of public attitudes toward foreign policy, for example, may come upon a respondent who, on hearing the purpose of the survey, says to him, "You don't want to talk to me about foreign policy. What I think about those fellows in the State Department would curl their hair. You'd better find somebody who is a more agreeable type." The interviewer will be likely to assure this respondent that the purpose of the study is not to find out the opinions of only those people who endorse current foreign policies. He will emphasize that the interview provides an opportunity for the respondent to register his views in a place where they may have some effect on public officials, whether they are critical or appreciative.

Introductions in sample surveys are rarely as individualized as the preceding example implies. It is usually possible to prepare a statement of purpose which appeals to goals shared by a large segment of the population. In any given interview, however, this statement of purpose may fail to motivate effectively, and the alert interviewer will try to adapt the statement to what he perceives will more readily tap the individual's motive patterns.

Analysis of Specific Types of Introductions

In some cases the relationship of the information-getting interview to the respondent's goals is clearly apparent to the respondent. An example might be the case of a worker who is asked to participate in a factory survey, the purpose of which is to attempt to place each person on his preferred work shift. Assuming the management's good faith, a frank response is obviously to the worker's advantage. In other studies this relationship is less direct and therefore less clear. These points will be made more specific by the analysis of interviewers' introductions in several typical situations.

A Survey Interview. The following example is an introduction, slightly modified, used by an interviewer from the University of Michigan's Survey Research Center on a survey of consumer finances.

INTERVIEWER: I'm from the Survey Research Center of the University of Michigan. We're doing a survey at this time in this city and in other places throughout the country, talking to people about how things are going financially these days. The Federal Reserve Board in Washington is interested in the public's ideas about this, and they've asked us to do this nationwide survey for them.

RESPONDENT: You say you're from the University of Michigan?

INTERVIEWER: Yes. The Survey Research Center of the University of Michigan. By the way, here's my identification.

RESPONDENT: Unhuh. Well, what's the purpose of all this? I never knew they did all this.

INTERVIEWER: Well, one of the chief jobs of the Federal Reserve Board is to look after the money matters of the country, you know. In order to know how to plan ahead they have to have information that is up to date about how people are getting along. We've been doing this work for them for six years now. They've put out a whole series of reports on it, like this one I have here. (Shows a report to the respondent.)

RESPONDENT: Unhuh, I see.

INTERVIEWER: You can see by this report that it's completely statistical. We never use any names on these surveys. It's all confidential and anonymous—we never identify the people at addresses we visit. We interview a sample of people in a large number of different cities throughout the United States, and the addresses themselves are picked by chance.

RESPONDENT: Well, what do you want to know?

Let us consider the way in which the preceding introduction meets the general requirements we specified earlier. The first of these requirements is that the introduction should explain the purpose of the interview and indicate the way in which the interview might contribute to the interests and goals of the respondent. Our sample introduction is thorough and specific with respect to the purpose of the interview. It mentions the agency collecting the data, the agency for which the data are being collected, and the broad economic purposes for which the Federal Reserve Board commissioned this research. The introduction is less specific with regard to the way in which the interview might relate to the goals and interests of the respondent. This point is not neglected, but is handled by indirection or implication, in the statements that the Federal Reserve Board is interested in the public's ideas, that the Board has responsibility for "looking after the money matters of the country," and that the surveys are carried on in order to "know how to plan ahead." The clear implication here is that the respondent interested in personal and national financial stability will be serving these goals, as well as the general one of supporting an official governmental activity, by cooperating with the interviewer.

The second requirement is that the intended use of the information should be made clear to the respondent. The sample introduction was adequate in this respect, also. The respondent was told not only the agency which would be utilizing the data, but also the specific ways in which the data would be used. He was shown a report typical of the final publication from previous studies, in order to reinforce the idea of statistical use of the information and to provide evidence that the information was treated confidentially and anonymously.

The third requirement for an interview introduction is that it should make the respondent understand what is expected of him. The sample introduction handles the indication of respondent role in a general way. The respondent understands that the interview has to do with his opinions on "how things are going financially these days," that the interviewer will also be asking about his "ideas about this." Later in the introduction this notion is repeated by the phrase "information that is up to date about how people are getting along." These phrases serve to communicate to the respondent that his function will be to provide information, not of an expert nature but having to do with himself and his views.

In general, this example represents an adequate introduction, although one which might be improved in several respects. It brought about willingness on the part of the householder to become a respondent.

A Reluctant Respondent. Unfortunately, approaching a respondent for a survey interview is not always as easy and free of resistance as the preceding example may seem to imply. To point out some of the kinds of problems that can occur in introducing such a study to a reluctant respondent, let us consider the following example:

INTERVIEWER: I'm from the Survey Research Center of the University of Michigan. We're doing a survey in this city and all over the country at the present time, getting people's ideas on how they think things are going in the world these days, how different countries are getting along together, and things like that. In order to get an accurate picture of how people all over the country feel about these things, we go to a lot of different cities and pick some addresses just simply by chance, and talk to somebody at those addresses. When we get through, we put the interviews all together and come out with a report that gives a general picture for the country as a whole. Of course, I want to be sure that you understand that we don't take any names, we don't identify anyone, we merely want to get something of how people feel about these important issues of the day.

RESPONDENT: Well, I'm sorry, I'm afraid I don't have the time now. I'm in the middle of my washing.

INTERVIEWER: Oh, I see. Well, maybe I could come in and talk with you while you went on with your washing. I wouldn't want to hold you up any.

RESPONDENT: Oh, I don't know. Actually I don't know much about foreign affairs anyway. I don't think you really want to talk to me. You ought to find somebody who knows a lot more than me.

INTERVIEWER: Well, you see, what we're interested in is getting the opinions and the ideas of all kinds of people all over the country. Now, we know that the notion of world affairs is pretty complicated. What we want is just to know how the people feel and what kinds of things they're thinking about. I guess there aren't any of us that know too much about the affairs of the world these days.

RESPONDENT: Well, I know I ought to read a lot more than I do, but I've got five kids, and I just don't have time to keep up with these things.

INTERVIEWER: I see.

RESPONDENT: What sort of things are you asking about anyway?

INTERVIEWER: Well, as I mentioned, this is part of a study that we are doing all over the country to find out how the people feel about world affairs. Just what kinds of things they're thinking about and what their opinions are. You see, the people in Washington are anxious to find out how the people in the country feel—what kinds of things they're thinking about.

RESPONDENT: I see.

INTERVIEWER: Why don't we try a few of the questions and see how it goes?

RESPONDENT: Okay. I'm willing to try a few, but I'm not sure I want to go through with it. Like I said before, I just don't know too much about these things, and I'm not sure as I'm going to want to continue. But a—all right, let's try and see how it goes.

Comparing the first statement of this interviewer with the introduction in the preceding example, one notices that the two are not very dissimilar. In this case, the interviewer gave an adequate explanation of the purpose and the value of the survey, explained how the information was to be used, and indicated what was to be expected of the respondent. At this point, instead of agreeing to be interviewed, the prospective respondent showed resistance.

Her first comment indicated that she was concerned about competing pressures of other activities, in this case the washing. At this early stage of the interview, the interviewer had little basis for evaluating the character and strength of her resistance. Was the pressure of the washing really so great that she could not spare the time for an interview, or was her statement merely a symptom of some other source of resistance? The interviewer made a rather direct approach to the problem and accepted her statement at face value—which accounts for his response, "Well, maybe I could . . . talk with you while you went on with your washing."

The housewife's next statement indicates what appears to be a more basic source of resistance. She has real feelings of inadequacy about her ability to play the respondent role. She answers that she hasn't time to read, that she is afraid she is uninformed, and therefore she does not wish to be interviewed. The interviewer handles her concern by re-emphasizing the role of the respondent and by attempting to correct her misperception of his purpose, stressing that a profound knowledge of international affairs is not necessary and what is wanted is merely opinions and attitudes. He also re-emphasizes the value of the interview by mentioning its use to "people in Washington."

At this point the interviewer feels that he has partially broken down the resistance and has brought about a level of positive motivation sufficient to warrant the risk of a little pressure. He suggests that they start the interview. He undoubtedly is convinced that once the respondent hears the type of questions the questionnaire contains, she will find herself adequate to the role and the interview can be completed satisfactorily. Somewhat reassured but still reluctant, the respondent agrees to start the interview. She does make it clear that at any time she may terminate the interview if it becomes too threatening.

Personnel Interviews. The following is an interview between a personnel officer and an employee of an industrial company.

INTERVIEWER: Joe, I asked you to come down to talk about a job on the drill press. Remember, when you first came on I told you that we'd consider you for promotion when an opening came up. Well, Fred Smith is leaving and we need someone on his job. How does that job look to you?

This introduction is simple enough to require little comment. The purposes of the personnel officer are clear to the respondent—that is, he knows what his role is, the purpose of the interview, and the way that the data are to be used. In fact, if Joe merely answers "Fine" to this question, we have a complete interview.

Another type of personnel interview offers a slightly more complicated example.

INTERVIEWER: Hello, Bill, come on in. We've got a job that is probably going to be opening up before long, and I thought that you might want to know about it. You remember that we always like to promote from within when these jobs come up, and I wanted to talk to you about an opening as a foreman.

RESPONDENT: Yeah, I heard something might open up.

INTERVIEWER: We're going to be needing at least one foreman within the next three or four weeks, and I wanted to see if you were interested. I wanted to talk over the job with you and with several other men who are in line for promotion, and get some ideas as to who might fit this job best.

RESPONDENT: Well, I sure would like to have it. I think I can really handle the foreman's job.

INTERVIEWER: Well, like I said, I'm interviewing three or four people who are eligible for promotion, and then the superintendent and I will get together and make a decision as to which one of the men should have the job.

RESPONDENT: I see.

INTERVIEWER: Of course, we've been going over your record and we know something about your qualifications. I thought today maybe we just ought to spend a little time getting your thinking about the job.

Let us see how this introduction to an interview meets the requirements stated earlier. In the first place, the purpose is made clear to the respondent in the opening sentence—that is, the foreman's job is opening up and he is being considered for it. The ways in which the data are to be used are also made clear; the interviewer says that he is going to talk to three or four people, and that these conversations will provide part of the basis for deciding who is to have the job. There is also the implied notion that this interview is to be used as an evaluation. This is not stated explicitly, but the implication is clear. This should be sufficient to structure the respondent's role.

The third example is a different sort of interview, between a plant superintendent and an employee. In this case the respondent has been reported as being insolent.

INTERVIEWER: I called you in today because there is a problem I want to talk to you about. Bill, your foreman reported to me that you were insolent to him the other day, and I thought that we had better talk about it and see what the situation was.

Let's stop the introduction at this point to see the implication of this statement if the interviewer fails to give any more of an idea of what this interview is to be. First of all, the purpose of the interview is in a sense clear—that is, the interviewer wants the respondent to talk about a particular situation and relationship. What is not at all clear is how the information from this interview is to be used. We can imagine that the respondent who has been notified to report to the superintendent's office has been anticipating the interview with some concern, and this introduction probably heightens his anxiety. He has no way of knowing whether this interview is to inform him that he is to be fired, whether he is to be disciplined in one way or another, or whether this is a constructive interview in which the unfortunate work situation is to be cleared up. Let's return to the interview and see how the situation is clarified if the interviewer adds this simple statement:

INTERVIEWER: Yes, I thought that we ought to get together and see how we can work this thing out. After all, you know that none of us can work our best when we're having troubles, and I thought if maybe we just had a chance to chat about this we could fix everything up.

The addition of these two sentences has given a very clear statement of how the information is to be used. The statement is sufficiently supportive that at this point the respondent should be greatly relieved. It appears that he does not have to be concerned about being fired or severely disciplined.

Medical Interview. In contrast with these types of introductions, we have the typical medical interview. In the medical interview the physician is likely to begin with the question, "What can I do for you?" or "What seems to be the trouble?" The interview begins with no introduction at all, and the interviewer starts his questioning with no prelude. The physician feels confident that the respondent role in the medical interview is so well understood by the patient that no introduction is necessary. Further, since the patient initiated the interview, the physician may assume a high level of motivation.

At times, however, the physician may have a naive patient, unaware of the need for a complete medical case history, or a patient who cannot understand the relevance of a particular line of questioning. In such situations the physician will need to use an introduction stating the purpose of the interview.

Summary. In the example of Mrs. Johnston and the poll interviewer who asked her opinion about women wearing shorts in the downtown area, we pointed out that some interviews make so few demands on the person and the questions are so short and simple that the elaboration of an introduction is unnecessary.

From the examples in this section we see that the precise way in which the interviewer introduces the idea of being interviewed and the topic of the interview to the respondent varies a good deal from situation to situation, depending primarily upon the amount of structure which the situation already has when the interviewer and respondent begin to interact. Several factors determine the degree to which the situation is structured prior to the interview, and the form which the introduction must take. One such factor is the extent to which the respondent has experience with the interview topic or knowledge of what is expected of him prior to the interview.

A second factor that determines the structuring of an interview situation, and therefore determines also the kind of introduction required, is the degree of the respondent's involvement and the level of his motivation to participate in the interview.

The level of respondent motivation, or degree of involvement, in beginning an interview is likely to be a resultant of positive and negative forces. Even in the introductory phases of the interview, the interviewer must recognize and deal with any feelings of threat which the respondent may have, any premonition on the respondent's part that the interview might in some way disadvantage him. In introducing an interview, the interviewer's assurances of anonymity, confidential treatment of the data, and beneficent impersonal uses of the research findings are typical devices to allay fear and generate positive motive forces.

Ethical Problems in Stating the Purpose of the Interview

In the preceding examples, the interviewer attempted to convey to the respondent as completely as possible the purpose of the interview and the procedure to be followed. There are interviews, however, in which the situation is more complicated with respect to the feasibility of communicating the full purpose to the respondent. In some cases, indeed, to discuss fully with the respondent the purpose of the interview would make it impossible to achieve that purpose.

Suppose that a person is being interviewed by a clinical psychologist for the purpose of determining his emotional stability. If the clinician announces this purpose to the respondent, any of several undesirable consequences may ensue. The respondent may distort information about himself, his reactions, and his experiences, in a direction which he considers will give the impression of calmness and stability. Alternatively, the respondent may become so upset by the prospect of being examined for stability that he will display a degree of excitement quite unusual for him.

Clearly in such cases the interviewer must be selective in the information which he conveys to the respondent by way of introduction. At the same time, to offer the respondent a fictitious purpose for the interview, or to misrepresent the process or the role which the respondent will be required to play, raises serious ethical problems. Without attempting to write a treatise on the ethics of such situations, we can point out some principles which should guide the interviewer.

First, the interviewer should tell the respondent as much as he can, without negating the purpose of the interview. In cases where information must be withheld from the respondent, the interviewer should state the general purpose of the interview, withholding some information rather than making a fictitious statement. Second, the interviewer should, in these cases as in all others, make clear to the respondent what the process of the interview will be, and what will be required of him during the interview.

The following quotation from the American Psychological Association's *Ethical Standards of Psychologists* will illustrate the point of view which we are advocating: "The psychologist is justified in misleading research subjects only when, in his judgment, this is clearly required by the problem being investigated, and when the above provisions regarding the protection of subjects are adhered to." Central

to these provisions is the statement: "Only when a problem is significant and can be investigated in no other way is the psychologist justified in exposing human subjects to emotional stress or other possible
harm. The psychologist, like other scientists, should protect the welfare of his research subjects."

A specific example will clarify this point. Suppose that we wish to
evaluate candidates for a position in which one of the major requirements is ability to think on one's feet, to answer unexpected questions
clearly and quickly, and in general to interact spontaneously and effectively with others. We might conclude that one way of evaluating
the abilities of a candidate to hold such a position would be to interview him, attempting to create in the interview some of the kinds of
situations to which he would be exposed on the job. In introducing
the subject of such an interview to the candidate, it would be possible
and appropriate to inform him that he was being considered for a
position, and that it was decided that a personal interview would give
him an opportunity to learn more about the job and give the interviewer a chance to learn something about his interests and abilities.
The interviewer would not, however, go on to explain that an additional and specific purpose of the interview was to present the respondent with the kinds of situations he might encounter on the job,
as a basis for evaluating his ability to handle such situations.

In such a case, the purpose introduced to the respondent is true as
far as it goes, but it is incomplete. The only valid reason for limiting
the respondent's information about the interview, even to this degree,
is that providing him with more complete information as to the purpose would invalidate the appraisal function of the interview.

SUMMARY

In Chapter 2 we discussed two major sources of respondent motivation, the direct psychological rewards of the interview process and the
perception of the interview as a means to respondent goals. The first
of these is less tangible and more difficult to illustrate; yet the satisfaction which respondents obtain in talking to an understanding, permissive interviewer is undeniable. The second is more obvious; we are
used to thinking in terms of means and ends. We give information to
the doctor in order to get well, to the personnel interviewer in order
to be considered for a job we want, to the social worker in order to get
counsel or economic assistance, and so on.

The present chapter has been devoted to illustrating the techniques
by which these two motive sources can be tapped. These illustrations, by implication, make clear the shifting pattern of motivation

that is typical of the information-getting interview. When the interview begins, the interviewer must depend almost entirely upon making it meaningful to the respondent in terms of his needs and goals. This is the reason for emphasizing so strongly the introduction of the interview to the respondent, and the ways of handling skepticism and resistance at this early stage. The potential information-giver becomes a respondent or a nonrespondent primarily on the motivation of such an introduction; he can hardly have begun to sense, at this point, whether the interview will be of value and satisfaction to him in itself.

As the interview progresses, however, the interest, support, and understanding of the interviewer increase in importance. The respondent, who may have agreed to the interview only for instrumental reasons and with little enthusiasm, finds it increasingly interesting and rewarding for its own sake. The external purpose that justified the interview in the first place may even become less salient in the more mature phases of the interview. As we have seen, new material or the intrusion of an "out-of-context" question may raise again, at any point in the interview, the questions of relevance and purpose which were important in the introductory phase. In general, however, the steady development of the permissive psychological climate is accompanied by an increasing reliance on this source of respondent motivation.

Unfortunately for the person learning to interview, it is very difficult to provide conveniently small "samples" of this climate. The brief exchanges and excerpts quoted earlier in this chapter cannot show the gradual development of the relationship between interviewer and respondent, and as a result such excerpts are almost certain to convey less than the full importance and flavor of this relationship. In Chapters 8 and 9 we will return to a discussion of the techniques by which the interviewer achieves such a psychological climate—in Chapter 8 as part of the task of meeting content objectives, and in Chapter 9 in the context of learning to interview. The reader will obtain a clearer picture of the psychological climate of the interview and its importance, however, from the complete transcripts of interviews which comprise the second part of this book. In these the development and interplay of the two major kinds of respondent motivation can be traced with greater clarity.

The Formulation of Objectives

In Chapter 3 we discussed the techniques by which a high level of respondent motivation could be achieved. There is much more to the interview, however, than establishing a favorable pattern of interaction between interviewer and respondent. An interview is initiated for a purpose; one of the participants wants information from the other. For the interview to be successful, therefore, it must produce that information; for the interviewing process to be at all efficient, it must exclude other irrelevant material. In short, the interview must be focused on certain specific content objectives. These assertions are illustrated in the following example.

The National Manufacturing Company has just completed, with great difficulty, the rush of orders which is typical of its busy season. The president of the company, Mr. Gordon, relieved of the backlog of work which has been oppressing him, calls in his industrial relations director, Mr. Brooks.

"Bill, you know as well as I do what a terrible time we've had for the last few months trying to get on top of this rush of orders. Now that things have eased up just a little bit, I've been trying to figure out what the difficulty was, so that we won't get into this kind of a box again. During the last few days, I've been working over the problems in the manufacturing end with Joe and the rest of his staff, and we think we've got some hunches as to what the trouble is. The way it looks to them is that a big share of the trouble has been the high absence rate in the plant. It's as if just at the time we needed the men most, something interferes with their being here regularly. At this point, Bill, it begins to look as if the problem is more in your bailiwick, and I decided I'd hand it over to you to see if you can't do something to cut down on these absences."

Bill Brooks goes back to the industrial relations office and sits down to think over how to tackle the problem of finding out why people are absent. He has always kept in close touch with the men in the plant, and he prides himself on his ability to have an effective informal conversation or interview with any one of them. He believes that if you want to know something about a person, the most straightforward and the most effective way to find out is simply to ask him. Believing this, and confident of his ability to get people to talk to him—to "bring them out"—he decides to talk to some of the men whose attendance records are particularly spotty. The first of Mr. Brooks' conversations goes somewhat as follows.

BROOKS (approaching a lathe hand in the engine plant): Hi, Fred, how are things going?

RESPONDENT: Oh, they're going all right, Mr. Brooks. I can't complain.

BROOKS: Feeling okay?

RESPONDENT: I sure am, I feel fine. Why?

BROOKS: Well, I've been doing a bit of figuring on our absence rates, and thinking about some of the reasons for people being off the job. I noticed that you'd been absent quite a few times in recent months, and as a matter of fact that you were out yesterday.

RESPONDENT (interrupting): Well, I had a real bad stomach ache yesterday. I don't really know what did it. It must have been something I had for dinner, I guess, but I really had some bad pains.

BROOKS: Well, that's too bad, Fred. I'm glad that you're feeling okay today. But how about some of the other times? What was the trouble then?

RESPONDENT: Well, it was always sickness. Nothing really serious, but you know how it is. Once in a while a fellow gets a bad cold or an upset stomach or something. That's about all there is to it.

BROOK: I see. Well, thanks, Fred. Be seeing you.

Later that day, as Mr. Brooks continues his informal survey of the causes for absence, he approaches a molder in the foundry.

BROOKS: Tom, you may have heard that I'm going around talking to some of the men, trying to get some hunches as to reasons for absence in the plant and whether there's anything we ought to be doing to make things better.

TOM: Yeah, Mr. Brooks, the fellows have been talking about it.

BROOKS: Well, you know there's nothing personal in this. We're not suggesting that anybody stayed out when he didn't need to. I'm just trying to learn a little bit about what it is that makes it necessary for people to be absent. I thought maybe there's something we can do that would take care of some of these problems. I've noticed that in the last few months you had to be away quite a few times. Is there anything special the matter?

TOM: Well, I wouldn't really say so. Now take yesterday; you probably noticed I was out. I wouldn't say I was really sick, but sometimes lately when I wake up in the morning I'm just so doggone tired that it doesn't seem I can get out of bed and go to work. Course, we moved

into a new place lately, and I've been trying to do a lot of chores getting the house fixed up. I don't stay away from work if I can help it.
I know that I'm needed on the job, and I need the money too. But,
like I say, some of these days I just can't make it.

BROOKS: Well, Tom, I certainly didn't mean to give you the idea that I
thought your absence was unnecessary, but now that I've heard you
tell the way you've been feeling, I think there's something you ought
to be sure to do. You know, the reason we have Doc Anderson on the
payroll is so that when any of us is feeling under the weather we can
get checked up. Now, within the next day or so I want you to make
it a point to go over and see him, tell him how you've been feeling, and
have him give you a thorough examination. Probably nothing at all
serious, but it won't hurt to find out. Let me know what Doc has to
say.

For his last interview in the foundry, Brooks has selected Stanley Peters,
one of the shake-out men, who's had a particularly large number of absences during the past few months. By this time, Brooks has questioned
quite a number of men, and as he appears on the shop floor, Peters leaves
his work and opens the conversation before Brooks can introduce the topic
of absence.

PETERS: Okay, Mr. Brooks, I know why you're here. You're worried about
my attendance record. Well, I can tell you that I'm a lot more worried than you are! I can't afford to be absent and I'm scared that I
may lose my job just because of my absence, but my wife's been sick
off and on all winter and when she's sick I just can't leave her alone,
not with three kids to take care of. What's more, I can't get help in
the house. Can't afford it. And both her folks and mine live out of
town. I've thought about this from every angle, but I'm just boxed in
and I don't see what I can do about it. You want to know why I've
been absent, that's it!

BROOKS: Stan, I don't know what to say. I didn't have the least idea of
what your home situation has been. I don't want you to feel that the
company is putting any pressure on you on this absence thing. As a
matter of fact, maybe there's something we can do to help you work
this thing out. How about dropping into my office in the next day or
two, and we'll see if between us we can't dope out something that will
help you out of this situation.

The next day, Mr. Brooks sits down with the transcribed notes of his interviews to piece together what he has been able to learn from them. As
he reads the transcriptions, he is increasingly impressed with the difficulty
of trying to keep in mind all the things that were said in the twelve interviews he took. He decides that it would be more useful and more methodical if he sorted the interviews into stacks according to the kind of reason
given for the absence in each case.

After completing the process of reading and sorting, he finds that all except one of the interviews fall into two stacks. One stack contains those
interviews in which the reported reason for absence was personal illness.
The other stack contains those interviews in which the reason for absence
was some unpredictable and unavoidable family emergency. The single

remaining interview is with a worker who lives out of town and drives to work each morning. Three times lately his car has broken down and he was unable to get to the plant. With the exception of this interview, the two stacks represent the sum total of Brooks's results. He somewhat disgustedly assesses the evidence in the following terms.

"Apparently all that people will say about being absent is that they couldn't help it, and that their absence was caused by their own illness or some difficulty in the family. What can I do with responses like these? I can't really believe that these reasons explain all the absences in a company the size of ours. Maybe people simply won't tell the truth about things like this. If that's right, I've been wasting my time, and the interview just isn't the way to get information on the problem. On the other hand, maybe the men did tell me the truth. If so, these absences are due to family illness or problems of personal health, and there really isn't a thing we can do about them except through medical means. I don't know how to treat this material. I don't know whether it's all true or a pack of lies."

As he broods about his interviewing experience and wonders what to do with the interviews, Mr. Brooks is suddenly struck by the fact that in his travels through the plant looking for men with frequent absences on their records, he entered only a few departments. Is this just a matter of chance, or does it mean that the absences are clustered in certain departments?

An inspection of the absence records from which Mr. Brooks selected his respondents tells him that his hunch is correct, that absences are distributed very unevenly. There are heavy clusters of absence in certain departments, whereas in others the number of absences is negligible. Brooks wonders whether this means that family emergencies and illnesses are distributed in this capricious way, or whether there are some departmental factors that are influencing absence rates. He decides to sound out one of the general foremen about this question.

Brooks arranges to have lunch with Cal Johnson, one of the general foremen. As soon as they have settled at one of the cafeteria tables, he asks Johnson what he thinks accounts for worker absence.

JOHNSON: Well, there are lots of different things that make men stay off the job, of course, and over the years I've probably seen most of them. I often think that if a supervisor keeps his eyes open he can get some pretty good hunches as to what accounts for absenteeism. Take Bert Jones, now. He's really a good steady fellow, and I know he hasn't been sick, yet in the last six months he's been absent a dozen times. Well, I happen to know that Bert's got a pretty tough situation at home. His wife has been a heavy drinker for years, but this year the thing's really gotten out of hand. She's become a confirmed alcoholic, and she's sick enough that she probably ought to be hospitalized, but Bert hesitates over the expense, and besides that, he just can't bring himself to commit her. So when Bert stays home I'm usually pretty sure that what he's trying to do is straighten out his wife. Of course, I'm not suggesting that all the liquor troubles are of that kind.

George Smith is absent for a day every couple of weeks, and we know that it's because he's gone off on a drunken spree. He's a good man, he gives us a good day's work when he's here, but every once in a while he just has to hang one on.

BROOKS: Well, Cal, you make it sound as if a lot of our absence troubles come out of bottles.

JOHNSON: I don't really mean to suggest that. I think a lot of our absence problems are made right here on the job. For instance, there's Fred. Now, he means well and he's a good hard worker, but the fact is that he's on a job that's just too big for him. He's got responsibilities and decisions to make that he hasn't been used to, and I think that every once in a while it just gets to be more than he can take. I'm not sure he'd admit even to himself that this is what his trouble is, but that's my feeling about it, and frankly I'm not sure what I ought to do.

Another case I'm worrying about is Al. Now, he's been a foreman for a long time. He's a strong man technically, and he really gets out the work. But he rides his people awfully hard in order to get it out. He cracks the whip all the time, and when anything goes wrong, he really rides the fellows he thinks are responsible. I can't prove it, but I've got a feeling that some of the absence in his group is a result of that kind of treatment. The men get to where they can't take it, and somebody calls in with a headache or digestive upset, and there it is. Well, I don't doubt that they're feeling bad, but the question is, why? I'll bet that if you look up the records on Al's group, you'll find they have more absences than any other of my sections.

Back in his own office, Mr. Brooks begins to think over what he may have learned from Cal Johnson. He has some new ideas about the possible causes of absence, and he has some ideas also about why the workers to whom he talked the previous day failed to mention these factors. He realizes that he never asked about some of these important potential causes of absence. He knew in a general way the purpose of his interviewing, but he had not thought through the kinds of information he required or the individual topics into which he should lead the interviews. He now recognizes that he should have found out specifically how the worker felt about his job and about the kind of work he was doing; and whether or not he was getting along well with his foreman. Brooks also thinks that he should have asked about things off the job, and especially the home situation of the worker.

These topics, or interview objectives, come quickly to his mind at this point, but he realizes also that it will be necessary for him to consider whether there may not be other topics of equal importance which he needs to include in his interviews. He thinks, for example, that the foreman's behavior probably has a good deal of influence on the work group and the way the men get along with each other. How a man feels about going to work could be influenced by his relationship with other men in the group. Mr. Brooks decides to ask about informal cooperation among workers in the same group, and about feelings of tension among group members.

Determining the Content of the Interview

Mr. Brooks' initial failure and his efforts to get ready for a second series of interviews illustrate an important fact about interviewing. There is much more to the interview than establishing a favorable pattern of interaction between interviewer and respondent and achieving a high level of respondent motivation to communicate. The interview, as Bingham and Moore[1] said, is "a conversation with a purpose." The implication of their phrase is that in a successful interview not only does communication take place frankly and freely, but the content of that communication is so focused and so controlled that the initial purpose of the interview is achieved.

Moreover, a general statement of purpose will not in itself make clear on what content the interview should focus. Mr. Brooks had well in mind his general purpose of finding out the reasons for absence. This, however, was not sufficient to guide the interview into the particular topics or content areas that would allow him to achieve his purpose. Mr. Brooks's original plan did not extend beyond the oversimplified procedure of asking the men why they were absent. Thereafter he could only follow where the respondent led him. It would be unusual if the respondents themselves directed the interview in a systematic fashion which thoroughly explored the subject Mr. Brooks had in mind. Such direction must rest with Mr. Brooks, and it is only by planning in advance, as he is now beginning to do, that he can hope for this systematic exploration.

Mr. Brooks now takes up his pencil and marshalls his new ideas into orderly written form. This is what he writes:

A. Find out the worker's attitudes toward his job.
B. Find out how he gets along with his foreman.
C. Find out whether he feels accepted or rejected by the other men in his work group.
D. See if he has serious sources of tension at home— recurring problems that keep him away from the job.
E. Get a general assessment of his physical well-being.

The step Mr. Brooks has just performed for his small study is standard operating procedure in the planning of large-scale interview surveys. Every interviewer, even if the scope of his interviewing problem is much narrower than those faced by researchers who use interviews to gather mass data, may learn much by observing how they plan questionnaires. In rough outline, their planning operations can be reduced to the following steps:

1. Stating the purpose of the survey fully.
2. Thinking out what kinds of information must be obtained in

---

[1] Walter Bingham and Bruce V. Moore, *How to Interview* (3rd ed.), Harper and Brothers, New York, 1941.

order to meet this purpose, and stating them in the form of *specific objectives.*

3. Drawing up a questionnaire in such a way that the answers will fulfill the specific objectives of step 2.

Mr. Brooks had performed step 1 before starting on his first interview. That is, his purpose was clear; it was to find out the causes of absence so that he could carry out the assignment his boss had given him to "cut down on the absence problem." The work he did after his failure—the pondering, the consulting with Cal Johnson, and finally the orderly listing of what he wanted the interviewer to cover —constituted step 2.

Developing Specific Objectives

The specific objectives, if properly drawn, define for us the precise kinds of information that will be needed to meet the purpose for which the interview is to be held.

These objectives are links between the general purpose or the problem that is to be solved and the specific questions which must be asked in the interview. They specify the individual topics about which information must be obtained. The objectives, in other words, "look both ways"—back toward the problem to be solved and forward to the specific interview questions yet to be formulated.

The development of specific objectives for an interview depends not upon the application of techniques but upon the ingenuity, insight, and experience of the interviewer. The determination of interview objectives is primarily a matter of getting insights and hunches as to what things may be important in explaining the problem to be solved, or what factors may be related to the broad question which constitutes the purpose of the interview. There are no set rules or procedures for getting such hunches or insights; we can, however, mention some of the sources from which they may be derived.

Sources of Objectives. In the example just described, Mr. Brooks got his hunches as to the causes of absence partly because he was insightful enough to notice departmental differences in absence rates and partly by drawing on the experience of other people, especially the general foreman, Mr. Johnson. The experience of others is certainly an important source of the hunches and insights upon which to base specific objectives. Insight may also come from one's own experience. This is perhaps the method by which most specialists (physicians, lawyers, etc.) determine the objectives of the interviews they conduct. Their own specialized experience and training is a continual source of hunches, insights, and hypotheses which may help to explain the professional problems they encounter.

Still another source is the professional literature which accumulates in many areas of specialization. Such writing is, of course, only another way of making available the experience of other people. If, for example, Mr. Brooks had been familiar with recent research on absence, he might have remembered that among the many factors related to absence are the worker's feelings about how well his skills are being utilized on the job, how he feels about his wages, and whether or not he feels his chances of promotion are good. From such research reports Mr. Brooks might have developed additional specific objectives.

Finally, in some situations hunches and insights are derived in a more formal way, and are usually stated as hypotheses. In some fields there are such hypotheses, derived from well-developed bodies of theory, which offer possible answers to the problem to be solved. But for Mr. Brooks there was no "theory of industrial absence." Suppose, however, that an industrial psychologist was confronted by a worker who had recently gotten into a fist fight with his foreman. Of the many possible explanations for such impulsive behavior, one involves the well-known psychological theory that aggression is often the result of frustration experience. If the psychologist were convinced of the potential importance of this theoretical approach to understanding the worker's behavior, he would arrive at the interview objective of determining the current sources of frustration in the worker's life, both on the job and off it. Hypotheses may be developed from observation as well as from theory. Cal Johnson's idea that some workers were absent because the boss was overly strict was in effect a hypothesis based on his observations.

Variations in Different Situations. Not every interviewer is in a position to formulate his specific objectives in advance as Mr. Brooks was. Physicians, lawyers, social workers, and others often must conduct their interviews under circumstances which do not permit advance planning. Usually these interviews are initiated by the patient or client, not by the interviewer. This means that the interviewer does not know the purpose of the interview until it is divulged by the respondent. The doctor who is confronted by a person in his office can assume only that the person wishes to talk to him about a personal medical problem, and even that assumption may be incorrect—the visitor may turn out to be selling pharmaceuticals or insurance.

Another respect in which the interviewing situation of the doctor differs from that of Mr. Brooks is the rapidity with which the steps leading up to the interview follow each other. The sequence of steps leading from the general purpose to the formulation of specific objectives, and then to the wording of individual questions and the interaction with the respondent, may take weeks or months in the case of the research interview, but may occur almost simultaneously in certain other kinds of interviews. An observer would find it impossible to state the moment at which the physician moves from the formulation of a specific objective to the asking of a question, and the doctor himself may often be unaware of the separateness of the steps leading to the interview conversation itself. Nevertheless, the process through which he goes follows the usual sequence. He is merely performing the series of steps described for Mr. Brooks, in telescoped form.

What actually happens when a patient is brought into a doctor's office? The first step is likely to involve an attempt by the doctor to determine the general purpose of the visit. He may ask the patient directly what is bothering him or what kind of help he wants, or he may simply wait for the patient to begin a description of his difficulties. In any case, the doctor must begin by getting the patient to announce the general purpose of the interview. As the patient talks and describes his symptoms, the doctor begins to get hunches as to what may be wrong with him. Almost at the same time, the doctor begins to formulate specific objectives, consisting of additional information he must obtain from the patient in order to eliminate or confirm the diagnostic possibilities which have come to his mind. The doctor has in mind the specific syndrome or set of symptoms that represent the unique characteristics of each of several diseases, and his specific objectives now involve obtaining from the patient such information as will fit one or another of these syndromes. At the same time he must obtain information to eliminate other syndromes. If the patient complains of severe abdominal pain, the doctor will immediately think of many possible explanations of such a symptom. In order to single out the correct one, he sets himself specific objectives, which may include learning the exact location of the pain, its duration, quality, frequency of occurrence, accompanying symptoms, and so on.

On what sources does the doctor draw for the formulation of such specific objectives? The major source is his training and experience as a physician. This training combines theory and the experience of others, which he has learned through textbooks, laboratory work, and a period of internship or supervised medical practice. In addition he has knowledge of the current medical situation in the area, including the prevalence of contagious diseases. Finally, he may have a case history on this particular respondent if he has previously consulted him as a patient.

We do not mean to imply that the only information obtainable from an interview is that which has been preplanned. Often the interviewer may gain fortuitous information, volunteered by the respondent, that relates directly to the interviewer's major purpose. He cannot depend upon respondents for such information, however, and the burden remains with the interviewer to assure himself that major topics are covered. He will also want to provide the respondent ample opportunity to bring up topics which the interviewer may not have considered but which may be pertinent to the general purpose of the interview.

Formulation of Questions

There is, of course, more to preparing for an interview than the process of moving from general purpose to specific objectives. The objectives can be thought of as specifications for information. They tell the interviewer what kinds of information he wishes to develop in the course of the interview, but they do not indicate how to formulate questions that will evoke the responses called for by the interview objectives. The specific objectives, in other words, remind the interviewer of what is wanted, but not of how to get it. The next step leading up to the interview itself is to formulate questions that will present the specific objectives in a form which can be successfully used with a respondent.

Mr. Brooks is faced with this problem. He reads over his objectives and thinks back to the interviews he took in the plant. If, as he suspects, many of the answers the men gave him were merely excuses for their absences rather than real reasons, how can he ask questions that avoid this problem. He thinks, for example, about his objective of finding out how the men get along with their foremen.

How can I ask questions about their attitude toward their foremen? If I ask a question like "How do you feel about your foreman?" some of the men are likely to balk at answering. And some of those who do answer will probably give me incorrect information.

This will defeat my purpose in asking the question. Perhaps I should start with less direct questions, like "We're interested in how supervisors in the plant go about supervising the men. We're not trying to identify any supervisor, or anything like that. We just want to get a general picture of supervision. How does your supervisor go about his job?" This might not frighten the man, and will help to introduce the subject. This question, with some additional subquestions, ought to obtain a lot of information.

Then I can probably follow up with another major question—"I'd like your opinion about the kinds of things supervisors do that the men like." Then I could ask the negative, since I will have a good setting for it. "What do supervisors do that the men don't like?" If I make the question general ("supervisors" instead of "your supervisor"), the man will feel freer to talk. Then I could probably go directly to the personal side in terms of his reactions to his own supervision. These questions will get the answer to the objective, and the man ought to feel free to talk about them, especially if I tell him he is one of several picked at random, and that his name won't be associated with the interview.

The problem of asking questions of respondents is, as Mr. Brooks is now discovering, often not a simple matter of knowing the objectives and then communicating the objective to the respondent. A number of decisions must be made: whether to ask for the information directly, or whether some indirect method is needed; how to word questions in order to communicate to the respondent exactly what is wanted. Such topics will be discussed in Chapters 5 and 6.

Analysis of Findings

In this book we are principally concerned with problems of designing questions and with interviewing. Other steps must follow these, however; something has to be done with the information that is the immediate product of the interview. Mr. Brooks' interviews with absentees will be of little use to him unless he can analyze his findings and obtain from them a pattern that provides an answer to the command which launched this research: "Cut down on these absences." Similarly the doctor will find the information from his patient meaningless unless he classifies the information, compares the symptoms with textbook descriptions or with those of other patients he has treated.

There are, then, stages following the interview itself which involve analyzing the information in order to answer the specific objectives. The ultimate aim of such analysis is to fulfill the general purpose, that is, to answer the broad question or to solve the problem for which the interview was initiated. Just as the objectives anticipate the questions, so do they anticipate the analysis which will be made of the information obtained in the interview. It is useless for the interviewer to obtain information which he is then unable to analyze in terms of the specific objectives for which the questions were devised.

Analysis methods and the complexity of analytic techniques vary greatly. Where one's purpose is the analysis of a single interview, as in the case of the doctor or lawyer, the analysis is often little more than a mental classification of the information as it is revealed by the respondent. In the survey or the research project, where many interviews may be taken with the same set of questions, elaborate procedures for coding or classifying responses to each question are often necessary. These codes may be transferred to punched cards, and the data may then be tabulated and subjected to statistical analyses.

As the following diagram (Figure 9) indicates, the interview is one of a sequence of steps, some preceding and anticipating the interview itself, others following directly from it. Each step is dependent upon the one preceding it, starting with the general purpose.

Figure 9. The context of the interview.

Importance of Adequate Preparation

Those who are accustomed to thinking of the interview as a separate event, uninfluenced by specifically formulated objectives or prepared questions, may find it difficult to appreciate the importance of these preliminary phases for a successful interview. They perform much the same function a topical outline or a set of notes would serve for a man about to make a speech.

Few speakers address an audience without some definite topic or purpose in mind (notwithstanding occasional impressions to the contrary). Similarly, few interviewers would begin a conversation with a respondent until they had decided on the subject of the interview. Mr. Brooks was given the purpose of this interviewing by assignment —"Find out what is responsible for the high rate of absence." But knowing the general purpose, whether assigned or of one's own choosing, is not enough. The speaker who goes before his audience without any more preparation than this is likely to perform very poorly unless he has unusual ability and experience. He will be uncertain as to the major topics he must cover in order to do justice to his subject. He will risk the uneven pacing and embarrassing pauses that result from searching for the appropriate word or phrase during the speech. He will be plagued with problems of sequence and continuity, and will be likely to think of things which he "forgot to mention." The chances of a boring, ineffective, repetitious speech will be at the maximum for such a speaker, and it is just so for an interviewer; adequate preparation is crucial.

But how much preparation is desirable, and what form should preparation take? Even the experienced speaker will find it advisable to analyze his subject, breaking it down into the subtopics which he wishes to discuss and deciding upon the order in which it will be most effective to present them. Such a topical outline for the speaker would be analogous to a list of specific objectives for the interviewer. They ensure the coverage of the content necessary to meet the general purpose for which the speech or interview was begun, and they give some sequence and structure, which would otherwise be lacking.

The speaker is now much nearer ready to face an audience, but he is not fully prepared. If he is to speak only from his list of topics, he must depend entirely on improvisation within each of them. In doing so, he assumes in lesser degree the problems already described; he must select vocabulary and formulate sentence structure as he proceeds. Most experienced speakers solve this problem by expanding the outline of topics to be discussed. They will jot down key words or sentences, or even occasional paragraphs, to make sure that they express their major thoughts in the most effective way. In this way the speaker is freed from dependence on the inspiration of the moment; he can work out in detail and polish to perfection the major point he wants to communicate. This formulation of key sentences is much like the development of a questionnaire to guide the interviewer.

SUMMARY

The major implication of our discussion is that the interview is not to be regarded as an isolated event, but rather as one of the steps in a sequence. The interview takes place in a context or matrix of such steps, and it can be understood and successfully practiced only if the interviewer is aware of this context. In this chapter, we have considered two of the elements which are common to all interviews: (1) the existence of a general purpose for which the interview is undertaken, and (2) the translation of this general purpose into a series of specific objectives or requirements for information.

As the contrasting examples of the industrial relations expert and the physician illustrate, these steps may take considerably different form in different kinds of interviews. They may be elaborate and strung out over a period of weeks or months in some research projects, or they may be nearly simultaneous as in the case of the physician. Nevertheless, each interview is undertaken for a general purpose, and somewhere between the establishment of the general purpose and the actual conduct of the interview there must be a translation of this purpose into specific objectives.

The specific objectives tell the interviewer what information he needs, but do not tell him how to obtain it from a respondent. This he must accomplish by wording questions in such a way as to convey his objective to the respondent.

Once the information is obtained, the interviewer needs to use some technique for analyzing the responses in order to answer the original purpose for which the interview was initiated.

The Formulation of Questions

Mr. Brooks and the physician, in the previous chapter, each started with a general purpose and developed specific objectives. Each also has to word questions and develop a questionnaire. Mr. Brooks can do this, as he did his objectives, with considerable forethought. He can write out questions, study them, try them out on a few people, revise them in the light of experience, and finally arrive at the ultimate questionnaire. He can have this questionnaire typewritten and can use it as a guide in each interview. The physician, since he cannot prepare all his specific objectives ahead of the interview, cannot prepare a fixed set of questions. He must devise some objectives and word questions as the interview progresses. But his lack of preparation time is partially compensated for by his extensive practice in questioning, especially as his particular kinds of interviewing problems are likely to recur with different patients. If he is observant of the effects on his patients of what he says, his questions improve with experience.

In terms of our analogy between interviewing and public speaking, the physician is like the speaker who is called on for a few extemporaneous remarks. His success will depend upon his experience and knowledge of his subject, and also on how well he understands and puts into practice the principles of public speaking. Furthermore, it is more difficult for him to make an effective speech than it is for the speaker who has ample opportunity for preparation and rehearsal. So it is with the interviewer. Experience and research indicate that the interviewer who arms himself with a carefully formulated set of questions is more likely to communicate accurately to the respondent and obtain the information he requires. The interviewer who cannot take time for such planning, or who cannot know in advance what the interview content will be, has a much more difficult task. He will increase the possibility of a successful interview if he knows the principles of question wording and has had some experience in formulating questions on related subjects.

This chapter is written for the interviewer who knows in advance the purpose and objectives of the interview and can plan his questions accordingly, but it will serve as well the interviewer who must depend upon spontaneously worded questions. Though we emphasize the importance of advance planning, the principles and techniques of question formulation are no less applicable to the interviewer who must improvise as he goes.

The Functions of Questions. The first purpose of interview questions is to translate specific objectives into a form in which they can be communicated to the respondent with maximum effectiveness. As we saw in the preceding chapter, effective questions can be developed only after adequate attention has been given to the formulation of specific objectives. To achieve their purpose the questions must convey to the respondent the idea or group of ideas required by the objectives, and must lead to responses which can be analyzed or interpreted so that the objectives are achieved.

In addition to this function of the questions there is a second of major importance. In Chapters 2 and 3 we paid considerable attention to the importance of motivating the respondent to participate in the interview, and to the psychological atmosphere which enhances the relationship between interviewer and respondent as a basis for free communication between the two. Since the interviewer is asking questions, the type of interaction he achieves will depend to a considerable extent on the quality of the questions he asks. Skillfully worded questions can do a great deal to assist and guide the interviewer in developing respondent motivation to communicate. Conversely, a skillful approach on the part of the interviewer in initiating a promising relationship with a respondent can be neutralized if the questions are such as to provoke embarrassment or hostile reactions. In short, the questions have a dual purpose: to provide a basis for the interviewer to obtain information to answer his objectives, and to assist the interviewer in his job of motivating the respondent to communicate freely.

Decisions in Question Forming. What are some of the decisions involved in preparing questions which are adequate to the dual purpose of meeting objectives and motivating communication? They involve three different kinds of problems. One is the problem of the actual choice of words; we have to frame our question so that the respondent understands it and so that it means to him what we want it to mean. As we shall see, this is by no means merely a matter of vocabulary, although vocabulary is one consideration.

Another decision is whether to ask an "open" or a "closed" question. Anyone who has taken college examinations will recognize the distinction if we give it another of its various sets of names, "multiple-choice" and "essay-type." Should a particular question be asked so that the respondent is restricted to choosing his answer from a pre-arranged list, or so that he must answer in his own words? This may appear at first blush to be a choice that only those preparing survey questionnaires (or college examinations) are confronted with, but both kinds of questions occur in spontaneous interviewing, although the interviewer's choice of one rather than the other is often, unfortunately, inadvert.

The third decision is of the kind we saw Mr. Brooks beginning to face when he said to himself, "If I ask the men, 'What do you think of your supervisor?' they are going to balk." It involves the choice between a direct and an indirect approach to a particular objective. There are many degrees of indirectness, and the purposes served by indirect approaches vary. In this chapter we shall talk mainly about the wording of questions, reserving for Chapter 6 most of our discussion of the choice between open and closed questions, and of indirect approaches to interview objectives.

LANGUAGE AND VOCABULARY

In the construction of a questionnaire, the primary criterion for the choice of language is that the vocabulary and syntax should offer maximum opportunity for complete and accurate communication of ideas between interviewer and respondent. More simply stated, the language of the interview must conform to the shared vocabulary of interviewer and respondent. The idea of "shared vocabulary" does not imply that the interviewer must make use of the same colloquialisms and speak with the same inflection as the respondent. Rather it means that the language the interviewer speaks must be understandable to the respondent, even though the respondent himself might have expressed the same idea in somewhat different fashion. Similarly, the answers of the respondent need not be offered in the terminology that the interviewer would have used, but must be understandable to the interviewer. Vocabulary and manner of expression are shared in the sense that there is a common basis for understanding.

The Area of Shared Language

The extent of shared language and vocabulary may be large or small in any given interviewer-respondent situation, depending on the characteristics of the individuals involved. For example, the shared vocabulary of two highly trained people in the same profession, two doctors or two lawyers, would be very large and very specialized. Moreover, the chances are that the shared language in such a case would include most of the vocabulary of each of the two persons, especially on the subject of their profession. On the other hand, two people may come together as interviewer and respondent with only a minimum sharing of language and therefore a minimum potential basis for understanding and communication. Suppose, for example, that an educated man whose background is entirely urban becomes a candidate for political office. He may find himself conducting a campaign that involves him in an occasional discussion with people of drastically different background. Picture our candidate attempting to interview an immigrant farmer with two years of formal education. Between the extensive vocabulary of the candidate and the limited speech of the farmer, the amount of overlap might be very small.

It is not always, of course, a requirement for a successful interview that the shared vocabulary between interviewer and respondent be large. The extent of common vocabulary required for a successful interview will depend upon the subject under discussion and the demands which the interview places upon the respondent. The question is not whether the shared vocabulary is large or small, but whether it is adequate for communication on the topic of the interview.

What can be done where the shared-language area of interviewer and respondent is judged insufficient for a successful interview? The obvious solution lies in increasing the vocabulary of one or the other of the principals in the interview. This is extremely difficult in the case of the respondent, although there are some limited possibilities here. For example, suppose that officials of a city government wish to determine the attitudes of local residents toward civil defense. The volunteer interviewers will quickly discover that some of the householders on whom they call do not understand the term "civil defense." If the interview is to be meaningful, therefore, the interviewer will have to resort to some lengthy definition and avoid the term civil defense entirely, or he will have to undertake to teach the respondent what the term means so that both of them can thereafter use it in the same fashion. The interviewer confronted by such a respondent might say, "I want to talk to you briefly about your views on civil defense, that is, the organization of volunteers to protect and help people in case of an enemy attack or other disaster."

It is more feasible and much more common to attempt to increase the shared language of interviewer and respondent by enlarging the vocabulary of the interviewer to include language familiar to the respondent. For example, the Survey Research Center recently undertook a study that involved interviewing several hundred corporation officers to determine how they handled some of the fiscal problems of their businesses, and especially what use they made of banking services. It was clear that the interviewing staff, which had been selected for professional background and interviewing competence, was being asked to obtain information on a special subject in which the interviewers were relatively ill-informed. Distinctions between primary and secondary banks, demand loans and floating loans, and the like, were completely outside the experience of most of the interviewers, as was the bulk of corporate fiscal terminology. The solution in this case was to provide special training for the interviewers, in which they were educated with respect to the vocabulary relevant to the interview and already part of the working equipment of their respondents. An alternative solution would have been to obtain interviewers who were more expert in matters of corporation finance. In this case it was deemed more efficient and feasible to provide some additional specialized knowledge to interviewers who were already skilled in the basic process of interviewing.

There is some danger of oversimplifying tne solution to language differences between interviewer and respondent. The solution does not consist merely in giving the interviewer the vocabulary and language level of the respondent, although it may be desirable under some circumstances to teach him certain words and expressions which the respondent will use. But the fact that a respondent may speak with poor grammar or use coarse language or may have some pronounced regional inflection does not mean that the interviewer should attempt to imitate these characteristics. He need not do so in order to make himself understood, and he might seriously offend the respondent by attempting to speak in a way which his background and position make incongruous.

The key point here is that the respondent has certain expectations of the language and vocabulary of the interviewer, depending on who the interviewer is and what his position is. Certain kinds of expression are appropriate to the interviewer's role, others would fit it very badly. For example, a poorly educated respondent may have great trouble expressing himself, but when he goes to a doctor or a lawyer for help, he will be little reassured if the professional man appears to have the same problems of language that he himself struggles with. What the respondent wants from the professional is a kind of language which is at once appropriate to the professional background and position and understandable to the respondent. If Professor Smith of the Great Lakes University Sociology Department is interviewing a population of Skid Row residents, he is likely to do better by relying on basic English than by attempting to assume the language of his respondents. If he attempts the latter, they are almost certain to perceive this as unusual behavior on the part of the professor, and to feel that he is somehow patronizing them, talking down to them. The result will be restricted motivation to communicate rather than an increased basis of understanding.

We are now in a position to be somewhat more definitive about the importance of common language between interviewer and respondent for the success of the interview. We see common language as essential to the interview. For communication to take place at all, it is necessary that interviewer and respondent have vocabulary and language in common. However, the existence of even a large shared vocabulary between interviewer and respondent does not guarantee effective communication or a successful interview. Shared language is a necessary but not an all-sufficient condition for communication.

Language and Empathy

Language plays an additional role in the interview by supplying cues to both interviewer and respondent as to the kind of person which the other is. Some of the first indications which the respondent gets as to whether the interviewer is a person very much like himself or very different will come from the language the interviewer employs in introducing himself and his subject. By extension, if interviewer and respondent "speak the same language," they are more likely to have had similar backgrounds and experience and are therefore more likely to be capable of understanding each other. Some authorities on interviewing carry this point to what we consider an illogical conclusion by arguing that the interviewer should attempt in all circumstances to talk as the respondent does, and that the respondent will then perceive the interviewer as capable of understanding him. We feel that although the interviewer may need to make adjustments or enlargements in his own vocabulary to accommodate that of the respondent, he cannot effectively and gracefully attempt to speak in a way that denies his own background, education, and role.

Moreover, we are convinced that the necessary basis for effective communication from the respondent lies, not in the respondent's perception that the interviewer is a person like himself, but rather in the respondent's realization that the interviewer is an empathic individual, a person who can understand him. It follows that what the interviewer must do is to show the respondent that he is capable of understanding him, his experiences and his feelings. This can be done more effectively by the kinds of techniques described in Chapters 3 and 8 than by an attempt to assume the alien vocabulary of the respondent.

Suppose, for example, that a respondent has with some difficulty brought out a groping, half-coherent statement of his own feelings at a time of crisis. He pauses, wondering whether he has been able to get these complicated ideas across and painfully aware of his own inadequacy in expressing them. If the interviewer makes a succinct and insightful summarization of what the respondent has said, he thereby provides the most effective evidence to the respondent that communication is actually taking place between them and, by the same token, does most to motivate and encourage the respondent to continue and enlarge that communication.

Language Level in Question Formation

When a questionnaire must be formulated to communicate to a large heterogeneous population, compromises on language level are unavoidable. The solution of the problem consists in using language that communicates successfully to the least sophisticated respondents involved and at the same time avoids the appearance of oversimplification. The process of formulating questions to communicate to the respondent at his own level of language is frequently a problem in word and idea simplification. This is true, for example, in a survey or research process when the sophisticated and highly trained researcher sets himself the problem of communicating to a technically naive population. It is also true in most of the interviews conducted by the physician, social worker, or business executive, where the respondent is usually a person of lesser experience, training, or expertness in the field under discussion.

The commonness of this situation is reflected in the bulk of the literature on question formation, which emphasizes the desirability of simplifying language. Though it is true in many cases that putting questions into the language of the respondent is a matter of simplifying, it is important to keep in mind that in all cases the goal is the language level of the respondent, not simplification for its own sake. If we must err, it is probably safest to make the error in the direction of oversimplification, but this mistake has its own risks. When we simplify too much or too little, the motivation of the respondent to communicate is likely to be impaired, because the language emphasizes rather than minimizes the social distance between him and the interviewer.

A question which, in terms of vocabulary and language, is beyond the understanding of the respondent, creates two problems. One is the obvious difficulty of communication when the respondent does not understand what is wanted. The second problem is motivational. The respondent, reacting to the difficulty of language, may sense such a gap of understanding between him and the interviewer that he concludes that he is talking to a person who can never really understand and empathize with him. When this happens, one of the major motives for communication has been lost.

The problems of oversimplification are also serious. The sophisticated respondent can understand an oversimplified question, but he may resent it as an insulting underestimate of his intellectual capacity. To borrow an example from Stanley Payne,[1] one person in ten may not readily understand the term "income tax," and for him we might devise such a question as "How do you feel about your income tax— that is, the amount you have to pay the government on the money you take in during the year?" But the remaining nine out of the ten might feel insulted by such a question because of the implication that they have to have the term explained to them.

FRAME OF REFERENCE

Whitehead[2] once wrote that "language is always ambiguous as to the exact proposition which it indicates." The basic reason for the ambiguity of language is that each individual interprets spoken or written communication from his unique experience and personal viewpoint. As a result, in some degree the meaning which an individual attaches to a communication must be uniquely his own and not shared by others. For many practical purposes, of course, the ambiguities of everyday communications are so inconsequential that we can ignore the truth of Whitehead's statement; the people between whom these

---

[1] *The Art of Asking Questions,* Princeton University Press, Princeton, 1951.

[2] Alfred N. Whitehead, *Process and Reality,* Macmillan, New York, 1929.

communications are exchanged have a sufficient body of shared or similar experience so that the meaning they extract from them is substantially the same. For example, if we invite a small American boy to go to the drugstore for a chocolate shake, the chances of our being misunderstood are remote. In our culture this represents a common idiom and appeals to common experiences. In another culture, even one where English is also the spoken language, this same phrase may not communicate anything to the respondent, or may convey something other than was intended.

Personal Frames of Reference

The essential point with respect to frame of reference is that each individual, on receiving a communication, must understand and interpret the information in the light of his own relevant past experiences. It is this process of providing a context out of experience that gives meaning to the communication. Communications differ in the extent to which they demand interpretation by their recipients. On the whole, the more fragmentary and ambiguous the stimulus, the more the individual has to draw on his own experience and on his own point of view and attitudes in order to give the stimulus meaning.

Suppose, for example, we meet an acquaintance on the street and greet him with the standard question, "How are things going?" Our question provides him with almost no frame of reference except an invitation to respond in general terms of satisfaction or dissatisfaction. Moreover, we have no way of knowing from his reply of "Fine," or "So-so," or "Not so good," whether he is answering our question in terms of his job, the state of his wife's health, or the fact that his favorite ball team just dropped a double header. He has provided his own frame of reference in answering our question, and the chances are that we have few clues to the context from which he replied.

In some cases the frame of reference is provided by the specialized roles or role relationship of the people involved in the communication, so that a verbal stimulus no more specific than that given in the previous example may acquire a more precise frame of reference. Suppose that the same question—"How are things going?"—is put to a man by his supervisor on the job. The ambiguity of the verbal stimulus may be considerably reduced by the role relationship of the two persons involved. A specific frame of reference is provided, not by the words used but by knowing that when the supervisor in the shop asks how things are going he is thinking about the job, not about the worker's family affairs or financial situation.

Often the respondent is so dominated by his own immediate needs that all communications must be interpreted in relation to these needs. Such strong needs will then determine his frame of reference. The father whose son is fighting in a war may be so concerned about his son's welfare that he is unable to discuss current affairs in any other context. The worker who has an acute grievance with his foreman may be quite unable psychologically to discuss any aspect of the work situation without getting into the nature of his grievance, or at least permitting the emotion generated by that grievance to condition his discussion of other aspects of the work situation.

The effects of such highly personal frames of reference can be illustrated from surveys. In a survey conducted during World War II regarding public attitudes toward the effectiveness of fuel-oil rationing, it was found that people whose homes were heated with fuel oil tended to answer the questions in personal terms; they spoke about the adequacy or inadequacy of their own allotments, and the temperatures which they were able to maintain in their own homes. People whose homes were heated with gas or with coal, on the other hand, had a more external frame of reference; they responded largely in terms of national policy and the problems of a war economy.

In the projective tests used in psychological diagnosis, ambiguity is deliberately employed to uncover the frames of reference characteristic of the person being examined. In such tests the psychologist provides his subject with a purposely ambiguous stimulus in the form of a partial statement, an incomplete story, or a vaguely defined picture. The subject is then asked to describe the picture, or to complete the statement or story. In doing so, he is necessarily thrown upon his own experience and attitudes, since the content of the stimulus itself is fragmentary and acquires meaning only as the subject endows it with the product of his own experience.

Broad Frames of Reference

Thus far we have been talking about individual frames of reference. For many topics, however, the frame of reference we encounter is much more likely to be national or regional in extent, or to be a characteristic of subgroups in our culture—occupational groups, social classes, or the like. The New Yorker and the rural Arkansan are likely to disagree on whether Little Rock is a big city; the Alaskan and the Texan will have different ideas of what constitutes a hot summer; the airline pilot and the timid passenger will have different answers when asked if a trip was pleasant and uneventful.

This discussion is probably sufficient to provide us with a definition of what is meant by frame of reference, and also to demonstrate that the frame of reference which an individual brings to a communication is an important psychological factor in determining what the communication will mean to him, and therefore how he will respond to it. Having learned these things about frame of reference, we must now face the problem of what to do about it in our role as interviewer. There are several possible answers to this question.

The Interviewer's Problems in Dealing with Frame of Reference

Interpreting the Response. We may wish to ascertain the frame of reference within which a respondent answers a question so that we can interpret his response in light of that frame of reference. Often the interviewer will ask a respondent to tell him *why* he feels as he does about a topic, in order to make explicit the frame of reference from which he answered the question.

Let's say we are doing a study on people's opinions about the economic outlook for the next couple of years. There have been reports in the newspapers that car dealers are badly overstocked. Many columnists and economists are saying that the automobile companies should cut back production to prevent the surplus from getting larger. They predict dire results to the economy if this is not done.

One of our objectives in the study is to discover whether all this talk is affecting people's feelings about the future. So we ask the question: "What do you think about car production these days—the number of cars being turned out by the factories?"

About half the respondents say that too many cars are being produced, 10 per cent answer too few, and the rest feel production is about right. Our first interpretation of these responses may be that half the people are being influenced by reports on overproduction and see this as an economic problem. But if we ask these people why they feel the way they do, we discover that four different frames of reference are represented in the answers.

One is the future of the total economy (as in the case of the respondent who says, "I read how they've turned out so many this year they're going to have to cut down production next year, and that could mean unemployment—not only for auto workers, but in the industries that supply the auto plants, and then in retail trade, and so on and so on, all along the line.") A second is the decline in morals ("If people didn't have so many cars to ride around in, they'd go to church on Sundays and there wouldn't be all those parties in parked cars you read about, and all that juvenile delinquency and crime.") Third is the overcrowding of the highways—more properly, the frame of reference of the car driver ("It's got so we just stay home on Sundays, hardly ever get into the country any more—the traffic jams are so bad; and you can't park anywhere—my wife says unless she goes to the supermarket first thing in the morning, she might as well plan to spend the day there, waiting for somebody to pull out of the parking lot so she can pull in.") The fourth involves one's personal status as a car owner ("They turn them out so fast they have to keep changing the styles so people will want new models, and by golly, I just can't afford to trade in my car every couple of years.")

The moral to be drawn from these examples is that an accurate interpretation of answers can be made only when we know the frame of reference which the respondent is using.

Controlling the Response. The most usual situation with respect to respondent frame of reference in an interview, however, is that we want to control it. Without taking time to make a particular frame of reference explicit to the respondent, and without attempting to ascertain the frame of reference each respondent is using, we want nevertheless to be reasonably confident that the respondent has the same frame of reference as we had when we designed the question. Moreover, if we are speaking to many respondents, we wish to be sure that each of them is answering the question from the same frame of reference, so that their responses are comparable. If we include in a public-opinion interview a question about the cost of living, we want to be sure that the respondents to whom we address the question are thinking of the same basic factors when they use the phrase "cost of living."

Techniques for Controlling Frames of Reference

How can we control the frame of reference within which a respondent will answer a question, or be confident that we understand the frame of reference which he is employing? There seem to be three major possibilities.

Learning the Respondent's Frame. We can ask the question, discover the respondent's frame of reference, and interpret the response accordingly. Suppose a young sixth-grader has a new teacher and his father is interested in finding out how the boy likes the teacher. The father also wants to find out the basis, or frame of reference, which his son uses for his evaluation of the teacher. The following interview takes place:

FATHER: Well, Johnny, how do you like your new teacher?
BOY: Gee, she's swell. All the kids like her.

FATHER: That's good. Why do all the kids like her?
BOY: Oh, she's easy. Doesn't make us work hard. Yesterday afternoon we
spent extra time in gym and never had spelling or reading at all. Miss
Strong would never have let us miss spelling and reading.

From this short interview we see that Johnny is evaluating his new
teacher in terms of how easy she is on the students. Other pupils,
possibly more diligent, might evaluate her teaching skills; still others
might have commented on her appearance.

Often the interviewer, particularly in a research project, is as much
interested in the respondent's frame of reference as he is in the
respondent's feelings or attitudes on a given subject. During World
War II the Office of War Information sponsored several surveys to
investigate the state of civilian morale. Early results showed that it
was of major importance to determine the point of view of the respondents when they talked about the progress of the war. Many
respondents reacted to the war primarily in terms of their husbands
or sons in the armed forces; for others the frame of reference was the
scarcity of consumer goods; some thought of the international conflict in broader perspective.

These varying frames of reference were important considerations in
the interpretation of the over-all feeling that the war was progressing
satisfactorily or unsatisfactorily.

Indicating a Specific Frame. A second way of controlling frame of
reference is to incorporate some specific frame of reference as part of
the question. In effect the respondent is instructed, as a part of the
question, with respect to the frame of reference which he is to employ.
For example, we might say to a respondent in a public opinion survey,
"How have you people been getting along this year? Financially, I
mean." The parenthetical "Financially, I mean" is simply an in-
struction to the respondent to use the economic frame of reference in
answering the question, rather than answering in terms of health,
family arrangements, job situation, or any other frame of reference
which might be paramount in his own mind. The supervisor who
says to a subordinate, "Now, how are things going on the job, I mean
between you and Ed?" is doing exactly the same thing. He is instructing his subordinate to answer the question in terms of a specific
interpersonal relationship.

Selecting a Common Frame. A third possibility for controlling
frame of reference is to use a stimulus or question for which the frame
of reference is common for the entire group serving as respondents.
A simple example is that of a survey in a single city, where the question is asked, "Do you think we should spend the money necessary to

build a new city hall?" In this case it is so apparent that the frame of reference is "this city" that it does not need to be specified.

Suppose two physicians meet in the corridor of a hospital and one asks the other, "How is Mrs. Smith getting along?" It is clear that the question refers to the state of Mrs. Smith's health, not her financial situation or her domestic life. The frame of reference is specified by the professional role of the physicians. This use of frame of reference is not actually a technique. It is rather a recognition on the part of the interviewer that the frame of reference is similar for the interviewer and respondent and therefore does not need to be controlled.

Obstacles to Control. When we attempt to understand or control the respondent's frame of reference, a number of special problems arise. Control sometimes becomes almost impossible if the respondent is under a good deal of emotional tension with respect to the topic under discussion. In such a situation, one frame of reference may be so strong that any other will be disregarded, even if a question is so worded as to rule out that frame of reference.

A factory worker goes to his family physician because he is feeling run down and tired and has developed back pains. The doctor examines him carefully, then gives the following verdict. "Tom, you know you aren't as young as you used to be. There's nothing that I can find that's wrong with you except that you're working too hard. As I say, there's nothing wrong with you *now*, but if you don't cut down on your work, there may be some very serious consequences."

The next day at work Tom is approached by an interviewer from the personnel department, who informs him that he was chosen, by random methods, as part of a sample of workers to be interviewed to find out what the company can do to increase employee satisfaction. The chances are that Tom's recent advice from his physician will be so salient that the phrase "the work is too hard or too demanding" will crop up repeatedly in the interview. This frame of reference will probably dominate all others, whereas a day or so previously Tom might have answered in terms of pay or supervision.

The interviewer's solution to this kind of problem lies in permitting a full response in terms of the worker's frame of reference, and then asking him for other things that might make the company a better place in which to work.

Problems of Frame of Reference in Question Wording

To say that the questionnaire should be cast in language the respondent understands is relatively unequivocal and straightforward.

It is equally important and considerably more difficult, however, to phrase questions that take account of the frame of reference which respondents bring to the subject under discussion. Nevertheless, the interviewer must introduce each topic in a way that ties in with the frames of reference of the respondent and is consistent with the respondent's notion of what is and is not relevant to the topic under discussion. The development of a topic from one question to another must meet not only the researcher's criteria for reasonableness and logic, it must also meet those of the respondent. Hence, frame of reference becomes another dimension on which the researcher must begin at the point "where the respondent is."

Bancroft and Welch[3] present an example of what happens when researchers have a frame of reference that is not shared by the respondents. They found that the series of questions used by the Bureau of the Census to ascertain the number of people in the labor market consistently underestimated the number of employed persons. When asked the question, "Did you do any work for pay or profit last week?" respondents reported in terms of what they considered their major activity. Young people attending college considered themselves to be students even if they were also employed on a part-time basis. Women who cooked, cleaned house, and raised children spoke of themselves as housewives, even if they also did some work for pay outside the home. The effect of the respondent's frame of reference was to classify as nonworkers many thousands of people who met the census definition of workers. The solution involved revising the questions, beginning with the acceptance of the respondent's classification of himself. People were asked first what their major activity was; those who gave nonworker responses were asked whether in addition to their major activity they did any work for pay. The effect of this change was to raise the official estimate of employment by more than a million persons.

It is instructive for the question writer to keep in mind the issues involved in the distortion which Bancroft and Welch report. The respondents' frames of reference with respect to what constituted work were different from that of the researchers who formulated the questions. Respondents tended to consider as work only those jobs which made up their major activity during the week. The research people had defined as work any service performed for pay during the week, even if the proportion of the respondent's time devoted to this activity was extremely small. The result of this difference in frame

---

[3] Gertrude Bancroft and Emmett H. Welch, "Recent Experience with Problems of Labor Force Measurement," *Journal of the American Statistical Association,* **41**, 303–312 (1946).

of reference meant that the simple word "work" failed to communicate to the respondent the meaning which the researchers intended. As a result the respondent's answer, accurate enough in terms of his own frame of reference, was in error with respect to the frame of reference of the researchers.

RELEVANCE OF QUESTIONS

A problem closely related to frame of reference is that of the relevance of a question from the respondent's point of view. In discussing the motivations of respondents to communicate (Chapter 2), we indicated that one of the major motivational forces stems from the respondent's perception that by communicating he will move toward certain of his own goals. As we there pointed out, an employee may feel that by cooperating with the industrial relations interviewer, he may bring about improvements in his own work situation. Similarly, the respondent in a public-opinion survey may feel that by making his attitudes known, he will in some fashion influence government policy in the direction which he considers desirable.

The negative side of this motivational picture is that if a respondent perceives a specific question as irrelevant to the topic under discussion, or as inappropriate to the goals and purposes of the interview, the effect will be to decrease his motivation to communicate. In fact, if the respondent perceives a question as irrelevant to the purpose of the interview, his attitude may well be one of skepticism or distrust. His trust of the interviewer may be lowered, and a negative force blocking communication may develop. For these reasons it is important that the questions in an interview be perceived by the respondent as appropriate to the topic under discussion, congruent with the purpose announced by the interviewer, and relevant to the respondent's own goals.

We also pointed out earlier that interviewers may sometimes find it desirable, when introducing a new topic, to reiterate the general purpose of the interview and explain the way in which this new topic fits into the general context. Such efforts on the part of the interviewer may actually be attempts to compensate for defects in the wording of specific questions. Careful attention to question wording should eliminate, in most cases, the necessity for special explanations. The important principle here is that the perceived relevance of a question can be thought of as a special type of frame of reference, which is likely to be important in determining whether a respondent will communicate a given piece of information.

Reluctance to communicate often develops quickly when the respondent fails to see the relationship between a question and his own perception of the research objective. A survey respondent who has talked freely about foreign policy may suddenly balk at being asked his age or his education. These questions in themselves may not be threatening, but they do not fit the respondent's perceptions of the purpose of the research. The example of collection of data on family income, referred to earlier, provides another case showing the extent to which a respondent's behavior may depend on his perception of what is relevant. The collection of detailed data on personal income, unsuccessfully attempted in many early surveys, was achieved by introducing a request for income data as part of a program to assess problems of consumer credit, spending, and saving. In the context of discussing saving, plans for consumer purchases, and attitudes and expectations about economic conditions and personal financial status, the question about family income appears to the respondent as reasonable and relevant.

The point may be made more dramatically in the following example from industry. Suppose that a supervisor has summoned an industrial foreman to his office to discuss a current problem of achieving higher production. After some considerable questioning about the impediments to achieving the norm that the supervisor considers appropriate, he looks at his subordinate and says, "By the way, Joe, how long have you been with us now?" From the point of view of the foreman, this question is not relevant to the solution of the production problem, which was the announced subject of the interview. However, it is highly relevant to another and particularly threatening context, that is, the possibility that he is to be fired. It is likely that the foreman will respond to this question in a guarded way and will be on the alert for signs of threat in the remainder of the interview. The irrelevance of the question to the stated purpose of the interview has had the effect of worsening the interviewer-respondent relationship, and probably reducing the amount of unbiased information which the supervisor will be able to elicit.

The principle involved in both these examples is that the content and substance of the interview, and the interviewer-respondent relationship which has been developed, establish a context within which certain questions appear to the respondent to be appropriate, relevant, and nonthreatening. Questions outside this context appear to him at best irrelevant, and possibly threatening.

INFORMATION LEVEL

A question must be worded so that it ties into the respondent's level of information in a meaningful way. It is all too easy to make unrealistic assumptions about the expertness of a respondent or about the amount of information he possesses. The importance of avoiding such assumptions lies in the fact that when the interviewer, with the authority of his role, asks the respondent a question, there is an implication that the respondent should be in possession of an adequate answer, and that if he cannot answer he is somehow discredited. If, for example, in a cross-section survey dealing with public attitudes toward problems of atomic energy, an interviewer were to ask, "What precautions should a technician take in handling radioactive isotopes?" a very common and immediate reaction from respondents would be embarrassment and resentment at being asked a question they were unable to answer. Not only would the researcher have lost the answer to a question, but he would also pay a price in terms of decreased motivation to communicate. Another possibility is that the respondents will feel obligated to show knowledge which they do not possess.

The *expertness* of the respondent is one aspect of information level which is an important consideration in wording questions. There are other components of information level which have to be considered. One of these is *language*. A respondent may be unable to answer a question simply because the words or concepts are beyond his vocabulary. The question "What is your ethnic background?" may well yield no information because the respondent doesn't know what "ethnic background" means.

A further problem of information level occurs when the respondent is asked for information that is a matter not of expertness but of *experience*. The question "About what was your father's income when you were a child?" is an example. Apart from the problem of memory involved, children quite commonly do not know their parents' incomes, and unless the respondent chanced to acquire the information years later, he is unlikely ever to possess it.

Finally, there is a problem which, while not wholly one of information level, can perhaps best be considered in this category. This has to do with the *psychological accessibility* or *inaccessibility* of information. Some questions request information that is within the respondent's experience but is beyond his psychological capacity to communicate. A naive research psychologist might inquire of a long-suffering subject, "Are you an autocrat?" The problem here is that the respondent probably does not know the answer to the question, because it requires a degree of objectivity about himself, his motivations, and his relationships to other people that is beyond the reach of most individuals. This kind of problem is likely to arise whenever we ask people to produce judgments about themselves, their values, or other emotionally charged topics. A seemingly straightforward question like "Are you a generous person?" becomes extremely difficult to answer accurately, for the kinds of reasons just specified.

Effects of Faulty Adaptation

Misjudging the respondent's information level affects both the answer to the question being asked and the interpersonal relationship between interviewer and respondent. The immediate effect is likely to be that the respondent is either unable or unwilling to answer the question at all. Another possibility is that he may attempt to answer the question but may unwittingly provide the interviewer with misleading information. A further complication is that the respondent may feel threatened because of the implication that he should be able to answer the question, and this may result in an impaired relationship between respondent and interviewer.

Most of the problems resulting from failure to adapt questions to the information level of the respondent fall into the category of what we may call *expert error*—that is, the error of ascribing to the respondent a degree of expertness in a particular field which he does not actually possess. Consider the following questions:

What is the state of morale in your plant?
Do you think it is possible to send a rocket to the moon?
Do you want to bring a criminal or a civil suit?
Do the people in your city favor an increase in taxes for new schools?
Some people who live near jet aircraft bases complain about the noise of the jets. What could be done to cut down on the noise?

There are experts for whom some of these questions might be appropriate—a lawyer could answer meaningfully the question about criminal or civil suits, and the rocket expert could discuss intelligently the question about a rocket to the moon. These questions require specialized information which the ordinary citizen does not possess.

Questions on plant morale and public attitudes toward taxes may be even more difficult, in the sense that no one can be certain of how a large group of people feel unless a recent referendum or a research project has ascertained the facts. The worker cannot know all the facts about the morale of his plant; the citizen does not know how the entire population feels about increased taxes for new schools. If the objective is to ascertain such facts, the question will fail. But such questions may be useful and appropriate if the objective is to investigate the perceptions or feelings of the respondent. The worker doesn't *know* the state of morale in his plant, but he may well have some feelings on the subject.

The general point to be made here is that a respondent should not be asked questions that require a degree of expertness he does not possess.

Techniques for Dealing with Problems of Information Level

We can now consider some solutions to the informational problems which have been discussed. The situation in which the problem is simply a linguistic one is perhaps the simplest to solve. In such cases we have only to reword the question in such a way that it uses the respondent's language. A slight and often effective variation on this solution is to incorporate in the question a definition which translates the concept the interviewer is using to a framework which is familiar to the respondent. If a physician wished to find out whether his patient had ever had a streptococcus infection, he might ask, "Did you ever have a sore throat that forced you to go to bed and caused a high fever of some duration?" The physician has to compromise in order to provide this operational definition of a streptococcus infection, but his compromise wording is likely to result in more accurate information than would adherence to precise medical terminology.

Sometimes, of course, our purpose is not to make a question conform to a respondent's experience, but rather to find out what the extent of the respondent's experience is. In such a case it is still possible to word the question in a way that minimizes the psychological impact of being unable to answer a question. Our previous question on handling radioactive isotopes might have been asked in the following way: "Many people haven't had an opportunity to learn a great deal about the technical problems of handling atomic material, but some have picked up information on this subject. Do you happen to know what precautions are appropriate for a technician handling radioactive isotopes?"

The problems of reaching material which is psychologically inaccessible are more complex. There is probably no way in which we can put the direct question "Are you an autocrat?" with any expectation of objective response. The solution to such a problem lies in an indirect approach to the objective. This may involve asking a number of questions about specific situations or specific behaviors which the respondent can report, but which do not ask him to evaluate himself. A still less direct approach to the same objective may involve the use of projective devices or indirect measures, some of which will be discussed in Chapter 6.

TECHNIQUES FOR HANDLING PROBLEMS OF SOCIAL ACCEPTABILITY

A basic characteristic of the respondent-centered questionnaire is its emphasis on the acceptability of a wide range of responses. No question should confront the respondent with the necessity for giving a socially unacceptable response; that is, a statement which he feels puts him in an embarrassing position in relation to the interviewer, or puts him in a position which he sees as inappropriate for a person of his occupation, family situation, or social class. In a sense we have already given considerable emphasis to this aspect of interviewing in our discussion of interviewing techniques. It is appropriate, however, to consider the special contribution which the questionnaire itself can make to solving the problem of social acceptability.

If we expect the respondent to answer freely and spontaneously, we must help him to feel that the entire range of possible responses to a question is acceptable to the interviewer, and to the respondent in terms of his own standards for himself. To a considerable extent this is a goal we can achieve in the wording of questions only by being sensitive to the needs and values of the people whom we wish to question. We must have in mind enough of the respondent's values and ethics so that we can try to avoid questions which he might perceive as socially unacceptable. An apparently innocuous question about social drinking, for example, would be seen as highly inappropriate by some segments of the population.

Perhaps the most frequently used technique for making a delicate question acceptable is to incorporate in it a brief statement intended to "educate" the respondent about the nonjudgmental character of our interest in him. In a survey among adolescent boys, the researcher wanted to find out whether there were differences of opinion between the boys and their parents about what time the boys should come home at night. The researcher felt that it was important to make it acceptable for respondents to admit that there might be family disagreement on this point. The question was worded, therefore: "In talking with young people all over the country, we find that many have disagreements with their families on what time they should be home at night. Do you have disagreements with your parents on this?" This wording did two things; it informed the respondent that he was not unusual if he had such disagreements, and it let him know that the interviewer considered such a response acceptable and normal.

Sometimes we communicate a nonjudgmental attitude by incorporating an excuse into our question for behavior the respondent might be reluctant to report. Instead of asking, "Did you vote in the last election?" we may say, "Were you able to get to the polls for the last election?"—implying that we know the respondent had a good reason if he did not vote. But the technique of the built-in excuse must be carefully applied. A supervisor who wishes to know whether a subordinate has completed a certain set of reports may preface the question by saying, "Bill, I know you've been extremely busy with the grommet order lately, but have you had a chance . . . ?" The form of this question neutralizes for Bill the unacceptable aspect of a negative reply, but it also handicaps the supervisor if he then wants to ask Bill *why* he hasn't finished the report.

Not every topic can be made socially acceptable to every respondent. When we have a sensitive topic, we may do better to attempt to overcome the barrier of social unacceptability by developing a counterforce of positive motivation. The respondent may be motivated to give an embarrassing or socially unacceptable answer if he is convinced that by doing so he is taking an important step for his own well-being or toward the achievement of certain of his own goals. The physician who wishes to find out whether symptoms he has encountered in a patient are due to excessive use of alcohol might put the question in the following way: "Mr. Jones, the symptoms which you describe and the condition which I find on examination can be caused by any of a number of things. The treatment varies a good deal depending on the cause. One of the most frequent causes of this illness is alcohol. About how much do you drink in a week?"

The preceding example is the interviewer's last resort. The more desirable solution is the kind we cited in our earlier examples, which meets the problem of the social acceptability of a topic by means of questions that satisfy the respondent's criteria of social acceptability.

LEADING QUESTIONS

A leading question is one which makes it easier or more tempting for the respondent to give one answer than another. For example, a question designed to elicit general attitudes toward rent control might read, "How do you feel about rent control?" A form of the same question that is leading is, "You wouldn't say that you were in favor of rent control, would you?" This kind of leading is so easily recognized that we avoid it almost without effort. A more subtle form of the same question might be, "Would you say that you are in favor of rent control?" This question makes it easier for the respondent to answer "yes" than "no." In answering "yes" he is merely agreeing with the language of the question. It is more difficult to respond "no," because this response seems to contradict the interviewer, or at least appears to be counter to the ideas of the person who worded the question.

The effects of the leading question are likely to be especially serious if the respondent is subordinate to the interviewer. The physician speaking to a patient, the lawyer questioning a client, the supervisor in conversation with a subordinate, or the social worker interviewing a client, is playing the interviewer role in relation to a respondent who is in a position of dependency. This is likely to mean that the respondent will be particularly sensitive to the interviewer's language and highly suggestible in reacting to questions that make one response easier than another. When the physician examining a suffering patient nods his head encouragingly and says, "It hurts there, doesn't it?" he is more likely to get an affirmative response than he would be if he worded the question in a more balanced fashion.

The aim in phrasing the question should be either to give no indication of possible responses, or if that is not feasible, to indicate the possible responses in such a way that the alternatives are balanced.

Another kind of leading question uses words that have become emotionally loaded either favorably or unfavorably. In our culture there are many words so emotionally charged that it is virtually impossible to expect a respondent to avoid a stereotyped reaction to them. Consider these two questions: "Did you vote in the last election?" and "Did you exercise your right as an American citizen to vote in the last election?" We can predict that the second question would turn up many more "voters" than did the first.

A third way in which a question may encourage a particular response is by associating one of the alternative responses with a goal so desirable that it can scarcely be denied. The question "Do you favor or oppose higher taxes to prepare for the dangers of war?" associates higher taxes with defense against attack, and thus implies that a negative answer means indifference to the menace of attack. Even if the respondent is permitted an unstructured reply, such a question does much to bias his answer. If he is given only the alternatives of acceptance or rejection, the biasing effect is even more serious. Another example might be taken from a journalist's interview with a member of the United States Senate: "Senator, a recent poll in your state shows that 74 per cent of the voters favor the housing bill. How do you stand on this bill?" The senator, who is concerned about reelection, will be more likely to express favorable attitudes toward the bill than he might have if the reporter had not included his first statement.

A final matter for consideration at this point is that the loaded question is not necessarily undesirable, and sometimes has a valuable place in a questionnaire. The problem is to avoid loading if one is looking for an undistorted response. For an example of a strongly loaded question used purposely, consider the following: "Would you favor sending food overseas to feed the starving people of India?" This question, after an "unloaded" series, was used to determine the number of people who were so strongly opposed to shipping food to other countries that they rejected the idea in spite of the strong emotional context of "starving people."

THE SINGLE IDEA

Questions should be limited to a single idea or a single reference. The reason is illustrated by this question, asked of an aspiring candidate for political office by a cub reporter: "Do you favor or oppose increased job security and the guaranteed annual wage, Candidate X?" A yes or no answer to this question by the suffering candidate makes it impossible for the reporter to determine whether he is in favor of or opposed to increased job security in general, the guaranteed annual wage in particular, or both of these things. The most acceptable formulation of this question would depend to some extent on the journalist's specific objective. If his purpose is to find out the candidate's attitude toward job security in general and the guaranteed annual wage in particular, it will be necessary for him to ask two questions, one referring to each of these subjects. If, on the other hand, the purpose of the question is merely to get some general notion of the candidate's attitude in the area of worker benefits, it might be possible to ask a global question such as, "How do you feel about some of the current proposals to increase job security, Candidate X?" It must be kept in mind, however, that if a global question of this type is asked, the interpretation should be very conservative. In other words, a positive response to a global question must be taken only to indicate favorableness in the general area, and cannot be interpreted as indicating the respondent's support for any of the specific examples that might be cited in such a question.

SUMMARY

In this chapter we have attempted to present the general principles underlying the formulation of questions and to point out some of the most common dangers. We have emphasized the dual function of interview questions—translating interview objectives into language familiar to the respondent, and assisting the interviewer to achieve a high level of respondent motivation.

The actual choice of words for questions is discussed in terms of such criteria as the area of "shared language" of interviewer and respondent, the empathic implications of language, and the appropriateness of language for the interviewer role.

The point of view advocated is that the language chosen for the interview must consist primarily of terms within the common experience of both interviewer and respondent. Expedients for increasing their shared vocabulary are considered, with emphasis on the practice of instructing the interviewer in the language of the respondent. The importance of language as symbolic of social distance is accepted, but the emphasis is on other means of conveying to the respondent the ability of the interviewer to understand and empathize. The efforts of interviewers to assume an unnatural idiom are rejected as ineffective and ill-advised.

The concept of frame of reference is introduced as an important determinant of what a question means to a respondent and how he will react to it. Three techniques for taking account of the respondent's frame of reference are analyzed: (1) we may elicit from him information which makes explicit the frame within which his answers originate; (2) we may instruct him regarding the frame of reference which we consider appropriate; (3) we may select a frame of reference common to an entire respondent group (if we are able to do so).

In addition to frame of reference, three related concepts are considered, each representing a potential source of respondent motivation or resistance. These are the *relevance* of the question as seen by the respondent, the respondent's *information level* in the area under question, and the degree of *social acceptability* which is imputed to his answers. The chapter concludes with two common problems of the question writer—the tendency to "lead" the respondent, and the confusion which results from attempting to combine several questions into one.

chapter 6

The Design of Questionnaires

We have said that three different kinds of problems are involved in preparing questions which are adequate to the dual purpose of meeting objectives and motivating communication. The first of these problems—the actual choice of words—was the major topic of Chapter 5. In this chapter we will consider two more problems related to question construction—the choice between open and closed questions, and between direct and indirect approaches to interview objectives. We will then turn to the problem of questionnaire organization and design—the patterning and sequence of questions which are most effective for different interview purposes.

OPEN AND CLOSED QUESTIONS

A major decision in the formulation of questions has to do with the form of the response; that is, whether the respondent is to reply in his own words, or is to select from a series of preassigned categories the answer that best approximates his own opinion. Questions of the former type are termed "open" or "unrestricted." The latter type of question is "closed" or "restricted." The open question simply establishes the topic for the respondent, and leaves him to structure his answer as he sees fit. The following example of an open question is taken from the questionnaire of an industrial study: "How do you feel about Negroes and whites working together in this factory?" The respondent answers *ad lib.*, and the interviewer makes a verbatim transcript of his answer. In the closed question the possible responses are contained in the question, so that the respondent merely has to select the category that comes closest to his position. An example of a closed question is: "Do you think your income will be higher, lower, or about the same this year as it was last year?"

The partisans of both the open and the closed question have been extremely vocal in advocating the advantages of their respective techniques. Some years ago, however, Lazarsfeld[1] pointed out that the appropriateness of open or closed questions depends upon a number of situational factors. We are in agreement with this general point of view, and would list the most important of the "situational factors" as being:

(1) The objectives of the interview (or of the part of the interview under consideration).

(2) The respondent's degree of knowledge or level of information about the topic in question.

(3) The extent to which the topic has been thought through by the respondent, so that his ideas and opinions about it are well structured.

(4) The ease with which the material in question can be communicated by the respondent, or the extent to which he is motivated to communicate on this topic.

(5) The extent to which the respondent's situation with respect to these matters (his information level, attitude structure, motivation, and ability to communicate) is known to the interviewer in advance of the interview.

The Objectives of the Interview

The basic principle here is that the closed question tends to be most successful when the interviewer's objective is to "classify" the respondent, that is, to lead the respondent to express agreement or disagreement with some stated point of view. If the interviewer's objective goes beyond the classification of the respondent and includes the wish to learn something of the respondent's frame of reference or the process by which he has arrived at a particular point of view, an open question is likely to be more appropriate than a single closed question or even a combination of closed questions.

Suppose we wish to learn what proportion of the workers in a plant consider it a good place in which to work. The objective can

---

[1] Paul F. Lazarsfeld, "The Controversy over Detailed Interviews—An Offer for Negotiation," *Public Opinion Quarterly*, **8**, 38–60 (1944).

be realized by asking the following closed question: "On the whole, would you say that this was a good or a poor place to work?" This question is clear and straightforward, and asks the respondent to place himself in one of two categories. If our objective does not go beyond this two-way classification of workers according to their over-all judgment of the work place, the question is adequate. Moreover, it is an efficient and economical way of getting the limited amount of information which we seek; the response satisfies directly the objective of the question, with no inference or interpretation by the interviewer.

Suppose, however, that our objectives include learning something of the structure of the worker's attitude, the basis for his over-all judgment of the company, and the intensity of his feelings on this subject. For these purposes the previous closed question is inadequate, and we would suggest instead that the topic be approached with an open question, such as: "Would you tell me how you feel about this company as a place to work?" Depending on the respondent's answer, this question might be followed with one or more supplementary questions, such as: "That's very interesting; can you tell me a little more about it?" or "I see. Would you explain exactly what you have in mind there?" or "Now, will you tell me why you feel that way about it?" (In Chapter 8, the technique of framing and using such supplementary or "probe" questions will be a major topic of discussion.)

Let us turn to a specific example in order to understand some of the differences between the responses evoked by open and by closed questions. Imagine that the open question "Would you tell me how you feel about this company as a place to work?" has just been asked of four employees in the same factory. The first is an enthusiastic company man of twenty-five years' seniority.

FIRST EMPLOYEE: You ask me if this is a good place to work; man, it's the best. I've been here for twenty-five years, and before I came to this company I had a taste of what other outfits were like. Here they treat you fair; you've got security; the pay is good; they're fine people to work for. I just couldn't ask for a better break.

SECOND EMPLOYEE: Well, I'd say it was as good as any. The hours are long and the work's tough and my foreman's no prize, but then none of them are. The point is that when you're a working man, you got to expect things to be like that. That's the way plants go, although you probably wouldn't know it, and this one's as good as most, better'n some.

THIRD EMPLOYEE: Well, in some ways I think this is a pretty poor place to work. The foreman just rides you all the time and the work is dirty. The fact is, I'm here for only one good reason, and that is that they pay better than any place around here. I'm willing to put up with an awful lot of this other stuff as long as I can make enough money, and from that point of view this is the best place in town.

FOURTH EMPLOYEE: Well, I can't very well answer that question for you. You see, I'm brand new here; I just came to work yesterday for the first time. The other guys seem to think it's O.K. I'd say that this is a good place to work.

Each of these four men, had he been asked the closed question—"On the whole, would you say that this is a good or a poor place to work?"—would probably have responded "good." The differences among the four, however, are pronounced and important. The first respondent has real enthusiasm for his job and his company. The category "good" would have given only a mild indication of the intensity of his positive feeling for the company. Moreover, his positive attitudes obviously were based upon experience in other situations and on a long work history within the present company.

Our second respondent provides an example of ambivalent attitudes toward industrial employment, and considers his present place of work no exception to the general rule that such employment is arduous and unpleasant. On an absolute scale, he indicated no great liking for his place of work. He did tell us, however, that in comparison to other still less attractive places, he considered his present company relatively good. Thus, in spite of his criticisms and ambivalence, he concludes by putting himself into the category of favorable responses.

The third respondent provides more striking evidence of the importance of frame of reference. He speaks about working conditions and supervision in specific and negative terms, but goes on to give the company a very high rating with respect to rate of pay, and tells us further that this characteristic is for him the crucial one in judging a place of work. He concludes that the favorable pay rate outweighs the negative attributes of the company, and that the company is therefore a desirable place to work.

The major characteristic of the fourth respondent is that he has no real basis for making a judgment of the company. He tells us this, and then goes on to say that his first impression from his meager experience is that the company will be a satisfactory place in which to work.

In summary, then, we have four respondents, all of whom would have been classified as answering "good" to our closed question, who present interesting and significant differences with respect to the intensity of their attitudes, the frame of reference or basis of their response, the amount of information or experience on which their response is based, and the amount of ambivalence or polarization of their attitudes on this question. To some extent we can generalize from this example to the kinds of situations for which open or closed questions are particularly appropriate.

The open question appears to be more appropriate when our objective is not only to discover the respondent's attitude toward some issue, but also to learn something about his level of information, the structure or basis on which he has formed his opinion, the frame of reference within which he answers the question, and the intensity of his feelings on the topic.

The closed question is appropriate when our objective is limited to the classification of the respondent with respect to some attitude or perception. Even this decision needs to be made with caution, since there are other factors which may make the closed question inappropriate even for such classification purposes. Some of these qualifications are taken up in later sections. We can, of course, attempt to measure intensity by asking an additional closed question to get at this dimension. Similarly, we can ask additional closed questions to illuminate to some degree the respondent's frame of reference and the structure of his opinion. If our objectives tend to be ambitious, however, and if the respondent's attitude structure is complex, the process of formulating batteries of closed questions often becomes more difficult and less satisfactory than the use of an initial open question to meet the same objectives.

The Respondent's Level of Information

A second factor in the choice between open and closed questions is the respondent's level of information regarding the topic to be discussed. Some minimal level of information is necessary for him to answer any questions, of course, and it is purposeless to raise questions which the respondent cannot comprehend, or which refer to things beyond his experience. It is less obvious, perhaps, that the choice of an open or closed question should be based in part upon the criterion of respondent knowledge. Let us develop this point by means of an example from survey research.

Consider the case of the householder answering his door to find a public-opinion interviewer, who asks, "How do you feel about the peacetime uses of atomic energy?" Our hypothetical householder may be an atomic physicist who has made a special study of this complex topic; he may be an informed layman who has strong opinions on the desirability of peaceful technological development in addition to military uses of atomic energy; or he may be a naive person who can only respond by saying, "Gosh, I don't know. You mean bombs?" Obviously, the length of the response and its entire character will be vastly different for these three respondents.

Consider the same situation with the interviewer asking a closed or poll-type question. The householder swings the door open, and our "closed questioner" says, "Are you for or against the peacetime use of atomic energy?" Any one of our three respondents is equally able to answer "for" or "against." If our research objective is limited to a classification of citizens' opinions on this subject, this is perhaps acceptable for the first two respondents. It may not be important for us to distinguish between the layman and the professional. The third respondent, however, presents the researcher with a real problem if he answers either "for" or "against." Not only does he not have an adequate amount of knowledge on which to base an opinion, he very likely has no opinion. To the extent that our closed question leads him to classify himself as for or against instead of "don't know," we have been misled.

The key generalization is that the open question provides an opportunity for the interviewer to ascertain lack of information or uncertainty of feeling on the part of the respondent, whereas the closed question does not. If there is reason to believe that the topic under discussion will be outside the experience of many respondents, it seems desirable to adopt the open question and avoid the closed form. It is possible to use a sequence or battery of closed questions to ascertain the respondent's level of knowledge, but this process has its own risks. The questions may be many, and potentially embarrassing to a respondent who must reveal his ignorance by a long string of noes. On the whole, the open question appears more appropriate for inquiries directed to a population in which level of information is extremely variable or is unknown to the interviewer.

Structuring of Respondent Opinions or Attitudes

This point has to do with the extent to which the respondent has already undertaken the cognitive process at the time that the interview begins. In other words, does the respondent have a clearcut attitude on the topic in question? Has he acquired enough information, and has he given the topic sufficient thought so that his attitude or position is already well defined? To the extent that such a process has taken place, the interviewer's problem is simply one of motivating the respondent to verbalize the attitude which he has already formulated. To the extent that this process has not occurred in advance of the interview, the interviewer may face the dual problem of motivating the respondent and assisting him to think through and formulate his opinion on the topic in question, so that he can verbalize it.

Consider the following example of a personnel interviewer approaching a factory foreman: "Mr. Smith, you've been with us now for over a year; we're much interested in finding out how you feel about your job." The chances are that since Mr. Smith's job is conspicuously within his experience and is an important part of his life, he has well-structured opinions about it. Assuming that he is motivated to communicate on this subject, he is well able to do so and his opinions are clearly defined. He can answer the foregoing open question, and he could answer equally well a closed question on the same subject, such as the following: "Mr. Smith, you've been with us for over a year now; we'd be interested in knowing whether you are satisfied or dissatisfied with your job situation."

Contrast Mr. Smith's ability to answer such a question, in an area where his information is well structured, with his ability to answer one he has never considered before: "Foreman Smith, do you think that your work group would do its best work on a piece-rate basis or an hourly wage?" Assuming that Foreman Smith has not previously thought the problem through, he must now marshall the relevant experience, consider the implications of that experience, and develop from his first ambiguous reactions a specific formulation in favor of the piece rate or the hourly wage. Mr. Smith must think the question over on the spot if he is to be able to answer it.

In the first situation, the closed question is likely to be quite appropriate, provided that its brief answers will satisfy our basic objectives. Mr. Smith's opinions about his job are sufficiently structured so that he can presumably give them readily. In the second situation, the open question is much more appropriate. We want Mr. Smith to recall, order, and evaluate his experience. A question that merely asks him to express in a word his preference for one of two alternative responses provides little incentive and less assistance for him to go through the complex process of "making up his mind." The open question, on the other hand, calling for a full response, gives Mr. Smith reason and opportunity to pull together his experience. It also creates a situation where the interviewer, through skillful probing, can assist him in the process. The encouragement and careful urging of the interviewer may be necessary to bring Mr. Smith to a full formulation of his opinion.

The open question, therefore, is to be desired in situations where the respondent has not yet formulated his opinions clearly. The use of a closed question in such a situation involves the serious risk that the respondent's first choice of an offered alternative may in fact be quite different from the conclusion he would reach if he went through the process of recall, organization, and evaluation of his own experience.

Motivating Power of the Question

In the early chapters of this book we discussed the importance of developing adequate motivation to communicate on the part of the respondent. We pointed out that absence of such motivation was likely to result either in lack of communication or in the communication of distorted or biased material. We discussed a number of ways in which the respondent might indicate that an adequate motivational base had not been developed. A respondent might give no answer at all to a question; he might state explicitly his reluctance to answer; or he might answer in a way that evades the objective of the question. When the interviewer receives responses of this sort to an open question, he then attacks the problem of developing more adequate respondent motivation, using the kinds of techniques which have already been presented. For example, he may offer reassurances of confidentiality; he may restate the reasons for the question or emphasize the importance of the interview purpose.

The closed question has both strengths and weaknesses with respect to the solution of this kind of motivational problem. On the one hand, the closed question requires less motivation to communicate on the part of the respondent. Not only does it demand less effort of him (particularly in cases where his attitudes are not really crystallized), but also the response itself is usually less revealing and potentially less threatening than in the case of the open question. For these reasons, the interviewer who uses the closed question will be confronted less often with absence of response, blunt refusal to respond, or a "don't know" answer. This apparent advantage of the closed question, however, entails certain risks. These risks are important in situations where the respondent is interested in avoiding an embarrassing answer or in concealing ambiguity in his own thinking. The closed question allows him to make an easy choice of word or phrase without betraying his anxiety or embarrassment. The attendant risk is that his choice may be dictated more by these avoidance wishes than by the motivation to communicate valid information. Consider a student whom the school principal engages in a conversation regarding his difficulties in mastering algebra. "John, before we discuss your problems in algebra, I want to know something about your study habits. Are you putting at least an hour a day on algebra, or not?" This is a closed question, and the youthful respondent has only to say, "Yes, I am," or "No, I'm not."

With only slight changes in phraseology, the principal might have asked the question in more open form. "John, before we discuss your problems in algebra, I want to know something about your study habits. Can you tell me about how much time you put on algebra each day?"

What are the likely effects of these two forms of the question, assuming that the topic is a painful one for the respondent and the situation not without its threatening aspects? The closed question is more easily answered; he need only repeat one of the suggested responses. The open question requires him to think through and phrase his own answer. This is more difficult, and he is correspondingly more likely to remain silent, make a hopeful attempt at changing the subject, or retreat to the safety of "don't know." On the other hand, the relative ease of response of the closed question, helpful as it is to interviewer and respondent at the time, carries more risk of a biased response. The student learns from the question that one hour's study time appears to mark an important boundary, and he knows which side of that boundary he had better be on. The forces on him to shade his response in that direction are strong, indeed.

We conclude that the closed question may be appropriate when such biasing forces are not present, or when the respondent is not likely to perceive one alternative answer as more acceptable to the interviewer. If these conditions are not met, the interviewer would be better advised to use the open form, and cope with the problem of respondent motivation in terms of the purpose of the inquiry, the safeguards for the respondent, and the quality of the personal relationship between them.

Interviewer's Insight into Respondent's Situation

It is the opinion of the authors that for many interviewing situations, the open question involves less risk than does the use of closed questions. The open question is less likely to involve the researcher or practitioner in difficulties arising from the four kinds of factors just discussed. The lesser risks and increased harvest of information which the open question provides, however, are achieved at relatively high expenditures of time and money and require a higher degree of interviewing skill. These administrative considerations in the use of open questions are fully discussed elsewhere.[2]

There is an additional point involved in the choice between open and closed questions, a point which has been implicit in the considera-

---

[2] Mildred Parten, *Surveys, Polls, and Samples*, Harper and Brothers, New York, 1950; Hadley A. Cantril, *Gauging Public Opinion*, Princeton University Press, Princeton, 1944; Paul F. Lazarsfeld, *op. cit.*

tions that have already been discussed, but which should now be made specific. Since the respondent's degree of knowledge, level of cognitive structuring, and motivational level are all important considerations in determining the choice between open and closed questions, it follows that the researcher or practitioner, in order to make this choice, must be in possession of substantial information and insight into the respondent's situation in respect to these variables.

Specifically, in choosing to investigate a topic by means of closed questions, the interviewer is saying that he is in possession of substantial information about the respondent's degree of knowledge or expertness in the area, that he can make realistic assumptions about the extent to which the respondent has thought through or structured his attitudes on the topic, and that he is in a position to make equally good assumptions about the respondent's motivation to communicate. The importance of such knowledge as a basis for formulating closed questions can best be shown by referring to the results of some empirical research on this problem.

Crutchfield and Gordon[3] have provided an excellent documentation of the effects of the improper use of the closed question. A national polling organization asked the following question in one of its studies: "After the war, would you like to see many changes or reforms made in the United States, or would you rather have the country remain pretty much the way it was before the war?" The answers indicated that the majority of people wanted things to remain as they were before the war. The results were interpreted as referring only to domestic economic issues. Crutchfield and Gordon repeated the study, having interviewers ask the same question followed by nondirective probes to ascertain what the respondents meant by their answers. The responses showed that respondents answered from any of seven different frames of reference. Some were concerned with domestic issues (employment conditions, standard of living, etc.), others with political affairs, and so on. Because the original researcher was unaware of these varying frames of reference, his interpretation of the findings was quite in error.

This faulty use of the closed question ties into the first of the points which we have already discussed. The researcher had objectives which required him to understand and interpret the answers in terms of the respondent's frame of reference. It turned out, however, that the respondents' frames of reference were many and variable, that the

---

[3] R. S. Crutchfield and D. A. Gordon, "Variations in Respondents' Interpretations of an Opinion Poll Question," *International Journal of Opinion and Attitude Research*, 1, No. 3, 1–12 (1947).

researcher did not have advance knowledge of them, and that the closed question failed to give him information that would permit correct interpretations.

Another illuminating example of the difficulties which arise from differences in interpretation of closed questions is cited by Angus Campbell.[4] During the early months of World War II, a plan to move German and Italian aliens away from the East Coast was being considered. In order to assess public feeling on the issue, a polling survey was conducted in several eastern cities, which included this question: "I'm going to ask you about several groups of people in this country. First, take Germans who are not citizens—that is, German aliens—do you think most of them are loyal to the United States, about half are loyal, or only a few are loyal?" The survey finding was that a large percentage of the public thought that only a few of the German aliens were loyal. This finding, along with certain other data from the same survey, was taken as the basis of a recommendation for rather drastic action regarding East Coast aliens.

Because of the fact that this recommendation was inconsistent with recommendations made by another survey organization on the basis of data obtained by a different technique, a small-scale study was undertaken by the Division of Program Surveys of the U. S. Department of Agriculture, to determine what respondents meant by their answers to this question. The researcher presented the original polling questions to a small sample of people in Philadelphia, but followed each question with nondirective probes to bring out the meaning the question had for the respondent.

Considering now only the question of loyalty stated above, the researcher found approximately the same proportion of people choosing the "only a few are loyal" category as the poll had reported. When these respondents were encouraged to expand on their answers, however, it was found that the terms loyalty and disloyalty as interpreted and used by the respondents did not generally refer to traitorous acts or utterances. A third of the respondents took "loyalty" to mean a by-product of citizenship; that is, citizens are loyal, noncitizens are disloyal. Another third defined loyalty in terms of sentimental factors such as "forgetting the old country" or "having affection for the United States." The remainder of the people interviewed had quite diverse ideas. Only one in ten meant that "disloyal" people would do things or say things harmful to this country. In other words, only a small

---

[4] "Polling, Open Interviewing, and the Problem of Interpretation," *Journal of Social Issues*, November 1946.

fraction of the people who said they thought most alien Germans were disloyal were actually expressing hostility or serious suspicion.

These examples are illustrative of the problems that arise when the researcher uses closed questions without adequate advance knowledge of the respondent's level of information, frame of reference, and structure of opinion. In some cases it is possible for the researcher to inform himself in advance on such points by pretest procedures, scouting interviews, or other means of studying the population which is to be questioned. Lazarsfeld[5] has suggested that for statistical studies or research projects of large size, the appropriate allocation of functions between the open and closed techniques consists of using open questions for the pilot work and closed questions for the data gathering. In this arrangement, the closed questions can be formulated on the basis of direct experience with at least a small sample of the population, and can take into account the level of information and frames of reference characteristic of this population. The researcher can thus take advantage of the savings in time and effort which the closed questions offer in dealing with a large respondent population.

Even assuming such preliminary knowledge of developmental procedures as Lazarsfeld recommends, it seems to us that the choice between open and closed questions has to do also with the basic simplicity or complexity of the topic to be investigated. Generally speaking, the closed question is well adapted to situations where (a) there are a limited number of known frames of reference from which the respondent can answer the question, (b) within these few possible frames of reference there is a known range of possible responses, and (c) within this range there are clearly defined choice points that accurately represent the position of each respondent.

Two examples will help to clarify these points. The first is the classification of respondent by marital status. In this case there is a known range of possible responses; a person is single, married, divorced, separated, or widowed. Within this range the choices are clear and the question has but one frame of reference for all respondents. Here the closed question is desirable and can be worded, "Are you single, married, divorced, separated, or widowed?" The respondent merely has to select the response which defines his marital status.

Another example of the closed type used appropriately is the question, "Would you say your present income is higher, lower, or about the same as your last year's income?" In this question the respondent is asked to compare facts which are known to him. The frame of

---

[5] *op. cit.*

reference is limited to an income comparison for two years, is specified in the question, and the choices are clear.

In short, the closed question represents a kind of efficient small-bore ammunition. If the objective is clearly in sight and not complex, and if the interviewer is confident of his marksmanship, all is well. For more ambitious game or in less well-defined situations, the greater range, spread, and fire power of the open question is indicated.

INDIRECT APPROACHES TO DIFFICULT MATERIAL

In the discussion of question wording and the use of open and closed questions, there has been an implicit underlying assumption that the respondent can and will report the information which is wanted, provided the interviewer can make clear what he is to report on and establish a favorable relationship with him. There are several situations, however, in which the respondent may be unable or unwilling to report the information which the interviewer wants.

In earlier chapters we have discussed the difficulties of obtaining adequate responses on certain subjects or in certain circumstances. We have emphasized the interviewer-respondent relationship as the major means of resolving these difficulties. But some problems in communication persist in spite of a supportive relationship between interviewer and respondent. A particular subject may so embarrass the respondent that he protects himself by giving partial or biased information. He feels that his own behavior or attitude violates some social norm, or conflicts with the image he must present to the world. Suppose that we wish to know whether a respondent sometimes drinks to excess, or whether he has strong feelings of prejudice toward certain minority groups, or merely whether he neglected to vote in the last presidential election. Some respondents may find it so ego-threatening to answer such questions that no interviewing skills will be adequate to motivate a full and frank response within the limitations of time which the situation imposes.

Another kind of information may be inaccessible to the respondent himself. If we wish to know whether a respondent has feelings of envy and hostility toward his father or whether he suffers from basic and persistent insecurity, we are raising questions into which the respondent may have little or no insight.

On other topics the respondent and interviewer may not have a common vocabulary or conceptual framework. In a recent study of mental health, it was found that most respondents had given little thought to the topic and were unacquainted with even the most elementary concepts and vocabulary of psychiatry. Matters that the specialist considered problems of mental health, these respondents classified as moral or disciplinary. It was, therefore, very difficult to discuss problems of mental health with them.

In such a circumstance the interviewer has to make decisions that are more basic than those of question wording and whether the question should be open or closed. The first decision is whether the objective can be met at all through the interview or must be discarded. If the interviewer feels that the objective can be fully met, or that it is so important that even partial information is better than none, a second decision remains. Is it feasible to word questions so that they get at the objective directly, or must some indirect approach be used?

If we were limited to direct questions, much information would be lost to the interview process, and interviewing would be a far less important method of data collection than it is. Fortunately, researchers and practitioners are becoming increasingly interested and skilled in the use of indirect approaches to objectives. We shall discuss here several of the kinds of problems that require the use of indirect techniques.

In the other chapters of this book, when we mention techniques for one purpose or another we proceed to a description of how to develop and use them. In considering indirect approaches, we intend to give the reader only a general orientation to the subject. The reason is that many of the techniques are highly complicated and are still in a very early stage of development. The design of an adequate sequence of indirect questions or a picture-story device is a research problem in itself. The validation of such techniques is especially important, and too often neglected. We believe that the design and testing of specialized techniques is best restricted to situations in which staff and facilities make feasible the necessary developmental research and studies of validation.

Potentially Embarrassing or Threatening Data

This is perhaps the most frequent reason for utilizing indirect approaches, and several examples can be given to illustrate the successful solution of this type of problem through indirect means. Recently the Survey Research Center undertook to discover how adolescent boys reacted to parental rules and requests, and what attitudes were reflected in this behavior. Preliminary informal interviews indicated that many of the boys found this topic an embarrassing one to discuss with an adult interviewer. They saw the interviewer as a representative of the world of adult authority epitomized by their own parents, and they imputed to the interviewer the attitudes of approval and disapproval which their parents expressed. Responses to direct questions were so meager that an indirect approach was indicated.

Respondents were shown two drawings. The first was intended to evoke the adolescents' reaction to the direct personal imposition of parental authority. The drawing shows a man and woman sitting in a living room. They are apparently speaking to a boy in his early teens, who is wearing a coat and seems about to leave the house. The father, according to the words printed above his head in cartoon fashion, has just said, "Be sure to be home by ten o'clock. We're going out ourselves and will be late getting back." Above the boy's head is a blank cartoon "balloon," suggesting that he has made some response. The interviewer presented this picture to the respondent, and asked him to supply the missing response. What does the boy reply? Does he argue with his father or agree to come home promptly? Does he consider the father's request reasonable or arbitrary? Does he really intend to keep his promise, or is he answering with reservations of his own? Information of this kind was supplied readily by the respondents, and from it the analysts inferred the respondents' own relations with their parents.

The second picture shows the same boy later in the evening. He is at a drugstore with a group of other boys and girls. A clock on the wall points to 9:57 P.M. The boy is saying, "I have to go home now." A friend replies, "Oh, stick around. Your folks aren't home anyway."

The interviewer presented this picture to the respondent and asked him what the boy decided to do. Again, the responses were readily given. They were used to infer the extent to which the adolescent boys had internalized the parents' standards. Would they obey, even when the risks of disobeying were pretty well eliminated?

Another example of the successful use of indirect questions comes from a market research project conducted by Mason Haire.[6] The problem was to determine some of the sources of consumer resistance to buying "instant" coffee. Haire felt that these resistances reflected prejudices rather than rational decisions, and that people might be reluctant to admit their prejudices. He felt that the potential embarrassment of such admissions would lead the respondent to elaborate rationalization·or to refusal to answer. There was also, of course, the possibility that people might be unaware of the real reason for their avoidance of instant coffee.

Haire suspected that one of the sources of resistance to this product

<hr>

[6] "Projective Techniques in Marketing Research," *Journal of Marketing,* **14,** 649–656 (1950).

was the feeling of some housewives that certain labor-saving devices, especially in the preparation of food, were somehow improper. He believed that some women would feel they were "cheating," or shirking their housewifely duties, if they stopped brewing or percolating in favor of instant coffee.

To test this hypothesis, a group of housewives were given a shopping list which contained approximately twenty items typical of the usual grocery list. A second list was prepared, which was exactly the same as the first with one exception. In list A was included a pound of regular coffee; in list B was included a jar of instant coffee. Another group of housewives was given the second list. All the respondents were asked, on the basis of the list which they had received, to describe the woman who was doing the shopping, attempting to guess what kind of person she was. Subsequent coding revealed that respondent perceptions of the woman using the list including the instant coffee could be classified easily into two groups. Some respondents were unfavorable, describing her as a lazy, slovenly housewife who thought little of her husband's well-being. Other respondents concluded that the woman buying the instant coffee was obviously a busy person who was saving time and had her work efficiently organized. The housewife whose list contained regular coffee was described in neutral or in mildly positive terms by most respondents. From this research, Haire learned that housewives differed in their attitudes toward the use of instant coffee, that many housewives had serious prejudices against this product, and that the basis of these prejudices involved their perceptions of themselves and their role as wives and housekeepers.

A similar approach was used by the Survey Research Center to determine some of the sources of resistance to using the telephone for making long distance calls. The following questions were asked of a state-wide sample of Michigan residents.

1. Mrs. Jones is a woman who makes a long distance phone call to her relatives once or twice a month just to visit with them.
   a. Why do you think she does this?
   b. What kind of person is she?
2. On arriving at a distant city, Mrs. Smith says to her husband, "I ought to call Mary and tell her we're all right now, but I just don't like to make the call."
   a. Why do you think she feels that way?
   b. Anything else?

Some respondents described Mrs. Jones as being a thoughtful, friendly person who recognized that the telephone could bring her closer to her friends than the more impersonal practice of writing letters. For other people, any woman using the long distance phone for social purposes was a thoughtless person who just didn't care how much of her husband's money she spent.

In similar fashion, some people found Mrs. Smith's hesitancy to use the telephone an evidence of thrift, others thought it irrational and inconsiderate. In both cases, the use of indirect questions produced better insight into the respondents' attitudes, and enabled the interviewer to discover the irrational blocks, prejudices, and stereotypes which the respondent might well have been unable to communicate directly.

This type of problem becomes much more serious when we want a respondent to give information that might require him to report violating some moral or ethical norm, or at least as exceeding the bounds of what is socially acceptable. Questions about moral beliefs, the use of alcoholic beverages, and racial and religious prejudice may represent an acute threat to the respondent.

Perhaps the simplest indirect approach to such problems is to use a question that directs attention to a person other than the respondent. This may be done as a substitute for or a preamble to a more direct approach, on the assumption that once an individual has been able to verbalize his own behavior by attributing it to another person, he is more ready to admit to it as his own. During World War II there was a good deal of social pressure against cashing war bonds, and many people felt that such behavior might be interpreted as being unpatriotic. One successful approach to studying the causes and incidence of bond redemption began with the following question: "Why do you think it is that some people cash war bonds?" This provided a respondent with an opportunity to justify cashing bonds, if he wanted to—such as "Well, I suppose a lot of people cash them because they find they need some money for something they didn't expect. They probably feel bad about cashing them, but sometimes it's necessary." It was then relatively easy to ask him whether he himself had experienced similar pressures, and even whether he had responded to them by cashing some of his own bonds.

Several researchers studying attitudes toward minority groups have encountered reluctance on the part of respondents to relate their attitudes directly, and have used successfully the pictorial type of stimulus described in connection with the Survey Research Center's study of adolescents. Radke, Traeger, and Davis[7] studied the reaction of

[7] M. Radke, H. G. Traeger, and H. Davis, "Social Perceptions in Attitudes of Children," *Genetic Psychology Monographs,* **40,** 327–447 (1949).

children to racial and religious groups by using a set of pictures as stimuli. One of these pictures showed several groups of children, one consisting entirely of white children, one a white group except for a single Negro, the third predominantly a Negro group. The child respondent was asked which group he would prefer to play in, and why he would prefer to play in that particular group. The presumption was that children who felt prejudices against Negroes which they were unwilling to verbalize directly would reveal them by indicating avoidance of a group in which there were Negro members.

Jahoda, Deutsch, and Cook[8] report the use of a sentence-completion test in conducting research on the same problem. The sentence-completion technique appears to offer somewhat greater ease of interpretation than the pictorial approach, but it does not lend itself quite so well to complete avoidance of threat. The following examples are taken from the work of Jahoda and her colleagues.

a. When a Negro sat down next to him on the bus, John _____.
b. Negroes are _____.
c. The sight of a Negro always _____.
d. A walk through the Negro section is _____.

The examples in this section demonstrate some of the many ways in which indirect techniques may be used to obtain data which the respondent might find embarrassing or threatening to communicate in answer to a direct question. Such indirect approaches have in common the use of an external stimulus or object of discussion, including such devices as pictures, a description or a brief anecdote, or merely the introduction of an imaginary third person who is to be described by the respondent. These techniques are also applicable to meeting other kinds of objectives that respondents are reluctant to discuss.

Lack of Common Vocabulary or Conceptual Framework

In a simpler form, this problem appears as a matter of language, and its solution consists in defining terms and concepts for the respondent. Survey interviews often include such definitions if common usage cannot be relied on. The problem becomes more complicated, however, if simple definitions cannot be given, or if the act of providing such a definition would introduce bias by suggesting the "right" answer. In such cases, less direct means become appropriate, as the following example illustrates.

A few years ago the Survey Research Center undertook a study in

---

[8] Marie Jahoda, Morton Deutsch, and Stuart W. Cook, *Research Methods in Social Relations*, Dryden Press, New York, 1951.

which one of the objectives was to learn something of people's knowledge about and attitudes toward mental illness. Additional objectives of the study included learning what behavioral or emotional symptoms people considered as being evidence of mental disturbance, and how they thought abnormal behavior should be dealt with. More specifically, the researchers wanted answers to such objectives as these: Do people consider all individuals with behavior disorders or eccentricities to be mentally ill? Do they consider behavior problems as problems requiring psychological understanding and remedy, or as problems to be handled through legal or disciplinary action?

The first difficulty the researchers encountered in making this investigation was the lack of common terminology between interviewer and respondent. The term "mental health" had little meaning for most people, and respondents' notions of "mental illness" ran all the way from slight nervousness to profoundly psychotic behavior. For the interviewer to have provided a definition of mental health or illness would have largely destroyed the value of the interview, because it would have suggested to the respondent what the expert included under the various categories of mental illness, and would thus have supplied him with the very knowledge the researchers wished to test. This was avoided by approaching indirectly the definition, symptoms, and treatment of mental illness.

The stimulus consisted in reading to the respondent brief anecdotal descriptions of several neurotic problems, behavior disorders, and psychoses. The respondent answered questions that described behavior within the range of common experience, in language which he understood. Analysis of the responses to these cases enabled the researcher to infer what symptoms were classified by respondents as indicative of mental illness, and which they considered to be within the range of normalcy. Two examples of the question sequences used in this study are given here.

Example 1

We would like to talk with you now about the *kinds* of problems that people might come up against. For example, take the case of a woman—let's call her Mrs. Jones. She's a terribly unhappy woman. She's afraid she's going to have a nervous breakdown.

Do you think many people have problems of this kind, or only a few people?

Why do you suppose some people get into a condition like this and others don't?

Could you tell me more about this?

If answer is in terms of internal "causes": How does a person get to be like this?

What do you think Mrs. Jones can do about it?

If no outside source is mentioned: Is there anywhere or any way she can get some help for her condition?

Ask everyone who has mentioned an outside source: If this didn't work, do you think there is anywhere else Mrs. Jones could go to get help?

If a person felt that he (she) was really getting into a nervous condition, do you think he (she) would go for help right away, or would he (she) wait?

Why do you think they would do that?

What do you think you yourself would do?

Do you feel a person is apt to talk with friends about this condition, or is he (she) more likely to keep quiet about it?

If answer is "keep quiet" or "some would, some wouldn't": Why wouldn't he (she) want to talk about it?

Ask everyone: How about yourself—do you think you would talk about it or not?   Why is that?

Do you think that women are more likely to get into a condition like this than men, or isn't there any difference?

Why do you think that is?

Example 2

Now here's the situation of Johnny, a ten-year-old boy.   His parents have found out that he's been stealing things for quite some time, and they are very much upset about it.

Why do you think some children behave this way and others don't?

Could you tell me more about this?

If answer is in terms of internal "causes": How does a boy get to be like this—(insert mentioned personality variable or type)?

What kinds of things do you think could be done in Johnny's case?

If some type of help for child or parents is mentioned: Suppose that didn't work—is there anywhere (else) they could go to get help with the problem?

If treatment for child is not mentioned: Johnny has been doing this for quite a long time.   Do you think there is any place the boy himself could be taken for help?

The use of indirect questions in such situations as this offers the same basic advantages and disadvantages that we have seen in other contexts.   They permit us to collect data which would not otherwise yield to the interview technique, but they involve inevitable difficulties in development, wording, and interpretation.   Such questions must therefore be worked out with special care prior to the interview, and tried out with a number of respondents to see whether they convey the impression for which the interviewer is striving and whether they evoke the required responses.   It would be virtually impossible to frame such question sequences without repeated trial and error. The questions on mental health in the examples cited here went through a series of ten or more revisions before they were judged adequate.

Reaction to a Complex Stimulus

Sometimes we need to use an indirect approach when we want the respondent to react to a complex situation or stimulus. The use of pictures or other visual material enables us to avoid verbal descriptions or definitions of excessive length or complexity.

Suppose that we wish to learn which of two classroom teaching situations a student would prefer—informal, democratically led discussion sessions, or conventional lectures with restricted student participation. To describe each of these situations adequately would require at least a paragraph, and might give the respondent more information than he could retain. He might therefore answer on the basis of only a part of the question—some key word which had particular impact for him. We run the risk also that in writing descriptions the use of such "loaded" words as "democratic" or "autocratic" might be difficult to avoid and biasing if used. (Many people might choose the "democratic" group because of the label alone.)

As an indirect alternative, one might offer the respondent two pictures. One might show a class listening attentively to a lecture from an instructor standing at a lectern, facing orderly rows of seats. Another picture might show a group of similar size surrounding the instructor at a conference table, in the midst of a give-and-take discussion. The respondent might then be asked which group he would like to be part of, why he made that choice, and what differences he would predict between the two groups.

The advantage of the picture for such objectives is obvious. The respondent can study it at length, and react to it without the need for complicated verbal instructions. Such pictures sometimes can do a much better job of presenting a complex stimulus successfully than can the more direct and conventional verbal approach.

Information Not Accessible to the Respondent

Perhaps the situation in which the indirect approach is most clearly indicated occurs when the objectives require that we obtain information about the respondent which he is unable to report. Theories of personality, the observations of therapists, and the experiences of everyday life combine to remind us that there are insights about our own behavior that all of us lack; there are characteristics of our own personalities of which we are unaware; there are sources of anxiety and pain that take their toll unrecognized.

A central concept which will be useful in thinking about the problem of what information is accessible to the interviewer by direct questions and what is inaccessible is the "cone of consciousness." A

schematic diagram of this cone is shown in Figure 10.   Just above the
cone is the environment in which the individual lives; at the bottom
is the basic personality level.   Between these two are various levels
or strata of the individual's psychological life.

At the first or top level we find sensory observations, or that information about the environment which reaches the individual through

ENVIRONMENT. . . the "real" world of objective facts

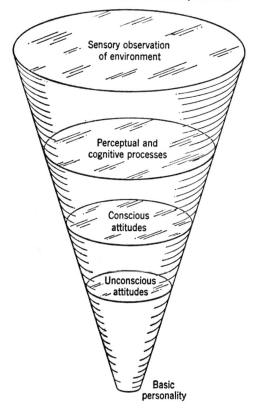

Figure 10. The cone of consciousness.

what he observes of the world.   These observations or stimuli are
organized and take on meaning through the processes of perception,
thinking, learning, and so forth, represented as the second level.   Attitudes are at the next levels.

For the purposes of this discussion we have identified two levels of
attitudes, conscious and unconscious.   It should be clear that these
levels are not actually discrete stages but shade one into another with
no sharp line between.   Furthermore, the various strata are contin-

ually interacting, and each is modifying and changing the other. For example, perceptions near the top of the cone are drastically affected by unconscious attitudes near the bottom of the cone.

When an object or fact from the environment is observed, it must be given meaning or structure by the individual. This structuring may modify the object or fact, making it different from what it is in the real world. To the extent that the perception differs from the objective fact, it does so because perception is determined only in part by the fact itself and in part by deeper levels of personality organization.

For our purposes in this chapter, the importance of this phenomenon is that the closer we get to the basic personality structure of the individual, the more difficult it is for him to communicate accurately to us about himself. As the diagram indicates, we soon approach an attitude level where the person is unable to report because these attitudes are unconscious. We have been emphasizing, however, that unconscious attitudes are interacting with higher levels. Psychologists and psychiatrists have learned to take advantage of this fact. They have found that if one is insightful enough (and has adequate theory), it is possible to ask questions relating to higher conscious levels of the cone that permit inferences to be made about attitudes or personality factors at deeper levels.

Psychologists are often concerned with the personality characteristic (or basic attitude) of security or insecurity. Many people react to other people and to various aspects of life in a self-assured manner, as persons who feel competent to deal with their world. Others have the opposite approach to the world. It is impossible for some—perhaps most—to answer correctly the question "Are you a secure or an insecure individual?" This is true in part because they do not know what the psychologist means by "secure" or "insecure," and partly because their self-image may keep this characteristic hidden from them. We can, however, ask a person questions at a perceptual and conscious attitudinal level that permit us to infer his level of security. He can report, for example, whether or not he likes to meet new people, whether or not he feels "nervous" in meeting new situations, whether he avoids some situations because he may not know how to act, and the like. Responses to questions like these provide a general picture of the person's basic security pattern. By inquiring how he reacts to situations in which secure people will act or feel one way and insecure people another, we can assess his position.

The accessible manifestations of personality characteristics are sought by psychologists and psychiatrists by means of specialized indirect techniques, the so-called "projectives." In Chapter 2 we discussed the personality dynamics of projection. Projective techniques require the respondent to react to a stimulus which offers him very little structure, in order to permit his unconscious attitudes to play a much more important part in determining his response. Perhaps the best known of the projective techniques is the Rorschach test. This test consists of a series of cards, each containing an ink-blot design. The design is meaningless; in other words, it has minimal relation to the real world and to objects which the individual may have seen. The respondent is asked to tell what he sees in the cards. Since the stimuli are without structure, the meaning which the subject assigns to the cards must come from within, from his personality. The psychologist then attempts to infer from these responses certain attributes of the subject's personality.

When our objectives are to gather data about such deep-lying material, only indirect approaches are open to us, because we wish the respondent to tell us things he does not know. We use the term "projective" to refer to such approaches when they are used to study personality. Modified projective techniques have been used for other purposes, however. The following example illustrates their use to learn something about unconscious attitudes.

Several years ago the Survey Research Center undertook the task of discovering whether people in this country felt anxiety over the possibility of being bombed in an enemy air attack. Some exploratory work, as well as derivations from psychoanalytic theory, convinced the researchers that many people were unable to verbalize their anxieties on this subject, and were themselves unaware of their fear of being bombed.[9] They had, in other words, protected themselves from consciously experiencing such fears; they had repressed them. If this hypothesis was correct, then a direct question about fear of bombing would produce a negative response from such people, but an indirect question might produce evidence of the fear and anxiety working at subconscious levels.

In accordance with this reasoning, an indirect approach was devised to measure the extent and intensity of anxiety over possible bombing. The indirect material consisted of a series of pictures drawn in a purposely ambiguous fashion, exhibited to the respondent one at a time. As each picture was shown to him, he was asked to describe what he saw, what he thought was happening, and what things he

---

[9] William A. Scott, "The Avoidance of Threatening Material in Imaginative Behavior," *Journal of Abnormal and Social Psychology*, **52**, No. 3, 338–346 (1956).

thought *other* people might see in the pictures. One of these pictures shows a woman standing in what might be a doorway; she is scanning the sky, in which some distant objects are visible only as formless specks. A second picture shows a woman hurrying along; a child trots beside her, holding one of her hands; a large bundle is held in her other arm. For some people, the first of these pictures represented only a woman watching a distant flight of geese or other birds; others saw a young wife watching her husband's Air Force squadron as it passed overhead; still others saw a mother whose house had been bombed and family injured or killed, watching the attacking planes as they left their ruined target. Interestingly enough, some people who gave for themselves very unmilitary interpretations of the picture mentioned the bombing theme promptly in answer to the questions of what *others* might see. The experience with the second picture was similar. Some respondents saw a young mother hurrying home from a trip to the grocery store to avoid an impending thunder shower; others saw a woman fleeing a bombed-out city, with her remaining possessions in a bundle and her weeping child beside her.

The findings from a series of such pictures were consistent in the following respects. Fewest respondents revealed anxiety over possible enemy air attack in answer to a direct question. More respondents saw the pictures as portraying such attacks. Still more thought that other people might see such things in the pictures. It seems clear that the indirect approach was producing data that more direct questions could not evoke.

Other examples might be cited to describe further the use of indirect questions for getting at facts about the respondent which he would be unable to admit directly—to himself or to an interviewer. Sanford[10] used simple line drawings of human figures to get at sources of anxiety and concern. He presented these drawings, which showed the characteristic postures and expressions of worry, and asked the respondents to speculate as to what the man in the picture might be worrying about. Sanford presents results which suggest strongly that this procedure yielded information about sources of worry and intensity of worries which went beyond what the respondent "knew" in any conscious sense.

The interviewer's enthusiasm for the ingenuity and power of indirect, semiprojective techniques must be tempered by the difficulties in their development and the serious problems of interpretation that they impose. These are well summarized by Jahoda, Deutsch, and Cook:

[10] Filmore H. Sanford, "The Use of A Projective Device in Attitude Surveying," *Public Opinion Quarterly*, **14**, 667–709 (1950–1951).

. . . It would be an oversimplification, however, to assume that one can directly infer the characteristics of the subject from the behavior, the wishes, the ideology, etc., of the characters with whom he identifies. Since different levels of personality—primitive wishes, conscience, defense mechanisms, perceptions of reality, etc.—may be "projected," the interpretation of such material is usually complex and involves a considerable degree of training and skill.

Although projective techniques have, in recent years, come to be an essential tool in the kit of clinical psychologists, the use of projective methods in attitudinal measurement is still rather exploratory and tentative. The clinical psychologist has at his disposal several well-developed projective techniques—the Rorschach, the Thematic Apperception Test, the Word Association Test, the Bender-Gestalt, etc.—which have been subjected to much investigation and have proved their value. Standardized methods of administration, scoring methods, and interpretative procedures have been published, making possible their widespread use.

The social scientist, in contrast to the clinical psychologist, has no well-developed projective techniques at his disposal. The development of standardized projective techniques to measure social attitudes, however, is to be expected in the not distant future. At present, there exists a considerable variety of ingenious techniques which have been developed by individual investigators for specific purposes. Few of these techniques have been employed in more than one investigation; none is supported by a wide body of experience. The techniques vary in the effectiveness with which they mask their purpose, the richness of personality material which they reveal, in the ambiguity of the stimulus which is presented to the subject, and in the expenditure of skill and effort necessary to the collection and analysis of responses.[11]

ORGANIZATION OF THE QUESTIONNAIRE

Thus far in this chapter we have been concerned with the form of questions—direct or indirect, open or closed. Whatever the form of the questions, there are a number of considerations regarding their order or sequence. The sequence of questions may do much to influence the success of the interview. These considerations include the necessity for providing an appropriate introductory phase to the interview, making easy and reasonable transitions from one interview topic to another, and formulating an appropriate conclusion to the interview.

Use of Multiple Questions

Even within the confines of a single objective, however, a number of questions may be required. In fact, it is common interviewing technique to use several questions to meet a single objective.

Perhaps the most common reason for using a number of questions

---

[11] *Research Methods in Social Relations, pp. 211–212.*

to meet an objective is our inability to phrase a single question to fit all situations encompassed by the objective. In the exploration of a given area of attitudes or perceptions, we can seldom be sure that any one question will be completely "on target." For this reason we typically ask a number of questions all aimed at the same target area. The assumption in this procedure is that the responses to several questions will be more accurate or reliable than the results achieved by any one question. The concept involved here is one which is encountered in any situation where there is some question of the precision of aim. The naval officer who wishes to demolish a target will certainly order a number of guns trained on that objective. His assumption is that while the aim of any one weapon in his arsenal may be faulty, the effect of a number of guns is likely to be successful. The framer of questions operates on the same assumption.

Another criterion determining the number of questions which will be asked stems from the complexity or breadth of the objective. Though the objective of determining a respondent's age can be covered easily with one question, ascertaining the annual income for a family may require several questions in order to cover the potential sources of income. There are, however, some circumstances in which a single question on income would be sufficient. If we want merely to divide people into broad income categories, we may be willing to tolerate the error that would result from the single question. Thus the degree of precision required is another criterion for the number of questions necessary. A further criterion is the importance of the objective in the over-all purpose of the interview. If the objective is of great importance we will use more questions simply to be sure that the objective is reached.

Generally speaking, ascertaining attitudes or beliefs requires more questions than discovering objective or factual information, because these psychological phenomena are usually more complex in nature. It is convenient to think of a belief or attitude as an area in the psychological field of the individual. The interviewer's purpose is to explore completely the area of the psychological field represented by the particular belief or attitude. Suppose we are interested in learning on what bases an industrial worker evaluates his foreman. The worker's attitudes may be based in part upon the foreman's technical skills, in part upon his supportiveness of the men, in part upon his effectiveness in dealing with his own superiors, and so on. It is unlikely that a single question will evoke a response which will explore fully all three of the sub-areas of the worker's attitude to his foreman.

The exploration of an attitude area may be accomplished by a series of closed questions, by an open question with probes or follow-up questions,[12] or by a combination of these. It may be useful to look at these approaches schematically in order to illuminate the conditions under which each is appropriate. Consider first the use of the open question. What we attempt to do with an open question is first to make a "hit" in the general attitude area to be explored. We might ask such a question as, "Would you tell me how you feel about your fore-man?" The responses to this question will of course vary for different respondents. Some may proceed to relate all of their feelings with respect to their foreman in response to this single question. Most respondents, however, will report their attitudes only partially. The function served by supplementary probe questions will be to lead the respondent to verbalize the remainder of the relevant material. The probing will be continued until the objective is fully explored.

An alternative way of exploring an attitudinal area is to use a number of closed questions, in which each question obtains material relating to a narrowly delimited sub-area of the total area to be explored. The assumption is that the interviewer is capable of framing a number of closed questions which *in toto* are adequate to obtain all of the material in the attitudinal area. For this approach to be successful, the interviewer must be able to specify the boundaries of the area to be explored and must be able to cover it completely with a number of complementary closed questions.

The contrast between these two approaches clarifies some of the criteria for the use of open and closed questions discussed earlier. It is clear that the closed question is most appropriate when the attitudinal area to be explored is limited in size and complexity, and when its configuration is generally well known to the investigator. On the other hand, if the area to be investigated is a complicated one, or if the investigator does not know its configuration and boundaries, the open question followed with probe questions represents the safest procedure for him.

THE SEQUENCE OF QUESTIONS WITHIN A TOPIC

The Funnel Sequence of Questions. Regardless of the form of question employed, the interviewer has a decision to make about the order or sequence in which the questions should be asked. A number of considerations determine this decision.

One ordering of questions is called a *funnel sequence.* The term refers to a procedure of asking the most general or unrestricted ques-

---

[12] The use of probe questions is the subject of Chapter 8.

tion in an area first, and following it with successively more restricted questions. In this way the content is gradually narrowed to the precise objectives. One of the major purposes of the funnel sequence is to prevent early questions from conditioning or biasing the responses to those which come later. The funnel sequence is especially useful when one wants to ascertain from the first open questions something about the respondent's frame of reference.

The following series of questions illustrates the funnel sequence used to determine whether the respondent thinks our foreign policy toward Russia should be relaxed or restricted, and why he holds his opinion.

1. How do you think this country is getting along in its relations with other countries?
2. How do you think we are doing in our relations with Russia?
3. Do you think we ought to be dealing with Russia differently from the way we are now?
4. (If yes) What should we be doing differently?
5. Some people say we should get tougher with Russia, and others think we are too tough as it is. How do you feel about it?

The reader will notice that the first question is very general. It does not establish a frame of reference for the respondent, but permits him great freedom in discussing the topic. In replying to this question the respondent is very likely to state his frame of reference. In the second question we have restricted the topic to one country, Russia. The third question is aimed at the respondent's opinion of how the United States ought to deal with Russia. And the fifth is specifically aimed at whether we should exert more pressure or be more lenient. If question 5 had been asked any earlier in the sequence, it might have conditioned the answers to the other questions.

Although the questions in this funnel sequence are all open in form, an effective funnel sequence can often be devised in which the early questions are open but the later questions are closed. If the sequence illustrated had been expanded to include the attitude of the respondent toward some specific issue of the day, or his opinion with respect to some specific point of present foreign policy, the closed form of the question might have been selected as most appropriate. Our foreign-policy series might have included the following closed question: "Do you favor or oppose the continuation of diplomatic relations with Russia?"

The funnel sequence also assists the interviewer in maintaining a good relationship with the respondent and motivating full communication. It permits the respondent, in the early stages of the sequence, to verbalize as he will those things which are salient for him. A sequence that began with highly specific closed questions might force the respondent to postpone or refrain completely from talking about any of his salient attitudes.

Inverted Funnel. There are times when it is desirable to invert the sequence and start with the specific questions, concluding by asking the respondent the most general question. It is clear that this inversion eliminates the basic advantages of the funnel sequence. It offers, however, other advantages that make it useful in some situations. The inverted funnel sequence compels the respondent to think through his attitudes in a number of the sub-areas which make up the objective. If the interviewer wishes to be sure that certain points have been considered by the respondent in reaching his evaluation, or to make sure that all respondents base their evaluations on similar specific dimensions, the inverted funnel may offer some assurance of these objectives.

The inverted sequence is especially appropriate for topics in which the respondent is without strong feelings or on which he has not previously formulated a point of view. In such cases it represents one way of leading the respondent to think through a particular area and arrive at a point of view during the process of the interview itself. This kind of logic might lead us to formulate such a sequence of questions to learn how a respondent evaluates his work situation. We might lead him through specific questions regarding his foreman, the physical conditions of his work, the content of the job, and so on, ending up with the most general query, "Now taking all these things into consideration, what do you think of this company as a place to work?"

Attitude Scales. There are, of course, a number of other patterns by which the ordering of questions may be prescribed. Among the most common is the attitude scale, in its many forms. Each of the various methods of scaling specifies or implies its own criteria for ordering questions. The techniques of Thurstone, Guttman, Likert, and Coombs are relevant examples. Consideration of these specialized techniques for attitude measurement is beyond the scope of this book. For a general description of scaling techniques the reader is referred to Jahoda, Deutsch, and Cook.[13] A description of Coomb's methods is found in his "Theory and Methods of Social Measurement."[14]

---

[13] *Research Methods in Social Relations.*

[14] C. H. Coombs in *Research Methods in the Behavioral Sciences,* L. Festinger and D. Katz (eds.), Dryden Press, New York, 1953.

Organization of Topics

In addition to problems of sequence within a particular topic or objective, we have the problem of how the various topics or sequences of questions should be put together into a questionnaire. How should we begin the interview? What should the sequence of topics be? How should we go from one topic to another? These questions can be answered with the general statement that the topics and the questions should be so arranged that they make the most sense to the respondent; that is, the sequence of ideas in the questionnaire should follow the logic of the respondent. For this reason, questions closely associated with each other in terms of the interview objectives may have to be widely separated in the questionnaire.

The Logic of the Respondent. A well-designed questionnaire facilitates the progress of the respondent from topic to topic, and often leads him to anticipate the next topic because it seems to him the next logical subject to discuss. A properly designed questionnaire provides a firm basis for the interviewer-respondent relationship and assists materially in the motivation of the respondent. The sequence of topics, then, is not haphazard or random; it is an organized, systematic progression.

The design of the questionnaire for the Survey Research Center's Surveys of Consumer Finances illustrates this point.[15] The objectives of these annual surveys are to ascertain the respondent's income, his savings patterns and the amount he has in various forms of savings, his buying intentions and major items purchased over the past year, his indebtedness, and his feeling about his own financial situation, both present and anticipated. The questionnaire starts with broad attitudinal questions on how the respondent feels about economic conditions generally, and moves to questions on his feelings about his own financial position and his expectations for the next few years. The interview then considers the respondent's assets, beginning with home ownership. How much is the house worth? When did he buy it? Does he have a mortgage? How much does he still owe on the mortgage? Similarly, ownership of automobiles is discussed. Then other major purchases are discussed. Next comes the topic of plans to purchase goods in the near future, which leads logically to the problem of sources of funds for such purchases. Will the money come from savings, from current income, or where? This introduces the topics of

---

[15] For a full description of these studies and their uses, see George Katona, *Psychological Analysis of Economic Behavior*, McGraw-Hill, New York, 1951.

how much income is available and how much savings the person has. Last, to round out the picture, the amount of money already committed (debts) is discussed.

This design was worked out with great care and after many preliminary interviews, so that the topics are logically organized in a sequence which carries the respondent along. Many times interviewers find respondents saying, "I thought you were going to ask me that next," or even anticipating questions in their responses.

We start the questionnaire where the respondent is—that is, with topics which are relevant from his point of view. We then try to follow each topic with another which appears to arise out of the previous one. The more we know about the structure of these topics from the respondent's point of view, the better job we can do of following a sequence that makes sense to him. A sequence that does this is of great value in achieving a successful interview.

Opening Questions. When we discussed the techniques of the interviewer-respondent relationship, we mentioned that a crucial point of the interview occurred when the introduction had been made and the first question was asked. At this early stage the respondent is not sure of his role; he does not know what is expected of him; he may be somewhat apprehensive. Because these opening questions are crucial, the interviewer must use special care with them. They should be such that the respondent can answer them without difficulty. They should not touch on the more important or possibly embarrassing areas. They should help the respondent reassure himself that he can successfully play the role expected of him. They should be such that he learns from them what his role is. At times interviewers use opening questions designed solely to get the interview started successfully, the content of the questions being of little interest to the researcher. In general, however, it is unnecessary to make special opening or so-called "can opener" questions. The interviewer needs merely to select with care the items which he puts at the beginning of the interview.

Criteria for Sequence. In Chapter 5 we talked about arranging questions on a topic in such a way as to prevent setting up undesired frames of reference for the respondent. We need also to be concerned about *conditioning* in arranging the topics in the questionnaire. As the respondent talks about a topic, he develops a "set" or a particular frame of reference. It is likely that this frame of reference will carry over to other topics, and later responses may be conditioned by it. Suppose we are interviewing a worker about how he feels toward the company in which he works. We want to find out how he feels, what he likes, what he doesn't like, what topics are salient and relevant to him, and so forth. If we have already talked with him about his relations with his foreman or how he feels about his wages, the chances are that in discussing his general attitude toward the company he will think in terms of the particular aspects of the company we have already introduced. In general, then, the interviewer needs to be alert to avoid conditioning the respondent to topics in a questionnaire through the order in which he brings them up.

Another criterion for sequence of topics is that of the difficulty of the subject matter for the respondent. This difficulty may be either in the amount of work a topic demands of the respondent or in the amount of threat it implies. If we need to discuss subjects which are threatening to the respondent, we should do so only when we have established a high degree of motivation. In the temporal sequence of the interview, this means such subjects should be left for the middle or toward the end of the questionnaire, when maximal rapport has been established.

Transitions from Area to Area. In spite of our most diligent efforts to make the flow of the questionnaire smooth and the sequence from topic to topic meaningful to the respondent, it is sometimes impossible to avoid an abrupt jump from one topic to another. In such cases, the interviewer will help the respondent to "shift gears" if he introduces the new topic with a transition. The transition is a statement informing the respondent that one topic has been completed, and the subject is about to change to something different and unrelated to what has just been covered. Such a transition might read, "Well, I guess that covers all we need to talk about in terms of the job; now let's turn to something else. Let's look at the subject of supervision and how you feel about your supervision." Transitions also help to avoid the respondent's carrying over a frame of reference to the new topic.

PRETESTING THE QUESTIONNAIRE

No matter how astute the interviewer has been in the wording of the questions, in developing the proper sequence of questions, and in the design of the questionnaire, he needs, wherever possible, to try it out before collecting the actual interviews. A research questionnaire usually is pretested with a small sample of respondents, and the results are analyzed to see whether they meet the research objectives. In this sense the pretest is actually a miniature study. Frequently some of the interviewer's "best questions" fail to elicit the kind of response that meets the objectives. An analysis of the pretest interviews in relation to the objectives will increase the probability of fulfilling these objectives. The pretest will often call for major revisions of questions, and several pretests may be required before a workable questionnaire is achieved.

The second objective of the pretest is to determine the extent to which the questionnaire meets the needs of the respondent, is realistic in its demands on him. Does the questionnaire promote an appropriate relationship with the respondent? Does the respondent understand the questions? Can the questions be asked without having to be explained or reworded? These doubts can be resolved only by pretesting the questionnaire and evaluating the results according to the reactions of respondents.

In Part II of this book appear transcriptions of several interviews, with comments on the questions used in them. By studying these interviews and comments the reader will see how the principles we have talked about in this chapter apply in practice.

SUMMARY

This chapter examines the structure of the interview as a whole—the design of questionnaires. The emphasis, therefore, is not on single questions but on the type of questions to be used, the general approach of the questionnaire, and the organization of topics within the questionnaire. Among the problems considered are the relative advantages of open and closed questions, the strengths and weaknesses of direct and indirect approaches to interview objectives, the patterning of questions within a topic, and the orderly linking together of topics.

The point of view advocated with respect to the choice between open and closed questions is that neither is superior for all purposes and situations. The following criteria are proposed as a basis for choosing the appropriate question type: (1) the interview objectives, (2) the respondent's level of information on the interview topic, (3) the degree of structure which characterizes respondent opinions on the topic, (4) the ease with which the material can be communicated, (5) the interviewer's knowledge and insight into the respondent's situation.

It is argued that the closed question is most appropriate when the interviewer's objective is to classify the respondent, when there is little question as to the adequacy of respondent information, when the respondent's opinions on the topic of the interview are well structured, when there are no major barriers to communication, and when the interviewer is well informed about the respondent.

Conversely, it is proposed that the open question is preferable when the interviewer's objectives go beyond classification of the respondent and include the discovery of his reasons for feeling as he does, when the level of respondent information is low or is unknown to the interviewer, when the respondent must think through problems or formulate opinions at the time of interview, when the barriers to communication are serious, and when the interviewer is uncertain as to the thinking and characteristics of the respondent.

The use of indirect approaches in the interview is discussed, and examples of indirect questions and pictorial material are described. Difficulties in the development and validation of such interview stimuli are emphasized, but their use is considered appropriate when interviewer and respondent do not share a common vocabulary or frame of reference, when it is necessary to present to the respondent a stimulus too complex for verbal communication, or when the communication of the required material poses extreme problems for the respondent, either in terms of psychological inaccessibility or ego threat.

The use of multiple questions to permit thorough exploration of an interview topic is discussed, with emphasis on the funnel sequence of questions. The problem of how to order topics within an interview is considered in the light of the major criterion of making the interview experience conform to the logic of the respondent's thinking rather than to the requirements of the interviewer. The chapter concludes with a discussion of the importance of testing the questionnaire in advance of its actual use as an instrument of data collection.

chapter 7

The Interview
as a Method of Measurement

Clarice Smith is a social caseworker for a local Red Feather agency, specializing in marriage counseling and family problems. Her own impressions and experiences tell her that her efforts are meeting with some success, but she is not satisfied with impressions. She wants to *know* whether her clients have made progress toward more harmonious family relations since she has worked with them. She wants to know which of her clients have made such progress, and *how much* they have made.

Arnold Johnson is on the market research staff of an automobile manufacturer whose share of the market has been on the wane. Johnson is given the job of finding out how recent purchasers of his company's cars feel about them—what percentage are satisfied, what percentage dissatisfied, and what reasons underlie these attitudes.

Professor Clyde Baker is a specialist in methods of mass communication. In recent years he has been working on problems of change of attitude, and especially the effects of television programs on political opinions. He has become convinced that short, frequently repeated messages are more effective, minute for minute, than hour-long productions. He wants now to prove his point in a way that will persuade even the most skeptical of his colleagues.

Edwin Greene is office manager for an insurance company. There is an opening in his office for an administrative officer, and Mr. Greene has applications from five people who are apparently well qualified. He wants to select the candidate who will work out best on the job, and he wants to have something more to go on than what he calls his intuition. The last two employees hired on this intuitive basis have not lived up to Mr. Greene's original expectations of them.

These four people, in different fields and facing different kinds of problems, have at least one thing in common—each requires some sort of *measurement* in order to provide a definitive answer to his questions. Furthermore, each of them might attempt to obtain the necessary measures by means of interviewing. Characteristically, the purpose for which the information-getting interview is undertaken involves some sort of measurement. The survey or research interviewer exemplifies this point very clearly; he wants the results of his work in quantitative or numerical terms. Mr. Johnson and Professor Baker may well set up interviews which look forward to such quantitative analysis. Miss Smith, the social worker, may be satisfied with something less precise in the way of measurement. If she can collect information which will permit her to compare the present adjustment of a client with the condition of the same client six months earlier, she will have achieved her purpose. But comparison is a form of measurement. Mr. Greene also may be satisfied with relative rather than strictly quantitative measurement. He wants to make a sound comparative judgment among five men. The physician who compares symptoms of a patient with the textbook description of a certain disease is engaged in a similar process of comparison and measurement. Broadly speaking, whenever we attempt to compare the statements of one individual with those of another, or with some external standard, or with statements made by the same person at another time, we are engaged in a process of measurement.

In these terms most information-getting interviews involve measurement; the questionnaire or interview schedule can usefully be regarded as a measurement device, and the interviewer as a measurer. Science involves measurement, and to the extent that the interviewer uses the interview as a measuring device, he faces problems in common with scientific technicians in other fields. The physicist with his electron microscope and the engineer with his micrometer might be slow to recognize their kinship with the interviewer, who attempts his measurements armed only with the relatively crude device of the questionnaire. In principle, however, the relationship exists; and the problems which the interviewer faces in using the questionnaire to achieve successful measurement and to avoid error are not too dissimilar from the problems which face scientific workers in fields characterized by greater technological development. In this chapter we will be concerned with those concepts of measurement which are relevant to the interview, and with the practical problems associated with the measurement aspects of the interviewer's role.

SOURCES OF MEASUREMENT ERROR

Consider for a moment the homely example of a father trying to determine the height of his five-year-old son. He stands the boy against the wall, sights over the top of the boy's head, and marks his height on the wall. Then he measures from the floor to the mark on the wall. The resulting figure is duly entered in the baby book as the child's height.

We can readily list some of the possible sources of error in this exercise in measurement. The child may slouch or he may stand on tiptoe as he backs up to the wall, or he may have his heels some distance from the wall. The father may be careless in sighting across the top of the boy's head to mark the wall and may mark below or above his son's actual height. If the family yardstick is misplaced as usual, Father may use Mother's cloth measuring tape instead, thus introducing additional possibilities for error. Tape measures can stretch after long usage, and the measurement may be inaccurate for this reason. Moreover, poor light or obscured marks of calibration on the tape may add to the list of potential difficulties.

Random Errors

If we wish to become more systematic about these different kinds of mistakes, we can distinguish between inaccuracy resulting from the measuring instrument itself, such as the stretching of the tape measure or its obscure calibrations, and inaccuracy resulting from the manner of its use, such as the parent's failure to read the measurement correctly or the child's failure to stand straight. We can distinguish also between error which originates with the measurer (father) and that which begins with the object of measurement (son).

There is another way in which we can classify the kinds of inaccuracies involved in this measurement. Some of the kinds of mistakes which we have mentioned can be thought of as *random errors;* that is, they are chance variations, which are as likely to give us an overestimate of the child's height as they are to give us an underestimate. We would expect that errors in reading the measure due to poor light would result in reading too high a figure on some occasions and too low on others, and that when the light was good a correct reading would be obtained. Similarly, the process of sighting over the top of the head to the wall might sometimes result in a mark above the actual head level and sometimes below.

If a large number of measures were taken under such circumstances, we would obtain a number of more or less imperfect estimates of the boy's height, some overestimating it and some underestimating it. The characteristic of random error is that it produces estimates which vary from the true value, sometimes above and sometimes below, on a random or chance basis. Accordingly, over an infinite number of measures, random errors cancel each other, or average out to zero.

Bias

A different type of inaccuracy is generated by factors which tend to produce mistakes only in one direction. If the parent always takes his son's measure with a tape which has been stretched, he will consistently underestimate his height. Or if he is eager to show his son as tall as possible, he may consistently mark the wall slightly above the boy's head level. Such errors are not random, because each has a characteristic effect and direction. The father's generous marking will consistently overstate the actual height; the stretched tape will consistently understate it. When errors of measurement result in a *systematic* piling up of inaccuracies in a single direction—either a consistent overestimation or a consistent underestimation—we refer to the measurement as *biased*.

Problems of error and bias are easy to identify in so simple an example. They are illustrative, however, of measurement difficulties which are encountered in some degree no matter how refined the instrument or how precise the technician.

Example: Measurement Error in Medicine

To develop further our approach to measurement and to problems of error and bias, consider the case of a physician attempting to get accurate readings of a patient's blood pressure. As with the father measuring his son's height, inaccuracies can arise from the measuring instrument, from the manner of its application, or even from some behavior of the patient. Moreover, these inaccuracies may be random errors, giving variously greater and lesser values than the true one, or they may be of a systematic sort, resulting in consistent underestimation or overestimation of the patient's actual blood pressure.

We can begin with the possibilities for error in the measurement device—the familiar rubber sleeve which is wrapped around the patient's arm and inflated until the pressure of the sleeve stops his pulse, the pressure required to stop the pulse and the pressure at which circulation resumes being read from a gauge or from a column of mercury in a calibrated tube. If chance differences in the position of the instrument or in temperature and humidity were to result in small variations above or below the true value, these would exemplify random errors due to characteristics of the instrument. Errors of a random sort may be the result also of the physician's use of the instrument. The inevitable human limitations in observation may cause him occasionally to record a reading somewhat above or below what the instrument actually showed. Finally, there is the patient's potential contribution to error. If his blood pressure is taken just after he has walked two blocks to the doctor's office and sprinted up the stairs to keep an appointment for which he is already late, the reading will probably be higher than if he saw the doctor after a leisurely half-hour of magazine reading in the waiting room. All these factors we can think of as random in their effects, contributing to readings which may be above or below the "normal" one.

But let us turn to inaccuracies of the systematic variety which might arise in the same situation. It is not difficult to think of biasing factors which could lead to persistent underestimation or overestimation of the "normal" blood pressure. Perhaps the instrument was not calibrated accurately at the factory, or perhaps subsequent wear or damage has upset the calibration. Using an instrument with either defect, the physician will invariably give inaccurate readings of his patients' blood pressure, which will deviate from the true value in the same direction and in the same amount. Such bias might occur also in the physician's use of the instrument. If he regularly placed the instrument in such a way that he had to look up at a sharp angle in order to read it, he would tend always to record a higher reading than the true one. The patient also may create biased results. If a visit to the doctor always produces in the patient a reaction of fear and anxiety, that reaction will be reflected each time his blood pressure is taken, and the physician will report for such an individual a figure higher than his "true" blood pressure (that is, blood pressure under normal, unstressful circumstances).

We can follow the implications of this example by expanding it to include the "consumers" of blood pressure readings—patients, insurance companies, even doctors themselves. When an insurance company receives from a doctor the statement that James McIntyre, aged 59, has a blood pressure of 180/94, the company assumes that the reading was accurate, unbiased, and without error. Moreover, the company assumes that repeated measures of Mr. McIntyre's blood pressure by the same doctor and with the same instrument (provided no changes in his physical condition have occurred), or measures taken with other instruments or by other physicians, will give the same results. Finally, one other assumption is made, perhaps more subtle than the rest—that the instrument and procedure employed really measure blood pressure, and blood pressure only, rather than some other physical characteristic.

In short, the users of data on blood pressure, like the users of most other kinds of measurement, make two major assumptions about the information they receive: (1) that the results would be identical if the measurement were repeated many times, and (2) that the procedure and instrument used really measure the thing which they purport to measure. In both assumptions, the insurance company may be on firm ground. There are a number of fields, however, in which it is not always certain that the elaborate devices for measurement are actually measuring the attribute in question. Some "intelligence" tests, for example, have been shown to measure unintentionally such attributes as education, vocabulary, and cultural background rather than intelligence alone.

MEASUREMENT IN THE INTERVIEW

So far we have developed the concept and problems of measurement by means of examples from fields other than interviewing. We have asserted, however, that interviewers are engaged in taking measurements (of a special kind), just as are technicians in other fields. In interviewing, as in other fields, the goal is to achieve measurements which are accurate, which reflect the true value of the attribute they purport to measure. And in interviewing, problems of measurement similar to those described are met in abundance. There are problems of the adequacy of the measuring instrument (questions or interview schedule), problems in its use by the interviewer, problems in the reactions of the respondent. Some of the errors in interviews are random, varying from one interview to the next and from one interviewer to another; others appear as biases, causing persistent deviations of the interview results from the true value of the attribute in question.

It will be useful, in our discussion of error in the interview, to make clear what we include in the concept of error. We can think in terms of a *true value*, which represents the level of the attribute we want to measure, and in terms of an *observed value*, which represents the measurement we actually obtain. The difference between the true value and the observed value then becomes the *total error*, which includes the effects of both random and nonrandom factors.[1]

Determining True Value

The concept of the true value of any attribute which we want to measure is a useful one. It serves as a goal or a target for our measurement, and also as a bench mark against which we can estimate the amount of our error. But in some situations the true value of an attribute may be an abstraction, which can be approximated but not definitely fixed. In other cases it may be impossible even to define a single true value, so that the concept becomes relative. These points can be clarified by examples involving interview data.

Let us begin with a case in which the true value is clear and absolute. Suppose that our objective is to ascertain a respondent's age. There is little difficulty in defining what is meant by the true value. The respondent was born on a certain day in a certain year, and there is only one response which can be correct or true.

The determination of true value becomes more complex if our objective is to learn a respondent's annual income. There is the problem of what constitutes an individual's income. Shall we restrict our definition to money income or include reimbursement in kind? Do we mean income before or after taxes? We must decide how to allocate income received jointly with spouse, and a number of similar technical questions. Since the term "annual" is ambiguous, we must decide whether we mean the last twelve months, the last calendar year, or the average of a certain period of years. Even after we have made these decisions, of course, it is likely that there will be some amount of error in the response obtained. Such error may occur because we have failed to define precisely what our concept of income is, or because we have failed to communicate that concept adequately to the respondent. There is also the error which comes from such respondent motives as fear of the Bureau of Internal Revenue or the wish to appear more prosperous than he really is. Regardless of these problems of error in obtaining a valid and accurate response, once we have set our definition an unequivocal true value becomes our target; we know the characteristic which we are trying to approx-

---

[1] In a single interview it is not possible to differentiate between random error and bias. This differentiation can be made only over a number of interviews. The differentiation is important, however, when we come to consider methods for overcoming error and bias.

imate, and we know that there is only one true or correct value that will meet our objective.[2]

The True Value of an Attitude

The concept of true value becomes even more obscure when we wish to measure attitudes. Consider, for instance, the question "How do you feel about your supervisor?" Many motivational factors may prevent a frank response to this question. An employee may make a nice distinction between his public and his private sentiments on such topics, but even then the problem of true value remains, for it is likely that the employee does not have a single, enduring attitude of liking or disliking his supervisor. Instead of one "true" attitude which he holds unvaryingly, regardless of the circumstances, the employee probably has a number of somewhat different attitudes toward his supervisor, depending upon the immediate situation.

The worker might have attitude A at the time his supervisor recommends him for promotion. On the day the same supervisor calls him in and reprimands him severely for a mistake which be believes was not his fault, the worker may have a quite different feeling toward his supervisor, which we shall call attitude B. Attitude C may characterize the employee's feeling for his supervisor one Sunday morning when he leaves church after a particularly moving sermon on the meaning of brotherly love, and attitude D may be generated in the course of a long union meeting called to consider management's rejection of a demand for a wage increase. Moreover, none of these may be the same as the evaluation that the worker reaches in a moment of solitude, when he is neither interacting with another individual nor reacting to some recent experience involving his supervisor.

Which of these represents his "true attitude"? And which should be our target in an interview? We may argue that, in one sense, only the attitude which he recognized in solitude is his true one, and that the others were modified in greater or lesser degree by some temporary situation or the presence of other people. And yet, we must recognize that his attitudes in these other situations have a validity of their own. During the local union meeting, the worker may feel differently toward his supervisor than he feels about him in a face-to-

---

[2] In practical terms it is seldom possible to obtain the true value for so complex a concept as family income. The researcher therefore specifies a degree of "required precision." He decides how closely the observed figure must approximate the true one in order to be considered accurate. A variation of a few dollars in annual family income, for example, is inconsequential for most purposes.

face conversation. Moreover, the attitude which the employee speaks only to himself may be relatively superficial, because he is unable to recognize and verbalize some of his deeper feelings without the skillful assistance of another person. Under these circumstances it becomes extremely difficult to argue that some one of these attitudes is the true or actual value.

We can, however, differentiate attitudes along several dimensions. One of these is depth. It may be useful to think of different levels of attitude. There may be a superficial level at which an attitude is much influenced by the experiences and associations of the moment. The worker leaving his supervisor after the reprimand feels that the boss is an arbitrary, ill-tempered character for whom he has an active dislike. At a deeper level, however, his attitude toward his supervisor has been developed over a long period of time. Reflected in it is the sum of all his experiences with the boss, threatening and supportive, as well as some basic orientations toward authority which were established early in life. Even at this level, his attitude is affected by a new experience; it was out of experience that the attitude was formed. But though day-to-day events may displace this deeper attitude slightly in a positive or negative direction, and a consistent series of new experiences might alter it drastically, it has a stability that does not characterize the surface reaction.

At this deeper level, then, attitudes change more slowly, and usually as a result of a succession of experiences of a consistent, undeniable character. An unvarying diet of aggression and severity from the boss would create a major alteration in the worker's attitude toward him; occasional outbursts of anger or praise may have some effects at this level, too, but they are dampened by the weight of past experience. The surface waves of affect may show a good deal of movement with each gust of wind; the deeper currents are relatively unaffected.

Can we now argue that it is this deeper level of attitude that represents.the goal of the interview? Certainly this attitudinal level is accessible to the interviewer if he wishes to obtain it. In answer to the question of how he is getting along with his supervisor, the employee's initial response may vary a great deal, depending on whether we interview him just after a raise or after a reprimand. In either case, however, the interviewer can accept this initial response as representing material that is salient for the worker at the moment. He can then determine, by means of encouraging and searching supplementary questions, the deeper-lying attitude. The very stability of this deeper attitude suggests greater truth or validity, and experience has taught us that such attitudes have greater general predictive value than do the more temporary moods. If we wish to make a general prediction about the tenor of this worker's life on the job, his deeper attitude toward his supervisor is likely to be more useful to us than any of the surface reactions.

But this does not imply that truth necessarily lies deep. All the attitudes of the worker toward his supervisor are true in the sense that all of them exist. The problem for us as interviewers is to decide which of these attitudes we want to measure, which one is our target value. The answer to this question depends almost entirely upon the objectives of the interview. Suppose that our purpose is to predict how an employee will behave after receiving criticism from his supervisor, or to understand his psychological reactions to such criticism. For these objectives the most relevant attitudes are those that the worker expresses in a comparable situation—attitude B in our example. In the same way, the target or true value may be any one of the several other attitudes previously described, depending upon our objectives. Once the objective has been defined, there is then a true value which is the target.

The Relativity of Error

We have seen that the concept of true value, at least when applied to attitudes, must be regarded as relative. By definition, then, the concept of error also becomes relative. Error can be appraised only in terms of the relationship between the measurement we actually obtain and the value which represented our target. If we accept the fact that the true value or quantity which we want to measure is defined by our objectives, it follows also that no question wording and no interviewing technique can be regarded as intrinsically biased. Whether or not a given technique or formulation is biased depends upon the objectives we want to achieve, and bias can be evaluated only in relation to those objectives. It accordingly becomes impossible to call a question biased or unbiased merely by reading the question. We must know both the question and the objectives before we can reach a judgment.

Consider the "stress" interviewing techniques employed during World War II for selection and assignment by the Office of Strategic Services. The purpose of this type of interview was to discover how men would behave under extreme conditions, the kinds of conditions they might encounter if captured by the enemy. To meet this general objective, some of the interviews were conducted under conditions of intimidation, embarrassment, extreme emotional stress, and even physical exhaustion. If such techniques were employed in order to predict how people would behave under the normal conditions of social interaction, we would judge them to be hopelessly biased. To meet the objective of predicting behavior under extreme conditions, however, the stress techniques may have been the best possible choice.

But the extreme problem faced by the OSS during the last world war is far removed from the interview problems which most of us are likely to encounter. Let us consider an example more within the range of ordinary interviewing experience. The following question was asked in a nationwide survey: "Would you favor sending food to relieve the suffering of the starving people of India?"[3] Is this question intrinsically biased? In the light of the argument we have been building, we would answer that it is not *intrinsically* biased. Words like "starving" and "suffering" obviously will increase the proportion of positive responses to this question. In this case, however, the purpose of the question was to sort out those who were opposed to the United States' sending aid to foreign countries under any circumstances whatsoever. The question was therefore designed to put the case in favor of foreign aid with sufficient strength and poignancy so that only those extremely opposed to such a policy would answer in the negative. For such a purpose the question is unbiased. But it would be seriously biased if we interpreted the responses to mean that people who answered this question favorably were favorable to the present government of India or would approve of sending aid under less extreme circumstances.

We can now give a more precise definition of bias: it is the intrusion of any *unplanned* or *unwanted* influence in the interview. This definition is important, but is not sufficient to guide us in practice. In the remainder of this chapter, we will examine the research evidence regarding sources of bias in the interview, and the suggestions which research offers for improving the interview as a measurement device.

The Prevalence of Error and Bias in the Interview

The advent of large-scale interview studies raised many questions about the accuracy of data obtained by means of personal interviews. Some of the sources of error in interview data have become the subjects of intensive investigation, and a considerable literature on the accuracy of sample survey interviews has been published. Most of what is currently known about the ways in which an interviewer may

---

[3] This question was included in a study made by the Division of Program Surveys, U. S. Department of Agriculture, in 1945.

affect the data he collects has been learned from research on the survey process. Fortunately, these findings are generally applicable to nonsurvey interviews. A brief review of some of these studies will make clear the prevalence of error and bias in the interview.

Some of the early work on the influence of interviewers on survey data began when investigators noticed what appeared to be suspicious or unusual patterning of interview responses. They then attempted to find the causes of these response patterns, and to determine by means of research the factors which were responsible. Stuart Rice published in 1929 an article entitled "Contagious Bias in the Interview,"[4] which reported a pioneer study of interviewer effect. Rice, in working with some survey data, was struck by the fact that the interviews of one interviewer seemed to be similar to each other and different from the results that another interviewer obtained. The purpose of the original study had been to determine causes of destitution by interviewing men in flophouses and cheap hotels. Rice found that respondents interrogated by one interviewer consistently assigned a high importance to overindulgence in liquor as a cause of their destitution, whereas the respondents of another interviewer tended to emphasize social and industrial conditions.

Myers'[5] study of age data obtained by interviewers in the decennial census provides an example of a similar approach to suspicious patterns in reported data. Myers found that when he plotted an age curve for the population of the United States based on the decennial census, there was a marked "heaping" of ages ending in zero (10, 20, 30, etc.). Beginning with such studies as these, there have been a number of successful attempts to identify and understand the sources of unexpected response patterns in reported interview data.[6]

Many studies are reported that measure the accuracy of interview data by comparing results obtained through personal interviews with information from independent objective sources. Twila Neely found, for example, that one out of every nine families receiving city relief failed to report this fact when asked the specific question in the course of an interview.[7] In another study she found that victims of auto

---

[4] "Contagious Bias in the Interview: A Methodological Note," *American Journal of Sociology*, **35**, 420–423 (1929).

[5] Robert J. Myers, "Errors and Bias in the Reporting of Ages in Census Data," *Transactions of the Actuarial Society of America*, **41**, 395–415 (1940).

[6] For a thorough review of research on interview bias, see Herbert H. Hyman *et al.*, *Interviewing for Social Research*, University of Chicago Press, Chicago, 1954.

[7] *A Study of Error in the Interview*, privately printed, 1937, pp. 72–83.

accidents tended to exaggerate the amount of work time they had lost, and to report inaccurately the amount of pay lost.

Hyman[8] reports several such studies. In one study, made during World War II, he found that in the upper income groups nearly half the respondents who had cashed government bonds during the previous week failed to report having done so on being asked directly.

Parry and Crossley[9] reported a study in which five sets of experienced interviewers took more than 900 interviews in a single community. These interviews included data on a number of the respondents' characteristics that could be checked from objective sources. On almost every topic, significant differences were found between the data obtained by interview and those obtained from the records of appropriate agencies. The differences are summarized in the following tabulation.

	Respondents Giving Inaccurate Reports, per cent
Voting and registration	25
Contributions to Community Chest	40
Ownership of library card	10
Ownership of driver's license	10
Auto ownership	3
Age	17
Home ownership	4
Possession of telephone	2

Other studies demonstrate differences found when the respondent was reinterviewed on the same questions. Kinsey,[10] in his study of male sexual behavior, reinterviewed over 150 respondents and found a considerable amount of variability between the two sets of interviews on some items and relatively close agreement on others. Agreement between items in the two waves of Kinsey interviews ranged from a correlation of .90 to a low of .40.

Hansen[11] and his colleagues of the Census Bureau conducted reinterviews with 150 families in the Baltimore area regarding their status in the labor force. Significantly different responses were obtained on approximately 40 per cent of the items in the interview.

---

[8] Herbert H. Hyman et al., op. cit.

[9] Hugh Parry and Helen Crossley, "Validity of Responses to Survey Questions," Public Opinion Quarterly, 14, 61–80 (1950).

[10] Alfred C. Kinsey, Wardell B. Pomeroy, and Clyde E. Martin, Sexual Behavior in the Human Male, W. B. Saunders, Philadelphia, 1948.

[11] Morris H. Hansen, William N. Hurwitz, Eli S. Marks, and W. P. Mauldin, "Response Errors in Surveys," Journal of the American Statistical Association, 46, 147–190, (1951).

Hovland and Wonderlic[12] had two employment interviewers independently question twenty-three job applicants regarding their work experience, family history, and social and personal characteristics. Comparison of the two sets of interviews showed considerable lack of agreement, with an average reliability of .71 for all items.

These are only a few of the many studies that show persistent and important differences between interview data and data obtained from other sources, and between two sets of interview data obtained when respondents are reinterviewed. The seriousness of the evidence is undeniable. The interview must be considered to be a measurement device which is fallible, and which is subject to substantial errors and biases. All this does not suggest, however, that the interview should be discarded as a means of collecting information.

A more temperate conclusion is that the interview, like other measurement techniques, has great value and unique advantages, but that it also has many possibilities for inaccuracy. We therefore need to learn more about the sources of bias and to develop methods for eliminating them. We need to think through the process of the interview from beginning to end, in terms of its vulnerability to bias.

POTENTIAL SOURCES OF BIAS

For the most part, our emphasis in this book has been on the *behavior* of interviewer and respondent. The interviewer asks questions, probes for full responses, motivates the respondent to communicate, and records the information. The respondent contributes to the interaction by answering questions, giving information, formulating his own thoughts, asking for clarification, and occasionally by refusing to respond to questions or by giving irrelevant answers. To some extent, manifestations of bias can be found in these overt behaviors.

To uncover the sources of bias, however, it is necessary to look behind the interaction itself. This we have already done in Chapter 2, in another context. We were interested then in exploring the behavioral dynamics of the interview, and we did so in terms of motivational forces generated in the psychological fields of respondent and interviewer. In this chapter we will return to the motive patterns of interviewer and respondent in our search for sources of bias. We will be interested also in some of the characteristics which each participant brings with him to the interview. Such factors are important both for the cues which they give us to the individual's own motives and be-

[12] C. I. Hovland and E. F. Wonderlic, "Prediction of Success from a Standardized Interview," *Journal of Applied Psychology*, **23**, 537–546 (1939).

havior during the interview, and because of the reactions which they evoke in the other participant in the interview.

Background Factors

Each person comes to the interview with many firmly fixed attitudes, personality characteristics, motives, and goals. Each participant has also a constellation of characteristics suggesting group memberships and group loyalties—age, sex, race, religious background; income and educational status. Such characteristics may be important as potential sources of bias in the interview.

Consider Evelyn Andersen, white, age 25, who is collecting data for her doctoral thesis. The subject of her dissertation is ways in which Negro children learn to handle conflict in their relations with white children. She is interviewing Negro parents in a southern rural county, to learn about the values they attempt to teach their children in this respect. Working down her list of sample households, she has just arrived at the home of a Negro sharecropper and is greeted at the door by the sixty-year-old head of the household. He tells her he has seven children, and has had two years of formal education. As she moves into the questions central to her topic, he assures her that his children have learned in all circumstances to be respectful and obedient toward white people. Miss Andersen finds herself wondering whether this respondent is being entirely frank.

In this example interviewer and respondent differ greatly in background characteristics. Will these divergent characteristics result in biased information? What are likely to be the dynamics of biasing influences if they occur? Research has shown that such influences do exist and that biased information is often associated with differences in background characteristics.

Hyman[13] reports a study in which Negro and white interviewers each interviewed a random sample of Negroes on problems of discrimination. Negro interviewers obtained significantly more information on resentment over discrimination than did the white interviewers.

Robinson and Rohde[14] conducted an experiment in which several groups of selected interviewers were assigned to interview samples of New York City householders on the subject of attitudes towards Jews. One group of interviewers included persons who were judged to be non-Semitic in appearance and in name. A second group included interviewers who were judged to be Semitic in appearance but non-

---

[13] *op. cit.*

[14] D. Robinson and S. Rohde, "Two Experiments with an Anti-Semitism Poll," *Journal of Abnormal and Social Psychology*, 41, 136–144 (1946).

Semitic in name; a third group of interviewers consisted of persons who were judged to be Semitic both in appearance and name. The responses obtained by these interviewers showed significant differences among the three groups with respect to the number of expressed anti-Semitic attitudes or stereotyped anti-Jewish statements they obtained in the course of discussing attitudes toward Jews with their respondents. Robinson and Rohde concluded that the more likely respondents were to identify the interviewers as Jewish, the less likely they were to make anti-Semitic statements in the course of the interview. Respondents apparently were motivated to avoid making statements which they anticipated would be painful to the interviewer or of which the interviewer would disapprove.

Katz[15] found that interviewers from working-class backgrounds consistently obtained more radical social and political opinions from respondents than did interviewers from the middle class. The differences were marked on labor issues, particularly among respondents who were members of trade unions. For example, working-class interviewers found that 44 per cent of their respondents favored a law against sit-down strikes; the middle-class interviewers found that 59 per cent favored such a law.

Several studies[16] have found that answers obtained when interviewers and respondents were of the same sex differed from those obtained when they were not of the same sex. Communication of critical or personal data was facilitated in the former situation. The same tendency was discovered when interviewers questioned respondents of similar age to their own, rather than respondents of markedly different age.

These studies give little indication of the manner in which background factors enter the interaction of the interview and how they bring about biased responses. Our explanation must therefore be considered tentative. It appears, however, that background characteristics enter into the interaction in two ways, both of which are indirect.

(1) Background characteristics are the source of many of our attitudes, perceptions, expectations, and motives. For example, individuals of high socioeconomic status tend to be somewhat more favorable toward big business and somewhat more critical of labor

---

[15] Daniel Katz, "Do Interviewers Bias Poll Results?," *Public Opinion Quarterly*, 6, 248–268 (1942).

[16] Herbert H. Hyman *et al.*, *op. cit.*, pp. 164–166; Mark Benney, David Riesman, and Shirley Star, "Group-Membership Effects in the Interview," unpublished.

unions than people at the other end of the socioeconomic scale. The extent to which an individual's age determines his attitudes toward many topics is so much a part of our day-to-day observations that little documentation is needed. In the same way, the other background factors—education, race, sex, religion, etc.—play their part in conditioning the psychological characteristics of interviewer and respondent, including those perceptions, attitudes, and motives which have particular relevance for the interview process. If the interviewer and respondent are widely divergent in their background characteristics, we would anticipate widely differing attitudes and motives. Such divergence makes mutual understanding more difficult, and therefore has serious consequences for the type of interaction which can take place between the two. This kind of problem we will consider more fully later in this chapter.

(2) Background characteristics may affect interviewer-respondent interaction through the cues which such characteristics provide to each participant about the other. If, for example, the respondent perceives the interviewer to be of a different race, this perception may have profound effects on his attitude toward the interviewer, on his behavior toward the interviewer, and therefore on the results of the interview itself. We cited earlier the case of a Negro sharecropper in the deep South who is approached by a white interviewer doing research on certain aspects of race relations among children. As the interviewer introduces herself, what are the perceptions of the sharecropper? He sees that he is to be engaged in conversation by a person of another race and of markedly different socioeconomic position. He attempts to understand this situation in terms of his previous experiences with people of similar characteristics, experiences in which the sharecropper was likely to be subordinate to a white supervisor or employer. Almost before the interview begins, therefore, he has formed a set of attitudes toward the interviewer, and has certain expectations regarding the interviewer's attitudes and probable behavior toward him.

These kinds of cues are as important for the interviewer as for the respondent. They provide the interviewer with some of the earliest cues to which he may react. The respondent's skin color or facial cast, his apparent economic status, and other observable characteristics, may lead the interviewer to certain expectations regarding the respondent's probable attitudes on certain topics, his level of information in various fields, and the like.

In summary, then, background factors are important in the interview because they constitute a kind of subsoil in which many of an individual's attitudes, motives, and perceptions have direct roots. But the background characteristics of each participant in the interview have additional importance because they provide cues for the other participant. Certain attitudes, motives, and stereotypes are triggered in the respondent's mind by his perception that the interviewer possesses certain background characteristics. The interviewer may be influenced in the same fashion by his initial perceptions of the respondent. Such reactions may in turn influence the behavior of both participants.

Psychological Factors

We stated that background characteristics provide a basis for the formation of attitudes, expectations, and motives. We want now to consider the research evidence that the interaction of the interview is affected by these latter factors. Among the early discoveries in this area, which interested (and troubled) survey technicians, were findings showing that the responses which interviewers obtained tended to be related to their own opinions and reactions. Cahalan, Tamulonis, and Verner[17] report a study in which interviews taken by more than 100 different interviewers were tabulated separately. About three fourths of the 51 interview questions showed significant differences in the responses obtained by different interviewers. Many of these differences were in the direction of the interviewers' own opinions. Apparently, the interviewers tended to see respondents in their own image.

A study by Ferber and Wales[18] on opinions toward prefabricated houses showed that the respondents of interviewers who favored such housing themselves were more favorable to prefabricated houses than were respondents of interviewers who were unfavorable.

Blankenship[19] reported similar results in 300 interviews dealing with political attitudes. Of the 31 questions on the questionnaire, 7 showed significant interviewer differences, and 3 were in the direction of the interviewer's own attitudes.

---

[17] D. Cahalan, V. Tamulonis, and H. W. Verner, "Interviewer Bias Involved in Certain Types of Attitude Questions," *International Journal of Opinion and Attitude Research*, 1, 63–77 (1947).

[18] Robert Ferber and Hugh Wales, "Detection and Correction of Interviewer Bias," *Public Opinion Quarterly*, 16, 107–127 (1952).

[19] Albert B. Blankenship, "The Effect of the Interviewer upon the Response in a Public Opinion Poll," *Journal of Consulting Psychology*, 4, 134–136 (1940).

Several studies in the literature deal with the effects of interviewers' expectations, rather than of their opinions. Stanton and Baker[20] had 200 students study twelve geometric designs. Several days later the students were interviewed to measure their recognition of these designs. Five experienced polling interviewers conducted the interviews. Each interviewer had been given a key supposedly indicating the "correct" responses, but some received keys that were actually incorrect. In general, the interviewers obtained results in favor of the responses they thought were correct. The results showed significant differences among the interviewers in this respect.

A study similar to the Stanton-Baker research was carried out by the Psychological Corporation.[21] Again, some potential respondents were shown nonsense materials. One group of interviewers was correctly informed of the materials which the respondents had seen. Another group was told that the respondents had seen items which had not really been shown to them, and a third group was told nothing. Each group of interviewers then interviewed the respondents to get them to identify the items they had seen. In each case the respondents "identified" a relatively high number of the items which the interviewers thought were correct.

Of course, not all the studies that have been done on these problems show evidence of interviewer bias. The disparity in research results seems to argue that while the potential danger of bias is great, it is not an inevitable part of interviewing. What is needed (and is still in the future) is definitive research to show precisely under what conditions the attitudes and expectations of interviewers and respondents can affect the interaction and bias the results of the interview. We can attempt a tentative analysis of this kind, consistent with the research findings available and with the approach to the interview as a process of interaction.

The psychological factors that influence behavior in the interview have a variety of origins. We can think of them to some extent in terms of the individual's personality, and regard certain attitudes and stereotypes as expressions of personality characteristics. To some extent also we can find the origins of attitudes in the background factors already described, and can trace the linkage between a person's experiences and environment and his present attitudes on a variety of

[20] F. Stanton and K. H. Baker, "Interviewer Bias and the Recall of Incompletely Learned Materials," *Sociometry*, **5**, 123–134 (1942).

[21] "Further contributions, 20th Anniversary of Psychological Corporation and to Honor Its Founder, James McKeen Cattell," *Journal of Applied Psychology*, **26**, 16–17 (1942).

subjects. It is not necessary, however, to undertake the impossibly difficult job of tracing the origins of each of the interviewer's and respondent's attitudes. Not all of the infinite number of attitudes or motives which an individual possesses are relevant to any particular interview. Each of his attitudes can be considered as a *predisposition* to behave in a certain way, or to react characteristically to a given stimulus. But the stimulus to action must be present if the attiude is to become effective as one of the determinants of behavior.

The stimuli or trigger mechanisms in the interview are likely to be of three main types. The first of these is the *content of the interview* itself. If an interviewer of strong pacifist persuasions is assigned the task of conducting an interview on attitudes toward the hydrogen bomb, it is entirely possible that his attitudes toward force as a means of settling international disputes will influence the end product of the interview. The same attitudes on the part of a doctor who was conducting an interview with a patient would probably be irrelevant to the interview and would have no effect on it. Attitudes and motives, other things being equal, will affect the result of the interview in the degree to which the content of the interview itself makes those attitudes relevant.

The second stimulus which may trigger relevant attitudes on the part of either interviewer or respondent is his *initial perceptions* of the other person's background characteristics or other visible attributes. A survey respondent of low economic status, somewhat sensitive to and resentful of his lack of means, might generate considerable hostility toward an interviewer merely because he perceives the interviewer to be relatively well dressed and driving a late-model automobile. Even if these perceptions were not sufficient to lead the respondent to feelings of hostility, they might suffice to create an attitude of skepticism of the interviewer's ability to understand the kinds of problems which he faces.

The interviewer may be as liable to such effects as the respondent. The respondent's age, race, sex, and socioeconomic status may relate to attitudes or stereotypes which the interviewer holds. Accordingly, the interviewer expects the respondent to behave in certain ways and give certain answers. It is only a short step for him to lead the respondent in the expected direction or to interpret his responses in ways which fit his own preconceptions. Suppose that Miss Andersen, the aspiring Ph.D. candidate whom we left interviewing a Negro sharecropper, is a person who regards Negroes of low economic status as invariably poorly educated, ill-informed, and inarticulate. The mere appearance of the sharecropper is sufficient to bring these stereotypes into operation. She forms certain expectations of the way in which the sharecropper will behave, certain expectations of his ability to respond. In the interview situation, these expectations may very well be of the self-fulfilling variety—that is, she may behave in such a way that her stereotypes of the sharecropper respondent will be reflected in the interview product, irrespective of the attributes of the respondent himself.

A third source of stimuli which may make certain attitudes of the interviewer or respondent operate to bias the results is the *behavior* of either participant during the course of the interview. The process here involves reactions much like those triggered by characteristics more immediately apparent. The interviewer or respondent finds, in some remark or expressed attitude of the other person, a stimulus which evokes certain attitudes and expectations on his own part and leads him to "fill in" a more complete picture of the person. If a respondent tells an interviewer that he votes for a certain political party, or that he reads a certain newspaper or belongs to a certain labor union, the interviewer will expect to discover—and may even assume he is discovering—a whole set of attitudes that he associates with the reported behavior or attribute. The remainder of the interview may reflect these expectations and attitudes of the interviewer, even if the respondent himself fails to fit the stereotype so neatly.

For the interviewer's stereotypes to come into play, it may not even be necessary for the respondent to characterize himself explicitly. An attitude or opinion expressed by the respondent may be sufficient to trigger the interviewer's stereotypes and provide him with a basis for classifying the respondent. The interviewer who has a stereotype of the *Chicago Tribune* reader need not be told by a respondent that he regularly reads this newspaper. It may be sufficient for the interviewer that he express certain opinions or attitudes which fit the interviewer's stereotype of the *Tribune* reader.

The respondent's sensitivity to the interviewer's attitudes, particularly the interviewer's attitudes toward him, is likely to be great and can readily bias the interview results. The interviewer's behavior can reinforce or modify initial impressions. If the interviewer addresses the respondent in language beyond his comprehension, or uses a tone or manner which suggests superiority and condescension, we can expect that the respondent's feelings of distance and resentment will be strengthened. If, on the other hand, the interviewer indicates unexpected ability to understand the respondent's situation, and a sincere interest and respect for the respondent, the perception of these behaviors is likely to lead rapidly to a new set of favorable attitudes toward the interviewer. The volume and validity of communication can be expected to vary with these attitudes.

Behavioral Factors

Thus far we have been talking about the attitudes, motives, and perceptions of the respondent and the interviewer. These psychological characteristics are *potentially* biasing, but not necessarily so. It is only through *behavior* that these predispositions to bias can become operative.

The specific behaviors of interviewer and respondent are infinite in number and variety. A limited number of categories, however, is adequate to describe the behavioral sources of bias. On the part of the interviewer, these behaviors include (1) asking questions, (2) probing for additional information, (3) recording responses, and (4) motivating the respondent to communicate. Except for number 3, they are primarily in the form of speech, but may also include movements, postures, facial expressions, and other nonverbal manifestations.

The behavior of the respondent that is relevant here consists almost entirely of his reactions to stimuli from the interviewer. The respondent answers questions—giving full information or withholding it, speaking frankly or distorting. Except for the interviewer's misinterpretations or errors in recording responses, it is in the respondent's answers that all the preceding bias factors have their effects. Mutual perceptions of background characteristics, reciprocal influences based on psychological responses to other behavioral cues—all are reflected in the end product of the interview, which consists of the respondent's answers, his verbal behavior.

A number of studies have been oriented toward examining the effects of different kinds of interviewer behavior during the course of the interview. In most cases, the researcher has inferred interviewer behavior from other evidence. Shapiro and Eberhart[22] report a study in which four experienced interviewers who had done graduate work in sociology and psychology each interviewed between 80 and 90 respondents. The respondents were veterans of World War II, and the purpose of the interview was to collect information about on-the-job training, financial status, occupational and educational history, and so forth.

Of the 38 questions in the questionnaire, 10 showed important

---

[22] S. Shapiro and J. C. Eberhart, "Interviewer Differences in an Intensive Interview Survey," *International Journal of Opinion and Attitude Research*, 1, No. 2, 1–17 (1947).

differences among interviewers. The authors say about these findings, "These [differences in response obtained] appear to result not from variations in the interviewers' own attitudes toward the topic covered by the questions, but from differences in the interviewing methods used." They then attempt to analyze the differences in methods which might have accounted for these findings. In the first place, it appeared that some interviewers were more likely than others to rely on the initial responses which the respondents gave, without additional probing. In other cases, the responses were incompletely reported. Occasionally the interviewers had to decide whether or not to ask a question that already had been partially answered in another context. There apparently was considerable variation among interviewers as to whether or not all the questions were asked. In this study, therefore, the differences appeared to be largely attributable to different techniques of probing, of reporting, and of selecting the questions to be asked, rather than the expectations or attitudes of the interviewers.

Findings which in some respects go beyond this study are reported by Guest.[23] Guest used as interviewers fifteen college students. He so arranged their assignments that each of these interviewers interviewed the same respondent, who had been previously instructed to give identical answers to all fifteen. The interviews were recorded by wire, and the wire recordings were subsequently analyzed to discover the frequency of errors and the types of errors made by the interviewers. One of the most startling findings of the study was the sheer number of errors. There were in the fifteen interviews 66 failures to ask supplementary questions when inadequate responses were given, and many failures to record significant material provided by the respondent. These errors were concentrated to some extent among interviewers, although every interviewer made some. The number of errors per interviewer varied from 12 to 36. Guest concluded from analysis of the wire recordings that the interviewers' attitudes were a source of contamination in the interview, because interviewers tended to introduce their own ideas into the conversation with the respondent, either by commenting on an answer which he made or by suggesting appropriate answers when he appeared to be hesitant.

Findings generally in accord with Guest's original study are reported in an unpublished manuscript of the Department of Scientific Research of the American Jewish Committee. In this study, fifteen

---

[23] L. L. Guest, "A Study of Interviewer Competence," *International Journal of Opinion and Attitude Research*, **1**, No. 4, 17–30 (1947).

interviewers were assigned a number of respondents, of whom three were "plants." The planted respondents had been rehearsed in the roles of "punctilious liberal," "hostile bigot," and "miscellaneous problem respondent," respectively. The method of analysis involved obtaining tape recordings of the planted interviews and examining them to determine the incidence of error and the kinds of errors which occurred most frequently. The categories included errors in asking questions in the interview schedule, errors in formulating supplementary questions, errors in recording responses, and flagrant cheating—that is, the fabrication of responses or the intentional omission of interview questions.

The findings of this study indicate that the most frequent errors occurred in the manner of asking questions, either in the original asking or in the way in which supplementary questions were improvised to improve inadequate responses. It is apparent from this study and from that of Guest that when the interviewer is thrown on his own and required to improvise questions to elicit a more adequate response from an uncertain or reluctant respondent, he tends to influence the respondent in ways which he does not intend. If the respondent is sensitive to the interviewer's attitudes and concerned about giving the "correct" answer, the responses actually obtained become a complex mixture of the respondent's own attitudes, the interviewer's attitudes, and the respondent's assessment of what the interviewer would consider the correct or appropriate answer. In this fashion, bias enters and the effectiveness of the interview as a means of data collection is compromised or negated. We turn now to the specific ways in which bias may result from the four major kinds of interviewing behavior—asking questions, probing for additional information, recording responses, and motivating the respondent.

Interviewer Behaviors Leading to Bias

Errors in Asking Questions. One of the interviewer's more common errors[24] is to reword a question in order to fit his perception of what

---

[24] In our discussion of deviation of observed value from true value, and in the subsequent description of research on the accuracy of interview data, we have distinguished between error and bias, that is, between chance fluctuations around a true value and a systematic tendency to underestimate or overestimate that value. In the individual case, this distinction is not feasible; it is only in making comparisons among many interviews that error and bias emerge as separate. In the discussion which follows, therefore, this distinction will not be attempted. Any factor in the interview that causes a difference between an observed and a true value will be referred to as bias. The term error will be used in the colloquial sense of "mistake."

the respondent is capable of understanding. Such modifications in wording frequently represent the interviewer's need rather than the respondent's. The interviewer who feels that the respondent is impatient may shorten the questioning to spare himself embarrassment. The timid interviewer, afraid of antagonizing a respondent, may preface a question with "I don't suppose you've thought about . . . " The interviewer who is faced with a highly educated, intelligent respondent may affect a higher level vocabulary than usual because it is important for him to feel that the respondent perceives him as an intellectual equal.

A related error consists in the interviewer's asking the question in a way that incorporates his own opinion of what constitutes an appropriate answer. Suppose that a survey interviewer questioning a poor farmer in a remote area reaches a point on the questionnaire where he is expected to ask about the respondent's current information on problems of controlling monopolies. The interviewer's stereotype of this respondent as a poorly educated, ill-informed person might express itself in a biased wording of the question, such as: "You haven't read any recent material on monopolies, I suppose?" The respondent's picture of the interviewer as a person of superior information could come into play at this point, complementing the bias already initiated, and regardless of his actual level of information, he might well reply, "That's right, I haven't."

Errors in Probing. Errors in probing (that is, supplementing a prepared question during the interview process) can sometimes occur through behaviors more subtle than speech. For example, an interviewer may fail to give a respondent sufficient time and opportunity to answer a question because he is convinced, on the basis of the respondent's background characteristics, that the respondent has little to offer. Probing errors of a more explicit kind can be found in such interviewer comments as "I guess that's all that you wanted to tell me on this subject, hm?"

Still more flagrant is the kind of probe question occasionally used by interviewers who feel they can anticipate in near clairvoyant fashion the answers which the respondent is about to give. It is all too common for interviewers in such circumstances to introduce questions with such phrases as "I suppose you would also agree that . . . " or "I suppose you would feel that . . . " The tendency of the respondent to avoid contradicting the interviewer, especially when the interviewer is perceived as having higher status, makes it likely that the question will result in biased information.

Errors in Recording. The third category of interviewer behaviors leading to bias is errors in recording. The interviewer may simply fail to "hear" a respondent's statement that threatens him or runs counter to his own attitudes, or is contrary to what he expects the respondent to say. Recording errors also occur because of interviewers' tendencies to round out, amplify, or otherwise modify responses. The interviewer may attempt, for instance, to make logical or articulate in his recording an illogical or incomplete response, or even a response which he is convinced the person interviewed was "about to give."

This type of error seems at first glance to be improbable. Yet the experience of many people in working with recorded data and write-ups of interview material confirms the fact that such errors occur all too frequently. It is a common observation that an electronic or other verbatim recording of an interview, or of any other conversation, is characterized by incomplete sentences, thoughts begun but not finished, and the like. The notes of interviewers, experienced and inexperienced, tend to be more finished pieces of composition, with very few incomplete thoughts or sentences. By what process is the raw material of spontaneous answers converted into the finished and relatively complete form of the interviewer's write-up? To the extent that this has been accomplished by careful probe questions and accurate recording, we have gained; to the extent that it is accomplished by the interviewer's own filling in and "improving," we are likely to have a biased report.

Errors in Motivating the Respondent. The last category of interviewer behavior which we want to consider is perhaps so general that it includes much of what has gone before. Almost everything the interviewer does has some bearing on the respondent's motivation to communicate adequately. This motivation, as we have seen, depends upon the ability of the interviewer to create a situation in which the respondent sees frank and full communication as being likely to fulfill his own needs and to contribute to a relationship that acquires value for him in the course of the interview.

A common error in this aspect of interviewing is lack of attention by the interviewer to the motivation of the respondent, with consequent *undermotivation*. In such cases, the respondent may continue the interview, but without that effort and involvement which the objectives require. Either an inadequate job of making the interview meaningful in terms of the respondent's own values and goals, or failure to make the interview experience itself rewarding, can create a situation in which the respondent is not sufficiently motivated to meet the requirements of a successful interview.

Another common error is *inappropriate motivation.* For example, new interviewers, learning of the importance of "rapport," frequently think it implies that interviews are based on a friendship relationship or require a "pally" bridge-club atmosphere. They miss the essential point, that the interviewer-respondent relationship should be based on understanding and acceptance and not on an imitation of friendship. When the interview is based on the latter, the respondent may be motivated to withhold his true feelings if he considers that they will hurt his new friend, or he may distort his own reactions to conform more nearly to what he thinks will please the interviewer.

The motivational demands of interviews vary a great deal, as we saw in Chapter 3. It is possible, therefore, for the interviewer to expend an inappropriately large amount of effort on the motivational aspects of the interview—to press on the respondent lengthy explanations for trivial requests, or to attempt a quasi-therapeutic relationship in order to obtain the answers to questions about trivial or superficial matters. Respondents are quick to sense and to resent the incongruity of such a situation. The more tractable may content themselves with an indication of impatience or a request to "get on with it." Others may refuse the interview.

Another error consists in tapping less desirable motive sources. For example, the interviewer may depend upon the status of his "office" to persuade some respondents to cooperate. We cannot argue that this kind of motivation will give poor results in all cases, but it does tend to emphasize the differences rather than the common interests of interviewer and respondent, and to this extent it makes some kinds of communication more difficult. The same difficulty, in reverse, may occur if the interviewer emphasizes his dependence and subordination. "I don't know what they'll say back at the office if I don't get this interview," the imploring survey interviewer may say. Such an appeal may lead a soft-hearted respondent to permit the interview, but it is not likely to motivate him to work at the job of making it a good one.

The last of the motivational errors frequently encountered in our experience stems from an interviewer's *lack of sensitivity* to the initial situation of the respondent. Basically, the interviewer must sense the respondent's needs, and adapt his efforts to motivate accordingly. He must "pick up the respondent where he is." Respondents will differ in resistance, in their interest in explanations and purposes, and in their need for encouragement and support. The amount of "motivating behavior" by the interviewer that appeals to one may repel another. These kinds of judgments the interviewer must make on the spot, and he must then adapt his behavior accordingly.

THE DYNAMICS OF BIAS

In reviewing some of the research on bias and error in the interview, we have considered the major sources of bias as derived from three factors: background characteristics, psychological attributes, and behavior in the interview itself. The results of such research do not add up to a complete explanation of the dynamics of bias nor to a clear set of instructions for eliminating it. They show that a variety of factors can generate effects which ultimately find their way into the interview product, but how these factors are related and by what paths they reach their effects remain to be determined.

Biasing Factors: A Model

We shall attempt now to put into a single scheme the several levels of bias-generating factors, and to show simultaneously their interrelations and the ways in which they affect the interview. Figure 11 presents a model based on the following assumptions: (1) the interview is an interactive process in which the background characteristics, psychological attributes, and behaviors of both principals are important determinants of the product; (2) interviewer and respondent are perceiving and reacting to the observable background characteristics and specific behaviors of each other.

The first pair of boxes, A_I and A_R (background characteristics), include some of the major attributes which interviewer and respondent bring to the interview situation. These factors are important because they influence behavior through the intervening variables of attitudes, expectations, and motives. In this way they can affect profoundly the results of the interview process. Moreover, background characteristics that are visible must be considered among the major targets for the perceptions and attitudes of the other person in the interview situation, affecting his behavior as well as that of the possessor.

The psychological characteristics of interviewer and respondent that are relevant to the interview appear as boxes B_I and B_R, representing perceptions, attitudes, expectations, and motives. The processes of perception and the formation of attitudes and expectations are of course common to both interviewer and respondent during the interview. It is only through these psychological processes that any factor can find behavioral expression in the interaction process and thus affect the end product of the interview. As we have already pointed out, certain background characteristics and specific acts of behavior can be perceived, and it is from perceptions of these characteristics and behaviors that the interviewer and respondent form attitudes toward and expectations of each other. We are concerned with interviewer and respondent attitudes because attitudes must be regarded as predispositions to behave in a certain fashion, and the behaviors of interviewer and respondent mean the success or failure of the interview process.

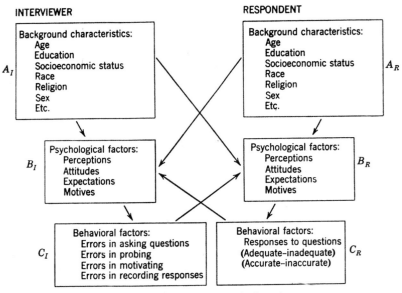

Figure 11. A model of bias in the interview.

This brings us to the pair of boxes C_I and C_R, behavioral factors. The behaviors which these boxes symbolize must be viewed as the resultant of background factors and psychological forces. Moreover, the behaviors of interviewer and respondent in the interview situation represent the major outcome of perceptual processes. During the interview process, each participant obtains from the behavior of the other the cues on which he bases his own behavior.

This figure reveals several attributes of the interaction pattern of the interview that deserve special mention. First, the interconnections of the various boxes in the diagram include no linkage whatsoever between the two boxes labeled behavior. In no instance does behavior of either interviewer or respondent occur merely as a physical reaction to the behavior of the other. The linkage is more complicated, involving a behavior on the part of interviewer or respondent, the perception of this behavior by the other principal in the interview, a cognitive or attitudinal development from that perception, and finally a resulting motivation to behave in a certain way. Only at this point is a behavorial act carried out, which in turn may be perceived by and in similar fashion reacted to by the other participant in the interview.

Each behavior in the interview thus can be traced back, at least in theory, to a perception. But only two categories shown in Figure 11 can be perceived. Each participant in the interview can perceive certain visible background characteristics and specific acts or behaviors on the part of the other. The important psychological factors of perceptions, attitudes, expectations, motivations, cannot be perceived directly, of course, and are inferred only as a result of perceived behavior or background factors. Nor are these inferences necessarily correct. Background characteristics that are perceivable, such as skin color, stature, apparent socioeconomic level, and the like, may lead to quite erroneous inferences regarding attitudes, beliefs, or level of information. In the same way, behaviors are easily misinterpreted and may lead to inferences that are incorrect and disfunctional for the interview process. Nevertheless, respondent and interviewer inevitably make such inferences in the search for cues that will assist them to understand each other and to carry out the requirements which the situation has imposed. Especially in the early moments of the interview, this means that the risks of reaching unwarranted conclusions, because of the fragmentary cues available, are very great.

Interaction and Bias

We need now to relate the foregoing description of respondent and interviewer interaction specifically to the problem of bias, and to illustrate additional ways in which bias may enter into the interview situation. We are approaching bias in interaction terms and defining it as the result of any unplanned or unwanted interaction in the interview situation. Bias is not the intrusion of any interviewer influence whatsoever. It is impossible to conceive of an interview as anything else but a process of interaction, and interaction means by definition that each individual is influencing the other and reacting to the other in a variety of ways. To say, therefore, that we want an interview without interviewer influence is a contradiction in terms. We want the interviewer to control to a considerable extent the subjects on which communication is to take place, and the depth and amount of material communicated. Certain kinds of influence and interaction are necessary and desirable in the interview situation. If the interviewer cannot influence the course of the interaction in these ways, that is, by adequately motivating the respondent, by conveying to him the objectives of the interview, and by guiding him to communicate in the appropriate subject matter areas, a successful interview cannot take place.

But certain other kinds of influences and interaction products are harmful in terms of the interview objectives, are not planned for, and their intrusion constitutes bias. For example, if the interviewer suggests to the respondent by some inadvertent behavior or even by appearance that he is uninterested in or incapable of understanding what the respondent is saying, bias may result. The bias may appear as a reduction in the general flow of communication between respondent and interviewer, or there may be withholding of some specific item of information that the respondent perceives to be beyond the interviewer's range of understanding and acceptance.

Any characteristic of the interviewer which produces this result, whether it is skin color, the act of smoking a cigar in the home of a fastidious respondent, or a brusque or supercilious tone of voice toward an insecure patient, constitutes a biasing factor in the interview. It represents the intrusion of an unwanted influence which will distort or reduce the information required to meet the interview objectives. A doctor who seeks information regarding a patient's symptoms ineptly may get a response that reflects partly the actual symptoms and partly the patient's fear of offending the doctor. In the same way, a public-opinion interviewer who has inadvertently conveyed to a respondent his own hostility toward the United Nations may obtain a response that represents a compromise between the respondent's own feelings of support for this organization and his wish to avoid controversy or to avoid appearing unsophisticated in the eyes of the interviewer. Such influences—unwanted, unplanned, and prejudicial to the objectives of the interview—produce bias.

METHODS OF ELIMINATING BIAS

What are the implications for the interviewer of this analysis of the origins of bias? The practical business of interviewing requires not only that we be able to identify biasing factors when they intrude in the interview, but that we develop techniques that will eliminate or lessen them.

We have seen that it is impracticable to eliminate bias by attempting to eliminate all interaction, because we wish to use the interaction process for the purpose of motivating the respondent to communicate and guiding him with respect to the content areas to be explored. We must find some way to make the most of the wanted aspects of interviewer influence and interaction and at the same time filter out the unwanted factors. Let us turn back to the interactional diagram presented in Figure 11, to consider which of the factors offer most promise for manipulation in order to avoid bias.

In general, the left side of the diagram, representing the attributes and characteristics of the interviewer, is more available for our manipulation than the right, which represents the corresponding characteristics of the respondent. Either we are doing our own interviewing, or the interviewer is ours to select and train. The respondent is accessible to us less directly, that is, only in terms of his reactions to the characteristics and behavior of the interviewer. If the respondent is part of a public-opinion panel, he is likely to be selected on a random basis, without regard to his cooperativeness. In other situations, such as those confronting the doctor, lawyer, or social worker, the respondent is likely to be self-selected. The interviewer, on the other hand, whether he is oneself or one's employee, is accessible for training. There seem to be encouraging possibilities for controlling those factors that are potential sources of bias on the interviewer's side of the diagram. With respect to the respondent's side, we must for the most part accept the fact that we can influence the respondent only by controlling the characteristics and behavior of the interviewer.

Control of Background Factors

Such characteristics as age, sex, education, race, religion, and socioeconomic status can be influenced, for the most part, only by the process of selection. It is quite possible to change the way an interviewer behaves during an interview, or even to change some of his attitudes toward his role. But it is impossible to bring about changes in background characteristics by training or by practice. There are some cases where the subject matter of the interview, or the intensity of respondent attitudes which the interview is likely to call forth, may require us to choose interviewers with certain background characteristics.

We cited earlier the research findings by Hyman to the effect that Negro and white interviewers obtain different information from identical respondents when questioning them about racial problems. The race of the interviewer appears to be the only factor that could account for the results which Hyman[25] obtained. Therefore, if we want

---

[25] Herbert H. Hyman et al., Interviewing for Social Research.

to conduct a field study which involves interviewing white respondents to determine their attitudes toward Negroes, we will be well advised to use only white interviewers. Conversely, if our objective is to determine attitudes of Negroes toward racial problems, we should limit ourselves to the selection of Negro interviewers.

Fortunately, experience and research indicate that for most subjects on which interviews are conducted the range of acceptable background characteristics is wide. The effects of divergence of background characteristics between interviewer and respondent can usually be overcome if the interviewer has adequate interviewing skills and is able to demonstrate that he can understand and communicate with the respondent.

The Survey Research Center, as part of its program of studying human relations in industry, often conducts personal interviews with samples of workers in industrial plants. Since the Center has more women than men on its interviewing staff, there is reason for using women interviewers in this work. The question was raised as to whether a woman could successfully interview industrial workers about their experiences on the job. Many managements felt that women interviewers would be unsuccessful. Their reaction was based on the assumption that workers would feel that the women, having had no industrial experience, would be unable to understand their work problems and that the men would not be willing to communicate with them.

Experience indicated that this was not the case. An analysis of the results of these interviews showed that the volume and content of the information obtained by the women interviewers did not differ from that obtained by experienced male interviewers. The fact that the women were skilled at their own job, and that they could convey to the men their interest in and understanding of job problems, overcame any initial resistance which might have existed.

We would like, at this point, to present a set of rules for determining when background factors are important as sources of bias and when they can be overcome by skilled technique. Unfortunately, this cannot be done; research findings on this problem are still meager. They do, however, support the idea that proper training can overcome many of the potential biasing effects of interviewer background characteristics. Experience shows that the atmosphere which the interviewer sets for the interview process, his reactions to the expressed attitudes of the respondent, and his technical skill are in most cases far more important than his background characteristics. These characteristics have importance primarily in that they affect first impressions, while the basic skills of the interviewer have deeper and more enduring effects upon the interviewer-respondent relationship, and therefore on the product of the interview. Earlier, we summed up the relevance of background characteristics of the interviewer by saying that a wide variety of background characteristics is admissible in most situations, and that to initiate the process of communication, it is necessary only that the interviewer be perceived as "within range."

The lists of "dos and don'ts" regarding dress, appearance, manner, language, and the like, that are frequently found in interviewing manuals usually have as their sole purpose helping the interviewer cloak his background characteristics sufficiently to avoid creating undesirable first impressions.

It is fortunate that the range of background characteristics permissible for the interviewer is broad, because interviews must often take place between individuals of quite different backgrounds in situations difficult to predict and control. It would be unfortunate if the physician were able to conduct a successful diagnostic interview only with individuals of specific background characteristics. The physician must proceed on the assumption (and so must his patients) that he can function successfully regardless of the background characteristics of individuals who seek his help. To some extent, of course, the clientele of any professional man has selected him on the basis of cues that include certain of his background characteristics. The fact remains, however, that doctors, lawyers, and people in many other professions do not select their respondents for their background characteristics, and that they must be able to interview successfully people of a wide variety of backgrounds.

Control of Psychological Factors

Let us consider now the psychological factors operating on the part of the interviewer, and the ways in which these factors can be modified or controlled for the purpose of avoiding bias in the interview. Basically, the problem here is to keep the attitudes and expectations of the interviewer from affecting his behavior in such a way as to introduce bias. The specific ways in which such bias is most frequently introduced are through the use of supplementary or probe questions by the interviewer, and through the recording or transcribing of material given him by the respondent. If the interviewer has concluded, because of his impressions of the respondent, that the answer to a particular question is likely to be negative, he may formulate a supplementary question in a way that makes it easier for the respondent to answer in a negative fashion. He may even record the negative response without actually obtaining it, convinced at the time that the respondent was about to give such an answer, and perhaps convinced subsequently that the answer was actually given.

To eliminate interviewer attitudes as sources of bias involves either changing the attitudes themselves, or devising some way of rendering them inoperative in the interview situation—that is, formulating a set of procedures and developing skills that will prevent the interviewer's attitudes toward the respondent from manifesting themselves. We cannot suspend the attitudinal and perceptual processes of the interviewer for the duration of the interview, and we would not even if we could. We need him to be as sensitive and perceptive an individual as it is possible for him to be. We require, however, that this sensitivity and perceptivity be exercised in his *role* as an interviewer, and in relation to the respondent as a *respondent*, not as a good or bad, likable or repulsive individual.

The interviewer's perceptions and sensitivities must be oriented toward the maintenance and enhancement of the relationship between himself and the respondent, and toward the fullness and adequacy of the responses in relation to his interviewing objectives. In his role as interviewer, he is not concerned with questions of agreement or disagreement with the respondent's sentiments; he is not concerned with the social and political implications of the information he is receiving; he is not concerned with moral issues which might be raised by the content of the interview. He is, in the interviewer role, essentially nonevaluative in his reactions to the content of the interview. He is, for the period of the interview, amoral in this sense.

If the demands of the interviewer role are as specific and as taxing as we have just indicated, it is clear that getting the interviewer to understand and accept the requirements of this role is of cardinal importance to his successful performance. We demand of the interviewer that he acquire the ability to get "in role" during the interviewing process, even if this requires him to compartmentalize or wall off many of the viewpoints and attitudes which he holds as an individual or a citizen. The techniques that we recommend to the interviewer are designed to aid him in playing his role successfully, and to provide a certain margin of safety at those moments in the interview when his ability to remain "in role" might otherwise wear thin.

The concept of the individual's "putting aside" his own attitudes when he assumes a professional role is familiar to all of us. We expect that a physician who is in private life a strong advocate of temperance can nevertheless treat an alcoholic patient successfully, and will be able to elicit from such a patient the facts regarding his experiences and behaviors that will facilitate treatment. We expect that the physician will be able to do this without indicating to the patient any revulsion he may feel regarding overindulgence in liquor, and we recognize that if such an attitude were communicated from physician to patient, it might very well lead the patient to withhold information of crucial importance to the physician in his role as healer. We expect the lawyer to be able to question a new client objectively without exercising his personal moral judgment in the process. We expect a nurse to be able to attend a patient without showing the revulsion or pity she may feel. Behavior in the professional role requires the suppression of personal feelings or beliefs during the exercise of the professional function.

These examples have important characteristics in common with the interviewer's situation. We require individuals to behave in certain ways when they are in the interviewer role. To function effectively, they require a theory and a concept of the role which they are playing as interviewers, and a knowledge and understanding of the specific skills and requirements which this role demands of them. They must then devote to the effective playing of this role the effort, skill, and training that it requires.

SUMMARY

Our purposes in this chapter have been to indicate some of the problems of achieving accuracy in the personal interview, to indicate the extent to which the interview product can be damaged by biasing factors, and to explain the ways in which such factors may enter into the interview process. To achieve these purposes, we have offered a conceptual scheme of the major kinds of factors that are potential sources of bias in the interview, and of the dynamic processes by which such factors may influence the interaction between interviewer and respondent, and thus affect the ultimate product of the interview.

The ample literature on the effects of bias on interview results emphasizes the importance of providing the interviewer with techniques adequate to achieve his purposes of motivating the respondent to communicate and controlling the content of that communication in order to meet interview objectives, and achieving these functions without the intrusion of bias. Only by so doing can he expect to obtain accurate information.

But as we have seen, there are many doors by which bias may enter the interview situation. There is no simple "anti-bias" device or procedure which the interviewer can be taught to use. The problem of avoiding bias is encountered not only at the moment of the interview itself, but at the earlier stages when questions are being formulated, when techniques for probing or asking supplementary questions are being decided upon, when methods of introduction and procedures for motivating the respondent are being devised.

The techniques and procedures described in earlier chapters, for achieving respondent motivation, formulating questions, probing, and so forth, have been chosen and developed because they offer minimum tendencies toward bias, as well as because they achieve the positive functions of data collection. In Chapter 3, for example, techniques are described for motivating the respondent to communicate. It is quite possible that under certain circumstances the motivating power of this kind of benign, neutral approach might be less than that of a strong expression of support and agreement on the part of the interviewer. But such expressions by the interviewer would tend to give the respondent the impression that certain kinds of attitudes or responses were more acceptable to the interviewer and more praiseworthy than others, and the remainder of the interview might well include attempts on the part of the respondent to win additional praise from the interviewer by exaggerating certain kinds of attitudes or behaviors and minimizing others.

What does the interviewer require in order to function effectively and without bias? We have answered this question by saying that he requires techniques for question formulation, for inducing respondent motivation, and for focusing the communication on the content objectives of the interview. We believe, however, that the interviewer needs also a deep understanding and insight into the dynamics of the interaction process of which he is to be a part. The interview process itself is complex, and each case sufficiently idiosyncratic so that no set of rules and procedures will suffice unless the interviewer has such insight into the psychology of the interaction. For this reason we have emphasized, throughout this book, the importance of a theory of interviewing, the importance of the dynamics of the interview process, and of the psychological forces which are active in that process.

Finally, in addition to insight, understanding, and adequate procedures, the interviewer requires training and practice in the use of his acquired skills in order to achieve a level of real proficiency. Chapter 9 discusses some of the techniques by which interviewing skills can be learned, but these skills are of course almost impossible to extract from a book alone. Finally, study of the last section of this book, which consists of transcripts of actual interviews with accompanying critical analyses of the interviewer-respondent interaction, will assist materially in learning the actual skills of interviewing.

chapter 8

Probing to Meet Objectives

In this chapter we will consider one of the most demanding and challenging of the interviewer's functions—probing to meet interview objectives. In spite of the care with which the interviewer has worded a question, the initial response may not be complete or may not be adequate to meet the specific objective for which it was devised. What can the interviewer do to encourage the respondent to amplify and expand his remarks? How can the interviewer provide this stimulation and guidance without biasing the responses?

A Problem in Interviewing Technique

Robert Case, the director of the Lakeside Hospital, is extremely interested in developing the best possible community reputation for his hospital service. It occurs to him that one way to approach this goal might be to find out from each departing patient how he feels about the quality of service. The director has heard, in indirect ways, that some patients have been rather vociferous in their criticisms of the hospital after they returned home. Mr. Case doesn't flinch from criticism himself, and he has the idea that the whole staff might benefit from knowing the sources of patients' dissatisfaction. If, on the other hand, patients are well pleased, this also is information he needs to have.

Thinking about ways of getting such information without launching a full-scale research project, the hospital director decides that a question or two about each patient's reactions to hospital service might be included as part of the ceremony of departure, which now involves the return of clothes

203

and valuables and the paying of the medical bill. Acting on this notion, he tells his cashiers that, as the bill is paid and the patient is signed out of the hospital, they should ask about the patient's reaction to his hospital experience. In order to make sure that the answers will be generally comparable, Mr. Case writes out the question which is to be used: "How do you feel about the service here at the hospital?"

A day or two later, in order to determine how his new plan is proceeding, he takes a seat in the cashiers' office, where he is within easy earshot of the three cashiers at their wickets.

One of the first conversations between a cashier and a patient goes as follows.

CASHIER: Well, Mr. Williams, you must be glad to be ready to go home. I'd like to ask you how you feel about the service here at the hospital.
PATIENT: Oh, it was O.K. Where's my receipt?
CASHIER: Here's your receipt, sir. We're very glad that you found the service satisfactory and liked it here.

The hospital administrator finds himself wondering whether Mr. Williams really found the service satisfactory or whether his hurried "It was O.K." was simply a means of getting his receipt promptly and getting on his way. At this point Mr. Case hears a second cashier asking the same question.

CASHIER: So you're ready to go home, Mr. MacAdam. How did you feel about the service here at the hospital?
PATIENT: Well, I was only here a day. I really wouldn't know.
CASHIER: Well, it's true you were here a short time, but tell me just generally, was it good or bad?
PATIENT: Good or bad? I'd say good.

The director listens now to a third cashier-patient conversation.

CASHIER: Would you please tell me how you feel about the service at the hospital?
PATIENT: There's one thing I want to know. Why is it that I couldn't get a cup of coffee except at meal time? Will you tell me that?
CASHIER: Well, I'm very sorry that you found the service unsatisfactory in any way. But you know how it is, we have a great many meals to serve and prepare, and if we tried to serve snacks between meals or do much in the way of individual menus, it would just take more time and cost more money than anyone would think reasonable. You understand, don't you?
PATIENT: Well, I understand that, but I still don't see why a person can't get a cup of coffee.

The last of the cashier interviewers Mr. Case observes follows a different pattern.

CASHIER: Well, Mr. Riley, we're glad to see that you're getting along so well. Before you leave, would you mind telling us how you feel about the service here at the hospital?
PATIENT: Well, it's kind of a mixed picture. Some was very good and some things were not so good.

CASHIER: I see. Can you tell me which things you liked and which you thought were not so good?

PATIENT: Well, I thought the nursing was excellent. The nurses seem to take a personal interest in you, and there was just no time of the day or night when I needed help and couldn't get it. That means a lot to a person when he's sick, you know. But some of the other services weren't really up to nursing. The food comes in cold from having stood around on these wagons they use, and I don't really think it was too appetizing even when it was hot. There's one other thing, too, that I ought to mention. I know that they can't bring up the X-rays and all the other special equipment to each patient's bedside, but I do think that they ought to schedule things so that a person who is still weak and sick doesn't have to sit around for a half hour or an hour on a hard bench waiting for an X-ray. That's pretty tough.

Mr. Case returns to his office and tries to think through the implications of what he has just heard. His thoughts run somewhat along these lines: "That last patient really told us the kind of thing that we need to know. Our hospital service could be a lot better if we got that sort of information from all our patients. But the other three didn't say much. Now why was it that of four patients who were asked the same question, only one of them really gave us the information we needed? Didn't the first three have anything to say? I'm not really convinced of that. I think maybe if they had been given the right kind of encouragement or direction, we could have learned something from every one of them. Maybe it was the particular cashier. Is there something about her personality or approach to people that gets results when the others can't? No, I don't think it's that. There must be some way by which we could make sure that every cashier every time would encourage each patient to give us all the information he can. Having them all ask the same question may be a step in the right direction, but it obviously isn't enough. I've got to think through what else we need to do."

CONTROLLED NONDIRECTIVE PROBING

The hospital director's problem is the one which will concern us in this chapter. He has discovered, as he himself says, that there is more to the job of interviewing than asking a specific question and recording the answer. A major part of the interviewer's job involves the use of techniques to focus and control the interaction after a primary question, in order that the objectives of the question will be met adequately.[1] This aspect of the interviewer's role is most demanding. When we say that an interviewer is skillful, we usually mean that he is adept at this part of his job.

Our immediate problem is to describe a general technique which

---

[1] By *primary question* we mean any question which introduces a new topic or asks for new content. *Secondary questions* (or probes), by contrast, are intended to elicit more fully the information already asked for by a primary question.

the interviewer can employ in the data-collection interview in order to evoke adequate responses. What should such a technique accomplish? First, it must enable the interviewer to motivate additional communication on the required topic. Second, it must enhance, or at least maintain, the interpersonal relationship between respondent and interviewer. Third, it must accomplish both these purposes without introducing bias or modifying the meaning of the primary questions. We need a technique which the interviewer can use when necessary in order to get the respondent to talk more, to talk in the relevant subject-matter area, and to do so without being influenced by the interviewer's attitudes in this same area.

Supplementing the Primary Question

In the following uncomplicated examples, the use of brief assenting comments, well-timed pauses, or simple encouraging requests for more information stimulate communication without introducing bias and without damaging the interviewer-respondent relationship.

Example 1

PHYSICIAN: Well, Mrs. Jones, tell me how you've been feeling since our last visit.
PATIENT: Not so well, doctor.
PHYSICIAN: Um-hm.
PATIENT: My appetite's not very good.
PHYSICIAN: I see.
PATIENT: I set down to a meal and nothing tastes good. (Pause.)
PHYSICIAN: Tell me more about it.
PATIENT: I eat so little I haven't any strength left.
PHYSICIAN: Um-hm.

Example 2

SOCIAL WORKER: You say you want to adopt a child. What kind of child were you thinking about?
RESPONDENT: Well, I don't really have too strong an idea on that. (Social worker waits patiently and expectantly, her eyes on the respondent, says nothing.)
RESPONDENT: I think we'd like a young baby, if we could get one. You know, one under six months. (Pause.)
SOCIAL WORKER: I see.
RESPONDENT: And I wouldn't want a baby that was sick or going to be dumb. (Long pause.)
(Social worker waits, in a relaxed fashion, apparently confident that there is more to come and that the respondent will resume when she wishes.)
RESPONDENT: I—that is we—wouldn't want one that's of a different race, that's . . . well, colored.

These examples illustrate three very useful and common ways of supplementing a primary question. The first is a *brief assertion of understanding and interest.* The "I see" and "um-hm" indicate to the respondent that he is communicating but has not yet given a complete response. A motion picture of the interview would show the interviewer nodding his head and giving other postural indications of interest and acceptance, in addition to his verbal responses.

The second example illustrates the use of the *pause,* which is the simplest and often the most effective way of encouraging communication. The novice interviewer is particularly conscious of silence, and he feels impelled to fill the quiet intervals himself. This may be ill-advised. The interviewer needs to be sensitive to the respondent's posture, facial reactions, and other cues in order to differentiate a "pregnant pause" from an "embarrassed silence." In many cases silence means that the respondent is thinking and considering how to respond further. Such a pause is fruitful and helps the interviewer-respondent relationship. The silence which comes when the respondent is truly "out of ideas" is embarrassing and is not conducive to an optimum relationship.

The third kind of supplementary device is illustrated in the foregoing examples when the doctor says, "Tell me more about it." There are many *neutral phrases* which can often be used to obtain a fuller, clearer response:

How do you mean?
I'd like to know more about your thinking on that.
What do you have in mind there?
I'm not sure I understand what you have in mind.
Why do you think that is so?
Why do you feel that way?
What do you think causes that?
Do you have any other reasons for feeling as you do?
Anything else?

Statements such as these indicate interest and make a direct bid for more information. Their successful use requires that the interviewer recognize promptly just how the respondent's answer has failed to meet the objective of the primary question. The interviewer must then formulate a neutral question or comment that will be appropriate to elicit the information he needs. As with the other kinds of supplementary questions, the manner of asking is at least as important as the wording. A harsh demand for clarification, with the implication that the initial response was unsatisfactory and the respondent inadequate, would handicap the rest of the interview. The same question asked quietly, and with the implication that the interviewer wants to understand fully and is concerned that he may not have done so, usually will arouse the respondent's desire to cooperate. The term which we will use for all such interviewer pauses, comments, and secondary questions is *probe*. This term differentiates the spontaneous, purposeful supplementary comments from primary questions. The probe, as the name implies, is a stimulus to further communication on the part of the respondent.

Origins of Nondirective Technique

The techniques of probing which are the subject of this chapter can be described as "controlled nondirective." By controlled nondirective probing we refer to a process which not only stimulates additional communication from the respondent, but does so in ways consistent with the basic approach to motivation and measurement in the interview developed throughout this book. Serving this process, probes have two major functions to perform:

(1) To motivate the respondent to communicate more fully—amplify his previous statement, clarify what he has said, or give the reasons or context out of which his statement developed. This motivating aspect of the interviewer's role was discussed first in Chapter 3, although at that time we were concerned with supplementary questions and comments only insofar as they provided a basis for an accepting, permissive relationship between interviewer and respondent.

(2) To control the interaction between interviewer and respondent by focusing it on the content objective of the interview. Probing thus serves to increase the efficiency and effectiveness of the interaction by instructing the respondent as to what is relevant and irrelevant, thereby reducing or eliminating the communication of material which would not serve the purposes for which the interview was initiated.

It is not enough, however, that the probe question should perform the two functions just described. A third requirement, equally important, is that the probe question accomplish these results without the introduction of any unplanned or unwanted influence into the interview; that is, it must not produce bias. It must increase the motivation of the respondent and focus the interaction on the content objectives of the interview, and must do so without suggesting to the respondent that one or another point of view is more acceptable to the interviewer, that one answer is right and another wrong, or that any relevant material need be withheld for any reason.

In naming this technique *controlled nondirective probing*, we are borrowing one of the concepts of Carl R. Rogers.[2]   He originated the term nondirective to describe certain aspects of client-centered therapy.   The client-centered therapist remains nondirective in the sense that he does not take the responsibility for deciding the topics to be discussed, the goals which the client should seek to attain, or the solutions to problems which the client brings up.   These are seen as necessarily the responsibility of the client, and it is the function of the therapist to help him assume these responsibilities.

In short, the client must determine the topics to be discussed at any given time.   He must determine also the manner in which these topics are to be explored.   These things the client *must* do because the therapist refuses to accept these responsibilities for him.   These things the client is *enabled* to do because the therapist provides an atmosphere of acceptance and permissiveness that gives the security and safety which the client requires.

Let us contrast this situation with that of the information-getting interviewer and his respondent.   The respondent in an information-getting interview cannot choose the topics to be discussed.   In the research interview the respondent will not even know the topics to be discussed until the interviewer communicates them to him.   When a patient approaches a doctor or a client approaches a lawyer, he takes the initiative in the beginning by introducing the problem or question that has led him to seek advice.   Once he has done this, however, the choice of specific topics to be explored or objectives to be covered becomes the function of the interviewer because of his expertness in the field of discussion.   The topics to be discussed in an information-getting interview are set by the content objectives of the interview.   They cannot be determined by the respondent during the course of the interview itself.   Moreover, the interviewer in the information-getting situation not only must accept the responsibility for being sure that the interview includes the topics necessary to his content objectives, but in the interests of efficiency he must also attempt to limit the extraneous topics into which the interview may ramble.   It is in this sense that the interaction in an information-getting interview is controlled, and it is for this reason that we have referred to our technique as controlled nondirective probing.

Once the topics to be discussed have been specified, however, the technique of the information-getting interviewer becomes in many ways comparable to that of the client-centered therapist.   Within the

---

[2] *Client-Centered Therapy* (1951) and *Counseling and Psychotherapy* (1942), Houghton Mifflin, Boston.

topic dictated by a given content objective, the information-getting interviewer permits the respondent to communicate material at his own pace and in his own way. Like the therapist, the interviewer is permissive and accepting, regardless of the point of view or values indicated in the responses.

Properly used, controlled nondirective techniques fulfill adequately the previously stated requirement for successful probes; that is, they motivate the respondent to communicate more fully, and they control the interaction between interviewer and respondent by focusing it on the question objectives. The techniques serve the dual purpose of motivating and measuring.

To the extent that the interviewer uses probes properly, the interaction is not biased. But the potentiality for bias is great. If, instead of motivating the respondent to amplify his responses in a nondirective manner, the interviewer suggests even to the slightest degree that certain responses are more acceptable than others, or if he hints at what the respondent might wish to include in his remarks, those probes are biased. The result of biased or directive probes is that the attitudes and opinions obtained in the interview are not truly the respondent's but reflect to some extent the respondent's reactions to the inadvertently expressed ideas of the interviewer.

In the terms used in our discussion of bias in Chapter 7, such probes introduce unwanted influence into the interaction between interviewer and respondent. Suppose that the social worker in Example 2 of this section, after the respondent stated that she didn't "really have too strong an idea" about what kind of a child she wanted to adopt, had said, "It wouldn't make too much difference how old the child was, then?" This probe would have informed the respondent that more information was required, but it would also have directed her to talk about age rather than health or race. Still less desirable, it might have suggested to the respondent that the social worker thought adoptive parents should not insist on a child of any certain age. For these reasons, and because the respondent might have felt that agreeing with the social worker was necessary for favorable consideration in adoption, this probe could have influenced the content and direction of the response, and we would consider it biased in spite of its effectiveness in stimulating communication.

The Summary Technique

In addition to the several ways of supplementing primary questions which we have already illustrated, there is a kind of nondirective probe that depends upon summarizing or reflecting the feeling which the respondent is expressing. This type of probe comes directly from the field of psychotherapy, where it is used extensively to assist the patient to examine his own attitudes as a basis for self-insight. The interviewer mirrors the patient's attitudes so that he can see himself better. The use of such probes is also appropriate in the information-getting interview when we want the respondent to explore his attitudes at greater length or depth. The three examples which follow illustrate the use of the summary and reflection of attitudes in a medical, an employment, and a survey interview.

Example 1

PATIENT: I just don't know. I've been taking these treatments for near to six months now and I don't seem to be getting any better.
PHYSICIAN: You don't see any improvement.
PATIENT: Heck no! I'm so dragged out all the time, I can't get going. I don't know. My treatments don't make me feel any better.
PHYSICIAN: You wonder whether it's worthwhile continuing the treatments.
PATIENT: Yes, frankly I do. Seems like if they were going to help me they would have done so before now. (Pause.) I wonder whether there is—whether *any* treatments will help.
PHYSICIAN: Wondering that must worry you.
PATIENT: Gosh, doc, tell me the truth now. Do you really think I'm going to get better or—or—I'm so worried I can't even sleep nights!

Example 2

EMPLOYMENT INTERVIEWER: What kind of work are you doing on your present job? Let's see, that's with the Blank Company, isn't it?
JOB APPLICANT: Yeah, I've worked for them for two years and I'm fed up.
INTERVIEWER: You want to leave them.
APPLICANT: I sure do. I'm the newest girl there, and I get all the junk to do that nobody else wants.
INTERVIEWER: You get the dregs, eh?
APPLICANT: I really do. I didn't mind at first, but I think now I can do much more than I have a chance to do there.
INTERVIEWER: Tell me what you have in mind.
APPLICANT: Well, one thing, I don't get a chance to use my shorthand. I don't take more than one letter a week. Most of my work is just typing reports with hundreds of tables and charts.
INTERVIEWER: You feel that you can do higher level work.
APPLICANT: I went to business school to be a secretary, and on my present job I don't have a chance.
INTERVIEWER: You'd like a secretarial job with more shorthand, is that it?
APPLICANT: Yes, I sure would. Do you have any secretarial jobs here?

Example 3

SURVEY INTERVIEWER: The next question I have here is about the United Nations. How do you feel about the way the U.N. is working out?
RESPONDENT: Boy, that's a big order. (Pause.) Well, frankly, I had great

hopes for the U.N. when it started. I thought maybe it was the answer to world peace, but now I don't know.
INTERVIEWER: You feel some doubts about it now.
RESPONDENT: Yes, I do. But I think it has done some good, too, and we should keep on trying to make it work.
INTERVIEWER: You feel it has done some good.
RESPONDENT: Oh, definitely. Particularly in the economic field. It has helped backward countries to improve their conditions. And I think it would have been a worse mess in Korea if the U.N. hadn't acted.
INTERVIEWER: So in some ways the U.N. is working out well, but in general not as well as you had hoped.
RESPONDENT: That's it exactly.

In these examples we have seen several uses of the interviewer's summary and reflection of respondent attitudes. Probes of this type convey permissiveness and acceptance of the respondent and his feelings, and in addition they stimulate further communication.[3] The summary probe lets the respondent hear succinctly from the interviewer what he has been struggling to say himself. In the process, he comes to understand better the implications of the material which he has been communicating. If the respondent finds that the reflection does not represent accurately or completely the meaning he wants to convey, he is then in a position to make modifications.

There is no doubt that this kind of probe question, when used adeptly, is extremely effective in stimulating communication and in assisting the respondent to formulate more accurately his feelings and opinions. Such a question can also serve the purpose of leading a respondent to a more frank communication of material which he has been handling in a rather defensive fashion. More directly and more effectively than any other kind of supplementary question, the summary or reflecting probe tells the respondent that he has been understood and accepted.

Summarizing a respondent's attitude or feeling is difficult, however, and demands a great deal of insight and ingenuity. The risks inherent in this technique are relatively great, and the interviewer should be well aware of them. Perhaps the most obvious danger is that the interviewer's own opinions will be included inadvertently in his attempt to summarize the respondent's attitudes. The respondent may accept the summary as accurate, rather than contradict the interviewer by denying its accuracy.

---

[3] See the supervisor-subordinate interview, Chapter 12 of this book, for a further example of the summary probe (I-14). The interviewer is able to sum up in a single statement the feeling which the respondent has been expressing in several preceding responses.

On the other hand, if the interviewer presents the summary probe in a form which the respondent is unable to accept as an accurate reflection of his own statements or feelings, his next response may be defensive. He may launch a kind of digressive argument with the interviewer as to what the respondent has really been saying. Such digressions are costly both in terms of inefficiency and in terms of a worsened relationship between interviewer and respondent. In addition, they are likely to result in bias, since the respondent's defensiveness often leads to distortion or concealment of information.

The effective use of the summary technique, therefore, requires that the interviewer be sufficiently quick and sensitive to formulate statements which the respondent can accept as accurately reflecting his own earlier responses, which he is then led to evaluate and either reinforce or modify. The interviewer must convey by manner and wording the impression that he is trying to understand the respondent's views and insure the accuracy of his representation of them, and not that he is expressing disbelief or attempting to trap the respondent in an extreme statement.

Formulating Appropriate Probe Questions

The preceding excerpts illustrate several kinds of probe questions without considering the alternative questions which the interviewer might have chosen. Since probing is a technique rather than a question or even an array of questions, it follows that experience and sensitivity rather than rules and rote phrases will determine the interviewer's success. The following three examples of alternative probe questions may help in the acquisition of skills and make clear some of the differences between adequate and inadequate probes.

Example 1. The first example presents the case of a survey interviewer who is working on the specific objective of learning what durable-goods purchases a householder has in mind for the coming year. This is an example of probing for factual information.

INTERVIEWER: What durable goods are you planning to buy in the coming year?

HOUSEHOLDER: Well, we're planning to buy a sewing machine next week.

This appears to be a valid response, as far as it goes, but the sewing machine may not be the only durable-goods purchase which this householder plans to make in the coming year. Therefore, the interviewer needs to devise probe questions that will ascertain whether or not the respondent plans to buy other durables. Here are some probes which an interviewer might use to obtain more information:

1. Are you planning to buy a TV set too?
2. You mean you aren't going to buy anything *else* but the sewing machine?
3. We find that people in your financial class often buy several kinds of durable goods during the year. Aren't you planning to buy anything else?
4. Are you planning to buy anything else?
5. I see. Do you have anything else in mind?

Consider the strengths and weaknesses of these probe questions. The major disadvantage of the first question is that it limits the respondent's frame of reference to a single purchase item. If the interviewer wanted to give equal attention to all durable goods, which the objective of the question requires, he would be faced with the necessity of asking a comparable question for every item in the durable goods field—a practical impossibility. The effect of the question, therefore, is to draw the attention of the respondent to a particular class of durable-goods purchases. The predictable result of such a line of questioning would be that the survey findings would show an overestimation of future television purchases relative to expected purchases of other durable goods.

Probe question 2 is the kind of question which can mean much or little, depending on the inflection. The implication of the question clearly is that the interviewer is skeptical of the respondent's first answer. The question suggests either that the respondent has not answered as fully as he should and that the interviewer is criticizing him, or that the respondent must indeed be in unfortunate circumstances. The probable effect of this question, like the first one, is biasing, but the bias is likely to be of a different sort. In this case the respondent is not led to reply in terms of any particular goods, but he may be led to an overstatement of his intended purchases. Moreover, the effect of this question on the interviewer-respondent relationship is likely to be damaging, since the respondent may well feel that the interviewer is either skeptical or supercilious.

Probe question 3 presents the problem of the previous question in an aggravated form. The respondent is left with the alternative of adding to his intended purchases, perhaps imaginatively, or of confessing that he is somehow a deviant member of the social group in which the interviewer has placed him. Again, we have an interaction that is likely to lead to resentment on the part of the respondent and consequent damage to the interviewer-respondent relationship, as well as the danger of an inflated statement of intended purchases.

Questions 4 and 5 are acceptable nondirective probes. These questions tell the respondent that mentioning a sewing-machine purchase is not necessarily a complete answer to the question, nor a fulfillment of his role as respondent. Further communication is desired of him. There is no suggestion, however, that this further response should take the form of listing additional purchases. Instead, the respondent is offered, by implication, either of two equally acceptable alternatives. He can indicate additional purchases, if he is planning them, or he can indicate that he plans to make no further purchases. The net effect of this probe is to elicit further information and, in addition, to teach the respondent his role by letting him know that the objective is to ascertain all the purchases he is planning. These supplemental questions are permissive and enhance the interviewer-respondent relationship.

Example 2. As a second example of the problem of stimulating complete responses, consider the case of a lawyer who is attempting to obtain information from a witness to an automobile accident. This involves an effort to get relevant legal facts in an informal interview outside a courtroom.

ATTORNEY: You mentioned that you saw an accident at the corner of Main Street and Third Avenue last Tuesday, I believe. Will you tell me what happened?
RESPONDENT: Well, this car came around the corner and hit this man.

This terse response obviously leaves the attorney with any number of unanswered questions. Here are some of the supplementary questions he might be led to ask:

1. How fast was the car going?
2. Where was the man?
3. Whose fault was it?
4. I'd like to get as complete a picture as I can of just what you saw and heard. Why don't you take your time and tell me everything that you remember, just as it happened?

Consider the advantages and disadvantages of these supplementary questions. The first two questions have in common the problem that they direct the respondent's attention to a specific aspect of the accident, and they do so inappropriately early in the interview. It is entirely possible that at some later moment the attorney might find it necessary to direct the respondent's attention to some specific points. In this case, however, the attorney would be directing the respondent's attention to problems of speed and position before getting the general picture of what the witness saw.

The third question has the more obvious defect of asking the respondent to make a conjecture or draw a conclusion from facts that have not yet been ascertained. Again, this is a question that under different circumstances or perhaps later in the same interview might be entirely appropriate.

The fourth probe question has the advantage of instructing the respondent in a way that indicates clearly the lawyer's interest in getting a full and complete response. Moreover, it tells the respondent that a literal statement of what was seen and heard, rather than any judgments or conclusions, is required in order to meet the interviewer's objectives. Within these limits the respondent is invited to speak from his own frame of reference and in his own terms.

Example 3. As a third example of probing techniques, imagine an interview taking place between an applicant for a factory job and a personnel interviewer.

INTERVIEWER: What kind of job do you think you're qualified for?
RESPONDENT: Well, I can run a lathe.

This remark on the respondent's part might be met by any one of the following comments:

1. We have no opening for lathe hands just now, but we do need someone to run a boring mill. Can you do that?
2. Everyone who comes in here says he can run a lathe, and I'm always suspicious of that answer. What makes you think you can run one?
3. Tell me something about your experience on a lathe.
4. I see. Do you have any other kinds of work experience?

The first probe question suffers mainly from the fact that it is leading and therefore likely to produce a biased response. A job applicant who is highly motivated to obtain a position is told that no job is available for his particular skill, but that a job is available for another, somewhat related skill. The forces on the respondent to invent some experience on a boring mill, in case he has none, would be extreme, and the validity of his response would be accordingly decreased.

The second probe is hostile in its approach, since it tells the respondent almost explicitly that his statement is not believed. The most likely prediction would be that the respondent would rise to the bait, first by overstating his experience in an attempt to impress an unfriendly and hostile interviewer, and second by behaving for the rest of the interview in a defensive or hostile fashion. Our placement interviewer is likely to have a difficult time getting statements of objective fact.

Probes 3 and 4 are both satisfactory as far as the interview process is concerned. They serve the proper functions of nondirective probing. They reorient the respondent to the interviewer's objectives, and they instruct him as to the subject he should talk about, without giving him clues to what he should say about it. The request, "Tell me something about your lathe experience," indicates to the respondent that his previous statement has been accepted and that the interviewer is sufficiently interested in it to want an elaboration. The other probe—"I see. Do you have any other kinds of work experience?"—also indicates the acceptance of the statement about having lathe experience, and then shifts to a clearly related although different subject. It is entirely likely that in any comprehensive job interview both these kinds of questions would be asked at some time in the course of the discussion, and it is optional with the interviewer whether he chooses to develop fully each kind of job experience, or prefers to get the broad outlines of job experience first and then develop details.

THE INADEQUATE RESPONSE

Despite the obvious differences among the preceding examples they have a common characteristic. In each case, the respondent replied to a question in a way which the interviewer judged to be inadequate. Inadequacy of response is the common denominator of all situations that necessitate probing, or the formulation of secondary questions. If the primary interview questions are successful in evoking adequate responses, probe questions are superfluous. The purpose of each probe or series of probes is to transform an inadequate response into one that meets the interview objectives.

How this is done will vary, of course. A probe must be tailored to fit the type of response inadequacy, and to take account also of the probable causes of the inadequacy. In the remainder of this chapter, we will discuss in sequence the symptoms or kinds of inadequate responses, the underlying causes for these symptoms, and (by example) the appropriate probing technique to resolve such problems.

Symptoms of Inadequate Response

Partial Response. This is one of the simpler types of response inadequacy with which the interviewer has to cope. It consists of material which is relevant to the question objective, but which does not fulfill it.

Nonresponse. This may be a complete blockage of communication, with the respondent remaining silent after a question has been put by the interviewer. Or the respondent may state directly that he will not answer the question. In either case, the nature of the probe will depend upon the interviewer's diagnosis of the basis for this reluctance to answer.

Irrelevant Response. Here the problem is not the volume of communication, but its focus. The respondent may talk without hesitation and at some length, but he does not speak to the objective of the interviewer's question. Before the interviewer can decide how to direct the respondent to the objective, he must judge whether the irrelevancies result from lack of comprehension or from an attempt, conscious or unconscious, to avoid communicating threatening or sensitive material.

Inaccurate Response. Such responses are common, and pose some of the interviewer's most difficult problems of diagnosis. The inaccurate response may be superficially complete and relevant to the question objective; it simply is not in accord with the facts, or presents a biased or distorted picture of the respondent's true feelings.

Verbalized Response Problem. Occasionally a respondent will make it unnecessary for the interviewer to diagnose the reasons for response inadequacy. In such cases the respondent replies to a question not by answering it but by stating why he cannot or will not answer it. Such reasons as the following may be given.

(*a*) Respondent does not understand the question.

(*b*) Respondent does not have the information necessary to answer the question. This may be the result of forgetting, inexperience, or lack of opinion.

(*c*) Respondent considers the question irrelevant or inappropriate to the stated purpose of the interview.

Causes of Inadequate Response

The first requirement of an interviewer in handling successfully the problems of inadequate response is that he be able to recognize response inadequacy in its various forms. But after he has identified an inadequate answer, he must formulate one or more probe questions that will overcome the problem. How is he to decide which type of probe is best suited to a given situation? Unfortunately, there is no simple answer to this question. There is no specific interviewing remedy for each kind of inadequate response.

The reasons for this complexity take us back to some of the theory presented earlier in the book, particularly in Chapters 2 and 7. We have assumed that all behavior is motivated, and that the motive patterns for a single act or segment of behavior are typically complex. Seldom does a human act involve only a single motive, nor does a motive always manifest itself in the same form of behavior. In order to probe successfully, the interviewer must decide not only how but *why* the initial response was inadequate; he must try to understand what factors motivated the response that was given. The interviewer needs to recognize an inadequate response as a *symptom* and then look for the cause.

Some of the underlying causes of restricted and distorted communication have already been rather fully described. In Chapter 3, for example, the major problems of respondent motivation were discussed at some length, and some of the forces urging and opposing communication were identified. Either a lack of positive motivation or a conflict of motives may lead to several of the symptoms of inadequate response which we have described.

Suppose that a survey interviewer asks a business man to list his sources of income. The respondent feels that the particular question is irrelevant to the objectives of the interview, and revealing the information might embarrass him with the Bureau of Internal Revenue. He may do one of several things: (1) he may give only a partial answer, (2) he may refuse to give any response, (3) he may avoid the question by giving irrelevant information, or (4) he may deliberately give inaccurate information.

This is a good example of a motive pattern which may result in the respondent's taking any of several paths to the goal of avoiding the threat. Which path he chooses will depend on factors of personality, habit, and on his perception of what the interviewer is most likely to accept.

Besides such problems of motivation and conflict of motives, there are many other "causes" underlying the symptoms we have described. Among them are the following.

(1) The respondent fails to understand the purpose of the question, or the kind of answer which is needed.

(2) The language or concepts in the question are beyond the respondent's comprehension.

These first two usually mean that the question as stated is deficient, and the interviewer must "translate" it or make it meaningful.

(3) The respondent may lack the information or background of experience necessary to answer the question.

(4) The respondent may not remember the information called for.

(5) The respondent may not be able to verbalize his feelings. This sort of respondent reaction is perhaps most common when the question taps intimate, "deeper" kinds of material, or content about which the respondent has not yet formulated his opinions. He may

have only scattered or conflicting impressions, which make it difficult for him to formulate a response.

(6) The respondent may feel that the question does not fit the purpose of the interview as it was explained to him and as it has been developed up to this point in the interview. For example, suppose a placement officer, in the midst of a personnel interview, asks the job applicant questions about his spare-time activities, or about his family relationships. The respondent may feel that these questions are inappropriate to the general subject of the interview, that they do not fit the stated purpose of determining whether or not he is eligible for a job. When a respondent perceives questions as irrelevant to his own goals and to the stated purpose of the interview, there is a high probability that his response will be inadequate in some respect.

(7) A respondent may perceive a question as going beyond the limits of what he is willing to admit to the interviewer. His relationship with the interviewer is inadequate to permit him to report the requested information.

(8) Finally, the respondent may consider the interviewer "out of range," unable to understand his true feelings.

Clues for Formulating Probe Questions

We have reviewed the kinds of inadequate responses which the interviewer is likely to encounter, and the perceptions and attitudes which produce such responses. To understand more clearly how these respondent attitudes and behaviors appear in the actual interview situation and how the interviewer resolves such problems, let us consider several examples of response inadequacy. In each case some overt behavior by the respondent serves as a signal to the interviewer that difficulty has been encountered, but he must gain insight into the causes before he can probe successfully.

Example 1

There have been persistent rumors that a man prominent in public life is going to enter on a strenuous campaign as candidate for governor. A journalist, sensing an interesting story, is conducting a general "human interest" interview. In the course of this interview he asks the direct question, "Tell me, Mr. Smith, are you planning to run for governor?" The respondent replies smoothly, "Young man, that all depends on the will of the people."

Example 2

A survey interviewer has been interviewing a relatively uninformed farmer on some major agricultural problems. At one point the interviewer asks, "What do you think of parity as a basis for price supports?" The respondent looks dubious for a moment, and then replies tentatively, "Oh, its all right."

Example 3

The manager of an industrial plant, considerably worried about the decreased effectiveness of one of his supervisors, summons the man to his office in order to examine some possible causes of his difficulty. In the course of the interview the manager says, "To tell the truth, Joe, you've been off your stride lately. Are you having any trouble at home?" The supervisor freezes somewhat and then says, in a tight-lipped fashion, "Oh, nothing worth mentioning."

These three examples have several characteristics in common. In each case the interviewer has asked a question to which the respondent gives an obviously incomplete or partial answer. To achieve his objectives, the interviewer must stimulate a more adequate response. But although the respondents' overt behavior is similar, their underlying attitudes or the basis for their behavior is quite different.

Our aspiring gubernatorial candidate wishes to be elected governor, but sees a blunt announcement of that fact as untimely. He avoids the question because he sees a complete answer as hurting rather than helping the attainment of his goal.

In the second example the poorly informed respondent has been confronted with what is sometimes referred to as a "flabbergaster." In other words, he has been asked a question which is beyond his level of information. He does not know anything about parity, and he may not even understand the question which has been put to him. At the same time, he is anxious to appear as well informed as possible and to retain his self-esteem and the respect of the interviewer. He therefore responds, not by indicating ignorance of the topic or lack of understanding of the question, but with the noncommittal, "Oh, its all right."

The third example indicates still another psychological basis for a partial response. The interviewer has asked a highly personal question in the context of a work-related interview. The respondent feels that the question is improper in the superior-subordinate relationship, and irrelevant to the work situation. At the same time, he is hardly in a position to tell his superior bluntly that the question is improper or that he is unwilling to answer it. He attempts to give a response which will be seen as meeting the minimum requirements of courtesy, but which will avoid any further discussion of the topic. Accordingly, he says, "Oh, nothing worth mentioning."

Two conclusions can be drawn from these examples, and from the analysis of the factors underlying the partial response in each case.

First, as we have said, the verbal behavior of the respondent is not sufficient to inform the interviewer of the basis underlying the inadequate response. Any one of the types of inadequate responses—partial response, irrelevant response, inaccurate response, etc.—can occur as a result of any one of the underlying respondent attitudes previously described. Yet the interviewer, if he is to be successful, must employ a probe appropriate to the particular attitude the symptom of which he is encountering. In short, the interviewer must provisionally diagnose the reason for the inadequate response, and this diagnosis frequently must be made on the basis of cues other than the verbal response itself.

Second, a major difference between a skillful and an unskillful interviewer lies in the ability to see beyond the mere words the respondent is using. Insight into respondents' attitudes and motives is the guide which the interviewer needs in order to make the appropriate choice of probe questions. What are some of the cues usually available to him?

Probably the most important cue for the interviewer lies in the nature of the stimulus which he has just employed—that is, the question that he has just asked. He would do well to ask himself how this question differs from others which preceded it. In the example of the supervisory interview, the question about the employee's home situation clearly introduces a more intimate and personal topic than the preceding material concerning on-the-job factors. Similarly, the question on parity might well be more demanding in terms of respondent information, and more laden with technological content, than other questions in a survey interview. So demanding a question asked of a respondent who has already demonstrated a low information level should lead the interviewer to the conclusion that he is dealing with a problem of lack of understanding, lack of information, and reluctance on the respondent's part to acknowledge these deficiencies openly. If the respondent who gave this answer had previously indicated a high level of information on agricultural affairs, a quite different conclusion might be reached as to the basis for his reluctance. It is important, then, for the interviewer to be constantly on the alert to the demands his questions make on each respondent. He needs to consider the question in relation to the respondent's interests, abilities, general level of motivation, and acceptance of the purpose of the interview.

A second basis on which the interviewer can appraise the underlying reasons for an inadequate response is the pattern of interaction which has characterized the interview up to that point. A respondent who has persistently shied away from certain topics as an unreasonable intrusion on his privacy can be assumed to be reacting similarly when he shows reluctance to answer a new question of similar kind. This means that the interviewer needs to be continually aware, throughout the course of the interview, of the level of the respondent's motivation or resistance to the communication process. The sensitive interviewer may be able to offer appropriate assurances and explanations before the respondent's problem manifest themselves in the immediate crisis of inadequate answers or complete blocking. Referring again to our second example on parity, it is likely that a poorly informed respondent will demonstrate lack of knowledge at frequent points throughout the interview. The problem for the interviewer is to identify the pattern as early as possible, and to adapt his behavior to minimizing it. How the interviewer can do this we shall consider specifically later in this chapter.

A third important way in which the interviewer can understand the basis for an inadequate response is by attention to nonverbal cues. In the preceding examples, the responses were similar in that each was pointedly brief and noncommittal. The nonverbal cues, however, would probably differ dramatically in the three cases. The possible candidate for governor responds heartily and with an enigmatic smile. It is apparent that he is by no means at a loss for words, nor is he in any doubt about the meaning of the question. He has simply decided to play it close to the chest. The other two cases present a considerable contrast. The uninformed farmer respondent probably gives his answer about parity in a tentative tone of voice, and with an air of discomfort and uncertainty. The supervisor who has been asked about his home situation gives a partial answer but shows also a noticeable cooling of attitude, considerable body tension, and a general sharpness of tone and hostility of expression that should suggest to the manager that he has definitely gone out of bounds.

TECHNIQUES FOR HANDLING INADEQUATE RESPONSES

From cues such as those indicated in the preceding section, the interviewer must make the best judgment of which he is capable as to the underlying basis for the respondent's behavior. On the basis of this judgment he then reacts to that latent attitude. He chooses a probe, or several probes, based on his assumption about the respondent's reasons for giving an inadequate answer. If he is completely in doubt as to those reasons, he may attempt to get from the respondent some explanation for his reluctance. In any case, it is clear that the inadequate response makes severe demands on the interviewer's skill and judgment. Errors and omissions in the technique of probing must be counted among the major causes of interviewer bias.

Our problem here is to consider what kinds of probes are best adapted to dealing with each of the underlying respondent attitudes previously discussed.

Failure to Understand Objectives

The first examples are ones in which the respondent fails to understand the objectives which the interviewer is trying to accomplish, or the kind of response which is required.

Example 1

INTERVIEWER: Do you expect to make higher wages in the next year or not?
RESPONDENT: Well, I sure hope so. We've had a tough time living on what I've been able to make this year.
INTERVIEWER: I can understand that. How about your *expectations?* Do you expect to make higher wages next year or not?

The answer is inadequate because the respondent answered in terms of his aspirations rather than expectations. The interviewer recognizes and accepts the answer, and with his second sentence makes a transition back to the objective. He then proceeds to repeat the primary question, in the hope that he has been able to clarify the objective for the respondent. This is a common problem for interviewers. It may be that the difficulty was not that the respondent failed to understand the question, but that preoccupation with his economic problems made it necessary for him to talk of his hopes before he could be realistic about his actual expectations. This the interviewer permitted without any implied criticism.

But suppose the interviewer had said, "Well, that isn't what I was asking you. I wanted to know what you think *will* happen." In this exchange the process of getting the respondent back to the objective involves unnecessary criticism. In effect, the interviewer has rejected the respondent, and probably the relationship which he is trying to establish will suffer. In cases of missed objectives, as in other interviewing situations, the interviewer should be accepting and permissive, without permitting the respondent to avoid the objective.

Example 2

INTERVIEWER: Why don't you eat in the plant cafeteria?
RESPONDENT: Because I carry my lunch.
INTERVIEWER: I see. Well, why don't you eat in the plant cafeteria instead of bringing your lunch?

This is one of the many ways in which a respondent may avoid the objectives without meaning to do so. When he says that he brings his lunch, he has answered the question to his satisfaction. But his answer is little more than a tautology. The interviewer accepts the response, but lets the respondent know that more information is required. The probe question also suggests that a "deeper" reason is wanted.[4]

Failure to Understand Requirements of Respondent Role

A related situation and also a common one, is created when the respondent fails to understand his role or does not realize how much is expected of him in answer to a question. When the respondent has no way of knowing how much information is wanted, he tends to give a short answer. The interviewer must then let the respondent know that he has not fulfilled his role adequately.

Example 1

INTERVIEWER: How do you feel about our foreign aid program?
RESPONDENT: I think it's O.K.
INTERVIEWER: I see. Can you give me more of your thinking on that?

In this example the interviewer uses an acceptable nondirective probe to get the respondent to say more. Such probes following inadequate responses help to teach the respondent that relatively full, elaborated answers are desired.

Example 2

PHYSICIAN: Tell me about how you've been feeling.
PATIENT: Well, not very well, I'm afraid, doctor.
PHYSICIAN: Well, that's too bad. Tell me more about it.

The interviewer indicates to the patient that he has not given enough information, and makes a direct request for more. In such cases, the interviewer can continue to use nondirective probes of this nature until he has information sufficient to answer the question objectives.

Failure to Understand Question

At times the respondent may fail to understand the question itself. Until the question has been communicated to him successfully, he cannot answer it.

---

[4] For a discussion of successive levels of "reasons why," see Paul F. Lazarsfeld, "The Art of Asking Why," *National Marketing Review*, 1, 26–38 (1935).

Example 1

LAWYER: Is it your considered opinion that the plaintiff was not exercising due caution in the operation of a motor vehicle?
WITNESS: What do you mean?
LAWYER: Well, I'd like your opinion on whether you felt the plaintiff, that is Mr. Smith, was driving carelessly.

This example is, we hope, not very typical. The reason that the respondent had a hard time is that the question was badly worded. The lawyer was using legal jargon to attempt to communicate a relatively simple idea. Presumably his rewording of his question is sufficiently clear, and the respondent will have no trouble with it. Let's look at another example which is somewhat more typical.

Example 2

INTERVIEWER: Do you think that we will continue to have inflation for the next year or two, or not?
RESPONDENT: Well, I don't know whether we will or not.
INTERVIEWER: What do you have in mind?
RESPONDENT: I think we will not have much unemployment.
INTERVIEWER: Well, thinking of the cost of living in general. Do you think it will keep going up for the next year or two, or not?

The respondent first offered a noncommittal answer, and the interviewer, to find out what this answer meant, used a nondirective probe. From the respondent's second answer it was not clear whether he understood what was meant by inflation, and the interviewer decided that he did not. He therefore attempted to explain what was meant by inflation, without changing the meaning of the question. We may question the adequacy of the definition, but the respondent's apparent misunderstanding forced the interviewer to attempt a definition or to ask the respondent what he understood inflation to be. We might note that this entire problem could have been avoided if the original question had defined "inflation" or had avoided the word altogether.

Example 3

PATIENT: Doctor, I feel tired a lot of the time, and I thought I had better see you about it.
PHYSICIAN: Do you think you are more fatigued than normal?
PATIENT: I don't know. That's why I came to see you.

This requires the patient to make a judgment he is probably incapable of making. The solution is not merely to reword the question. The physician may need to ask a series of questions in order to discover how the patient really feels and what he understands by normal fatigue.

Example 4

INTERVIEWER: Do you think that the present social security payments are adequate?
RESPONDENT: I just don't know.
INTERVIEWER: Well, do you think that the old-age pensions which the government pays are enough to get along on?

In this case the interviewer's diagnosis of an ambiguous "I don't know" was that the respondent failed to understand the question. He therefore repeated it in substance, using simpler language and risking the possibility of altering the meaning. The interviewer's problem stems from the ambiguity of the respondent's phrase. What is it that he does not know—the meaning of the question or the answer to it? Asking the respondent what he doesn't know is awkward. If the previous course of the interview has given the interviewer a reasonable basis for inferring that the respondent was having difficulty with the question itself, the probe seems appropriate. A more basic improvement in the question sequence, however, would have avoided the problem entirely. The question on adequacy of social security payments might have been preceded by a question to ascertain the respondent's level of information regarding the terms of such payments.

Respondent's Confusion or Emotional Ambivalence

Another source of inadequate response shows itself as difficulty in verbalizing, or as equivocal statements on the required topic. This difficulty may occur because a respondent is asked about an issue on which he has not yet formulated an opinion, or because his attitudes are submerged beyond his grasp, or because he is defensive about them.

The following examples illustrate these kinds of problems, and some ways in which they are handled by experienced interviewers. In the first, a social worker is speaking to an aged man, who has been attempting to care for his wife, who is incurably ill.

Example 1

SOCIAL WORKER: How do you feel about having your wife moved to a nursing home?
HUSBAND: I suppose she would get better care there. (Pause.) But we have been together for all these years, and we've always looked after each other whenever there was any trouble. (Pause.) I just don't know what to say.
SOCIAL WORKER: Yes, of course, I can understand. This is a very hard thing to think through. Why don't we just talk about it for a while.

The social worker in her response first recognizes and accepts the fact that this is a painful decision for the husband to have to consider. Her second sentence recognizes the real ambivalence of his feelings, and implies that difficulties in expression are entirely understandable. Finally, she offers to assist the respondent to clarify his own feelings in the matter.

Example 2

PERSONNEL INTERVIEWER: On the whole, are you satisfied with your job or would you like something else?

RESPONDENT: Well, the pay is good on the job I have now, and the fellows are good to work with. (Pause.)   But sometimes the work gets pretty monotonous, and then, too, I feel that I am not getting ahead as fast as I should on this job.

INTERVIEWER: You feel undecided; there are things on both sides.

RESPONDENT: Yuh, it's a tough kind of a decision to have to make. (Pause.)   I think though, that taking it all into consideration, I would really like to have a chance at another job, particularly if the job paid more money.

Notice particularly the interviewer's response "You feel undecided." The interviewer recognizes the ambivalence and gives the respondent a chance to talk about it some more.   It is entirely nondirective and permissive, and yet strongly encourages further discussion.

Example 3

REAL ESTATE SALESMAN: Well, Mr. Jones, what did you think you should get for your house?

MR. JONES: To tell the truth, I really don't know.   I would think somewhere between $10,000 and $15,000.   I know that some people in the next block got about $15,000 for theirs, and this house is almost as good.   I really don't know.   Mrs. Jones and I have been talking this over, and sometimes we think one thing and sometimes another.

SALESMAN: Well, you mention somewhere between ten and fifteen thousand.   Which figure comes closest to that which you would accept?

MR. JONES: Well, as I say, I would like fifteen thousand.   I think it is really worth that, but I don't know if I can really get that much for it or not. It has some disadvantages, I know.

SALESMAN: You think it might not bring as much as fifteen.

MR. JONES: No, I'm afraid it won't.   As a matter of fact, I think I would accept twelve thousand.   If we could get $12,000 I would be happy. I might have to actually accept ten, but I would hate to do it.

This example illustrates a more simple use of nondirective probing to help a respondent think through the problem and reach a definite conclusion.   The decision is certainly important to the respondent, and his thinking has been uncertain.   Consider how differently this interview might have gone if the salesman had attempted immediately to argue that the house was worth only $10,000. One suspects that Mr. Jones would have become defensive and insisted that his home was actually worth much more.

Example 4

DETECTIVE: Now, Mr. Stewart, I understand that you were in the store when it was held up. Will you tell me what happened?

MR. STEWART: Yeah, sure. A man came into the store and shouted, "This is a stickup!" and he started waving a gun around.

DETECTIVE: Can you describe the man for me?

MR. STEWART: Oh gee, I don't know. I really don't remember much about what happened.

DETECTIVE: Well, I wish you would try to give me as good a description as you can.

MR. STEWART: Well, I'd say he was middle-aged, and kind of skinny. And like I say, I can't remember too well, because as a matter of fact I was pretty scared.

DETECTIVE: Yes, sure, it's hard to remember too well in situations like this. Let's just see how well we can do. About how old would you say he was?

MR. STEWART: Well, I'd guess he was somewhere between 40 and 60 years.

DETECTIVE: Somewhere between 40 and 60. What would be your closest guess?

MR. STEWART: Well, I don't know. He had some grey hair. I would say he was probably about 45.

In this example, too, the interviewer accepts the confusion which the man feels, and indicates to him that he understands his problem in describing an individual who is observed momentarily and under such exciting circumstances. He then uses a series of probes to get the witness to think about the age of the robber, and emerges with a reasonably specific answer.

Example 5

COUNSELOR: I see that you have to elect one more course to fill out your hours for graduation. Have you thought about what you want to take?

STUDENT: As a matter of fact, I thought of two courses, and I can't make up my mind between them.

COUNSELOR: Yes, that can be tough. Which two are you considering?

STUDENT: There's Math 168 and Sociology 203. I think I ought to have the math for the work that I am going to do, but I hear it's really a tough course. The sociology course is a lot easier, and I don't want to work too hard my last semester. After all, I'd like to have some time for fun.

COUNSELOR: You're torn between the course that you feel you ought to have and the one that would give you some free time.

STUDENT: I sure am. I know I've got to decide by tomorrow, and I'm darned if I know which one to pick.

Counselor: Yeah, that's a hard choice.
Student: I think maybe I'll take sociology.
Counselor: That will give you the free time.
Student: Yes. (Pause.) I can always pick up the math later by reading up on it if I really need it, and after all, I'm not going to be in college again, so I might as well enjoy myself a little. I think as a matter of fact I will take that sociology course.

Example 6

Another factor which frequently gives rise to response problems is the respondent's feeling that a question is too personal or threatening. It is difficult to illustrate this kind of question out of the context of the entire interview because, of course, the relationship of the interviewer and the respondent determines in part what things will be seen as threatening. In general, however, when an interviewer discovers that a respondent is beginning to "block," or to give evasive answers to questions of a personal nature, it is quite likely that he is encountering reaction to threat. If the respondent verbalizes his difficulty, of course, the diagnosis is considerably easier.

Suppose that in an attempt to ascertain marital adjustment in a personnel selection interview, an inept interviewer produces the following exchange:

Interviewer: How are you getting along with your wife?
Respondent: I don't talk about my personal affairs with anybody!

One can be reasonably sure that the response means in this case that the interviewer has overstepped the bounds of the relationship he has established. The "cure" for this problem is obviously that the question should not be asked until the relationship will sustain it. This may mean that an interviewer must leave a question that appears to be particularly touchy until late in the interview. Often the fault is in the question itself; in this case a more oblique approach may be necessary.

Another factor in inadequate response listed earlier was the respondent's perception that the question is irrelevant to the purpose of the interview and to his motivation to participate in it. Two examples of this type of problem follow. The first is an excerpt from the latter part of a legal interview, conducted in an attorney's office.

Example 7

Lawyer: You've given me a great deal of valuable information, and I am very grateful to you for your help. I have one other question. Had you been drinking before the accident you witnessed?
Respondent: Well, er . . . . (Pause.)

LAWYER: Did you have anything to drink before the accident?
RESPONDENT: I don't see what business that is of yours.
LAWYER: I ask because if you were to testify at the trial and the defendant's lawyer could prove you had been drinking, your testimony might not stand up.
RESPONDENT: Oh, I get it. Sorry I blew up. Well, I had a couple of beers but that's all. What's more, other men were in the car with me all evening and can tell you so if you need them.

In this example, the respondent's first reaction to a threatening or embarrassing question was simply not to answer. The attorney repeated the question, a probing technique which is often appropriate but which indicates that in this case the interviewer had made a faulty diagnosis. The respondent had heard and understood the question; his problem was motivational rather than comprehension. The repeated question did, however, require some acknowledgment, and the respondent handled it by verbalizing his resentment and unwillingness to answer. The attorney then realized the basis for the response problem and explained the relevance of the question to the respondent's interests and the requirements of the law. As the respondent then says apologetically, he had not understood the purpose of the question. Without this positive motivation, the negative factor of embarrassment was enough to prevent response.

The last example, from a survey interview, reminds us that explanations of question objectives may be unavailing.

Example 8

INTERVIEWER: About how far through school did you get?
RESPONDENT: I don't see what that has to do with this interview. I don't tell people about my education.
INTERVIEWER: Well, as I mentioned to you, we're talking to people all over the country, and we're interested in how people with different amounts of education feel about public affairs. That's why we ask all the people we interview approximately how much education they had.
RESPONDENT: Yes, I see why you might like to have the information, but I'm afraid that I'm just going to have to refuse.

The interviewer's explanation was not sufficient to overcome the reluctance of the respondent. It is possible that the respondent was somewhat ashamed of his lack of education and did not wish to divulge it. The interviewer may abandon his efforts and move to other topics, or he may attempt to overcome the respondent's resistance by further explanation of the objective or by dealing directly with the probable basis for resistance. There is also the possibility of returning to the question at a later moment, when the interviewer-respondent relationship has been more fully developed.

SUMMARY

Examples and exposition of probing are continued in **Chapter 9** and in the second section of the book. The purpose of this chapter has been to illustrate the dynamics of the interview in terms of the probes or follow-up techniques which the interviewer uses to obtain full and accurate responses. Like the primary questions, probes have a dual purpose; they supplement the primary questions both in terms of respondent motivation and in terms of measurement.

As a motivation technique, probes must be accepting and permissive. They must help the respondent to verbalize his feelings and must help maintain the general receptive atmosphere that is most conducive to a productive interaction between the principals in the interview. As a device for measurement, the probes must focus on the question objectives. To avoid bias they must be nonjudgmental, conveying neither positive nor negative interviewer opinions on the topic under discussion. They must stimulate the respondent to give a full response.

Probe questions that meet these requirements will add greatly to fullness and accuracy of response, and to the cooperation of the respondent in the interview process.

chapter 9

Learning to Interview

A major aim of this book has been to give the reader an image of the ideal interview. To this end we have included chapters on interviewing theory and principles, and other chapters on techniques for the application of these principles. Although the interviewer requires this background and understanding, they are not in themselves sufficient. The successful interviewer is one who has developed the skill necessary to put the principles into practice. The purpose of this chapter and of the second part of the book is to give the reader an opportunity to acquire some skill in identifying and utilizing good interviewing techniques.

We hear conflicting things about learning to interview. Some folklore tells us that a person must be born with certain personality characteristics in order to learn how to interview successfully. The implication is that there is an "interviewer personality type" who has a natural talent for interviewing, in the same way that some people are endowed with a natural talent for music or art. This means that natural talent need only be discovered and we have a ready-made interviewer. Others maintain that everyone can be given a specific list of "dos and don'ts" and can be taught to apply these injunctions successfully. In that case, little thought or attention need be given to theory or principles.

The research that has been done on characteristics of successful interviewers is fragmentary, but it does not substantiate the idea that either inborn talent or rote knowledge of things to do and to avoid determines excellence in interviewing.

We do know from experience and from specific research that not all interviewers will be successful in getting accurate information from all respondents. Much of this evidence has already been reviewed in Chapter 7. We have generalized these findings by saying that for a successful interaction to occur it is essential that the interviewer be perceived by the respondent as being "within range" of communication. We have described some studies in which interviewers were not perceived in this way and biased information resulted. In most kinds of interviews it is unlikely that the respondent initially perceives the interviewer as being so different that they cannot successfully communicate with each other. What is probably much more important from the standpoint of successful communication is not how the interviewer looks or how he is dressed, but how he acts during the interview. His behavior will quickly improve or worsen the respondent's first impression of him.

Behavior that increases the probability of the interviewer's being perceived as within communication range has been described in earlier chapters. Its components have been identified as permissiveness, receptivity, and empathy. It follows that some people are more likely to be successful interviewers than others, partly because of their personality traits, but more because they somehow have learned how to create the psychological atmosphere in which respondent communication flourishes. The essential quality required to establish such an atmosphere is a sensitivity to human relationships, especially those relationships characteristic of the interview.

In discussing qualifications for doing personal counseling and psychotherapy, Rogers writes:

> The person who is quite obtuse to the reactions of others, who does not realize that his remarks have caused another pleasure or distress, who does not sense the hostility or friendliness which exists between himself and others or between two of his acquaintances, is not likely to become a satisfactory counselor. There is no doubt that this quality can be developed, but unless an individual has a considerable degree of this social sensitivity, it is doubtful that counseling is his most promising field of effort. On the other hand, the individual who is naturally observant of the reactions of others, who can pick out of a schoolroom group the unhappy child, who can sense the personal antagonism which underlies casual argument, who is alert to the subtle differences in actions which show that one parent has a comfortable relationship with his child, an-

other a relationship full of tensions—such a person has a good natural foundation upon which to build counseling skills.[1]

This sensitivity is important to the person who uses the interview as a technique for collecting information, as well as to the person who uses the interview as a means of effecting changes in people's attitudes. To some, this sensitivity to human relationships is a characteristic mode of thought. With sufficient training, most people can develop a considerable degree of sensitivity, but to some it comes more easily than to others. For a few, such a mode of thought and behavior is foreign and will remain so. These few are unlikely to achieve success as interviewers. For the rest, the sensitivity can be developed through appropriate training.

The twin goals of this chapter on training are (1) to help the learner develop a sensitivity to the human relationships in the interview, and (2) to help the learner to develop skill in the application of acceptable interviewing techniques, particularly techniques of probing for more information.

PRINCIPLES OF INTERVIEWER TRAINING
Skill Training

One of the first principles of an interviewer training program is that skill practice is more effective if carried out in a group rather than on an individual basis. Experience has shown that the behavior changes involved in learning new skills are made easier by group participation. This is especially true when the desired changes involve increasing sensitivity to human relationships.

A corollary of this principle is that skill training is best accomplished by observation, practice, critical review, and discussion of practical experience rather than by lecture. People learn to interact with others by interacting rather than by reading about interaction. Trainees learn more readily if they are actively involved in the learning process. The essence of this approach is the assertion of John Dewey that we learn by doing. "That education is not an affair of 'telling' and being told, but an active and constructive process, is a principle almost as generally violated in practice as conceded in theory."[2]

Bavelas developed this principle in relation to skill training when

---

[1] Carl R. Rogers, *Counseling and Psychotherapy*, Houghton Mifflin, Boston, 1942, p. 254.

[2] John Dewey, *Democracy in Education*, Macmillan, New York, 1916, p. 46.

he wrote about the problems of managers in acquiring the skills to establish good personal relationships with employees:

> Actually, both casual observations and research indicate that the quality of personal relationships depends upon specific social skills, and that like other skills they may be learned by practice. They cannot be learned out of books to any greater extent than skill in playing tennis can be acquired by reading a book . . . . What appears to be the most effective method of teaching skills is a common sense one—watch others, let others watch you, discuss and evaluate differences, and try again.[3]

Canter and his colleagues, agreeing with this approach, have attempted to specify the conditions under which it is most effective:

> People must have an opportunity to practice new ways of behaving if these are to become part of themselves. This fact lies behind the frequently stated principle that we learn to do by doing. The principle is true as far as it goes. But doing will lead to desirable learning only if certain conditions are present in the practice situation. What are these conditions?
> First, the learner must be free to try something new. This means that he must be free to make mistakes as well as to achieve successes . . . .
> Second, the learner must be able to see and know the effects which his behavior achieves if he is to weed out behavior which gets effects he doesn't want and establish those behaviors which lead to the effects he desires. Otherwise he doesn't acquire the *meaning* of his acts as he practices them . . . . This process of getting feedback on the effects of what we do, in order to improve what we do in terms of better achieving some desired effect, is a part of all intelligent practice.[4]

The application of these principles to training interviewers is obvious. It means giving each trainee an opportunity to discuss interviewing principles, to practice interviews, to describe his own successes and failures and discuss those of others, in an environment in which he feels secure. He must know that his clumsiest efforts will not excite ridicule, that his worst mistakes will bring help rather than blame, that the others in the situation share and understand his problems. He must be confident that he is accepted and valued by his colleagues, trainees and veterans, that they also want to learn from his experiences and help him acquire proficiency. The trainee learns not only from practice and interaction, but also from relating his practical experiences to principles and theory. He sees how poor interview techniques lead to inaccurate information or poor human rela-

---

[3] Alex Bavelas, "Role Playing and Management Training," *Sociatry*, 1, No. 2, (June 1947).

[4] See *Adult Leadership*, 2, No. 2 (June 1953), especially pages 5–8 and 31. The issue committee consists of Ralph Canter, Hubert S. Coffey, William P. Golden, Jr., Gordon Hearne, and Theodore C. Kroeber.

tionships. He learns to eliminate poor techniques by seeing why they are poor. He is motivated to use good techniques by seeing that they obtain more satisfactory results.

Use of Role Playing

There are a number of specific training methods which can provide an opportunity to practice and to analyze the results of practice under favorable conditions. One of these, role playing, is so well adapted to interviewer training that it deserves special consideration. The use of role playing or "reality practice" was pioneered by J. L. Moreno as a technique of psychological therapy. It has been adapted as a technique for training in various behavioral skills, especially those involving interpersonal relationships.

In the application of role playing to interviewer training, one member of the group plays the part of a respondent, identifying himself with some actual person whom he knows, and responds to the interviewer in terms of the role which he is playing. One of the other members of the group plays the interviewer. The rest of the group act as observers. When the role playing session ends, there is a general discussion of the techniques which the interviewer used, the problems posed by the respondent, and the strengths and weaknesses which were demonstrated.

The trainee who plays the interviewer role gets the benefit of practicing directly the words and techniques he must use in the interview situation. He also gets the experience of facing real problems without real penalties; the game has reality, but he is not playing "for keeps." As a result, he is freer in his approach and more able to observe himself than he would be in an actual interview situation. Bavelas has summarized this aspect of role playing as follows:

It is a common occurrence in role playing that a person makes the same mistakes that he has been observed to make unconsciously while on the job, and immediately after the play is over, points out himself that he has made errors. He becomes, as it were, sensitized to himself.[5]

The trainee usually gets as much out of playing the role of the respondent, however, as he does out of playing the interviewer role. As a respondent, he can perceive where the interviewer failed to get information that was potentially available, and when the interviewer used techniques that were irritating. Analyzing his own reactions to being interviewed, and experiencing directly the effects of different interviewing techniques, sensitize the trainee to reactions of respond-

[5] Alex Bavelas, *op. cit.*

ents.   Meanwhile, the trainees who are observers have a chance to see the performance in a more detached way and to plan the elimination of errors in their own interview techniques.

Barron evaluates the use of role playing as a device for training interviewers thus:

> The use of role playing or reality practice is being increasingly recognized as an effective means of translating principles into methods, of learning the how, of getting the feel of doing something in a situation where one is not playing for keeps.   In training which is directed toward improving skill in interpersonal relations, it offers an effective way of bridging the gap between formal study of principles, methods and techniques on a verbal level and actual work with those methods and techniques.   It offers an opportunity for practice in a kind of work like interviewing where close supervision and training on the job are very difficult.[6]

Other writers stress the value of the opportunity to play both roles in an interpersonal relation:

> Because role playing helps people to get insights into their own and others' feelings, it has been widely recognized as a method of helping people to broaden their understanding of and to empathize with other people; to see things from the point of view of the person on the other side of the table (or tracks or globe).[7]

Role playing is an effective technique for moving the learning of human relations skills from the level of intellectual understanding to that of living through interviewing experiences.

Techniques of Role Playing

We can now describe in more detail the mechanics of role playing. In setting up a role-playing session, the person acting as interviewer prepares for his role by thinking through (either by himself or with the group) his objectives and what he hopes to accomplish during the interview.   The person selected for the respondent role is given the general outline of the kind of interviewing situation that is to be played, and the broad aspects of his role are discussed.   He then leaves the group and thinks out his role in more detail while the interviewer is planning his own role.   To give the session a sense of reality, the situation and the roles should be well within the experience of the group members.   The role selected for the respondent must be one with which he can identify easily.

---

[6] Margaret Barron, "Role Practice in Interview Training," *Sociatry,* 1, No. 2 (June 1947).

[7] Grace Levit and Helen Hall Jennings, "Learning Through Role Playing," *Adult Leadership,* 2, No. 5 (October, 1953).

The rest of the group, acting as observers, are instructed to concentrate on process, to note examples of good and poor technique, and so forth. It may be useful to have some of the observers pay special attention to the interviewer, and others to the respondent. The actual role-playing scene is kept brief, ten or fifteen minutes. This provides enough behavior to discuss, without overwhelming the group with material. After the scene the observers report their findings. The respondent reports how he felt, where he reacted negatively to the interviewer's probes, at what points information he was prepared to give was not obtained, and why. The interviewer explains why he did what he did, where he felt he was especially proficient in his role, and in what respects he needs help.

The functions of the instructor or group leader are important. As a more experienced interviewer, he picks up points the group may miss, relates the experiences of role playing back to principles of interviewing, and encourages participation by trainees in the role playing and discussion. The discussion should center around such questions as: How did the interviewer, the respondent, and the observers feel about the participation of each person? Why did the respondent and the interviewer do what they did? What probe questions did the interviewer have to improvise? How did the respondent react to them? Was there evidence of bias? How could it have been avoided?

The pattern of role playing can be varied to provide many different kinds of experience. Starting with relatively simple situations will give the group members a feeling of assurance that they can all play their assigned roles. As they become more experienced at taking roles and making analytical observations, the sessions can be made more complicated.

Use of Recordings in Training

Recorded interviews are among the training aids particularly well adapted to interviewer training, and there are several ways in which they can be used to advantage. In the early stages of training they can be used to illustrate principles of interviewing and the components of an interview. For example, the Survey Research Center has made a set of six records which consist of short excerpts from different phases of an interview. There are several different introductions, and examples of asking questions of differing content and difficulty. Entire records are devoted to demonstrating probe questions and other techniques for encouraging communication. Such recorded material can be introduced early in the training to demonstrate how principles and techniques are used in actual interviews.

The recordings have the advantage of using examples from outside the group, and can therefore be subjected to criticism and analysis without threat to any member of the group. The new interviewer can enter into this process some time before he is sufficiently sure of himself to participate in a role playing interview. Standard recordings also provide the trainer with examples which have been carefully selected to represent specific points, so that he need not risk the possibility of their failing to emerge from the role-playing interview.

Recordings can be used in conjunction with role playing and with practice interviews, as well as to prepare for these training experiences. Parts of the recordings can be replayed when they are appropriate to illustrate points under discussion, or to refresh the trainees' memories. Recorded material helps greatly in the "feedback" part of the role-playing sessions, where it can be used to clarify points which were not thoroughly illustrated in the role playing.

Recording Actual Interviews

At times it is useful to record actual nontraining interviews. This raises questions about the procedures for making such recordings. Should the respondent be told that the interview is being recorded, or should concealed microphones be used? We believe that professional ethics requires that such recordings be made only with the knowledge of both participants. Fortunately, experience shows that the presence of a microphone is seldom a deterrent in the interview. Where there is some reaction to the recording, the interviewer is much more likely to remain aware of and nervous about the mike than the respondent. The respondent is usually willing to accept the recording apparatus, on the interviewer's explanation of its importance.

The procedure, then, is to tell the respondent that the interview is to be recorded in order that an accurate report can be obtained, and to reassure him of the confidentiality of the record. If the subject matter of the interview is likely to be very personal, it is advisable to tell the respondent that if he wishes to speak "off the record" the microphone will be turned off. Experience indicates that respondents seldom take advantage of this opportunity, but that it helps them to feel somewhat freer.

Use of Observation in Interviews

When recording equipment is not available or its use is not feasible, observation can be used as a substitute. In this case the trainer remains with the new interviewer during an actual interview. He can be introduced as a colleague, a supervisor, or as a friend, depending on the circumstances. The observer should remain as inconspicuous as possible. He should not participate in any way in the interview, and should attempt to keep out of the range of the respondent's attention as much as possible. Because observation puts some strain on the interviewer, it should be attempted only after other techniques of training have helped him to develop a good deal of self-assurance in the interviewer role. During the interview, the observer should take notes on technique and process, to provide a basis for the joint analysis of the interview.

RATING SCALES

To help the trainee focus his attention on the most significant aspects of the interviewer's job, and to help him become more sen-

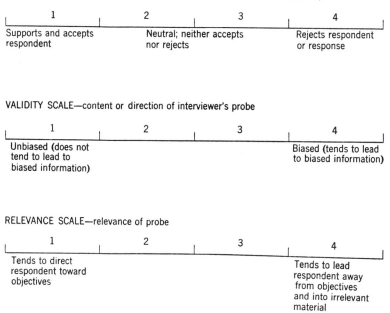

Figure 12. Rating scales for evaluation of probes.

sitive to the interactions of the interview, we have prepared three rating scales (Figure 12). These scales are designed primarily to evaluate the interviewer's effectiveness as he probes for more material. They can be used also to evaluate the primary questions in the interview, and are especially appropriate when the interviewer is formulating the primary questions spontaneously rather than using a prepared questionnaire.

Method of Use

The use of the scales does not imply a fixed criterion of correctness or incorrectness. A question is correct when it moves the interview toward the goal or objective. A question is incorrect when it blocks interaction, or when it leads to irrelevant or distorted information. Moving the interview toward its goals means not only meeting the stated objective of a question, but also achieving the psychological atmosphere that assures the respondent of understanding and stimulates him to participate freely.

Ideally, a probe question would be rated as 1 on all three scales; it would be accepting of the respondent, would avoid bias, and would focus the communication on the objectives. In practice, however, it is not always possible (or desirable) to formulate a probe question that will rate high on all three scales. In such cases, the interviewer must decide what will best serve the over-all purpose of the interview. If the respondent is reticent and suspicious, it may be more important for the interviewer to improve the relationship between them than to urge the respondent toward a specific question objective. If, on the other hand, a secure and loquacious respondent is happily communicating irrelevant material, the interviewer can well afford a probe question that rates neutral or even low on acceptance but reorients the respondent to the primary objective. We do not assume, in short, that each of the scales is equally applicable at all times.

The use of these scales is best described by example. Suppose that our purpose is to evaluate the probe question in the following interaction, in which the interviewer is attempting to ascertain the attitudes of an industrial worker toward his salary.

INTERVIEWER (primary question): How do you feel about your wages here at the company?

RESPONDENT: Well, I'm only making about $2.00 an hour right now. I expect to be doing better next month, though, because I'm being shifted to a new job.

INTERVIEWER (probe): You say you're making *about* $2.00 an hour now?

Let us evaluate this question on the scales of Figure 12.

Acceptance Scale: Ideally, the interviewer's rejoinder to information from the respondent should be accepting and supportive. Such a response would be rated 1. A neutral probe is not bad in this case, although it does little to motivate further respondent communication. The probe question actually used here we would rate as a 3. It tends to reject the respondent slightly by failing to recognize the importance of what he was saying about his new job.

Validity Scale: The ideal probe here can be rated 1. The probe as given is also rated 1, since it was entirely nondirective and did nothing to suggest that a greater or lesser amount would have been more appropriate.

Relevance Scale: In this case there is reason for leading the respondent toward the objective, but the probe did not do so. The probe actually used is therefore rated 4. The objective called for attitudes, yet the interviewer's probe does nothing to reorient the respondent. The probe is likely to lead to more factual information about the respondent's current wages.

Suppose now that the objective was to ascertain the hourly rate paid the worker. For this objective the same probe might have been used, but the ratings might be different, since the ratings of any probe are in terms of the question objectives.

INTERVIEWER (primary question): Would you tell me what the rate is on your job?

RESPONDENT: Well, I'm only making about $2.00 an hour right now. I expect to be doing better next month though, because I'm being shifted to a new job.

INTERVIEWER (probe): You say you're making about $2.00 an hour now?

Acceptance Scale, Validity Scale: Ratings on these scales tend not to be affected by the change in objective here. The probe would be rated 3 for acceptance and 1 for validity.

Relevance Scale: The ideal probe is 1, and the actual probe now becomes 1, since it communicates to the respondent the fact that his first answer was appropriate but not sufficiently exact to satisfy the objective. The same probe, then, may be rated quite differently depending upon the question objective.

In using the scales, the purpose should not be to "score" an interview. The scales are designed to help the interviewer think in analytical terms, especially in appraising his spontaneous formulation of questions in the interview. If the new interviewer becomes accustomed to analyzing his probe questions in terms of the criteria of acceptance, validity, and relevance, he will be well along the way to thinking in terms of unbiased interaction. In group training, the scales can be used to focus discussion and to evaluate the interviewer's success in achieving the objectives of the interview. They can be used to analyze recorded material or role-played interviews, and to facilitate discussion among the "raters" in reaching consensus regarding the interviewer's effectiveness.

Application of the Rating Scales

In this section a number of additional examples of probes are given. Some of them have been rated on the scales of Figure 12; those that are not rated can be used for practice. These examples are intended to help the new interviewer take the first steps in the learning process. They can be used to advantage for group discussions. You may find that you disagree with the ratings given. The ratings are admittedly judgmental, and the probes are not intended to be perfect.

The objective of example 1 is to determine the current market value of the respondent's home, according to his own estimate.

Example 1

INTERVIEWER: What would this house be worth if you sold it now?
RESPONDENT: Well, a real estate man offered me $11,500 cash last month.

Possible probes:
A. Do you think that's a fair price?
B. Would you take that little for it?
C. Yes, seems to me that's a good price.
D. Would it be worth more or less than that if you sold it now?
E. How do you feel about selling your house?

Rating of the possible probe responses:

	A	B	C	D	E
Acceptance	2	2	2	2	2
Validity	2	4	4	1	1
Relevance	3	2	2	1	4

Probe *D* comes closest to being rated an ideal probe. The others fail on at least one of the three scales. For example, probe *A* may bias the response and may lead away from the objective. Probe *B* is adequate on two scales, but is likely to yield a biased response; this probe makes it difficult for the respondent to say that he considers the house to be worth *less* than $11,500. Probe *C* is biased; the respondent must now contradict the interviewer if he estimates the value of the house at more or less than $11,500. Probe *E* is focused on the respondent's attitudes, which are irrelevant to the objective of the question.

The next two examples are similar to this one and are left for the reader to rate. Example 2 is from an exit interview with a stenographer who is about to leave her job. The interview is taken by a personnel interviewer, for the purpose of ascertaining why she is leaving. Example 3 is from the opening interaction in a medical interview. How do you rate the possible probes?

Example 2

INTERVIEWER: I see from this record that you're going to leave us [leave the employ of the company] after five years. How do you happen to be leaving now?
RESPONDENT: I'm going to work at the United plant.

Possible probes:
A. Are you getting more money there?
B. Don't you like it here?
C. Of course, I'm particularly interested in why you want to leave your job here. Can you tell me something about that?

Example 3

INTERVIEWER: Good afternoon, Mr. Jones. What can I do for you today?
RESPONDENT: Well, doctor, all day yesterday I felt awful! Last night and today I feel even worse.

Possible probes:
A. When did you start to feel bad?
B. Is it your stomach?
C. Tell me more about how you feel.
D. Do you feel nauseated or faint?

Example 4 is a different type of interview. Our ratings are reported below so that you can compare them with yours. The interview is between an assistant plant superintendent and an employee who operates a punch press. The objectives are somewhat complex: to "let the employee know that we know he's not making production" and to try to discover the factors which may be causing the difficulty.

Example 4

INTERVIEWER: Fred [the foreman] tells me you aren't producing up to standard these days, Bill. What's the matter?
RESPONDENT: Listen, if that jerk would get the damned machine fixed right I would. But no, he says it's my fault!

Possible probes:
A. Listen, Bill, I don't care what the trouble is, you'd better make production, or else!
B. Why the devil didn't you report it to me before now?
C. Oh, come on, that machine's O.K.
D. Let's talk about the trouble. Maybe we can talk it over and get it taken care of.
E. Then it's a problem with the machine. Is that it?
F. It's really a problem to you, I can see.
G. Bill, getting excited about this won't help. Let's talk things over calmly and see what we can do.

What are the considerations for selecting an adequate probe in this example? Acceptance appears to be extremely important. The respondent is quite emotional, and needs to "talk out" some of his anger and hostility before he can consider calmly the barriers that stand between him and an acceptable level of production. The interviewer is in a position of authority over the respondent, a fact more likely to inhibit than to encourage the communication of such emotional material. Clearly, a high degree of acceptance is needed.

The major content objective is to learn what really interferes with the respondent's making higher production. For the moment, however, this objective can be subordinated to the need for establishing a more satisfactory relationship and clearing the air. It can be argued, of course, that attention to content is always important, and that exploring the condition of the machine is what is called for. But the violence of the worker's reaction suggests that factors other than the machine, frustrations not yet mentioned, may be at least equally relevant to the objective. Too direct a rejoinder to his complaint about the machine may cut off communication about these other factors. Therefore, a response primarily to the worker's feelings, one that leaves him free to blow off steam, is likely to lead us more rapidly to a full achievement of the content objective.

Analysis of suggested probes:

	A	B	C	D	E	F	G
Acceptance	4	3	4	1	2	1	3
Validity	3	4	3	2	4	1	3
Relevance	4	4	4	2	3	2	2

Probe *F* comes closest to the ideal, and probe *D* next. The main differences between probe *F* and others are that it responds to the feelings which the respondent is expressing, and that there is a recognition and acceptance of this strong feeling with no criticism of the respondent. Probes *A, B,* and *C* reject the attitude and the respondent. It is quite unlikely that the approach they represent would lead to the data needed to make an accurate analysis of the situation; the interview would be likely to end up in recriminations, charges, and countercharges, and would not achieve its objectives. Probe *G* looks better on superficial inspection than it actually is. It sounds like an appeal to reason instead of emotion, but it will not serve this purpose. This emotional respondent will be rejected rather than made rational by this probe. The probe in effect scolds him for his outburst and denies his right to be emotional or indignant. As a result, he may feel that he must withhold certain kinds of material, and communication may be inhibited, with biasing effects on the interview.

Example 5 has 10 possible probes. Rate the ideal probe, and then **rate each of the 10. Which comes closest to the ideal?**

Example 5

INTERVIEWER: How do you like the men you work with on the job?
RESPONDENT: Well, most of them are O.K., I guess. Of course, when you're with the same guys all the time, things don't always go smooth.

Possible probes:
A. What do you mean?
B. You mean they're really not a very good bunch to work with?
C. What kind of things go wrong?
D. But you say most of them are O.K., eh?
E. Yes, I suppose that's how it is when people work together all the time.
F. You mean you actually sometimes get into fights?
G. Tell me more about it.
H. But in general its O.K., eh?
I. Things don't always go smoothly.
J. Well, taking it all into consideration would you say you liked the men or not?

The next examples are of a different type. In actual interviews we are unable to know, except indirectly, what the respondent is thinking and how the probing is affecting him. Example 6 is a fanciful example of an employment interview in which we have an opportunity to see both the manifest and latent content. On the left side of the page is the interview as it actually occurred. On the right side are the thoughts of both participants. The objective of the interview is to determine the qualifications of a job applicant. The interview is conducted by a personnel interviewer.

Example 6

MANIFEST CONTENT	LATENT CONTENT
INTERVIEWER: Good morning, Miss Jones. I understand you came in to talk about a job.	INTERVIEWER: Oh, my gosh. Here's another young girl who wants a job. She's probably no good. I don't think we would ever hire her.
RESPONDENT: Yes, I heard you were taking on some girls.	RESPONDENT: Boy, I hope there's a job here for me. I'm good enough at typing and speedwriting now to hold down a job here any day.
INTERVIEWER: Well, we are taking on a very few for special jobs. Can you take shorthand?	INTERVIEWER: I'll play this carefully —don't want to encourage her any.
RESPONDENT: No, but I . . .	RESPONDENT: For gosh sakes. He didn't let me tell him I can do speedwriting, and can do as well with that as most of the girls do with regular shorthand.

MANIFEST CONTENT	LATENT CONTENT
INTERVIEWER: Can you type?	INTERVIEWER: Let's get on with this. She was going to tell me she'd learn shorthand if she got the job. I've heard that ten times in the past two days!
RESPONDENT: Yes, and . . .	RESPONDENT: What's the matter with that old crab. He won't let me tell about my speedwriting!
INTERVIEWER: How many words a minute?	INTERVIEWER: Guess this'll slow her down some.
RESPONDENT: I don't know how many, but I can type as fast as most girls.	RESPONDENT: He thinks I'm no good. Not much chance for me here, I guess.
INTERVIEWER: Well, we'll give you a typing test to find out your speed. Have you held a regular job before?	INTERVIEWER: I'll bet she's just out of school.
RESPONDENT: Yes, I worked two hours after school as a typist in a store.	RESPONDENT: There! That's *some* experience. If I can tell him about all the things I did there, he will see that I'm really pretty good.
INTERVIEWER: I guess we wouldn't consider that a regular job, though.	INTERVIEWER: Just as I thought. No experience. Probably her old man runs the store, too!
RESPONDENT: Well, I worked regularly every day, five days a week.	RESPONDENT: He can't get away with that. I *did* have a regular job!
INTERVIEWER: Sure, but we don't call two hours a day regular.	INTERVIEWER: Oh, my aching back. Let's get this over with.
RESPONDENT: Oh.	RESPONDENT: I give up! To hell with him and his job.

This interview, while somewhat extreme, is in many ways not unusual. Clearly there was little of common understanding or real communication present here. The interviewer never gave the respondent an opportunity to tell her story, and each was frustrated by that fact. He found out almost nothing about the applicant, about her job skills, her interests, or her personal characteristics. It may be that he missed a potentially good stenographer, and he certainly established ill will for his company.

Example 7 is an imaginary interview of the same respondent with another interviewer.

Example 7

INTERVIEWER: Good morning, Miss Jones, I understand you came in to talk about a job.

RESPONDENT: Yes, I heard you were taking on some girls.

INTERVIEWER: Well, we don't have *many* openings right at present, but we do have a few. Also, we're interested in finding out about people who want jobs because we do have vacancies from time to time.

RESPONDENT: I would like to work here. A couple of my friends work here, and they say it's a good place.

INTERVIEWER: That's the kind of news we like to hear. Now tell me something about yourself. What kind of job are you interested in?

RESPONDENT: I'd like to be a secretary. I don't know whether I can be right away, but that's what I'd like to do.

INTERVIEWER: I see.

RESPONDENT: I just graduated from high school last month. I don't mean to brag, but I got all A's my last two years.

INTERVIEWER: That's good work.

RESPONDENT: Well, thank you. I took a year of typing, too.

INTERVIEWER: I see. Did you learn shorthand?

RESPONDENT: Well, no, but I did learn speedwriting by myself evenings.

INTERVIEWER: Have you had any experience using your typing and speedwriting?

RESPONDENT: The past year I've been working two hours each afternoon at the Acme store.

INTERVIEWER: What kind of work did you do there?

RESPONDENT: Well, I typed letters and took some dictation, but not as much as I wanted to. I got so I could type pretty well. I was doing as well as the other girl, who worked full time.

INTERVIEWER: You type pretty well, then.

RESPONDENT: Yes, and I had a little bookkeeping experience there too, when the other girl was out sick for a month.

INTERVIEWER: That's good experience.

RESPONDENT: Sure was. I was scared to death when I first tried it, but I made out O.K.

INTERVIEWER: That made you feel good, I bet.

RESPONDENT: It sure did!

INTERVIEWER: Well, suppose we arrange for you to take a typing and dictation test so we can see whether you might fit into any of the jobs we now have open.

RESPONDENT: Gee, that's swell! Thanks a lot. I hope I get to work here; I know I'd like it.

INTERVIEWER: Well, I hope it works out, too. Let's talk about it again after your tests, shall we?

In this example it is unnecessary to express separately the thoughts of the interviewer and the respondent. The tone of the interview itself makes it apparent that each is communicating with the other. The relationship is good, as the interviewer accepts the respondent.

In doing so he elicits much information about the respondent in contrast to the previous example. Try rating some probes in each example and see the extent of the contrast.

SELF LEARNING

The assumption of this chapter so far has been that the new interviewer is part of a group who are learning and practicing together. In many cases the readers of this book will want to learn to interview but must do so by themselves. How can this type of learning be carried out most effectively?

The most important ingredient of effective learning, which is missing for the single learner, is the opportunity for feedback, the help of the group in evaluating his performance. If he is to become proficient as an interviewer, he must find opportunities for evaluating his progress.

The scales will be particularly useful to him in this respect. He should study the preceding examples and make his own ratings before looking at the ratings which we have made. He can then compare the two sets of ratings, read the explanations, and evaluate his own probes.

The use of recordings of interviews will also be helpful. He can listen to records of his interviews, rate his probes, and analyze his own interviewing. A further technique which is useful in analyzing recordings is to rate the probe and then study the respondent's next few remarks. If the probe is inappropriate, its effect can often be noticed in what the respondent says or does. For example, if the respondent makes an irrelevant response, the interviewer should examine the earlier probes to see whether they might have caused this. If the respondent appears to become defensive, listen to the preceding probes and evaluate them carefully to see whether any of them might have been the cause. If the respondent gives information which appears to be different from or inconsistent with earlier information, the interviewer will want to consider whether any of his probes have been biased or leading.

The indirect type of feedback is based on the assumption that poor or inappropriate probes have an effect upon later responses and can be identified by the interviewer in listening to a recording.

The interviewer should use the scales described in this chapter to rate the probes in the interviews in Part II of this book. He should analyze the probes independently of the writers' comments, and then compare his ratings with the commentaries.

Another technique, which provides more direct feedback, is to discuss the interview with the respondent. Select a respondent (a friend or acquaintance) who will be sufficiently secure in the interview and in his relationships with the interviewer to discuss frankly how he felt during the interview. What irritated him? Did he always understand what was wanted? Ideally, the interviewer and the respondent should listen to the recording of their interview together, stopping the record frequently so that the interviewer can ask the respondent how he felt at that point, why he answered as he did, and so on.

More indirect learning experiences are readily available in listening to and analyzing informally the work of other interviewers—for example social conversations, business interviews, a sales attempt in which one is oneself the respondent, and the like. In all of these the essentials of interviews are present. What did the "interviewer" say or do? What happened as a result? How did I feel as a "respondent"? What could or should he have said so that I would feel differently?

All these experiences, which are common, give an opportunity to practice identifying the elements of human relationships, analyzing their components and predicting their outcome. As the learner becomes more and more sensitive to listening to discussions and conversations in this way, he will be surprised at what he hears about these interactions that he missed before. He will find that he listens and then "codes" what he hears.

In these ways, the "solitary learner" may hope to compensate in some degree for being deprived of the group learning situation, and to achieve considerable proficiency at interviewing for information.

SUMMARY

This chapter, the last in Part I, is intended to prepare the reader to use to best advantage the interview transcriptions and commentaries which make up Part II of the book. In this chapter, the emphasis is not on the content of interviewing but rather on the process by which interviewing skills can be acquired. The basic assumption of the chapter is that most people can become successful interviewers. We recognize that some people have formed habits of interaction and possess characteristic sensitivities which facilitate successful interviewing, but others are without these habits and sensitivities. We believe, however, that these are qualities that can be cultivated successfully by most people. Chapter 9 suggests some of the means by which they may be acquired.

The training approach advocated here is primarily one of skill practice, with emphasis on the group as the unit of training. Extensive use of role-playing is suggested, with the trainee being given ample opportunity to be successively interviewer, respondent, and observer. The analysis of recorded interviews is useful as a preliminary to actual interviewing practices. Recording the practice interviews of trainees is also suggested as a means of letting the novice hear exactly what he does in the interview situation.

A system of three scales is proposed to help the interviewer rate the effectiveness of his own techniques of probing for information. These include scales of acceptance, validity, and relevance. Each remark of the interviewer can be analyzed in terms of its effect on the interviewer-respondent relationship, in terms of its validity or avoidance of bias, and in terms of its relevance or contribution to achieving the content objectives of the interview. The chapter includes also excerpts from five interviews, with numerous examples of alternative probe questions and analyses of their relative strengths and weaknesses in terms of the three rating scales. In conclusion we consider the special problems of the "solitary learner," the person who wants to learn to interview or to improve his interviewing techniques but must do so without the help of others. Specific suggestions to such persons include the use of recorded material and interview transcriptions, with analysis in terms of the rating scales. It is suggested also that the solitary learner develop the practice of listening to and analyzing interviews in which he plays the part of respondent or observer. These include social conversations, business discussions, persuasive attempts by salesmen, and the like.

part II

INTRODUCTION

In Part I of this book we have attempted to do three things. First, we have suggested a general approach for understanding the interactions of the information-getting interview. Second, we have discussed specific techniques and procedures that the interviewer may use to gain information in an unbiased way. Third, in the chapter immediately preceding this, we have given the reader some suggestions for becoming a more proficient interviewer. The principles and techniques of interviewing have been illustrated by brief excerpts from interviews, some actual and some constructed by the authors. The purpose of Part II is to illustrate more fully the techniques of the information-getting interview. This we shall do by using actual interviews as they occur in actual interviewing situations.

Brief excerpts from interviews, although useful to illustrate specific points of technique, are not adequate substitutes for an entire interview in which one can see how the techniques are interrelated, and how an interview develops through its various stages. The interviews recorded in this part of the book are intended to give the reader a more complete and unified picture of various kinds of interviews as they actually are carried out by practitioners.

These interviews—a medical interview, two personnel interviews, a supervisory interview, and a social-work interview—are representative of different kinds of information-getting interviews. They were selected not for perfection of technique but as good examples from the particular fields which they represent, and because they serve to illustrate the practical application of principles and techniques discussed in the first part of the book. They are intended not merely to be read for their human interest, but to be studied and evaluated. In doing this, the reader should become increasingly sensitive to technique, and should gain a better understanding of interviewing principles.

The following approach will maximize their usefulness. Read only the respondent's answer, covering up the interviewer's probe that follows it. Before reading further, consider what interviewer probe is most appropriate. If you were the interviewer, what would you say, what type of probe would you use? Is this a situation that calls for more information, for clarifying information already obtained? Or has the present topic been thoroughly explored and is it time to switch to a new area? After deciding the most appropriate type of probe, decide how you, if you were the interviewer, would actually word that probe to best fit the objective. In this connection the three scales (Figure 12) in Chapter 9 will be useful. After a probe is formulated, rate it on the scales and then evaluate its adequacy. Now uncover the interviewer's probe and see what he did. Compare your probe with the one actually used. Study the interviewer's probe and decide whether you feel he used a poor probe or a good one and why it was good or poor.

Unfortunately, the reader must remain at a disadvantage; his interpretations must be based entirely on the printed page. He would interpret some of the comments quite differently if he were listening to a recording of the interview, in which he could hear and evaluate the varying inflections, intonations, bewilderments, tensions, and other audible cues. Hesitations and difficulties in phrasing the responses would become much more significant. The real interviewer obviously had the additional advantage of being able to see and interpret gestures and facial expressions, and his reactions to both audible and visible cues are reflected in his probes.

The authors' comments (in brackets) are intended to help the reader in his analysis of the interviews. These comments are inserted at points which the authors consider to be especially apt demonstrations of some of the principles expounded in Part I.

It may interest the reader to know something of the process

through which these interviews were obtained. With the exception of the role-played interview, these were recorded by means of a tape recorder temporarily installed at the location where the interviewer usually conducted his interviews. That is, the medical interview took place in the physician's examining room of a large hospital; the employment interviews were taken in the interviewing cubicles of the personnel department in a large corporation, and so on. A typed script was made from the tapes, and the transcript was carefully reviewed to be sure that it was a faithful reproduction of the original interview.

The recording of interviews has the disadvantage that it creates some pressure on the interviewer. It is interesting to note that the pressure on the respondent was virtually nil; it was the interviewer who felt nervous and under some strain. This is consistent with earlier statements that most respondents do not know what the role of an interviewer is. When the interviewer explains that a part of his role is to make tape recordings of the interview, as far as the respondent is concerned this is standard interviewing procedure and presents no problems whatever. In each case the respondent was informed that the interview was being recorded and that it was to be used for research purposes. In not a single case was there any hesitancy on the respondent's part. The respondent was told that if there was anything he wished to say that he did not wish to have recorded, the machine would be stopped. In no interview did the respondent take advantage of this offer. As one can see from reading the scripts, there appears to be no reluctance to talk about intimate personal matters. The interviewer, however, recognizing that the recording was somewhat unusual for his role, was not quite as much at ease as was the respondent. Virtually all interviewers reported that during the first few minutes of the interview they were much aware that the reel on the tape machine was revolving and each word they said was being caught. They said, however, that the nervousness quickly diminished and the recording machine was soon forgotten completely.

From many such recordings, the interviews found in this part of the book were selected. Several criteria were used in their selection, the first being that they were good illustrations of interviewing techniques. Although, as we have said earlier, they are not supposed to be perfect examples, each interviewer was skilled in his own particular field, and an attempt was made to select interviews representing the kinds typical of the different fields. Selecting any one interview to be typical of a whole class is of course difficult. Some attempt also was made to select interviews which were interesting in terms of content, although this was secondary to the other criteria.

The scripts of the recordings as you read them are entirely unedited, except that personal and place names have been changed and other identifying words have been removed to maintain the anonymity of the respondents.

chapter 10

A Medical Interview

Cardiac Symptoms and Neurotic Manifestations

This chapter contains an interview between a physician and a patient. Physicians conduct interviews at various stages in the therapeutic process and for a variety of purposes. A doctor may interview a patient to determine whether a particular course of therapy has resulted in changes in symptoms, or to reassure the patient with respect to treatment under way. One of the major purposes of medical interviewing, however, is to obtain a case history as a basis for an initial diagnosis. We have chosen an initial diagnostic interview for illustrating and analyzing the medical interview.

The purpose of the case-history interview is to determine the extent and nature of the patient's complaints and to permit the formulation of some tentative hypotheses by the physician as to the possible sources of those complaints. The interview also provides the opportunity for the physician to acquire additional relevant facts from the patient that may assist him to reject some hypotheses and to retain others. In theory, the diagnostic interview concludes when the physician has exhausted all the relevant information the patient can communicate. This may mean that the physician has reduced the possible explanations of the patient's condition to a single cause and the interview leads directly into the therapeutic phase, in which the physician attempts to eliminate this cause. On the other hand, it may mean that when the physician terminates the interview, he has developed several possible causes of the patient's complaint. In such a case, the interview leads into a second phase of the patient-doctor relationship, in which various tests and examinations are used to determine which of the possible explanations is the correct one.

The length and complexity of medical interviews vary over a broad range. Some patients arrive at the doctor's office with injuries so obvious in nature that no interview is necessary, and the physician proceeds immediately with treatment. The patient who arrives with his broken arm in a crude sling has no need for nor motivation to become the respondent in a medical interview. On the other hand, many patients arrive in the physician's consulting room with only the vague statement that they don't feel well or are worried about the state of their health. The physician must begin by attempting to narrow down the symptoms and possible causes of the complaint, and in some cases must discover whether or not the feeling of being unwell has any basic physical origin. Somewhere between these extremes lies the more usual case in which the patient's complaints are reasonably well defined and somewhat localized. Such a case is presented in our example.

Of the many types of information-getting interviews, the diagnostic interview as practiced by the physician is certainly one of the most complex and demanding of skilled interviewing techniques. The reason for this complexity lies partially in the fact that the physician must fulfill several roles at the same time. He must obtain sufficient information from the patient to formulate hypotheses as to what may be the nature of the medical problem. Next, he must frame additional questions to test the hypotheses he has developed. Third, he must reject some of his possible explanations in the light of further information obtained from the patient. Finally, the hypotheses remaining may be put to more stringent and specialized tests. In any case, having satisfied himself as to the most likely medical basis of the patient's symptoms, the physician must then act upon his best hypothesis by recommending and carrying out medication or other therapy. These stages are typical of many research operations extending over a substantial period of time and perhaps with the participation of a number of people. But the physician is typically the sole theorist, interviewer, analyst, and action agent. Such a combination of activities requires great skill and attention to interviewing as well as medical techniques if the physician is to obtain the unbiased and complete data necessary for making the most appropriate medical decisions.

A second complexity which is characteristic of the medical inter-

view stems primarily from the patient role and the ambivalences associated with it. Of all the information-getting interviews, the medical
interview probably puts the respondent in a situation where he has
most to win or lose. The patient-respondent must await a medical
verdict which may tell him that he is to undergo long and painful
therapy or none at all; that he is basically in excellent health or is
suffering from an incurable disease. As a result the medical interview
is often a real threat to the patient, and a great deal of emotion is
involved. The patient is likely to be ambivalent—on the one hand,
he wants the physician to discover and remedy the cause of his difficulty; on the other, he does not want the physician to discover anything that will require radical or extended therapy.

The result of these conflicting forces is likely to make the patient
an unreliable reporter of his own symptoms. He is also likely to approach the interview in an extremely suggestible frame of mind.
That is, he will attempt to read some medical significance into the
doctor's questions. He will also understand the implications of the
questions, and may attempt to frame his replies partly in terms of his
own symptoms and partly in terms of what he infers to be the import
of the physician's query. If, in asking about a particular symptom,
the doctor uses a choice of words and tone of voice which suggest
dire consequences for the possessor of the symptom, the patient is
perhaps more likely to conclude that he doesn't really have that
symptom. This is much less a matter of direct falsification than of
understandable biases in recollection and communication, generated
by the emotional forces in the situation.

A third source of complexity in the medical interview is the difference in language between patient and physician. The two participants in the interview do not share a common language, particularly
in reference to the descriptions of symptoms. In the medical interview which follows this introduction, we find that the patient describes his pain in terms which merely echo those used by the doctor
in his questions. When the physician asks the patient to characterize
the pain in his own words, the patient's difficulty in formulating a
description emphasizes the gap in vocabulary between the two.

Several characteristics of this interview should be noted. First, it
was conducted in a hospital. The physician was on the hospital staff,
and the patient had been admitted to the hospital the previous evening. There was therefore the possibility of physician and patient
having more uninterrupted time for the interview than might be
feasible in the office of a general practitioner. The interview is somewhat unusual also in the complexity and inconsistency of some of the

symptoms reported. The patient began by describing what appeared to be a fairly straightforward and understandable set of symptoms, but in the course of the interview the physician was led to discard his original hypotheses and to develop others. The process of eliminating one interpretation of symptoms and developing a more satisfactory one necessitated extensive probing into several aspects of the patient's life and interpersonal relationships.

The patient was a man forty years of age, who stated on admission that he had been ill for the past three weeks with severe chest pains on the left side. The interview took place in the early afternoon and was the second interview which the patient had had since his entry into the hospital. At the time of his entry on the previous evening, there was a brief intake interview. The patient was now about to have a full case history taken, following which a general physical examination would be made by the examining physician. The interview occurred in an examining room.

Before the recorded text of this interview began, the doctor introduced himself to the patient and explained the purpose of the interview and of the physical examination which would follow it. At this time, the physician requested the patient's permission to record their conversation for purposes of research. The patient agreed, and the interview then got underway.

In conducting this interview, the physician made use of brief notes taken at the time of the patient's admittance to the hospital. He also used a case-history form on which some of the specific information was recorded.

In general, we feel that this interview represents an insightful and successful handling of a difficult situation. The patient was cooperative but was largely without initial insight into the real source of his difficulties. Moreover, his descriptions of his own symptoms showed the kind of vagueness and inconsistencies that must present difficult diagnostic problems for physicians.

Interview[1]

1. I: Now, Mr. Blank, your trouble began, as I understand, three weeks ago. Is that right?

    [I-1. The interviewer begins by checking the records of the intake interview in order to meet his first objective: determining the onset of the patient's symptoms. The interviewer uses a question form which is clear but lacks balance. He em-

----

[1] Throughout these interviews, I refers to the interviewer, R refers to the respondent.

ploys the response of the previous interview as a question form which puts the respondent in the position of having to contradict the record of the previous interview in order to make any change or corrections.]

R: Yes.
2. I: And before that you were perfectly all right. Is that right?
R: Yes.
3. I: No difficulty at all.
R: No.
4. I: Nothing.
R: Like I mentioned, about fifteen years back it was the same symptom I had when I went to a doctor and he was more interested in the pain in my arm.

[I-2 to I-4. These three probes are used in a determined attempt to rule out possibilities of an earlier onset of symptoms than that which the patient reported on entering the hospital. The interviewer's persistence is commendable. At the same time we must wonder whether the interviewer might not have reached his objective earlier if he had asked the initial question in a more balanced form and had avoided the persistent use of negatively phrased probes. For example, the initial question might have been worded, "Now Mr. Blank, when was the first time you had any trouble of this kind?" Similarly, his probe questions might have been worded along the following lines: "Well, had you had any previous difficulty whatever?" The important point, however, is that the interviewer's persistence is finally rewarded with the material contained in R-4. This, then, becomes the lead which the interviewer is to follow in unraveling the background of the patient's symptoms. The interviewer is now well on his way to realizing his first major objective: to determine the time of onset of symptoms, to obtain a full description of the symptoms, and to investigate some of the situational factors associated with the symptoms. The full realization of these objectives will require an exchange of 35 or 40 questions and responses.]

5. I: How old were you at that time?
R: Well, let's say—go back to '39—in the year '38 or '39.
6. I: I see. It is about fifteen years ago.
R: Yes.
7. I: You are now forty, so it would make you about twenty-five?
R: Yes.

[I-5 to I-7 represent a straightforward kind of interaction to determine the respondent's age at the previous onset of symptoms. When the respondent encounters difficulty in stating his age at that time, the interviewer utilizes the respondent's statement of the year of initial symptoms, and then does the respondent's arithmetic for him.]

8. I: And what kind of pain was that—would you describe it for me?
R: Well it was just like—well, it was just like a sore spot—you know

—in other words just like the beat of your temple. When it hit, it would hurt—ache all the time.

9. I: Was it sore in between those beatings? Or was it a throbbing pain?
    R: A throbbing pain.
10. I: I see—
    R: Running from here to here. (Points to left arm.)
11. I: Did you have any pain elsewhere except in the inner side of that arm there?
    R: No.
12. I: You didn't have any pain in your chest at that time?
    R: No.
13. I: You did not?
    R: No.
14. I: You say it ran back and forth from your arm to your chest though?
    R: Yes. From my heart, it seems. — It seemed like it came from there.

[I-8 to I-14 represent the physician's attempt to elicit the respondent's description of his pain. These questions are an excellent example of interviewing technique. The physician begins with a question (I-8) which is broad, open, and free from leading or biasing factors. He then employs a series of supplementary questions in an effort to get a fuller description of the symptoms. This is a good example of the funnel approach described in Chapter 6. The physician follows his initial broad question with a series of increasingly specific supplementary questions to establish the type of pain and the exact location of the pain. In each case the physician's question builds on the response which precedes it. The balance and unbiased formulation of the questions is particularly important here, considering the difficulty of obtaining a description of internal pain from a layman and the possibility of a high degree of suggestibility on the patient's part.]

15. I: Do you remember what you were doing at that time or not?
    R: No. No, I don't.

[Beginning with I-15 the interviewer is attempting to discover some of the situational factors which might have had a bearing on the first experience of symptoms by the patient. The interviewer is flexible enough to digress to pick up other relevant information (for example, the duration of symptoms), but he persists in the attempt to discover environmental factors attending the onset of symptoms some fifteen years ago.]

16. I: And how—how long did it last?
    R: Oh—three or four days, I would say.
17. I: Three or four days.
    R: Yes, because when I went to the doctor, why he, like I say, was just—he was interested in that, and he told me to come back, and I never did go back.
18. I: Uh-huh.

R: And that was the end of that incident.

19. I: Do you remember anything else happening at that time except for this throbbing pain? — Was there anything else associated with the pain? Any other discomfort?

R: No.

20. I: And it lasted three or four days and then you were well again.

R: Yes.

21. I: No difficulty at all. O.K.

R: No. I said then—well, I'll tell you, another thing is—I will say that on and off that I did feel the pain in here and I never got anything in my—well, let's say in my heart—but even when I went into the service I tried to tell them that—I tell you the truth, I tried to tell 'em that I got pains right in here, and you know how they were—you know, you look healthy, get going! (Laughs.)

22. I: Sure. Did you notice that pain at any particular time?

R: No, see, I wouldn't remember.

[I-20 to I-22 provide some additional evidence of interviewing skill on the part of the physician. In I-20 he makes an accurate summarization of what the respondent has told him. This summary question serves the additional purpose of leading the respondent away from the response reflected in R-17, which the doctor apparently feels is digressive. Having got the patient's corroboration of the summary, the physician again demonstrates his caution and care in attempting to elicit other information with probe questions I-20 and I-21. The interviewer's use of the expression "O.K." (I-21) is interesting. The physician has been pushing the patient to make certain that there was no persistence of symptoms. In I-21 the interviewer tells the patient that he accepts his statements, and at the same time the inflection, permissive tone, and relaxed pacing of the interview are such that the respondent is encouraged to provide additional information. It is clear that introduction of a new line of questioning by the interviewer at this moment would have prevented the important additional information which the respondent offers in R-21, in spite of the fact that he has twice previously indicated that there was no persistence of symptoms.

We already have some clue as to the sources of the patient's anxiety. In R-14 the patient refers to the pain as coming from his heart. This appears to be more an expression of anxiety than an actual attempt to locate the pain. In R-17 the patient indicated that when the doctor became more interested in the pain of the arm, rather than in the chest area, the patient never returned to the doctor. In R-21 the patient enlarges on the picture of a man who has recurrent pain, is concerned with the possibility of a heart disease as a cause of that pain, but feels that the physicians with whom he has come in contact have not given him an adequate opportunity to talk about his symptoms, nor shown sufficient concern for them. The interviewer's "Sure" (I-22) deserves comment. In this case he is recognizing in a very human way the situation that the respondent is describing, and yet he is not making a great point of it. In listening to the interview, one notices that this interview is definitely directed toward a goal. Very little time is spent in idle talk or "rapport building" of a superficial nature. It is also clear that a permissive relationship has been established.]

23. I: Was there anything that brought that pain on, as far as you know —anything that you would do?
     R: No.
24. I: —that would bring that pain on?
     R: No—not unless when I was eighteen years of age I went to a boys' club in Detroit and picked up a weight—125 pounds. Well, I picked it up twelve times—
25. I: Yeah, um-hmmm.
     R: —just bragging off you know, and then the thirteenth time I keeled over—you see I barely got it half way and I keeled over. You see I had a sprained back for two years.

[In I-22 the interviewer returns to the objective. In R-22 it becomes clear that this question is not reaching the objective, so the interviewer asks another open question (I-23) aimed at the same objective. R-24 is interesting. The respondent first answers, "No." Then after a pause he mentions very tentatively an event which might possibly be related to his pain. The interviewer has been sufficiently permissive so that the respondent finally is able to bring out what appears to have been a rather embarrassing episode. The interviewer then follows this response with enough questions (I-26 to I-29) to satisfy himself that the symptoms involved in this specific episode are unrelated to the patient's present difficulty.]

26. I: You went over backwards?
     R: Yes, flipped right backward and the weight and all.
27. I: Did the weight hit you or did it end up behind you?
     R: No—it was right back. I threw it, and when it got back of me it dropped.
28. I: Where was your pain in your back at that time?
     R: The whole small of my back—I couldn't pick up anything.
29. I: Just in the small of the back? Nowhere else except for that?
     R: No.
30. I: O.K. Now this pain that you talk of, that has occurred since you were about age twenty-five—
     R: That's right.

[When the physician is assured of these facts, he (I-30) brings the patient back to a discussion of the present symptoms.]

31. I: Would that occur when you were doing anything similar to that, or would it just come on spontaneously?
     R: No, just spontaneously. In other words every so often I'd—

32. I: Did you ever notice it at night?

    R: Um—I wouldn't say that—couldn't say that.

33. I: No relationship with night.

    R: No, I—

34. I: No extra pain then?

    R: Hasn't been aching then, not until three weeks back—then it really knocked me out.

35. I: Yeah—but actually except for this discomfort which you had in your arm, before three weeks ago you were perfectly all right, is that right?

    R: Except, like you mentioned, spontaneously—I would, now and then, maybe a couple of years or so, you know, in between I would get this ache in my arm and—

36. I: You never knew what brought that on?

    R: No. I never did. No.

37. I: Never any association with doing anything, like lifting—or coughing or—

    R: Well, I did, er, I did work in a coal yard for three years, and I worked in a factory on a block, but that was never hard work—as far as the coal was concerned, I mean, it wasn't hard work.

38. I: Was it the kind of thing, the kind of pain that you would feel after you lifted something too heavy for you, or a different kind of sensation from that?

    R: Gee, I couldn't say. I've worked like a maniac for eight hours and nothing develops—nothing that hurts me at all—in fact I like to work.

    [I-31 to I-38. The interviewer is completing the description and symptoms of the initial onset of the patient's complaint, thus fulfilling the first objective. This summary takes the form of a series of questions asked by the physician to verify the information which he already has. Where necessary, the physician does not hesitate to cut off the patient's repetition of previously obtained information. Nor does he permit the patient to describe his present problems until the summary of the previous symptoms is complete.]

39. I: O.K. And then three weeks ago you had this pain all of a sudden—is that right?

    [I-39 is an example of the transitional statement described in an earlier chapter. The interviewer's "O.K." informs the respondent that one section of the interview has been completed and that the physician has sufficient information and is ready to move to other subjects. He then begins the second major objective, namely, determining the description and background of the patient's recent attack.]

    R: That's right.

40. I: Same kind of a pain you've had before over a past number of years?

    R: That's right. I got up one day, I can't remember whether it was in the morning or the afternoon—but I felt it, you know what I mean, I felt it between here and here, and I guess—I think I got one or two just slight jabs like, you know, and I held on and kinda tried to get my air again, and I told my wife about it, or ex-wife, let's say, and I sat around for a while and the pain went away, and I went outside and it never bothered me after that and—

41. I: This was when?
    R: About three weeks ago.
42. I: Well, is this the same time you talked about—you told me about last night, that came on all of a sudden?
    R: No—no.
43. I: It was before that.
    R: *That* stopped until Monday morning about eight o'clock.
44. I: Well, now talking about the time when it came on suddenly three weeks ago. You said you were working on a fence at that time?
    R: Yes, I was. But I think I was in the house at the time. I remember because—
45. I: In other words you weren't working on a fence at that time?
    R: Well, I'd been working on the fence, I tell you the truth—for—oh —two or three—
46. I: Well, that's what I'm getting at—you weren't working on the fence when this happened?
    R: No. No. I have been doing that for two, three months now and it's pretty hard pounding the nails, but I was in the house when it happened.
47. I: You were in the house. Do you remember when you woke up that morning if you had a pain?
    R: No, it didn't hurt me then.
48. I: Well, how did it come on?
    R: Just like you were going to jab—like a couple of days back, just a slight pain, and I got scared and I kinda hung onto it, and then I got another real *slight* one, you know—like—
49. I: This is the one you're talking about three weeks ago?
    R: That's right. It was—

   [R-39 to I-49 show problems of clarification. The respondent has difficulty in recalling the exact time at which the attack occurred and the circumstances under which it occurred. The respondent also succeeds in confusing the interviewer as to the specific incident and circumstances which he is describing. It seems likely that the interviewer's persistent and commendable efforts to get the respondent's meaning clear make the pace of the interview slower and the interaction somewhat bumpier than had previously been the case. Such a process of misunderstanding and clarification often poses a rapport problem. However, the interviewer insisted on clarifying the situation, and beginning with I-49 he is able to put together a reasonable summary of the information which the respondent has provided.]

50. I: And you were in the house?
    R: Yes.

51. I: What time of day was it?
    R: It was—I wouldn't say—I'd say it was either in the morning or at night—late.
52. I: Was it after a meal or not?
    R: No, I don't think so.
53. I: About the middle of the morning then, let's say?
    R: Because I don't eat—just drink coffee for breakfast, and I don't eat until about three o'clock in the afternoon and then I go to work, so I—
54. I: Uh-huh.
    R: I forgot to mention one other thing—maybe I did to you—
55. I: Well wait, Bill. Let's see if we can—let's clarify this thing that happened three weeks ago before going into that. Do you remember anything that day before you had this pain in your side that was bothering you? Was there any kind of discomfort in that region before this pain came on?
    R: Well, I would say no.
56. I: You'd say no. In other words it came on suddenly like a bolt from the blue.
    R: Yeah, that's it.
57. I: Never felt it before?
    R: Not that pain three weeks ago—maybe a few years back I did—
58. I: But not of that severity.
    R: No.
59. I: Or was it?
    R: No. No, not except fifteen years back it hit me a couple of times, just light pains.
60. I: But not like this?
    R: No. This time it really give me a kick.
61. I: What did it feel like?
    R: Well, just like someone took a knife and slashed it across your skin, just a sharp jab.
62. I: It felt sharp, in other words?
    R: Yeah, that's right.
63. I: Anything else besides that?
    R: No. Then it started to ache, then it started to ache and then it would keep running up and down here.
64. I: Running back and forth from where to where?
    R: From my arms—from here to here.
65. I: You spoke of it as being a throbbing kind of pain before. Was it this way again—or wasn't it?
    R: Was this the three weeks back?
66. I: Yeah—when you had the pain that time—
    R: Yeah.
67. I: Was it throbbing or I mean a dull ache, or—

[The interviewer now proceeds to elicit additional information regarding the character and circumstances of the patient's pain. By and large the interviewer does this skillfully, through the use of open questions. It is perhaps worth remarking that the confusion that occurs around R-64 to R-67 appears to result from the respondent's characterization of the pain as "sharp" rather than "throbbing," which has been the description used most frequently up to now.   In this connection it is interesting to find that the phrase "throbbing pain" was introduced into the conversation not by the respondent but by the interviewer, in an effort to break the deadlock occasioned by the respondent's inability to characterize the pain.   (See I-9 and R-9.)   In other words it now appears that I-9 was a biasing probe, and that the interviewer's misapprehensions about the throbbing character of the respondent's pain resulted from this bias.   The interviewer attempts to clarify this problem in I-67, failing to recall that it was he himself who introduced the notion of the throbbing pain.   In the patient's response we find that he is still unable to characterize the pain.   It seems clear that the doctor's vocabulary for the description of pain is something the patient simply does not share, and that this difference in terminology represents a serious handicap to their communication.]

R: Well, it was hurting me—my heart was hurting me for about an hour I'd say—I could hardly get my wind—then I went outside and forgot about it—it kinda stopped—

68. I: That long a time.

R: I fooled around, well I *did* work. — Well, I went outside.

[R-67. The patient, unable to characterize the pain as the doctor has requested, resorts to the communication of interesting but irrelevant data.   Unable to characterize the pain in the doctor's terms, the patient attempts to describe it in terms familiar to himself, giving expression at the same time to a repetition of the real source of his anxiety, "My heart was hurting me."]

69. I: Did it affect your breath at that time?

R: Well, in other words, I grabbed for it—maybe that's what made me go outdoors.

70. I: (Pause.)   Did you notice that when you coughed or when you sneezed, was it any worse at that time?

R: Not the one three weeks ago.   A couple of days back—yeah.

71. I: Um-hmm.   But not the one three weeks ago.

R: No—it just lasted, let's say about an hour or so.

72. I: This pain was sharp, is that right, Bill?

R: Yeah.

[This communications difficulty is by no means ended.   The doctor attempts again in I-72 to get a specific characterization of the pain, resorting to the highly directive question, "This pain was sharp, is that right, Bill?"   The patient naturally enough agrees with the physician at this point, that it was indeed sharp.   Several responses later, however, the patient demonstrates that he is basically unable to characterize the pain.]

73. I: It had no—there was nothing else besides that you noticed that bothered you at all?

R: No.
74. I: Was it at all burning in nature?
R: Um—ah—
75. I: Did it feel like a hot iron?
R: Just an ache.
76. I: Just an ache. It lasted for about an hour?
R: Yeah, and then it went away and I went outside and went to work.
77. I: You went to work again.
R: Yeah.

[The physician's attempt at translation (I-75) is a good rewording of the question (I-74) and retains its unbiased form, but does little to help the respondent. At this point the physician moves on to another of his subobjectives: the duration of the pain. In I-76 and I-77 the interviewer provides us with examples of successful probes which are merely echoes of the respondent's previous statement but result in elaboration on those statements.]

78. I: You were O.K.
R: I just couldn't stay there and worry about it—you know what I mean—I couldn't.
79. I: But you felt all right. You went to work on the fence?
R: Yeah. Oh—
80. I: Yeah, and then you were O. K. in *every way*—until just recently?
R: That's right.

[In I-78 the interviewer uses a probe that is unfortunately directive. It consists of a flat assertion to the respondent, and is so worded that the respondent would have to contradict the physician in order to state that he felt any symptoms. Moreover, when the respondent fails to agree with the physician that he "felt O.K.," and instead volunteers other information, the interviewer persists in his own line of questioning, again requesting the respondent to agree that he "felt all right."]

81. I: And this most recent episode began two days ago, is that right?
R: Monday.
82. I: Last Monday?
R: Monday.
83. I: Today is Wednesday, right?
R: Yes.
84. I: And that again in the morning?
R: Eight o'clock. I noticed it was five minutes after I ate—
85. I: Five minutes after you ate. — Did you have coffee for breakfast?
R: Yeah—I had three cups of coffee.
86. I: That is your usual breakfast, is that right?
R: Yeah.

[This is a reasonably straightforward question, and its directive character is perhaps understandable in the light of the fact that it is picking up a thread of response first given in

R-53. The question form "Is that your usual breakfast?" would have been preferable.]

87. I: You felt all right that night?
    R: Oh yeah.

[I-87. This is another example of the interviewer's tendency to frame questions in assertive form.]

88. I: No trouble at all.
    R: Until a couple of days back—three weeks back—I felt all right. I paid no more attention to that—until I come up with—

89. I: Was it the same kind of pain as before?
    R: Yeah, it was. But this was a *good* one. (Laughs.)

90. I: How long did that last?
    R: Oh, just a . . . (missed on recording). It felt like someone was shooting my arm and my back or something like that. By the time I walked ten *more* feet—why it got me again—gave me another one, see—and then I knew something was going wrong, so I sat in a chair for a few hours. (Part of response unintelligible.)

91. I: I see, and, er—anything else associated with this pain?
    R: No. No. It was just between my arm and side.

92. I: How did you feel?
    R: I felt weak—just like someone was squeezing the thing and pulling me down—in other words I just got limp like.

93. I: Squeezing like what?
    R: Well, like someone was hanging on to this thing.

94. I: Hanging on where?
    R: To the heart, we'll say. — Just seemed like someone was trying to pull it out or hanging on to it, you know?

95. I: Feel like it was inside or outside?
    R: Yeah—inside—just like inside.

[I-88 to I-95. In this series of questions the interviewer is attempting, with some success, to explore a number of dimensions of the respondent's experience with the pain. Specifically, the physician wants to know the duration, characteristics of the pain, and the like. Although this sequence of questions is effective in terms of the information he is able to develop, it seems likely that a funnel order of questions might have been more effective. Such a sequence might have begun with the doctor's inviting the patient to describe as much as he could remember of the circumstances and characteristics of the attack.

The probing in this sequence of questions appears to have been permissive and well phrased on the whole, but it appears also to have become specific before the respondent was really ready for it. For example, when the respondent in R-88 begins a description of a situation, the physician interrupts to inquire whether it was the same kind of pain he suffered before. In I-90 the physician suggests still another dimension, the duration of the pain. It is interesting that the respondent has

A MEDICAL INTERVIEW — page 271

generated sufficient momentum for a general description of his symptoms that he ignores I-90 entirely and proceeds with his own narrative. It is to the interviewer's credit that he responds to this description with a more insightful and generalized kind of probing (I-91 to I-94).]

96. I: Did that pain scare you, Bill, or not?
R: Pardon?
97. I: Did that pain scare you?
R: Well, I—I'll admit it did! After two *good* ones like *that*, why I got scared, yeah!

[I-96 represents a sudden change of pace. The physician changes the context of the discussion to inquire about the patient's reaction to the pain. It is difficult to evaluate this question. It is certainly a digression in terms of content, and since the physician does not pursue this line of questioning, we must assume that it does not represent an important objective at this point in the interview. Moreover, its effect on the respondent is to stop him completely for a moment (see R-96). It seems likely that the question is a result of a sudden insight on the part of the physician that the patient is showing a good deal of anxiety, and is an effort to bring that anxiety into the open. In this respect he is eventually successful (see R-97). It is possible that the remainder of the interview is benefited by the fact that this anxiety has been expressed and faced to this extent.]

98. I: Were you short of breath at that time?
R: Er, well, I wasn't really short of breath—I was more or less gasping, we'll say, a little bit but not much.
99. I: What position did you get in to make it feel better?
R: I just sat down in a chair and kinda leaned back.
100. I: Leaned back, um-hm.
R: Leaned back, I couldn't do anything. Just hung on to it. More or less I was waiting for it to hit me again. (Laughs.) And then I took about three breaths—a good three breaths and those three breaths, oh, not right away but let's say maybe an hour later I took a breath and got another one.
101. I: When you took a breath?
R: About three breaths I took and each one—so I *quit*—I mean I—
102. I: Did you move around at that time? When you were in the chair?
R: Yes, I moved.
103. I: Did it hurt when you moved at all?
R: No, but it kept on aching—it just ached—it ached all the way until night time. It ached all the way to night—until I went to bed.
104. I: Did you take anything to eat at all that day?
R: I had a bowl of soup, that is all I had.
105. I: Was it a strong soup, or what was—
R: Vegetable soup, ———'s soup.

106. I: Did that affect it at all?
     R: No.
107. I: You had no pain any place else?
     R: No.
108. I: Your bowels had been O.K.
     R: They are O.K. Been O.K. for years and years.
109. I: You never had any yellow jaundice at all?
     R: No.
110. I: Does any particular food bother you—any particular food give you trouble?
     R: No—I can eat anything.
111. I: Um-hmm. Did you ever have any pain in your belly at all?
     R: No, sir.
112. I: Did you ever have any trouble passing your water at all?
     R: No.
113. I: Or in your kidneys or in your bladder?
     R: No. — Not unless sometimes when I drink too much beer—it feels—it begins to hurt and then I quit.

[I-103 to I-113. In this series the interviewer is asking questions in an attempt to find out what might be related to the patient's pain. These questions would have been less susceptible to bias if they had been worded without the implied response. For example, in I-109 the question might better have been asked, "Did you ever have yellow jaundice?"]

114. I: Uh-huh.
     R: I mean my kidney, the right one—
115. I: Then after it started last Monday, then it went away Monday night, is that right? And you went to sleep.
     R: It really didn't go away. I laid down with it hurting me—with it aching, see—I put that electric hot pad on—and I must have fallen asleep because I was scared to lay down because you know how it is, you just think about different things.
116. I: What do you mean you were scared to lay down—scared to go to sleep?
     R: Yeah. (Laughs.) Scared I wouldn't wake up any more, and didn't know what to expect.

[In I-115 the interviewer makes two erroneous assumptions in the question—that the pain went away Monday night and that the patient went to sleep. Notice that the respondent had to go to some length to contradict this—"It really didn't go away." It is clear that he did fall asleep sometime during the night, but that he fell asleep sitting in a chair, as we shall see later on. In this case the respondent did correct the erroneous assumptions made by the interviewer. One wonders in how many more cases the interviewer has been left with false assumptions because the respondent did not go to the length that would be required to correct them.

The probe of I-116 is unbiased and simply asks the respondent to clarify his meaning. On the other hand, it appears not too well chosen in the light of the preceding response. In R-115 the respondent is obviously asking for understanding and reassurance—"You know how it is." The interviewer responds, not by offering this understanding and reassurance, but rather with a request for clarification. Although the respondent goes on to clarify his feelings, we cannot help speculating on the greater effectiveness which might have been achieved with some such response as "Yes, I can see how that sort of thing would frighten you." Such a probe would have represented an interviewer response to the attitude, as well as the content of the respondent's previous statement. Such a demonstration of interviewer sensitivity to respondent attitude almost invariably builds a stronger interviewer-respondent relationship, and in this case would probably have resulted in valuable information.]

117. I: Uh-huh.
    R: So that when I laid down with the pad like this here (a heating pad)—I just put my head back and must have fallen to sleep, because the next thing I knew it was morning and I was sitting the same way.

118. I: Did you feel all right?
    R: Yeah. Took the pad off and gave the kids breakfast, woke them up and sent them off to school, and then had my usual two or three cups of coffee—I usually drink three or four cups, it isn't strong coffee. And by gosh—not even an hour I would say, the damned thing took off and started aching again.   —It ached until yesterday.

119. I: And did you have that sudden pain again or just an ache?
    R: No, just an ache. A dull ache come on it and it stayed until I saw you last night.

120. I: I see, did it go away last night or not?
    R: Yeah—it went when I went to sleep. — You know when I was talking to you here, well, it was still annoying me—I mentioned it to you—but then when I laid down on my side and just didn't give a darn no more, you know, and— (Laughs.)

121. I: It went away.
    R: I got up this morning and haven't got it except, oh, twenty minutes ago it started aching right down here—right here. I was sitting . . . (unintelligible). It wasn't up here—the other one was here—just seemed like something running around in there and trying to get past the door and can't get nowhere. That is the way it seems to me. It seems like a bunch of blood clots. (Laughs.) That is the way it seems to me. (Snickers.)

122. I: How about—
    R: Nothing here though.
123. I: Nothing in your chest at all?
    R: No.

[I-120 to I-123 are attempts at getting more information about the individual's condition. An analysis of the respondent's answers in the same sequence indicates that underlying attitudes of fear, worry, concern, are being expressed. He is responding to the request for factual information in terms of attitude. He says, "I laid down on my side and just didn't give a darn no more," and "It seems like a bunch of blood clots." Other indications also show the tension and concern which he is suffering. The physician disregards these attitudes and focuses on facts. This may be correct in terms of the interviewer's particular objectives. We wonder, however, whether one objective of this interview should not be to permit the respondent to explore his attitudes somewhat more completely. The type of response which would have helped to get at the attitude would have been "You were really quite worried as to what would happen, weren't you?" This would appear to summarize what the respondent has actually been saying throughout this series.]

124. I: That's for today. How about yesterday—did you have pain just in the arm yesterday or—

R: No, this was aching—

125. I: Aching.

R: Yeah, it was aching all the time.

126. I: What kind of a feeling was that?

R: Well, that—a—dull ache—like a tooth.

127. I: And I understand this was not at all affected by anything you would do—is that right? That is, if you got up and exercised yourself, would that—

R: No—no, that wouldn't—no, nothing at all. (Long pause.) One more thing I was going to mention. Yesterday, well, not yesterday, but before I came here-ah-oh, I would say about five times through the day, through the whole day, I would notice while it was aching, just like water dribbling—you know what I mean—

128. I: In your chest?

R: Yes. Just like it was in the heart I would say—just like water getting through it. You can just feel it, just like you could feel something really loose (laughs) flapping like it was trying to go away. Just for a few seconds, then it'd go away. That was just about five times through the whole day, and I never felt it no more.

129. I: Just then?

R: Yes.

[The patient's response in R-127 is interesting. Notice that after his first statement there is a pause. Apparently the physician is writing some notes. After considerable silence, the respondent comes out with a careful statement describing how he felt, and what some of his symptoms were. He makes one of the longest statements about his condition that he has made thus far in the interview. This illustrates the value of the pause, which often is one of the best probing techniques the interviewer has at his disposal. The fact is that in the unhurried, leisurely pace of an interview much material comes out spontaneously without the need for the interviewer to fill gaps in the conversation with some sort of comment.]

130. I: Just then. Have you ever had any pain in your back at all?
R: You mean up?
131. I: Yeah.
R: No, not except a strained back—
132. I: Down low—
R: Had that for a couple of years—
133. I: I see.
R: And I couldn't do anything—
134. I: Um-hmm.
R: It didn't seem like it affected this here. It *might* have something to do in later years.
135. I: Have you ever had any venereal infections?
R: No—none.
136. I: Have you ever had any discharge down below at all?
R: No.
137. I: No infection from a woman or anything like that?
R: No.
138. I: Have you had blood tests for that at all?
R: Gee, I don't know.
139. I: You have had no particular pain in your back?
R: No.
140. I: No difficulty walking?
R: No.
141. I: No numbness of your arms or your legs?
R: No.
142. I: No tingling—as though your arm or your leg was asleep?
R: No—not unless this darn thing here (part unintelligible) . . . this came on about three years ago.
143. I: What?
R: This here.
144. I: Oh, that little bump there.
R: About three years ago I noticed it grew out and it stayed there. Maybe that has got something to do with this sore arm.
145. I: No swelling anywhere else?
R: No. No place on my body. (Pause.)

[I-127 to I-145 represent a straightforward series of questions in which the physician is ruling out the possibility of a variety of diseases. On the whole, these seem to be successfully asked and promptly answered. The only criticism here is the interviewer's frequent use of the assertive question form, which we have noted earlier.]

146. I: You say you—are you divorced now, Bill, or what?

[I-146. Here the physician is beginning to attack his fourth major objective: the discovery of relevant facts about the patient's family life and social adjustment. His opening question develops a good deal of important information.]

R: Well, I am divorced now for a little over a year. I'm making plans to marry her. It was just a big misunderstanding. She was running a restaurant with her brother, and then they used to stay out a little bit at night and I'd have to stay home and watch the kids and I got mad about it. I told my attorney to go give her a talking to and instead she says, "Well, if you don't like it, give me a divorce." (Laughs.)

147. I: So much for that, eh? (Laughs.)   That was her brother?
R: What?

148. I: With her brother?
R: They parted anyway. She's home now. — She is my age. She's a nice woman.

[I-147 and I-148 are requests for clarification, and the respondent ignores them to continue his narrative.]

149. I: How do you get along now, all right?
R: O.K.

150. I: You don't have any trouble getting along with her now, or what?
R: No, none whatsoever.

151. I: Live together now?
R: Yeah—but not sleep together—I just got a room— (Laughs.)

152. I: Yeah.
R: Just for—well, for different purposes—in other words not living in adultery, you see, at all.

153. I: Um-hmm.
R: I got three boys there, and I don't think . . . (end of statement unintelligible).

[I-149 and I-150 are examples of the difficulties which arise from biased question wording. The interviewer uses a question wording which leads the respondent to say that he is now getting along satisfactorily with his wife. Subsequently, contrary information is developed (see R-160 through R-163). It is likely that a general question, such as "Would you tell me something about your home situation," would have produced more satisfactory results. It is in answer to I-151 that the respondent begins to give information which provides the physician with some of his most valuable insights—and incidentally, contradicts entirely R-149 and R-150.]

154. I: (Unintelligible.)
R: I don't know, she just must have got—she is a Catholic and that is what I can't understand. She goes to church every Sunday and she gets home and gets (unintelligible) . . . out of the way and—Maybe she is a cold woman now, I don't know.

155. I: Uh-huh.
R: And I don't go out and . . . (unintelligible).

156. I: But you are able to get along with her sexually though, is that right or what?

[I-156 is another example of a biased question which the respondent corrects. The respondent is speaking softly and with considerable intensity.]

R: Oh yes, before that, sure. Well, she had a child, you see—like I told you, I got a boy fourteen months—well, after that she, well—wouldn't have anything to do with me.

157. I: She was scared.

R: Just scared. She had it at the _____ Hospital. She was just scared and wouldn't have nothing more— She don't want no baby—I can't even touch her now. I don't sleep with her. — I have my own room upstairs. I got a lot of tools and a lot of stuff there and I— I could have stayed with my folks but ain't no sense. I got a job at the _____ Airport for nine years. I got all kinds benefits and stuff—you know what I mean— I like the kid and like her. She just says, "When the time comes, I'll marry you again," and it's finished. — Otherwise we get along perfectly. In fact, if you want to talk to her she will be here at six o'clock or six-thirty tonight.

[I-157. This appears to be an insightful probe. The interviewer here seems to have caught the psychological import of the preceding response and, as the rich response in R-157 suggests, the question has a facilitating effect.]

158. I: Have you had any recent difficulty at all with her, or—or—

R: No. — Nothing at all.

159. I: How about during the past six months, say? Have things become any worse or any better?

R: You mean besides a slight argument?

160. I: Yes—

R: No, I never argue with her. I just get mad at her at times and I figure— Well, when I would get mad you know I wouldn't *feel* good, so I cut that out, completely, I mean I—

[I-159. Here again the interviewer shows considerable skill and insight. When the respondent insists on characterizing his present family situation as untroubled, in spite of the unusual facts which he has already communicated, the physician switches the frame of reference and asks the respondent whether things have been getting better or worse. As R-160 indicates, the approach is successful.]

161. I: What do you mean, you wouldn't feel good?

R: I would just start hurting like—aching.

162. I: What kind of pain was that?

R: About the same thing. It wasn't no sharp pain, just an ache, and I would have to hang on, and I *told* her, I said— Well, you know how a woman is, she'll always try to stick you one way or another, whether something is wrong or not.

163. I: What do you mean, "stick you"?

R: Well, in other words, she wants things this way, and I tell her it's not and (laughs) and then she starts— (laughs) yapping and all—so—so I get mad at her and walk out. And I figure as long as I get mad I can feel my blood pressure rise and then I'd get an ache, and I *told* her about it—

164. I: Um-hmm.

R: The kids got the same way like their old man—

165. I: When you feel your blood pressure rise—what do you mean by that?

R: Well, you know, you can feel your face burning, that you're getting mad about something or other—you know—

166. I: And how long after these things do you start having trouble with your chest?

R: It would last—oh, it would last maybe a couple of hours—two or three hours maybe, until I have to cool off myself—

167. I: Sure, sure.

R: I go outside and tell her to forget about it.

> [I-159 to I-167. In these passages the interviewer and respondent appear to be working together successfully. The interviewer has simplified and restricted his probe questions, and the respondent is playing a more important part in the interaction and contributing more of the total volume of communication. One reason for the success appears to be that the interviewer now is following the respondent's flow of thought, rather than pursuing his own paths. Here he is using questions which are more respondent-oriented. It is interesting that the successful probes in many cases consist of no more than a murmur of agreement or understanding (I-160, I-164, I-167).]

168. I: What can you do to forget about it?

R: Work—I mean just, just go outside and—well, work. Stay out there. — I got four acres there, and I just work around the garage. — Nothing heavy though.

169. I: That makes you feel better.

> [The interviewer is equally successful in summarizing and responding to the attitudes which the patient expresses (I-169).]

R: Yeah—just as soon as I get away from her, she gets—

170. I: What kind of work do you do when you—

> [I-170. Occasionally the interviewer misjudges the respondent's needs in rather conspicuous fashion. Here, for example, the physician has interposed a question about the kind of work the patient does, at a time when the respondent is motivated to continue the narrative about his way of resolving tense situations with his wife. It is significant that this question is relevant from the physician's point of view but appears irrelevant to the respondent at this point. The patient seizes the first opportunity to return to his previous line of discussion.]

R: Well, I got this shop in the garage—I got a great big garage—I

171. I: I see.

R: And she is pretty easy to get along with. I find for myself that I have to cool off, on account of this here—that something is going wrong. That's all there is to it. And I *told* her and I told the kids— Kids both have an automobile and they are always asking me one thing and another, and I am no mechanic but if I give them everything—they both have a car and the old lady have a car and I ain't got any. (Laughs.)   — And they are always asking, and between the baby and her old man, lives with us too, you know, and between him—he's an alcoholic—

172. I: Um-hmm.

R: and he's got booze there all the time and—

173. I: Does he get in trouble too, or not?

R: No. He's just—

174. I: What kids are you talking about now?

R: My children.

175. I: Have a car?

R: One boy, he goes to college.

176. I: Oh, these are other kids of yours now? By the first marriage?

R: No, the same one—same one—

177. I: Oh, I see—In other words this was your third child—this one that came—

R: Yes.

178. I: I see.

R: I got Frank, he is going to _____ (college) and Dick is going to high school and Tommy was born about fourteen months ago—

179. I: Um-hmm.

R: And—well, between all them people there I got a mess.

180. I: Sure— Before this trouble came up two weeks ago, did you notice any of the same kind of difficulties when you'd get in some kind of an emotional difficulty, that this thing would come on, or when you'd get mad?   — Or let us put it this way. Three weeks ago was there anything that you knew of that could have caused this pain to come on you—the one that came on you three weeks ago?

[I-180. This question begins with a rather cumbersome summary attempt on the part of the interviewer to see whether the patient can provide any additional situational factors to explain his symptoms. It concludes, however, with a well-worded invitation to the patient to search his memory for such situational factors, and it is significant that this open question is productive of additional information.]

R: I don't know, unless I— (Pause.)   No—well, I'll tell you frankly, I did drink whiskey up to three weeks ago until I got that first jab—

181. I: Um-hmm.

R: In the heart or wherever it was.

[R-181. Here the patient is beginning the difficult task of telling the physician that he has been drinking habitually and heavily. Throughout the interview, the interviewer has been accepting, permissive, and uncritical of the respondent. A good relationship has developed, and it is a result of the relationship that the patient is able to communicate this embarrassing information. The stammers and pauses which characterize R-180, followed by the sudden "Well, I'll tell you frankly," illustrate the respondent's difficulty in communicating this material. In I-181 through I-186 the interviewer continues successfully the uncritical drawing out of information regarding his drinking habits.]

182. I: You drank pretty heavy did you, or not?

R: Well—let's say a half a pint a day anyway—but that would be through the whole day put together.

183. I: And that was for—for how long had you been doing that?

R: Oh—guess for years. (Laughs.)

184. I: How many years? — Twenty years?

R: Oh—no, I didn't do it too much in the service. Er—well, when I came back later on I didn't touch it too much—as long as—

185. I: In other words, for about ten years you have been drinking that much?

R: As long as her old man was around, why I helped him on it. (Both laugh.)

186. I: Is there anything over the past—that happened three weeks ago —that you noticed that began this thing on you?

R: No—not—unless maybe it was the *whiskey*, but I—

[Here the interviewer attempts again to develop material regarding situational factors and onset of symptoms. The respondent answers by communicating his anxiety that drinking may have been responsible for his symptoms.]

187. I: Where was your wife three weeks ago?

[I-187. It is apparent here that the physician has become interested in the association of the respondent's symptoms and his recurring crises with his wife. In the language of Chapter 4, he has now developed a specific hypothesis, which becomes an additional objective for his interview and which he now proposes to test by means of additional information. Earlier in the interview it seemed that the physician hypothesized that his patient was describing a typical cardiac episode, and that his objective was to obtain an accurate description of symptoms prior to physical examination. It now appears that the physician has permitted himself at least one alternative hypothesis, namely that the patient's pains represent a psychosomatic reaction to interpersonal difficulties with his wife. It remains for him to explore and test this hypothesis.]

R: She was at home.

188. I: Your home?

R: Yes. She was at home.

189. I: And this was—what day was it? Was it Sunday you said?

R: Geez, I don't know what day it was. I would have to ask her, because I know it was one day when I was sitting in the house and I got that jab and at—at the same time she was barking about something and I told her to keep quiet and I said, "Leave me alone." I said, "I don't feel good." That is all I told her.

She must have caught on because—or rather she didn't catch on, because she kept on talking about one thing or another and I just got up and walked away.

[R-189. The new line of questioning is turning up important information.]

190. I: And when did you have the pain?
  R: Well, I had that just right about that time—in the morning.
191. I: Well, when did it come on real suddenly? You say it came on real suddenly before that?
  R: Yes.
192. I: Do you remember what you were doing when it came on?
  R: No, I don't. I was in the house, I know that.
193. I: Were you talking to your wife at all?
  R: I might have been.
194. I: Did you ever get mad at her at that time?
  R: (Laugh.) No—I wouldn't say—
195. I: Um-hmm, and what about that—
  R: If I had drunk too much the night before, would that have done it?
196. I: Well, I don't know. (Pause.) Did you have any trouble with your wife that day—do you remember, or don't you remember?

[I-189 to I-196. In this sequence the interviewer, following a funnel order of questions, attempts to lead the respondent further into a discussion of the situation immediately preceding the onset of symptoms, especially his interaction with his wife at this time.]

  R: No—not besides a little under—a little misunderstanding now and then. — I don't argue with her like that—I like the little kid and I don't want to go around arguing with her. She is a little choppy. I just walk away from her.
197. I: Uh-huh. — Your wife's like a little kid?
  R: No. I mean, I like the little boy I got.
198. I: Oh, I see—
  R: And—ah—a woman is a woman. — Well, especially the one I got. She's always yapping about one thing or another so I just have to get away from her— (Laughs.)
199. I: Sure, sure. — Ah—and—ah—when you want to get away from her, what do you usually do?
  R: Go outside for a couple—two, three hours and forget about it. I come back, I don't say no more.
200. I: Do you remember when you had this pain in your chest a long time ago? Do you know what caused it or brought it on?

[I-200 to I-208. In this sequence of questions it appears that the physician, feeling that the symptoms are related to the patient's crises with his wife, is trying to lead him either to corroborate or at least to share in this insight. It is clear, however, from I-200 and the succeeding responses, that the patient is either unable or unwilling to express this insight at this time.]

R: No, I don't. No—I just don't remember.

201. I: Do you remember when you got *mad* a while back, that you might have—

R: No—geez, that's been so many years back, I wouldn't—unless like you said—

202. I: Yeah—um-hmm.

R: It might have been from that straining myself with the weights. Maybe I was doing it wrong—see—but it was more or less like I say, bragging off. Picked this hundred twenty-five pounds twelve times. I'll remember that to my dying day.

[R-202 is an excellent example of the length to which the patient will go to avoid the pressure of linking his symptoms to his relationship with his wife. The discussion of weight-lifting is completely irrelevant at this point, and the erroneous statement on the part of the patient, that the physician suggested the weight-lifting might have been responsible, is especially interesting.]

203. I: When this happened last Monday, do you remember where you were—what you were doing?

R: Yeah. I sent the kids off to school. I fixed their breakfast, waked them up and sent them both to school. One goes with the bus and the other goes with the car—

204. I: When does your wife get to work?

R: She don't work.

205. I: She don't work?

R: She sleeps. She sleeps with the baby. I don't bother her.

206. I: Um-hmm. She stays in the house?

R: Yeah, she stays home. Then the kid gets up about seven o'clock and I get him his bottle of milk and give her a couple cups of coffee, and she gets up about two hours later—she has to stay up half of the night with that little guy.

207. I: You bring the coffee up to her, do you?

R: Yeah—she's all right.

208. I: Didn't have an argument with her—

R: No, no. — After I send the kids out, see, sometimes I get up late. After I sent the children to school I go down to the bathroom and wash up and brush my teeth and stuff. I went to the bathroom, I know that, and combed my hair, washed my face, and then I come up, and as soon as I got up and opened the door —she was up by then—yeah she was up—she was in the living room there, and as soon as I opened the door I just shut it—why bang, that is when it done it—just like that out of a clear sky.

209. I: Have you had any shortness of breath at all, Bill?

[Beginning with I-209 the physician resumes the methodical exploration for his case history.]

R: No—not since I don't smoke.

210. I: No swelling in your ankles?

R: No.

211. I: No shortness of breath at night?

R: No—never gasp for air—(unintelligible).

212. I: Anybody in your family ever have heart trouble?
R: No.

213. I: O.K.   And what kind of work are you doing?
R: Nothing.   (Laughs.)   I have been sitting for eight and one-half years.   See, I work at the airport and what they call the fuel dump—the gas storage.   And it is just like you were going to the gas station.   They come with their trucks, the airline trucks, to the bulk plant, and all I do is take the meter reading and, oh, and give them two or three thousand gallons, whatever they want, and they go on.

214. I: And you've been doing that for eight years, have you?
R: Yes.

215. I: Just about the same thing?
R: Yeah.   About the same thing.   No hard work out there.

216. I: Yeah.   Have you had the same job—have you kept it right along?
R: Yes, ever since I came home from the service.

217. I: Has your drinking ever interfered with your job?
R: Pardon?

[I-217. Here the physician interjects a question in a content area to which the respondent earlier has demonstrated considerable sensitivity.   The respondent's bland "Pardon?" is probably an expression of blocking or resistance rather than a simple misunderstanding of the question, although it is possible that the sudden shift of context has created a misunderstanding.   In R-96 we saw the same respondent behavior when a question was asked which presented some of the same psychological problems.]

218. I: Has your drinking ever interfered with your job?
R: No.

[I-218. The interviewer repeats the question and is rewarded with a specific response.   Responses 218 through 235 are a fairly routine process of obtaining historical information without any notable problems of emotion or understanding.]

219. I: You have been able to work right along every day?
R: Well—I wouldn't drink on the job.   I mean I have a little bit at home maybe, or a bottle of beer, or even two—but I never go to work drunk—I don't believe in that.

220. I: Um-hmm.   What did you do before the war?   Anything in particular?
R: Before the war, for two years I worked for the _____, the newspaper—

221. I: I see.
R: That was light work.

222. I: Where were you in service?
R: (Part missing.)

223. I: Where were you in this country?
R: First I got out of _____ and got shipped to_____ , _____,

for boot training. From ———, ———, well, I got a fur-
lough and came back—oh, I don't know how many days—anyway, when I went back we got sent on a train to San Francisco,
I believe. — We waited nine weeks at ———, I believe, to
be shipped. Nobody knew what was going to happen—so I got
shipped in nine weeks.

224. I: Excuse me, Bill, I wasn't listening then—where did you start out?
     R: After boot camp?
225. I: Yeah.
     R: To ———, ———.
226. I: Were you always in this country, or did you go abroad?
     R: I went as far as—Pearl Harbor was as far as I got.
227. I: And when was that?
     R: What year, you mean?
228. I: Yeah.
     R: Well, I would say in '45.
229. I: '45? You see much action, did ya?
     R: No, I don't believe I seen any. We'd get shakedown.
230. I: What is the total length of time you were in the service?
     R: Twenty-two months, I would say. I know I got in March 1,
         1944, to until about '46 in December.
231. I: O.K. You average half a pint a day drink—is that right?

        [I-231 appears to be a rather directive question form, but in
        fact it represents only a restatement of information previously
        given by the respondent.]

     R: Uh-huh.
232. I: And how much do you smoke a day?
     R: I don't smoke.
233. I: Are you taking any kind of medicine now at all?
     R: No.
234. I: Are your mother and father still living?
     R: Yes.
235. I: Are they well?
     R: Um-hmm.
236. I: Are they alive?
     R: Yes.
237. I: How old are they?
     R: Oh, they're—I would say they are sixty-three apiece. My dad
         works up there.
238. I: Any brothers or sisters?
     R: Yes.
239. I: And are they alive and well?
     R: Yes.

        [This is an excellent example of a double-barreled question
        and of the problem such a question entails. The phrase "alive
        and well," while common enough and easily understood, makes
        the respondent's "Yes" completely ambiguous. Is he stating
        that both his brothers and sisters are alive and that they are
        well, or is the "Yes" a qualified response?]

240. I: No trouble at all?
     R: No.
241. I: No illness?
     R: No.

[I-241. The interviewer responds to this problem of ambiguity by asking a separate (although directive) probe question about their health.]

242. I: You got three children?
     R: Yes.
243. I: And they are all well?

[I-243. This is another example, although not a serious one, of a persistent interviewer tendency to ask simple questions in directive form. The implication of this wording is conducive to an affirmative response. Preferable wording would have been, "How is their health?"]

     R: Yes.
244. I: Have you ever been exposed to tuberculosis?
     R: Pardon?
245. I: Have you ever been exposed to tuberculosis?
     R: No. I don't see how.
246. I: Anybody in the, uh, —say aunts or uncles or cousins ever have any serious diseases that you know about—cancer or mental disease or heart trouble or diabetes?

[I-246. This is a good example of the shotgun type of question, which has serious defects. The interviewer asks a general question and provides a partial definition by mentioning some specifics. This sort of question has two problems. First it taxes the respondent's memory, and second, it assumes that the respondent has the ability to define or complete the interviewer's definition of "serious diseases." If the objective is merely to get a superficial inventory of prominent family illnesses, this may be sufficient. If, on the other hand, the interviewer needs to know these facts in detail, it would be preferable to use a separate question for each illness in which he is interested.]

     R: Well, my—that I wouldn't know now, but I know one uncle died here about a year ago. He had a heart attack. Gee, he was fat.
247. I: Fat, was he?
     R: Uh-huh. He was sixty years old. He was pretty—pretty chubby.
248. I: No ulcers in the family anywhere?
     R: No, my sister got gall bladder stones, or whatever. That was years and years ago. That is about all I can remember.
249. I: Okey-doke. And did you ever have any serious illness as a child at all?

[I-249. Here the interviewer begins a series of questions on the respondent's own illness history. This question is parallel to I-246 and involves the same problem of definitions of the phrase "serious illness." In this case, however, the interviewer solves the problem by means of a skillful application of the funnel sequence of questions.]

    R: Double pneumonia when I was seven.
250. I: Um-hmm. Anything else?

[Here the interviewer uses a probe question to evoke further general responses in answer to the "serious illness" query.]

    R: No.
251. I: Did you ever, uh, have rheumatic fever?

[I-251. Having asked the general question about serious illness, and having probed for additional responses in that area, the interviewer now begins a series of probe questions relating to disease categories in which he is specifically interested.]

    R: No.
252. I: Any skin trouble at all? Did you ever break out—ever have a red rash, scarlet fever?
    R: No. Nothing like that, unless—I got a—one here on my knee. It's been on for years.
253. I: What's that?
    R: I don't know what the devil it is. It might be . . . (laughs a little, unintelligible words) something like this here.
254. I: You have had that for a long time?
    R: Yes, and that's about all. It keeps itching. I had one on this leg here.
255. I: Did you ever have, did you ever have measles, mumps, chicken pox . . . (unintelligible word)?
    R: I wouldn't remember that.
256. I: Did you ever have any kidney trouble that you know about?
    R: Kidney trouble? No, except too much beer puffed one of 'em out, this one.
257. I: What do you mean?
    R: I mean this would ache.
258. I: When you had a lot of beer?
    R: For a couple days, then I'd quit that.
259. I: I see. This was how long ago?
    R: Oh, a few years back, I'd say. I'd say about eight, nine years back.
260. I: Did you have any other trouble at that time, or just that one trouble?
    R: No. One day I drank just too many—twelve bottles of beer (laugh) and I—that was at my brother-in-law's.
261. I: Did you have any joint trouble when you were young?
    R: How do you mean that?

[I-261. Here we have a rather humorous example of a communication failure. The respondent has been preoccupied with his description of his indulgence in alcohol. The interviewer, however, is preparing to move on to questions regarding rheumatism and arthritis. Under the circumstances, the unintentional pun involving the phrase "joint trouble," and the resulting respondent confusion, were almost inevitable.]

262. I: Any kind of arthritis when you were young?
     R: No. No.
263. I: Uh-huh. Have you had any illnesses since you've been, since you've been grown up? Any kind of sickness?
     R: Just had flu. About every second year I get it for about seven or eight days.
264. I: Uh-huh. What's that consist of?
     R: Oh, just shakes. When I get the shakes and go get a shot from the doctor and some pills, and it will go away.
265. I: What do you mean "shakes"?
     R: Well it, well, you know how it, how it feels—like you are catching a cold, and you start shaking. — I knew it would be the flu, so I'd right away get in bed.

[I-264. This is the first of two good examples of interviewer probing for the purpose of defining a term employed by the respondent. In R-263 the respondent says that he has had the flu. The interviewer asks him for his definition of this disease. The respondent then defines it with a highly colloquial phrase (R-264). The interviewer's probe in I-265 evokes a more complete description.]

266. I: What kind of shots would the doctor give you?
     R: I don't know what it was. I'd go to the same one I was to yesterday. He'd give me something, give me some pills and—
267. I: Oh, it would fix it up pretty well?
     R: Yeah, hmmm, soon's the cold—I'd get a cold at the same time, runny nose—and that would—they'd both be right together always, but now there is a preventative. Company makes you go and get it, but I missed this year.
268. I: Uh-huh. O.K. Any operations?
     R: No.
269. I: No operations? Any serious injuries at all? Have you broken anything?
     R: No.
270. I: Any bones? Have you ever been in any serious accidents?
     R: No. (Pause.) One thing though. I don't know if you noticed yesterday, I did, when I was—well, I'd say I was about eighteen —seventeen, eighteen, nineteen—right in there, and a fellow did hit me right here. We was on the street corner and he was a pretty big, big guy. — I'll tell you how it happened. His brother called—

[R-270. The respondent's first answer is an unqualified negative. When the interviewer pauses, however, the respondent proceeds to communicate material which contradicts his previous negative statement. He has had an accident which he considers serious, and even after twenty years it is an event which calls forth a good deal of emotion. The initial negative statement and subsequent halting contradiction and bringing out of difficult material are typical of a respondent who is trying to verbalize emotional facts and attitudes. From the point of view of interviewing technique, it is of crucial importance that the pacing and atmosphere of the interview at this point permitted the respondent to verabalize this material as he felt able to do.]

271. I: Where did he hit you? No, I—

[I-271. The interviewer, concentrating on the medical aspects of the case, underestimates the implications of the preceding response. As a result he cuts off the respondent's incoherent narrative rather abruptly. At an earlier time in the interview this might have been destructive to the interviewer-respondent relationship. At this point the relationship apparently is sufficiently well established so that no real damage is done.]

    R: He hit me right here.
272. I: Oh. Yuh.
    R: Right in this spot. This is the spot now.
273. I: What'd he hit you with?
    R: With his fist. — I didn't expect it.
274. I: Uh-huh.
    R: He called my sister—he had two brothers—
275. I: How long did the pain last after you had that?
    R: Oh, for years. It lasted for years.
276. I: For years? Do you still feel it?
    R: No. No more. I don't know if I—if you noticed yesterday when I looked at you. It was right in here, this rib right in here.
277. I: Um-hmm.
    R: He just give me a good one. That did, that did affect something though, Doc. What I mean is, after he gave me one, the next day I really—I really *felt* that. It might have started from that time on, too. I dunno. 'Cause, boy, it was really achin' the whole time.
278. I: You were about eighteen years old then?
    R: Yes.
279. I: Do you get any headaches?
    R: Oh, not, not unless I don't eat in the morning or something.
280. I: I see. How has your weight been?
    R: Pardon?
281. I: How has your weight been?
    R: Oh, it's all right.
282. I: Stable? No change?

[This is another example of a mild but easily avoidable directiveness in question wording. Such a phrasing as "Has your weight changed lately?" would have avoided the gentle pressure toward a negative response.]

    R: Well, it's going down now.
283. I: How much have you lost in the past six months?
    R: Er—well, from 197—
284. I: Well, that's right. You have lost . . . (unintelligible).
    R: I am now about 175. I was too fat carrying that around, and

I started thinking about my uncle being fat, and figured I'd better get it down and *quit* everything.

[R-284. This is the latest of a number of cases (for example, R-272) in which the respondent answers a routine question by conveying something of the anxiety which he feels about his present physical situation. The interviewer largely ignores the attitudinal and emotional aspects of the response, and presses on with the inventory of physical symptoms. Whether or not this should be regarded as an error in interviewing technique must be determined in terms of the interview objectives. If the purpose of the interview includes therapy or even the ventilation of respondent anxiety, more sensitivity to such material is indicated. If, on the other hand, the physician wishes only to concentrate on the physical symptoms of his patient and is satisfied that the kind of anxiety expressed in R-284 is irrelevant for the diagnosis of those symptoms, then he is justified in not responding to the anxieties.]

285. I: Uh-huh.   Have any trouble with your eyes?
     R: No.
286. I: Ever see double?
     R: No.   The left one's 20/20.   This is 20/30.
287. I: Have any trouble reading a newspaper at all?
     R: No.
288. I: Any trouble with your ears?
     R: No.
289. I: Any ringing in your ears?
     R: No.
290. I: Any bloody noses?   You can breathe through your nose all right?
     R: Yes.
291. I: You have any soreness of your lips, cracking of the lips at all?
     R: No.
292. I: Tongue ever get sore?
     R: No.
293: I: Bleeding gums?
     R: No.
294. I: How are your teeth?   Have you had them checked?
     R: No.
295. I: Are your teeth all right?
     R: No.
296. I: Why not?
     R: I have four false teeth, and the rest of them are—
297. I: Do you take care of them very much?   Do you or not?

[I-294. This is a classic example of the double-barreled question and of the kinds of confusion which can result from such a question. Having asked two questions at once, the interviewer finds it impossible to interpret the single negative response obtained in R-294. As a result he has to ask half of the original double-barreled question. By this time the respondent (R-296) is enlarging his response to the second part of the original question. The resulting ambiguity makes it necessary for the interviewer to attempt a third rewording (I-297), which reveals quite clearly his growing irritation with the confusion—"Do you or not?"]

R: Well, I'll say this, it's too late. — I think I'd better get them all out one of these days.

[R-297. At this point the respondent expresses in his own way his reaction to the preceding confusion, "Well, I'll say this, it's too late." It is too late also to make any clear sense out of the foregoing exchange, and the physician, recognizing this, leaves the subject and goes on to inquire about sore throats.]

298. I: Any sore throats?
R: No. I used to get them a few years back, but no more.
299. I: Any change in your voice that you ever noticed at all?
R: No, except that I don't know how to talk English. (Laughs.)
300. I: Do you know that you have a cough at all?
R: Pardon?
301. I: Any cough?
R: No.
302. I: Do you ever cough anything up, any blood?
R: No.
303. I: Never cough any blood? Um-hmm.
R: No. (Pause.)
304. I: Do you ever feel your heart pounding real loud?
R: (Pause.) No, I don't think so. I wouldn't say so.
305. I: Ever feel your heart turn over?
R: How do you mean, "turn over"? I've noticed it skips. (Laughs.)

[I-304. This question introduces a sequence regarding heart symptoms, and illustrates the problem of trying to get a layman to communicate technical information. In this case the interviewer proposes colloquial phrases, such as "heart turning over," "heart pounding," etc. Some problem of ambiguity remains, however. It is clear that the respondent thinks of his own symptoms in words unlike those which the physician proposes. The dangers are that the respondent may misunderstand or misconstrue the physician's phrase, and that the respondent may fail to communicate important information simply because his own descriptive phrase has not been specifically included in the question. If the physician is attempting to translate from the patient's responses to these colloquially phrased questions to some specific coronary disease, the risks are great.

This is an example of the general problem, discussed earlier, of achieving a common language between respondent and interviewer. The general solution to this problem is to word the initial question in open form so that the respondent can use and define his own language and description. Such a sequence for this objective might be worded as follows:

1. Have you ever had any unusual feelings or sensations in your heart? (If yes) Would you describe them for me?
2. Have you had any other feelings or sensations? Now, I'd like to mention to you several ways in which people sometimes describe feelings they have had in or around their heart, and find out whether you have ever had similar feelings.
3. Does your heart ever feel as though it was turning over? (If yes) Can you describe for me how that feels?
4. Does your heart ever feel as if it was skipping a beat? (If yes) Can you tell me how that feels?]

306. I: Uh-huh. O.K. Your appetite's been pretty good, I gather.
R: Yes, I—
307. I: Um-hmm. No particular food bothers you? You don't have any trouble swallowing food?
R: No.
308. I: No heartburns, sour stomach, no pain in your stomach at all?
R: No.
309. I: Um-hmm. No particular cramps?
R: No.
310. I: Um-hmm. You've had no yellow jaundice, where your eyes get all yellow?
R: No.
311. I: Have your bowels been pretty regular?
R: Yes.
312. I: Do you go every day—or every three days, or—
R: No, every morning.
313. I: Um, every morning.
R: Right after the coffee. (Laughs.)
314. I: Pretty regular?
R: The same time always.
315. I: Notice any change in your stools at all, recently?
R: No.
316. I: Ever constipated or diarrhea?
R: No.
317. I: Ever see blood in your stools?
R: No.
318. I: Have you had much gas?
R: No. Oh, I used to but no more. I just watch the food now. In other words, I don't fool around with something like cabbage or beans, or stuff like that there, that's—
319. I: What does that do to you?
R: No, that is gassy. I eat any beans or cabbage or something like that, or green beans, why all day long, you know, I—
320. I: (Laughs.) You never had any blood in your stools at all, right?
R: No.
321. I: Ever had any burning when you pass your water? Any kind of urinary infection?
R: No. No.
322. I: Have you noticed any particular change of color in your urine of

any significance? Ever notice any blood in your urine? Ever been dark like coffee?

R: No.

[Here the physician asked questions about the respondent's sex activities. No particularly relevant information was divulged.]

323. I: How does your chest feel now?

R: It feels all right except just a couple of minutes ago, this, this, right in here—it seems like two or three run down.

324. I: Two or three what?

R: Well, like something wants to run through your passage or something, and it don't want to go.

325. I: I see.

R: It wants to run through there and it backs up or some darn thing.

326. I: I see.

R: It's here, where it aches. It's right here.

[I-324 to I-326. These represent a series of permissive probes in which the interviewer merely acknowledges his attention and acceptance of the information the respondent is communicating, usually by employing the simple phrase "I see." These nondirective probes lead to valuable information.]

327. I: How about your chest?

[I-327. With this question the interviewer initiates a question sequence dealing with specific symptoms.]

R: Nothing. Nothing the matter there now.

328. I: Fine. O.K. (Pause.) You have no trouble with your legs or your arms? I mean you can walk all right? No dizziness?

R: No.

329. I: Never get dizzy?

R: No.

330. I: Never had any unconsciousness?

R: No.

331. I: Do your arms or legs ever go to sleep, tingle, numb?

R: No, unless I put it under my can (laugh) and sit on 'em.

332. I: O.K., Bill. You haven't got any idea why you are having this trouble, have you?

[I-332. With this question the interviewer attempts a process which he has tried unsuccessfully in the past, namely, urging the respondent to indicate the extent of his insight into his own problems.]

R: No, I really don't. I haven't at all. What I'm afraid of is—what—what, of course I should listen, right here now, to what you people are going to do, but—this guy here last night, he's the guy that scared me. He has no cause to lie to me, but he maybe mentioned that that's what it could be.

[R-332. The respondent reacts typically to the interviewer's bid for insight, and demonstrates clearly the stress, emotion, and ambivalence which such a question evokes in him. These emotional reactions are apparent in the respondent's difficulty in verbalization, in his repeated negative statements, and finally in the rushed, incoherent breaking through of some of the fears about his physical symptoms and prognosis. The interviewer is content to encourage, with permissive murmurs and phrases, this rush of emotional communication. It is perhaps significant that the physician refrains from directly offering the respondent the reassurance for which he is so obviously bidding.]

333. I: What?
R: A plugged-up blood vessel. And he says that the spot around there where it can't get through eventually gets flabby, he said—
334. I: Um-hmm.
R: And it'll stop on me, he says, and they'll do something to open it up. He says they might prevent it, and they might not.
335. I: Sure. Um-hmm.
R: What he meant, "they," I dunno. "Hospital" is what he said.
336. I: Um-hmm. Uh-huh.
R: That is all I can tell you.
337. I: Uh-huh. You haven't any other idea why you should get pains like this? Can you figure out anything that could bring them on?

[I-337. The interviewer is unable to refrain from another demand for respondent insight. The respondent, however, is equally unable to respond until he has received some reassurance with respect to the immediate threat of his symptoms. This request he makes specific with the question "You don't think it's anything in the heart, do you?"]

R: (Pause.) Well, I don't know. Could be, maybe—what's— You don't think it's anything in the heart, do you? — I want to ask you—I mean it's, uh—
338. I: Well—uh—we're going to have to take a lot of studies on that. — At this point I would say no. I would say almost *surely*, no.

[I-338. This represents a balanced statement on the part of the physician, in which he relieves some of the patient's immediate anxieties, but does so without misleading him regarding the course of diagnostic procedures to be followed.]

R: That there is nothing in my heart?
339. I: There's nothing wrong with your heart.
R: Well, there is only two things I can figure—all these years—living with a woman like *I* got, she is a very nice woman but—there isn't one day that can go by—
340. I: Um-hmm.
R: That she didn't give me a hard time on something, plus, plus the whiskey—
341. I: Sure.
R: You see what I mean? I, I never would be myself. I try to keep cool and I just figure there's something is going to catch up with me some day, and that's about as far as I got—

342. I: Sure.
      R: Till three weeks back.

          [R-339 and following.   At this point, having reassured him-
          self of the physician's statement that he is not in the midst of
          an acute cardiac episode, the respondent can begin to focus his
          attention on other things.   He is now able for the first time to
          attempt to comply with the physician's request to search his
          own thinking and experience for insight into his symptoms.]

343. I: Till three weeks back.
      R: So, like I say, I did have some—uh, I did have—I did have
           enough whiskey the day before, because I had a slight headache
           the next morning and—
344. I: Do you think there is some relationship, then, between this trou-
           ble with your wife and this trouble you're having, or not?

          [I-344.   The interviewer tries a more direct probe to see,
          or to force the respondent to see, whether a relationship exists
          between the wife's behavior and the attacks which the re-
          spondent has been having.   Apparently the interviewer is now
          convinced that this relationship does exist, and he is either
          asking to have his own hypothesis confirmed or trying to see
          whether the respondent has insight into this relationship.]

      R: I don't know.   It could be, and it couldn't.
345. I: Um-hmm.
      R: I dunno.
346. I: Ah-hmm.   (Both speak.)
      R: Go ahead.
347. I: No, go ahead.   I want to hear you.
      R: I said I like the woman and I like the kids, and I like everything.
           But I don't like to have a person like *her* tell me something that
           is wrong.   She just sticks her two cents into something that she
           doesn't know about—about it, see.
348. I: Sure, uh-huh.
      R: And just like me trying to tell you what them two other doctors
           told me.   Well, you won't—no matter what you say.   (Laughs.)
           You don't care about me.   I just tell her to keep quiet, that is
           all.   And then when I have a couple of drinks or so it is worse.
349. I: Um-hmm.
      R: Well, I would just tell her off, that's all.
350. I: Um-hmm.
      R: I get mad about it—
351. I: Um-hmm.
      R: And I get madder, and I kinda got like the shakes.
352. I: Um-hmm.
      R: To tell you the truth, I kinda got the shakes, in other words.   I
           would get shaky—
353. I: Um-hmm.
      R: And I get so darn mad at her, I don't want to *hit* the woman—
354. I: Um-hmm.
      R: I never do that—
355. I: Um-hmm.

R: But it is just my nature to get mad at her, I guess. I have a temper after the old man.

[R-344 to R-355. In spite of the reassurance which the interviewer has given, and the somewhat increased freedom of the respondent's talk, it still takes some time before the respondent either can recognize, or at least verbalize, what he has suspected all along, namely that there is a possible connection between his relationship with his wife and the attacks. In R-347 the relationship is for the first time clearly made. The interviewer's behavior during this period is commendable. Notice the permissive, nondirective probing he uses, and the facilitation of responses which results from this. A great deal is going on during this period, and the interviewer merely acts to keep the respondent in motion.]

356. I: Now, when you get mad, do you notice any chest trouble, do you think?

[I-356. Here is another direct bid on the part of the interviewer to get the respondent to talk more about the relationship, and apparently in this case he made good.]

R: Yeah, I would get an ache in a little while.

357. I: Um-hmm.

R: And after I would start to shake.

358. I: Um-hmm.

R: And then when I would cool off and then something would start aching—

359. I: Um-hmm.

R: I would say, "Well, you done it again." I wouldn't feel good.

360. I: What kind of a person would you consider yourself to be, Bill?

[I-360. This question is what might be called a "flabbergaster." The interviewer is obviously pleased with the kind of information he is now getting, and the apparent insight which exists. He is making an attempt to increase the level of insight and to get more information. It is obvious, however, that this question does not really communicate to the respondent. Even if the respondent did understand what was wanted, it is doubtful whether he could or would give a frank appraisal. We do not know what the interviewer's specific objective was in asking this question. The most reasonable hypothesis is that we have here an instance of "expert error" (see Chapter 5). In other words, the interviewer was asking himself about the psychological make-up of the respondent. This question, one entirely appropriate for the physician to be propounding to himself, was inappropriate to ask of the respondent. He was demanding that the respondent show a degree of expertness, understanding, and insight which is unrealistic under the circumstances.]

R: Ah—gee, I don't know.

361. I: If you would have to say in a couple of words what kind of a person you figure you were, how would you describe yourself?

R: Is there any kind of names for it?

362. I: We . . . just in your words.
    R: What kind of a person I am?
363. I: I mean if you, say, if you were somebody else, and you were describing yourself to someone, what do you suppose you would think of yourself? What type of person?

> [I-361 to I-363. These questions represent an extension of I-360. The respondent and interviewer are sparring, the interviewer pursuing this line of questioning and the respondent either unable or unwilling to respond to it.]

    R: Well, let me ask you another thing before I answer that. If, er, —would worry, mental worry, have anything to do with that?

> [R-363. This is a difficult response to interpret. The patient gives the doctor a bit of the information for which he was striving, that is, the patient proposes a linkage between mental problems or anxieties and his physical symptoms. Whether this represents a real insight on the part of the patient, or whether the patient is obediently picking up the earlier suggestion of the physician, is almost impossible to determine.]

364. I: Do you think so?
    R: I mean is there, er . . . (unintelligible). I didn't get any toothbrush yet. I'm waiting for her to bring it tonight. I can brush my teeth with.

> [R-364. This is another response for which interpretation is difficult. The introduction by the respondent of the extraneous business of mouth hygiene and the missing toothbrush is problematical. It may be that the respondent is still attempting to escape from the interviewer's persistent demand for insights. It may be that this is the respondent's way of reintroducing into the conversation the business of his relationship with his wife. Still another possibility is that the respondent has reached a degree of neurotic adjustment that has led to very considerable discontinuity in his own thinking and verbalizations, and that his sudden reference to the toothbrush is entirely spontaneous.]

365. I: Why is that worrying you?

> [I-365. The respondent's discussion of the toothbrush has succeeded in turning the tables. It is now the interviewer who is flabbergasted and asking for clarification.]

    R: Pardon?
366. I: Why is that worrying you?
    R: I don't know. (Pause.) I never feel right unless I brush 'em twice a day.
367. I: Uh-huh.
    R: Ah—if a—let's say that if I had for the last three years, I'd say, I'll tell you what my mental trouble is—I have had— I'm not going to talk about being smart, or anything—
368. I: Um-hmm.

R: But I like music, for one thing. See, I can write songs, opera songs, but I can't get rid of them any place.

369. I: Uh-huh.

R: I try to make connections here and there, and always writing letters to somebody or another, and never get an answer.

370. I: Um-hmm.

R: And then I got an article I'm trying to contact somebody on here. In plumbing, I got an invention of my own, but I am afraid they're gonna grab it on me.

371. I: What is that?

R: Well, you tell it to somebody, then you tell it to somebody like yourself. After I met you, that's different. But these business-men, why they don't want it, and the next month it is out on the market. Then there is something else. Well, er, in writing plays, like for, let's say for movies, I can do that also—although I can't talk good English.

372. I: Uh-huh.

R: I can think faster than I can write.

373. I: Uh-huh.

R: I never had much schooling—

374. I: Uh-huh.

R: And, er, then there is something. — Let's say there is about eight different things I have that I could put out on the market—not to change the subject.

375. I: Yuh.

R: If I had the *opportunity*, see, I'm always on *my* job. I got eight hours to do nothing, so—I'm always writing letters here and never get any answer, see—

376. I: Uh-huh.

R: All that, maybe, plus living with her old man, and living with her, and maybe the two kids, and the whiskey up to three weeks ago— Maybe it ganged up on me, see what I mean?

377. I: Uh-huh.

R: And I have been with this one job so many years, and the more you sit you can figure out stuff, you know, you get an idea and you check up and there is nothing like it, especially in music, see. I can put the stuff on, but I can't get rid of it. Maybe I am looking for the big money end of it and it makes me nervous.

378. I: Uh-huh.

R: Do you see what I mean?

[I-365 to I-378. This represents a sequence in which the physician wisely uses minimum probe questions and occasional indications of continued interest and attention. This inter-viewer behavior is very successful in maintaining a continuing stream of respondent communication, and in helping the re-spondent to verbalize material which is obviously of an ex-tremely emotional and intimate nature. One indication of the interviewer's intelligent restraint during this sequence of ques-tions comes in R-366. At this point the respondent has answered the previous question by saying bluntly, "I don't know." Rather than move on to the next question, the physician waits through a pause at this point, which leads to further response on the part of the patient that in fact contradicts and enlarges upon his previous statement of "I don't know."

It seems likely that throughout this whole sequence the interviewer was uncertain as to the significance of the material that was being communicated, but was sufficiently sensitive to the respondent's mood and need for communication so that he did nothing to inhibit its flow. The short interviewer words and phrases exemplify this role.

R-376. This response is perhaps the interviewer's reward for his previous encouragement of the respondent, even in the face of rather incoherent communication. At this point the respondent, having made vague references to his unrealistically lofty aspirations, to his problems with alcohol, to his difficult relationship with his wife, and his rather complex family situation, sums up his responses and his insights by saying, "Maybe it ganged up on me, see what I mean?" By thus suggesting that his present difficulties are the result of a combination of situational factors, the respondent has finally been able to answer the question which the interviewer asked so much earlier (I-364). Both the delay and the gradual process by which the respondent brought out this difficult material are typical. Typical also was the respondent's previous avoidance of this difficult question by the communication of irrelevant information.]

379. I: Why does it make you nervous?
     R: I just get shaky—just get the shakes a little bit and forget it. Well, this darn thing will take off. I'll get an ache. That is why I am trying to get away from all of that.
380. I: Do you think there is a relationship between them, then?

> [I-380. The interviewer here appears to be asking the same question about linkage between situational factors and psychological symptoms which he has had so much difficulty getting answered previously. It is difficult to see why the interviewer poses this question again, considering both the previous difficulty and the fact that the respondent has just been able to answer what is essentially the same question (see R-371).]

     R: Pardon?
381. I: Do you think there is a relationship between them?
     R: Might *be*, Doctor, but I don't know.
382. I: Well, we'll sure find out.
     R: O.K., I hope we do. There is really nothing much wrong with my heart. I mean actually I don't care what you do to me. If I have to pay later on—I have my own house that is worth money—
383. I: Uh-huh.
     R: And I'll get rid of it—
384. I: Uh-huh.

R: And it don't bother me one bit because I am not going to take it where, if I should go some place, you see what I mean. I don't care.

[R-382 to R-384. At this point a number of things become apparent. First, the respondent still has considerable anxiety regarding heart disease. The glimmers of insight exhibited in the latter parts of the interview have not wrought any magical improvement in his level of anxiety. This response is important also, however, for at least two other reasons. The patient gives some indication of how important it is for him to be reassured. Finally, it is in this response that the patient for the first time refers specifically to the fear of death. It seems likely that this has been his basic concern throughout the interview, and the occasion for his visit to the hospital. The reference is colloquial and ambiguous, "I am not going to take it where, if I should go some place, you see what I mean." But the reference is unmistakable.]

385. I: Well, Bill, what we will do here, uh, I haven't been over you yet, and we've got a lot of studies to do. We'll do, we'll make all the studies and we'll be absolutely sure what we're talking about.

R: Yes, sir. O.K.

[I-385. The interviewer is getting ready to terminate the interview, and he is very wisely doing so by attempting to give the respondent some clear expectations as to what the remainder of the diagnostic process will be like. The respondent, however, in spite of his "Yes, sir. O.K.," is not sufficiently reassured to leave it at this.]

386. I: And if everything is all right, we'll let you know about it. I kind of suspect now by what you tell me, that your heart is O.K. and everything else is O.K. But we will take all our X-rays and all our studies, and make perfectly sure of that so that when we tell you one way or the other, you may be sure that we know what we are talking about. So until that time we won't give you a definite answer—but we will when we know.

R: One more thing, do you think that say three weeks back, very roughly, that after quitting—that after getting that one poke like that, that after I quit that, whiskey drinking, well—they claim that it stays in your system for thirty days roughly—

387. I: Uh-huh.

R: Ah, would, er—in other words, if I didn't have any—would that have brought it on again?

388. I: Well, Bill, I don't think we can really say. I—I don't think we can really say. Whiskey isn't good for a man, especially if taken in excess, but I am not sure we could say it causes what you have now.

R: I'm not, er—I'll tell you. I am not nervous in a way, unless I get angry, and that is what I am trying to get away completely from. I have to—like some people say—I have to find that out for myself—

389. I: Um-hmm.
    R: Or *find* myself, we'll say.
390. I: Sure.
    R: To get away from that. See, I am different natured—like you asked me before, and I am a different type of person now. My wife is different from me like night and day. You can—if you talk to that woman for an hour, or half an hour, or fifteen minutes, when—if she comes tonight or tomorrow, or any time, you will see what I mean. She is a very nice person.

    [I-386 to I-390. During this exchange the interviewer begins by resuming his attempts to close off the interview. The respondent counters by beginning to verbalize some of his remaining thoughts, questions, and anxieties. From a technical point of view, it seems desirable that the interview be brought to a close with such an exchange and a final statement of structuring and reassurance on the part of the physician. Unfortunately, however, the physician is tempted by the respondent's contrasting of himself and his wife, to return to a previously unproductive line of questioning.]

391. I: Uh-huh. Sure.
    R: But I can't figure it out.
392. I: What kind of person are you?

    [I-392. Here the interviewer resumes the previous attempt to get the respondent to give some characterological statement about himself.]

    R: Pardon?
393. I: What kind of person are you?
    R: Ah—(Laughs.) I don't know no—no—medical names.

    [R-392 and R-393. Here the respondent uses the polite devices of appearing not to hear the question and of disclaiming knowledge of medical vocabulary in order to avoid the impossibly difficult task which the physician is demanding of him.]

394. I: You don't need medical names. You see somebody on the street, what kind of a guy would you say he was? What kind of a guy would you say he was?

    [I-394. The physician rewords his request for a character analysis by the respondent.]

    R: Well, I can meet someone *else*—I can tell my wife. I mean I can tell somebody, and I know you're prob'ly a good-natured person, and take that chief over there—
395. I: Uh-huh.
    R: And take somebody like that, but I can't see myself. I can't—

    [R-394 and R-395. At this point the respondent is led to educate the interviewer by explaining that, although it is possible to make general character and personality judgments about other people, performing the same process for oneself is quite a different matter, incomparably more difficult.]

396. I: Does it bother you when things don't go the way they should go?
          [I-396. The interviewer pushes again in the same general
          direction, but with a more specific kind of question.]

    R: It does. I'll admit that it does. But I say I have got to find
          myself on that.
          [R-396. By this time, however, the respondent is ready to
          terminate the interview, and does so rather skillfully by quietly
          admitting the physician's suggestion that he is bothered when
          things don't go the way he thinks they should, finishing with
          the general statement that this is one of the problems he has to
          solve.]

397. I: Sure. Okey-doke, Bill. Do you want to take off your jacket
          and your shirt there, and we'll give you a going over.
          [I-397. The physician indicates that a physical examination
          will follow the interview immediately. In fact, the immediate
          proceeding to the physical examination does a good deal to
          handle the kinds of anxieties that the patient has previously
          indicated. It is likely that the negative findings of the physi-
          cal examination will provide a much more important kind of
          reassurance than anything the physician might have attempted
          to say at this point.]

Two Personnel Interviews:

Experienced and Inexperienced Applicants for a Clerical Job

The following personnel interviews have the common purpose of obtaining information about the past work experience, personal characteristics, interests, and abilities of job applicants. This information is to serve as a basis for an initial recommendation as to whether or not the person should be hired, and if so, for what sort of position. In the first of these interviews, the applicant has had no previous experience in the company. The applicant in the second interview has previously done clerical work in the company, but left to take another job.

Both interviews are conducted by the same interviewer, and both represent straightforward examples of the information-getting interview in a business or industrial situation. The interviewer has the primary function of obtaining information about the applicant. In this case the function of information-getting is coupled with that of making a tentative decision about the applicant's suitability for employment. The final decisions, however, are made by other people. A supplementary function which the interviewer is expected to perform is to communicate to the respondent certain information about the work situation in the company and the likelihood of employment. This necessitates a shift in role on the part of the interviewer, from information-getting to information-giving. Characteristically, this role change occurs rather late in the interviewing process.

These interviews are quite representative of the initial-selection interviews that take place in nearly all business and industrial concerns. Several other types of personnel interviews are equally common, including those which have for their major purpose the final selection of personnel, the evaluation of persons already on the payroll, and exit interviews conducted with persons who are about to leave the company. In all such interviews, the roles have become institutionalized and are well-known to both interviewer and respondent. Each understands why the interview is being conducted and the content area to be discussed. Very little in the way of introduction is necessary, and the basic job of information-getting begins almost immediately. The kind of rapport which this interview requires is achieved quickly, and the interview moves very rapidly to its basic purpose.

Both of these interviews take place in the small office of the employment interviewer. The office is one of a number of such cubicles in the personnel department of a large corporation. In both cases the interview has been initiated by the respondent's application for a job, and the interviewer has the respondent's written application in front of her during the interview. In the first case, the applicant is interested in a stenographic job. She is a young girl nineteen years old, with relatively brief experience since graduation from high school. In the second case, the respondent is a young woman with somewhat more work experience including, as we have said, brief employment in the company to which she is now reapplying for a position. The interviewer is a woman with a good deal of skill and experience at her job.

Personnel Interview 1

1. I: Have a chair, Virginia. It's a nice day, isn't it?
   R: It sure is.
2. I: We've been very fortunate this last week or so in getting this nice sunshine.
   R: That's right, it hardly seems that we can be having this weather in November, does it?

> [I-1 and I-2. These two introductory comments or questions by the interviewer merely serve to establish the first superficial relationship between the interviewer and the applicant, and to put the respondent at ease. Very little time is spent in this type of rapport building, however, and the rest of the interview is very businesslike in tone. The initial basis for communication between these two people is sufficiently explicit that a more elaborate introduction is quite unnecessary.]

3. I: That's right.   (Pause.)   Now, let's see.   It's Miss Virginia Smith, is that right?

   R: That's correct.

   [I-3 and I-4. After a pause the interviewer moves into the basic content of the interview, beginning with the open question I-4.]

4. I: And what can I do for you, Virginia?

   R: Well, I was looking for an office job.

5. I: I see.   Are you working now?

   [I-5. The objective of this question is to determine the course of the interview.   The present employment situation of the applicant and her previous work experience will influence the objectives of the interview and the questions which will be asked.]

   R: Right now I'm not.   I have been though.

6. I: Will you tell me a little bit about the work that you've done?

   [I-6. Having determined that there is previous work experience, the interviewer employs this well-chosen open question to encourage the respondent to begin a description of the jobs which she has held.]

   R: Well, I worked for the Real Estate Company for the last five months.   Kind of general office work.   I did a little bit of everything.

7. I: I see.

   R: They had apartments all over, it was just a small place, but they were building buildings in the country, where the farmers live . . .

8. I: I see.

   [I-7 and I-8 are merely permissive, encouraging response. From the single open question and the two nondirective probes, a considerable amount of information is obtained about previous jobs in a short space of time.]

   R: And so they moved too far out, and so I wanted a better place to work, and so I left there.

9. I: I see, and how long had you been with them, Virginia?

   R: Well, over a year.

10. I: I see.   And was that your first job?   And that was your first job after school?

   R: Well, I worked there—ah-h-h—a year while I was going to school, and then afterward I worked there full time.   And so I left there in October, about a month ago.

11. I: Office jobs are not very plentiful right at this time.

   [I-11. It is not clear why the interviewer made this comment. She may have intended it merely as a pleasantry, or as a further attempt to make the respondent comfortable in the role of job applicant.   It is possible also that I-11 is a reaction to the indication (R-10) that after more than a month of job-hunting, the respondent is still unemployed.   Regardless of her purpose, the interviewer seems to have struck a responsive note.]

R: That's right! I know! I've been looking all over for one.

12. I: You say this was out in West Branch. You live in West Branch?

     R: Uh-huh.

13. I: And do you want to work in that locality?

[I-13. The company has branch offices in various localities, so the girl could, in fact, work in her home town as an employee of this company.]

     R: Well, just so I have something. I have to have something.

14. I: Then would it be possible for you to go back and forth from there?

     R: Yes. I have extremely good transportation.

15. I: Well, that's very fortunate.

     R: Yes. This man that drives back and forth said that he would give me a ride anywhere around here. And there's a couple of girls that I know, that work here, and they have a ride, and I could ride with them.

[R-15. It is interesting to notice here how much information has been elicited in the interview thus far, relevant to the question of whether or not this applicant will make a satisfactory employee. Not only has the respondent given a good deal of descriptive and factual data about herself, but she has also expressed her need for work and her flexibility regarding place of work and type of job. The free flow of information is due in large part to the skilled interviewing techniques. Apparently a good relationship has been established between the interviewer and the respondent. The interviewer has made effective use of questions, usually beginning a topic with an open question, which she follows with nondirective, permissive probe questions. Contrast this process with an interview in which the interviewer merely follows an application form, asking the questions as they appear on the form—stilted, unelaborated, and mechanical.]

16. I: Uh-huh.

     R: And then the bus comes downtown.

17. I: I see. And what are the names of the girls that you know?

     R: Carol Blank and Sally Doe.

18. I: Sure, I know those girls. They started work for us around July or August.

     R: Yes, they're good friends. I've known them a long time.

19. I: Did you graduate from high school with them?

     R: Yes, we were classmates.

20. I: That was last June, wasn't it?

     R: Yeah.

[I-19 and I-20. Here we see a transition. The interviewer feels that she has enough information about the previous job and the possibility of transportation, and is now using these questions as a transition to the educational background of the respondent.]

21. I: What course did you take? What course did you take in high school?

     R: Commercial.

22. I: Can you tell me what courses that includes?
    R: Well, I took two years of bookkeeping, and two years of short-hand, and two years of typing. And then your English, and, ah, I guess that's all.
23. I: And how did you do in school?

> [I-23. Again the interviewer asks an open question, which brings forth an answer too general for the interviewer's objective.]

    R: (Laughs in a rather embarrassed fashion.) Well, okay I guess I wasn't a brain, but I wasn't the dumbest one in the class.
24. I: Well, good for you. What were your marks? What were your marks, on the average?

> [I-24. The interviewer recognizes the embarrassment which the respondent is expressing, murmurs a supportive "Good for you," and then asks a very specific question to learn the respondent's academic standing.]

    R: Well, average, about B minus.
25. I: Did you have some favorite subjects?
    R: Yes, typing.
26. I: Good, and how is your speed in typing?
    R: Well, when I finished school I had between 57 and 60 words a minute.
27. I: I see.
    R: Of course, I haven't been doing too much typing. With my job it wasn't required, and so I'm a little rusty right now.
28. I: Sure. That's something you have to keep up on and do every day.
    R: Yes, once you get your speed up there, I find, if you stop, it goes down to about 50. I went all summer, and when I started school it was down to about 35, but then it came right up again.

> [R-26 to R-28. The information obtained here also reflects the permissive relationship which has been established. Even in the collection of such factual information as the number of words per minute that the respondent can type, the attitude of the respondent toward the interview and the interviewer is relevant. In this case the respondent is sufficiently secure to be very frank in her evaluation of her own typing speed. Note especially R-27.]

29. I: Uh-huh.
    R: That's one good thing about typing.
30. I: Uh-huh, that's right, as long as you know the keyboard. As long as you know the keyboard, and you've achieved a certain speed.
    R: (Interrupting.) Yeah, you can get it right up again.
31. I: How about your shorthand, Virginia?
    R: (Laughing in an enbarrassed fashion.) Well, ha, ha, I had two years of it, but, ah, I haven't been working at it, and so I was wanting a clerk-typist job if I could get it. I was going to get a clerk-typist job if I could, but what do you require for shorthand?

32. I: Well, our dictation test is given at 80 words per minute.
    R: I see.
33. I: But we found that unless you can take it at school at 100 to 120 words per minute, that you won't be able to do 80 words a minute on the test.

> [I-33. This is a blunt statement, not unkind but intended to inform the applicant that something more than a casual knowledge of shorthand is required. At an early point in the interview, such a statement would have been difficult for the respondent to handle. At this point it presents no problems.]

    R: I see. Well, that was around what I had, but I never cared much for shorthand.
34. I: I see. Well, we'll forget about that for the present.
    R: Uh-huh. Yeah. But I would like to have a job where, that I could use it a little bit, and then gradually work up on it.
35. I: I see.
    R: Until I gain my speed back, and things like that.

> [R-32 to R-35 offer another example of a fairly frank explanation on the part of the respondent, this time with respect to her abilities in shorthand, as well as her aspirations.]

36. I: Uh-huh. Well, Virginia, as I mentioned before, it's been very slow, and we've had few openings. Unfortunately I can't give you much encouragement as to how soon we'll be able to consider you.
    R: Uh-huh.
37. I: At the present time, there aren't any openings.
    R: Uh-huh.
38. I: And there's still quite a few people waiting. June graduates like yourself, who haven't been placed. We still fill job openings, however, from the applications that we take, and so I'd be very glad to have you fill one out.
    R: Uh-huh.
39. I: Leave it with us and we can get in touch with you when there's a little more to offer in the way of job openings.
    R: Yeah, I see.

> [I-36 to I-39. Here we see a definite shift in the interviewer's role. Prior to this point the interviewer, for the most part, has been gathering information from the respondent. With this series of questions the interviewer becomes an information giver. As this phase of the interview is completed, the respondent has had a good opportunity to tell about herself, her aspirations, her strengths and weaknesses. She now receives from the interviewer a kindly but realistic assessment of the potentialities for a job in this company at this particular time.]

The interview proceeds for another several minutes, in which the interviewer takes up an apparent problem of overweight on the part of the respondent. The interviewer explains to the respondent that the company requires a rather strict physical examination prior to employment. She wonders whether the respondent has given thought to the possibility of rejection on physical grounds, whether the respondent has considered losing some weight. The interview ends with the respondent declaring that she will consult her family physician to see whether she should do something about her weight, and that after this she will return to see the interviewer, take typing and shorthand tests, and be ready for an eventual job opening.

Personnel Interview 2

1. I: I think we've met before, haven't we?
   R: Yes, I remember you.
2. I: And I remember you. I remember you working here, but I'm afraid I don't remember where.
   R: Well, I worked in the purchasing department.
3. I: Oh, yes.
   R: For approximately two years.
4. I: You were a typist up there, weren't you?
   R: Well, I did general clerical work. In field supplies I posted, did filing and general clerical work.
5. I: Did you come to us right from high school, Susan?
   R: Well, no. I went to school for a year, to college for a year.
6. I: Where did you go?
   R: ———— College.
7. I: ———— College, uh-huh. And then you started working?
   R: Then I started working here, and now I've just finished this comptometer school.

   [I-1 to I-7. This is an easy and uneventful beginning. The interviewer vaguely remembers the respondent as a former employee. She is attempting to refresh her memory and re-establish the circumstances of the earlier employment. The respondent contents herself with brief factual answers. The role relationship appears familiar to both, and is made easier by the earlier acquaintance.]

8. I: Uh-huh, I see.
   R: Now I heard you had a "comp" opening, and I thought perhaps, I just thought I'd inquire about it, and see if there was any chance of . . .
9. I: Well, a comptometer job is presently being posted. You probably heard about that. That job is presently being posted. You probably remember about the posting of jobs and promotion from within.
   R: Uh-huh, yes, I talked to an employee, and she told me that a job had been posted.
10. I: That's right, and I believe the posting expires tomorrow, so we won't know whether there are any bids from within the company, whether any employees will need to be given consideration, until that time.
    R: I see.

    [R-7 to R-10. The respondent answers the question, but then takes the initiative in the interview. She wants to move the discussion into the area of her new competence and present interest, comptometer operation.

I-7 to I-10. The interviewer accepts the respondent's change of subject and invites further communication. Having ascertained the respondent's interest in a job as a comptometer operator, the interviewer explains the company's policy of giving priority to present employees. With I-11 she returns to her major objective, completing the applicant's job history.]

11. I: How did you happen to leave, Susan?
    R: Well, I went down to Florida. I had an opportunity to go down there and live.
12. I: I see.

[I-11 and I-12. The interviewer uses questions like these with considerable effectiveness. I-11 is open, worded in a neutral, easy fashion; I-12 is a typical nondirective probe, the effect of which is well reflected in R-12.]

    R: And I didn't like it. I hated it. And I worked for the telephone company down there, and I transferred back here, and I disliked it so much that I thought I'd better get into something more— well, more genteel. (Laughter.)
13. I: Uh-huh, what sort of work did you do for the telephone company?
    R: Operating. And I liked it down there. It was wonderful.

[I-13. The respondent has communicated material with a good deal of emotional content, but it leaves a number of questions unanswered. Why did she transfer back from Florida? Why did she dislike the job so much after transfer? What are the implications of "more genteel"? The interviewer might well have probed this area more fully, rather than move to the new content of I-13.]

14. I: Yeah. I can imagine that just being in Florida itself would be nice.
    R: Yeah, I mean the job. We had afternoons off and went back to work in the evenings. We just sat on the beach. We were at a small town.
15. I: Wonderful. Were you right in (city)?
    R: Yeah. But then when I got back here it was just *horrible*. I just don't care for the telephone company at all.

[R-12. The respondent's dislike for the previous job comes through even more strongly here, but again the interviewer declines to explore the topic, or even to show acceptance of this reaction. Instead, there is "I see," and a shift in subject.]

16. I: I see. You wanted to return to New York. Was that your reason for leaving down in Florida? It was convenient to be transferred, wasn't it, from one state to the other?

[I-16. There are two problems of technique here. First, two questions are asked simultaneously, so that the respondent must choose which to answer. She answers the second question, and the first remains unanswered. The second problem is the

directive wording of the questions themselves. Each one begins with an assertive statement and ends with an invitation to
the respondent to offer corroboration.]

R: Yes, it certainly was. I appreciated that very much. And I took
my vacation in between.

17. I: Good . . . That gave you a chance to get moved.

R: Yeah. I went home, and had a little holiday at home before I
started working again. That part worked out just fine. But then
when I started working, I just didn't like that office, where I was.

18. I: Where were you, in the _____ Building here in this city?

[I-18. This question again uses the assertive form, in which
the interviewer includes the expected answer in the question.
The respondent must then contradict the interviewer in order
to give the correct answer (R-18). This is probably not important in so neutral a matter as place of work, however. More
important is the omission of a probe following R-17. Why is
it that the applicant "just didn't like that office"?]

R: No. (She names the location of the building where she worked.)

19. I: I see. Were you on the swing shift, where you worked?

R: Not here, no. I had fairly good hours.

20. I: Well, that was fortunate because most of the girls, I understand,
most of the girls start off on the split shift.

R: Well, down here I think it works that way because they have so
many more operators, but over at that other office they only have
a couple of split shifts. And usually they can find somebody who
lives in the neighborhood, and it works out good for them. Oh,
like married girls who have children, they can spend time with
them in the afternoon.

21. I: I see. How long have you worked for the telephone company
since you got back up here?

R: From July through November.

22. I: I see.

R: From July through November.

23. I: That's of this year?

R: That's right.

24. I: Five months.

R: Uh-huh.

25. I: I see.

R: No. No, it isn't *this* year, I left there last November, a year ago.
This last November.

26. I: Oh. A year ago. I see. (Pause.)

R: Then I went to comptometer school.

27. I: I see. You did that on a full-time basis?

R: Uh-huh.

28. I: Fine. Now, have you completed your course yet?

R: Yes.

29. I: Do you like "comp" work?

R: Yes, I like it very much. It got kind of tedious in school, because
I was so late, so I might have trouble with my adding.

30. I: I see.
    R: And I was doing the same thing constantly, and I think I got tired, but I like the work, calculation I did, it's interesting.
31. I: Uh-huh. What comptometer did you use?
    R: (She gives the name of a comptometer.)
32. I: Is that a manually operated?
    R: Well, they had both kinds.
33. I: Oh, they do?

> [I-26 to I-33. The objective of this series of questions is obviously to find out how much experience and skill the respondent has in the comptometer operation. Again, as in the previous interview, notice that the questions are in general open questions, which bring forth a good deal of information with specific details filled in when necessary (for example, I-31 and I-32). One gets the impression in this interview, as in the last, of a relaxed interaction, with a fine relationship between the two people. It is also clear that this relationship is built up not in terms of extraneous rapport-building "factors," but in terms of the permissive atmosphere which attends even the specific fact-gathering involved in this interview.]

    R: Yes, and I worked at both. Oh-huh. Altogether, when I finally *did* get my adding, it was on an electric machine.
34. I: I see.
    R: Because the touch is so much easier to get your speed on the electric one.
35. I: I see. Uh-huh. Will you excuse me while I ask for your files, while you were up at purchasing.
    R: Uh-huh.
36. I: And we'll get a look at that.
    R: Uh-huh. Yeah, uh-huh, I left right around Thanksgiving.
37. I: I see. (Pause. Interviewer dials telephone, waits. No one answers.) No one seems to answer.
    R: Yeah. It must be getting close to lunch time.
38. I: Yes, I suspect they're changing shifts. (Somebody finally answers phone.) May I have the files on Miss Blank? (Interviewer returns to conversation with respondent.) Well, the job, as I told you, Susan, is posted and the posting expires tomorrow. Now, I don't believe we've had any bids as yet, since most competent comp operators within the company would be doing that sort of work.
    R: Sure, uh-huh.
39. I: So that there's a good chance that we would be able to consider you for it, and you'd probably like to know a little bit more about it.

> [I-38 and I-39. The interviewer is giving the respondent a definite understanding as to what the job opening is, what the steps are to getting the job, etc. In I-40 and I-41 she is giving the respondent the specific job description. This job description is interrupted by the sequence in which the respondent

feels sufficiently free in the interview to ask some fairly detailed questions and get into quite a discussion with the interviewer about the different kinds of machines.]

R: Yes, I would. I'd like to know what department it's in, and everything.

40. I: Well, the machine used on the job is a _____ calculator, so that possibly would be different from the (gives name of comptometer that the respondent says she was used to operating). Altogether I would think that the basic principles would be the same.

R: Oh, yes.

41. I: Now, that is an electrically operated one, so that if you've worked on an electrically operated machine—

R: Oh yes, that's wonderful.

42. I: —it would be pretty much the same.

R: Could you describe the machine to me? Or do you know what it's like?

43. I: I'm afraid I couldn't, beyond telling you that it's similar to a standard comp.

R: Well, I was wondering whether it had two keyboards or one. If it has two, the calculations would be worked a little different.

44. I: I see. Well, I don't know about that. We can find that out, Susan.

R: Some of those, I forget what kind that is now, I know a girl from school, she went to apply for a job and they had a completely different kind of machine than we were used to. She did it, she took the job, but she practically had to learn the whole machine over again.

45. I: Well, now that's something that we would have to check.

R: Uh-huh.

46. I: Now, in addition to operating the calculator and making computations, the duties listed here are: performing clerical duties, which require mathematical knowledge, necessary to obtain average cost to five decimal places, to secure sufficient accuracy, and other—

R: (Interrupts.) Average cost?

47. I: —and other mathematical computations.

R: (Interrupting.) Well, that would be prorating, I guess?

48. I: Well, I would think so. It involves quite a bit of math, Susan. Did you have much of that in high school?

R: I had four years of math in high school, but I didn't have any courses that were business math, except the courses that I had at comp school, and we covered all the angles of it.

49. I: All the phases as they were used on the machine, I suspect? Which, of course, would be the . . .

R: Uh-huh.

50. I: Which, of course, would be the thing that you would be doing here.

[I-48 to I-50. The interviewer is checking specifically on the high math component of the job.]

R: Uh-huh. Uh-huh. And a lot of it was just grade-school arithmetic. It was more like a review than anything else.
51. I: Uh-huh, surely, well, I should think that would apply to the work
that you would do here on this job. It says apply percentages,
average cost, prorating expenses, and involving ratio and resolving unit cost. Now sometimes, some of those things sound more
involved, those things sound more forbidding than they actually
are.

[I-51. The interviewer is trying to reassure the respondent
by telling her that sometimes job descriptions can be forbidding
in sound though the work is actually not that complicated.]

R: Yeah, I know. It sounds like a job that wouldn't be all the, well,
that is, all the same thing.
52. I: Yes, that's right. That's right. It sounds kind of technical and
somewhat less routine than some of the work that you've done.
R: Yeah, it sounds wonderful.
53. I: (Looks at file which has just been brought to her.) I see that
you left us in November of '52. I see that you were "average"
in your records, and that they say that they would consider re-
employing you. So that everything is clear on that score. Now
we have an application that was originally filled out when you
first applied here, but I think it would be a good idea if you'd fill
out a new one, to bring your experience and training up to date,
and perhaps we could arrange to have you come back in tomorrow
morning to take any additional tests that are necessary. It was
four years ago that you came in, and they might not have the
same one that they have at the present time, and there are some
tests for this job specifically, and we'd like to get comp tests on
you, too. We have some other applicants who have been in over
the past several months to be considered for the job, but we'd be
very glad to give you a chance.

[I-53. Here the interviewer is reviewing briefly the record of
this respondent at the time of her last employment, and gives
the respondent some feedback as to what the record looks
like. In addition, she is giving the respondent some fill-in on
the new test which the company is using, and asking for an
application which will bring the old application up to date.]

R: Oh, I'd appreciate that so much.
54. I: And we will see what might work out.
R: Oh, I wanted to come back, and I think I wanted to so badly that
I thought it would be impossible. You know, until I heard about
this.

[R-54. The respondent is describing her attitude of wanting
to get back to work in the company, and one would suspect that
at least partially she is responding to the warm friendliness of
this particular interview.]

55. I: Uh-huh.
R: There are so few comp openings, you know, around the city.

56. I: They have lessened considerably in the past several months.
    R: Uh-huh, in the past three months the girls at school have been having more and more trouble finding . . .
57. I: Yes, there was formerly quite a demand for trained comptometer operators.
    R: You know what it is. It's this competition with IBM, with the IBM systems that they are using.
58. I: Oh, I see.
    R: Oh, it's *terrible*, and even the girls that they have on comptometers are getting laid off, and the new girls have little chance . . .
59. I: Sure.
    R: —to compete with the girls who are experienced operators.
60. I: Yeah.
    R: But I thought with my previous experience, I would not have as much trouble.
61. I: Well, that's right. You have some office experience, and an additional skill will always be valuable. Even though you might not be doing a job as a comp operator, in many of the clerical jobs in the company it's helpful to have a knowledge of comp.
    R: Uh-huh.
62. I: Well, fine. And if you will fill out an application for me, if I can find one for you here . . . (Looks in desk.) Now if you will take this down to room 126, that's two offices down, then fill it out and bring it back to me and I will arrange for the test.
    R: Okay!
        [At this point the respondent leaves to fill out the application form. The interview picks up when she brings the application back.]
63. I: (Looks over forms.) Well, I guess that's complete. Good. Now, is it possible for you to come in at two o'clock tomorrow and take the comp test?
    R: Uh-huh, sure.
64. I: Good. Do you know where the testing division is? Do you remember where the testing division is located? Do you remember that?
    R: Yes, it's in this little building right over here.
65. I: Yeah, that's right, and it's in room 255.
    R: 255, and I should be there at two o'clock?
66. I: Uh-huh.
    R: And I don't have to come here first?
67. I: No, but come here when you finish. They'll send you over here then.
    R: Is that all?
68. I: Yeah, that's it. Fine, we'll see you tomorrow.
    R: Oh, thanks ever so much, Miss Blank.
69. I: Well, I hope that everything works out for you. As I say, we have some other folks to consider, and when you were filling out your application, a bid came in for the job from an employee.
        [I-69. This statement on the part of the interviewer must have been very jarring to the respondent—that a bid for the

job came in from an employee. Notice how the interviewer is supportive (I-70) and shows the warm friendly attitude toward this respondent which has characterized this interview throughout.]

    R: No kidding!

70. I: So keep your fingers crossed, and we'll hope for the best.

    R: Well, one consolation I have, even if I had come sooner, anyone in the company would have been considered.

71. I: That's right. They have through tomorrow to apply for it.

    R: Uh-huh. Well, I'll keep my fingers crossed.

72. I: Well, fine. We'll see you tomorrow.

    R: Okay, at two o'clock. Over here at 255.

73. I: That's right, uh-huh. Good-by.

    R: Bye.

chapter 12

A Supervisor-Subordinate Interview:

A Production Bottleneck and an Office Feud

This is a role-played interview between a supervisor and one of his subordinates. The subordinate is the head of a typing and clerical pool in a large office, and the supervisor is the department head to whom he reports. Both are men and both have been with the company in their present positions for several years. The interview has been initiated by the supervisor, who has called the respondent into his office so that they can hold their conversation in private.

The supervisor's objectives in initiating the interview are several. It is an information-getting interview, in the sense that the major objective is to learn from the respondent the nature of some difficulties in the typing and clerical operation and any ideas he may have for their remedy. But the interview has other objectives. The interviewer, in his role as supervisor, has the job of arbitrating a disagreement between two of his staff and arriving at a generally satisfactory settlement. He has already received a communication of protest from one of his staff members, and his present interview with the other protagonist is a necessary preliminary to working through some administrative solution in a group meeting.

This interview illustrates some of the special problems involved in the information-getting interview as it occurs between a supervisor and a subordinate. It is clear at various points throughout the interview that the dual role of the interviewer as supervisor and interviewer, and the complementary duality of the respondent's role as subordinate as well as respondent, raise a number of difficult problems. Moreover, this duality reflects itself in a certain diversity of interview objectives. While information-getting is the major purpose for which the interview was initiated, we cannot ignore the administrative purposes of problem-solving and arbitration, which the interviewer must keep before him.

It seems likely that this interview is not unusual in these respects, that its problems are common to most information-getting interviews between supervisors and subordinates. It is difficult for a supervisor to shed completely the attributes of the supervisory position and assume fully the role of interviewer. It is even more difficult for the respondent to accept his superior in the interviewer role and to ignore, even for the brief period of the interview, the status and power differences which exist between them. This problem manifests itself in various ways. Among the more frequent is the tendency for the respondent to become defensive and to withhold or distort information. He must protect himself against the possibility of administrative action on the part of the interviewer when he resumes his supervisory role.

In our discussion of respondent motivation in Chapter 2, we emphasized the positive forces of the interpersonal relationship and the desire of the respondent to achieve some of his own goals through the interview. We emphasized also the necessity of avoiding negative forces or barriers to communication which might be caused by possibilities of reprisal or punitive action against the respondent. It was in this connection that we stressed the importance of anonymity and confidentiality. In an interview between a supervisor and subordinate, though positive motivating forces are present, several barriers to full communication are likely to be present, also. The supervisor is in a peculiarly good position to take remedial and constructive action as a result of the interview, but he is in an equally good position to take punitive or disciplinary action against the respondent. He might, for example, be in a position to arrange either the promotion or dismissal of the respondent.

It is worthwhile to explore some of the implications of the supervisory role for the information-getting function, and to consider what special approaches or procedures the supervisor should use. We must begin by accepting the fact that the supervisor can never divorce himself entirely from his administrative and supervisory functions. His subordinates are certain to recall that in addition to the information-getting function, he performs many others, some of which are intimately connected with their own well-being.   There are, however, some things which the supervisor can do in the information-getting role that may alleviate this difficulty.   To the extent that he can, he must differentiate the information-getting function from his other functions, and then make sure that this differentiation is understood and accepted by his subordinate-respondent.   In part, the supervisor can do this by specifying the information-getting purpose of the interview and disavowing any other purposes.   In part, he can achieve this by remaining completely in the information-getting role during the interview, resisting the temptation to make administrative pronouncements or exercise his authority.   In his information-getting function he must behave like any other interviewer; that is, he must be accepting, permissive, nonjudgmental.

Even at best, the supervisor-interviewer must expect that certain information will remain unavailable to him because of his dual role.   It is only as the supervisor builds up trust in his subordinates that real communication can take place between them.   He does this, not in a single interview but over time, by consistently respecting the confidences he may receive during such interviews.

Unlike the other transcripts that comprise this section of the book, the following interview was role-played.   To create the interaction, each of the authors assumed a role, one as supervisor-interviewer, the other as subordinate-respondent.   After agreement on the objectives, the interview itself proceeded on a spontaneous basis, without any rehearsal of content or language.   It will be of interest to the reader that the device of role-playing was resorted to only after repeated attempts had been made to record an actual interview between supervisor and subordinate.   For reasons which most supervisors and administrators will quickly appreciate, our attempts to record such material ended without success.

Interview

1. I: Well, good morning, Joel.   How are you?
   R: Oh, pretty good, Mr. Blake.
         [I-1. This begins some informal introductory material, which extends through I-7.   This introduction is considerably longer than that which has characterized some of the other interviews, and at first glance it might appear somewhat aimless and digressive.   The supervisory role relationships which exist between the interviewer and respondent, however, make it necessary and desirable that the business of the interview not be entered into before some manifestation of personal interest occurs.   Where a personal relationship exists prior to the inter-

view, an indication of such interest is both natural and appropriate. Moreover, the interviewer uses this introductory material to give some structure to the interview. In I-2, for example, he indicates that the reason for this appointment is to discuss some job-related topics. It seems likely that the interviewer recognizes that the experience of a subordinate on being summoned to the supervisor's office includes some feelings of insecurity and concern, and the interviewer is attempting to offer some reassurance and establish an informal and comfortable atmosphere before beginning the interview proper.]

2. I: Fine. It's been some time since we sat down and had a talk about the job.
R: Well it has, but I guess you're a busy man these days.
3. I: Oh, yeah. Always things seem to pile up; more than they ought to, I guess. How's your family?
R: Oh they're fine, they're fine.
4. I: Your boy home from college this year?
R: Yeah, he's, he's out of school now.
5. I: Oh, swell.
R: Trying to line up a summer job.
6. I: I was wondering. Got any plans, has he?
R: Yeah, I think he's, ah, likely to be working down at the department store for the summer.
7. I: Oh, fine. Well I hope to get to see him sometime this summer. Haven't seen him in a long time now.
R: Yeah, you wouldn't, you wouldn't recognize him. He's filled out a lot.
8. I: I bet—they do. Well, Joel, ah, as I was mentioning, it's been some time since we've talked about the job very much, and I thought it might be a good idea today to, ah, sit down and have a chat about, ah, about things, the way we do once in a while. Ah, how are things going?
R: Well, I guess they're going all right. We're, we're all working hard. Doing our best.

[I-8 begins the body of the interview. The interviewer repeats the statement made in I-2, that he wants to talk about the job, and poses his first direct question. This is put in broad, open form, permitting the respondent to answer in terms of any aspect of his job. In spite of the interviewer's efforts at informality and reassurance, the respondent's answer (R-8) appears to be defensive. He offers relatively little information, and instead makes a general assertion of virtue.]

9. I: Yeah, we've sure had a lot of work to do lately, haven't we? Things seem to be going pretty well?
R: Yeah, I'd say they were going pretty well on the whole. We're getting a lot of work out.

[I-9. The interviewer accepts the respondent's statement that he is working hard. Having done this in a reassuring fashion, he repeats the question. The question is not stated in as balanced a form as it was in I-8, but it reflects the respondent's previous statement that things are, on the whole, going satisfactorily.

R-9 to R-11.   In this series of interchanges the interviewer makes patient attempts to get the respondent to talk about the work situation.   The respondent, however, continues defensive and appears unwilling to reveal any of his problems at this point.   Implicitly, he continues to ask for reassurance and recognition of hard work.   He is perhaps reacting to the interviewer as a supervisor rather than in the information-getting role.   This supervisor-subordinate relationship poses a problem for the interviewer throughout the entire discussion.]

10. I: Yeah, Joel, I suppose your section does have a heck of a lot of work close to it, doesn't it?

     R: Well, it does.   Course, course we're always busy but, ah, in the last few months it seems to have been especially heavy.   I'll say this though, we've, we've got a good, good crew of girls this year.

11. I: Well, that's good.

     R: They, ah, they come in right on time.   They, they tend to business while they're there.   Some of 'em are, we've got some really fine typists.

12. I: Joel, I don't know about the typists, but I went by there the other day and you got some darn good looking girls, too.

     R: Ah-ha-ha.   Well, we, we don't pick them on that basis . . .

           [I-12 to I-14.   The interviewer attempts again to lighten the atmosphere a bit.   There is some suggestion here that the supervisor is attempting to persuade the subordinate that he is a "regular guy."]

13. I: Ah, come on, Joel, you know that . . . (Laughter.)

     R: Well, it's no handicap.

14. I: Yah, that's right, if they can type too, that's good.   You're, ah, I gather then that you're able to keep up with the, ah, work pretty well with the crew you've got.

     R: Well, I'd say that on the whole we were.   Course, ah, I don't like to ask to add to the crew.   That raises costs and I know we gotta keep our costs down.   I'd say that most of the time we keep up pretty well.   Course, there're some times of the day, late afternoon especially, where, where things really bulk up.

           [I-14.   Since the global questions (I-8 and I-9) did not produce much, the interviewer now tries a more specific question.   It is possible that a better balanced wording would have improved it; however, the interviewer appears to be phrasing his question in a way that catches the content and implications of what the respondent has previously been saying.   In any case, the question appears successful, and in R-14 it brings out some important material for the first time in the interview.]

15. I: Sometimes they kinda jam up on you at the end of the day, huh?

     R: Yeah, they do and, ah, well, I suppose when, ah, when things jam up that way you can't make everybody happy.

[R-15. Here the respondent, encouraged by the interviewer's accurate reflection and acceptance of his previous expression, gives further indication of the nature of the problems which he has hinted at in R-14. It is in this response that we get the first indication of interpersonal difficulties.]

16. I: Sometimes they gripe to you, do they?

R: Well, I, ah, I don't like to, ah, say that, that anybody gripes really. I, I'm not complaining.

[I-16. The interviewer attempts to reflect the attitude which the respondent has previously conveyed, for purposes of encouraging further response. However, perhaps betrayed by his knowledge of what has actually gone on, the interviewer offers a stronger statement of the respondent's attitude than he is yet ready to accept. The interviewer's statement is factually correct, but it goes somewhat beyond the respondent's previous statement and leads to some temporary difficulties. In R-16 the respondent resists and becomes somewhat defensive about the implication that he is complaining about anyone.]

17. I: Yeah, I didn't mean that. I thought you, ah, indicated a few minutes ago that, ah, every once in a while they complain.

R: Well, as a matter of fact, you can't please everybody. I guess that's what it comes down to. I don't want to point the finger at anybody as, as complaining. Let's just say that when things bulk up the way they do sometimes in the afternoon, you can't make everybody happy.

[I-17. At this point the interviewer gets defensive, probably realizing that he has used an unfortunate probe. He emerges from his role and attempts to explain and justify his previous statement. The result is further defensiveness on the respondent's part.]

18. I: Yeah, I suppose, Joel, that on a job like yours, ah, you can't give everyone exactly what they want when they want it.

R: Well, we, we try. We try most of the time, and most of the time I'd, I'd say, ah, we're pretty successful. But what tends to happen is that sometimes we just get so loaded in the afternoon that something's had to go over to the next day.

[I-18. Here the interviewer has recovered. He no longer attempts to justify his own wording, but focuses on the respondent's previous less personal statement about the work situation. This more appropriate interviewing procedure is rewarded with the communication of additional material in R-18. For the first time, the respondent volunteers the basis of the current difficulty.]

19. I: Hm. Your work bulks up then the latter part of the afternoon, huh?

R: Yeah, I, that happens. Now I, I can understand how it is. Ah, people, ah, do a lot of writing and dictating in the morning, and then it starts, ah, pouring in to us after lunch. Sometimes the girls aren't very busy in the morning, and then, ah, the afternoon is awfully hectic.

20. I: Yeah, well, of course we've been pretty busy, ah, all over the place, and I guess, ah, a lot of the boys are feeling under, ah, some pressures. Ah, tell me more. What, ah . . . Does this create special problems for you?

R: Well, frankly it does. Of course there's always a problem when people feel pushed, I suppose, but the thing that makes it most difficult is that when people bring us work, nobody seems to know or care what other work is tossed at us. They're, they're just thinking about their own stuff, and, ah, sometimes it gets to the point where, well, where we just can't get it all out in the afternoon. We have to tell somebody that they'll, they'll have to wait till the next morning.

[I-20. This again appears as a statement that incorporates unnecessarily in the interviewer role material which the interviewer has acquired in his role as supervisor. The interviewer has certain facts about the situation, and he is obviously laboring to get the respondent to bring forth material in the same area. Nevertheless, the question with which I-20 ends is well worded and effective. In R-20 the respondent begins to show the good effects of some of the reassurance which he has received, and he elaborates further the kinds of difficulties in which he has found himself.]

21. I: This must cause a real problem for you sometimes. How do the men, how do the men take this?

R: Well, some of 'em, some of 'em take it pretty well. Some of 'em understand that, ah, that we've got our problems, too. Most of 'em, I guess, ah, are thinking mainly about their, their own work and ah . . .

[I-21. Proceeding with the funnel sequence of questions, the interviewer now asks a somewhat more restrictive question focused on the respondent's relations with other people in the work situation.]

22. I: Yeah, I suppose that's natural.

R: . . . wishing they could get it out. Once in a while we get a guy who gets pretty nasty about it.

23. I: Yeah, I guess that's right, Joel. As a matter of fact, one of the, ah, reasons why I thought we ought to have a talk this morning was, ah, one of the men was in yesterday, ah, saying that he was having some real problems, ah, getting some of the work out of your group. Ah, he thought maybe we ought to have a general talk to find out what kind of problems we're having, you're having with your operation. See if there is anything we could do.

R: Yeah. Well, I thought that might be it. Well, whatever you say.

[I-23. This is a rather defensively delivered bit of communication by the interviewer. From the beginning of the interview he has been in a situation in which he had a good deal of information regarding the respondent and regarding the specific difficulties in which the respondent found himself on the previous day. However, the interviewer has chosen, in his supervisory role, to keep this information to himself while attempting as an interviewer to get the respondent to discuss some of the same material. This has posed a problem which is more one of administration and interpersonal ethics than interviewing technique. At this point in the interview, the interviewer apparently has decided that he can no longer pretend to be uninformed on the topic. Apparently feeling some defensiveness at not having communicated the information earlier, he admits the episode which led to this interview.

In order to communicate this material, it is necessary for the interviewer to get out of his interviewing role and assume the supervisory role. The result of this communication is by no means good. The respondent answers in a way that emphasizes the supervisor-subordinate relationship. Moreover, the response (R-23) clearly suggests that the respondent had his own suspicions about the basis for the interview, and that these suspicions have now been confirmed.

It is certainly questionable whether the procedure that the interviewer is following here is desirable. On the other hand, it is difficult to predict whether the interview would have followed a more effective course had it begun with a statement from the interviewer as to the circumstances which had caused him to summon his subordinate. It is entirely possible that such an introduction would have created difficulties more serious than those which are here encountered.]

24. I: Well, as I say, I wasn't, ah, I wasn't calling you in specifically for this, Joel. I don't want you to get the idea I brought you in here to give you hell or anything of this sort. But I know that when we, we have a lot of people working together like this, once in a while there's almost bound to be, ah, friction develop, unevenness of the work. It's particularly true when we've been working as hard as we have. We've all been putting in all kinds of hours, and I know as well as you do how hard you people have all been working. But I thought that, ah, it's been some time since we've had a general discussion and this, ah, just reminded me this might be a good time to talk things over generally. Ah, I just want to reassure you that I'm not really trying to put the finger on you at all here. Why don't you tell me a little bit more about what went on yesterday, and we'll see if we can't work something out.

   R: Well, I, I suppose if you come right down to it, it wasn't much. It was one of those things that happens. Ah, about four-thirty we were rushed as we could be. Johnson came plowing in with some work he said had to get out.

   [I-24. The interviewer clearly feels uncomfortable about the material he has communicated and the respondent's somewhat resentful reaction to it. He appears not entirely certain what to say. He is still out of the interviewer role, but is anxious to leave his supervisory role for the more comfortable interviewer-respondent relationship. He does reassert the constructive purpose of the interview and his desire to bring about a remedy to any existing difficulties. In R-24 the respondent shows some acceptance of the situation. He appears to be somewhat re-assured although still on the defensive.]

25. I: Well, just one of those things, huh.

R: Yeah, I, I guess that's, that's it. He, ah, he just kept yelling that work had to get out, and I began by not knowing how we could do it. I guess before he was done I sounded off a bit myself.

26. I: Well, Joel, I can see why this might have really got under your skin. Ah, I suspect it's not very pleasant, when you're doing a job, to have someone really land on you like this.

R: That's right, and I felt that he really wasn't justified. He stood there saying that he had to have the work out. Never thought to say, "Joel can you get it out?" No. "I gotta have it!"

[R-26. The respondent appears to be considerably reassured by the encouragement and patience which the interviewer has shown. He is now communicating material, but it is material not wholly relevant to the objectives of the interview. Appar-ently the respondent wishes to talk about the personal aspects of the difficulty, whereas the interviewer's objectives require a discussion of the situation apart from the personalities involved.]

27. I: Well, Joel, as I said before, I'm not particularly interested in this, ah, problem between you and Johnson. Ah, I don't want to get into that too much. What I am interested in is whether this represents a general kind of problem for you, and whether there's something we can do about it.

R: We're not servants just because we run a typing pool. We're a service section all right, but not a servant section, and it isn't up to him to treat us as if we were.

[I-27. The interviewer plays a purposefully directive role in getting the interview back on the objectives. It is especially im-portant to the interviewer to redirect the content of the inter-view at this time, because in his supervisory role he wishes to avoid a situation in which one employee is reporting some series of hostilities with another. In R-27 the respondent does not pay much attention to the interviewer's attempt at reorientation. Apparently there is good deal of emotion here, and he is intent on completing the ventilation process.]

28. I: Yeah. Well, ah, as I say, Joel, I can sure see why you would be upset by this but, ah, let's look at it more generally for a moment. Ah, is, is this problem of, ah, having to get out more work than you can at a particular time of day, ah, a general problem? I think that you've indicated before that the work tends to pile up, and I wonder whether there is something we may be able to do that would help out this situation.

R: Well, there're really a lot of things that could be done. If people would agree to do them.

[I-28. The interviewer makes a second attempt at reorienta-tion here, and in the process reasserts the constructive purpose of the interview. Apparently the respondent (R-28) has got rid of enough emotion so that he can now listen and pay attention to the interviewer's attempts to move the conversation toward a more constructive outcome.]

29. I: Ah, will you tell me more? What kind of things do you have in mind here?

   R: Well, for instance. Why, why can't we have a rule that anything that comes to our section after two in the afternoon doesn't get out till the next morning?

   [I-29. With this question we move into a series of questions and answers in which both interviewer and respondent are clearly in the area of problem-solving. In this discussion the interviewer is restricting his conversation to general kinds of probe questions.]

30. I: Ah, well, that might be one possibility. Ah, let's explore this a little more. Do you have any other thoughts in mind that might help out things?

   R: Well, I should think, ah, another possibility might be to have somebody make decisions about what's important and what can be delayed. If a couple guys come in toward the end of the day, each one waving a letter and saying that it has to be typed, and we only have time to do one of them, which one do we do?

31. I: What you're saying is that you'd like to have somebody who protects you from this, ah, problem of overload, so that you don't have to cope with that, is that it?

   R: Well, I don't know whether I mean just protect, but there are decisions to be made and somebody has to make them so they'll be accepted.

   [I-31. The interviewer asks a question that is essentially a reflection of the previous statements by the respondent, all of which imply that the solution to the problem lies in change on the part of others. Apparently the interviewer wants to see if the respondent is at all aware that a solution might involve action or change on his own part. It seems likely, however, that the interviewer has somewhat overstated the sense of the respondent's previous communications. The respondent (R-31) shows some tendency toward rejection of the interviewer's formulation, but on the whole he accepts the content.]

32. I: Yeah, I guess that's right. But let's, ah, let's look at it from another point of view for a minute. Ah, as I indicated to you earlier, I suspect, well, you know as well as I this kind of pressure is going to continue on us. Ah, is there anything that you think you could do in your section that might, ah, prevent some of the problems of this sort?

   R: I suppose we could always have more girls working, but that gets kind of expensive.

   [I-32. This question represents a further step-down in the funnel sequence, and requires the respondent to focus specifically on the question of changes in his own operation. The respondent's answers in this area are meager and grudging, but he does follow in the direction which the interviewer's question suggests.]

33. I: Yeah, particularly since you indicated that, ah, sometimes in the morning the girls weren't fully occupied as it is, huh?

R: Yes, I did say that. Of course, of course, it doesn't happen very often, and I suppose that there is the possibility of, of staggering the hours a little, of having some girls come in later. We could even have a night shift. I don't know. The girls don't like to work irregular hours. You know. Their free time is pretty important to 'em.

[I-33 represents a statement on the part of the interviewer which is factually accurate but is undesirable interviewing technique. Here he confronts the respondent with an apparent inconsistency in his point of view. It is difficult to specify what the intent of this question is, and it may indeed have been quite benign. Nevertheless, there seems to be some tendency to needle the respondent at this point. The respondent (R-33), either because of or in spite of the previous question, for the first time comes up with a suggestion that involves meaningful change in his own operation.]

34. I: Yeah, I can see why it might be. There is the one possibility you've mentioned of the, of staggering the hours. Ah, are there any other kinds of adjustments you think could be made that will help out?

R: Well, I don't really know. I have thought sometimes about having a night shift, or at least a skeleton crew on the second shift. It would raise some supervisory problems, but it might be more efficient than overtime in the long run.

[I-34 and I-35. The interviewer attempts to make the most of this line of response by stimulating the respondent to think further about the problem and the kinds of solutions which might be developed in answer to it.]

35. I: Uh-huh. This might be a possible solution. Is there anything else that you think might help out?

R: Well, I'm just going to tell you straight out, Mr. Blake, but I think the real solution doesn't lie in having the girls work odd hours or getting more girls. It lies in, in having the people who hand work to us understand what we're up against and, ah, if that doesn't do it, in having some system of priorities that will even things out for us.

[R-35. Apparently the respondent has no further ideas to contribute and here returns to the assertion that the most appropriate solution to the problem lies with people other than himself. This is a further rejection of the notion that he perhaps needs to change.]

36. I: Well, I gather, at least the implication of what you're saying, Joel, is that, ah, the solution to this problem lies not with you at all but with somebody else entirely. Is that the way you feel about it?

R: Well, that, that, that's, I suppose it did kinda sound that way. I don't mean that there isn't something we could do too. I, I'm willing to meet the other men halfway on this thing.

[I-36. Here the interviewer attempts to summarize the respondent's attitude. The notion of a summary at this point, to which the respondent can either accede or take exception, is probably appropriate. It seems, however, that the interviewer has overstated the content of the respondent's previous statements. A more neutral summary would clearly have been preferable. The respondent (R-36) feels the needle and reacts by becoming defensive, in much the fashion that characterized some of the early exchanges in the interview.]

37. I: Yeah. Well, I didn't mean to say that there wasn't anything you felt you could do, but it seemed to me what you were saying is that the most of the adjustment was going to have to be made by other people, and I just want to be sure that's the way you really felt about it.

R: Well, let's put it this way. I won't say that most of the adjustment has to be made by other people, but the way it looks to me now, ah, it would be cheapest and most efficient if we could work it out on that basis.

[I-37. This represents a disavowal on the part of the interviewer of any aggressive attempt. If this were an earlier phase of the interview, the interviewer would have the problem of getting back into role and out of the supervisor-subordinate situation. As it is, he can move more definitively into the supervisory role and proceed to bring the interview to a close. This he does, beginning with I-38.]

38. I: Well, Joel, look. This, ah, this gives me an idea. I think you, you're perfectly right that, ah, when we get into things of this sort there's no simple solution in sense of one person changing. Ah, why don't we do this. Why don't we, ah, set up a meeting in the next two or three days and let me get together a couple of people who have the most call on the pool and somebody from Personnel and you and me, and let's sit down and see whether we can't work out some different procedures that will help us out in this. How's that sound to you?

R: Well, that sounds pretty good to me. I'm, I'm not anxious to continue the present hassle that started yesterday.

[I-38, with its clear communication of an administrative or action decision, conveys the words of the supervisor rather than those of an interviewer.]

39. I: Well, O.K. then. Suppose, ah, suppose I try to set this up in the next day or two and I'll, ah, I'll let you know as soon as we can get it set up. I think that's a good idea. Thanks a lot for coming in, Joel.

R: That's all right.

40. I: We'll be seeing you soon, then.

R: Yeah.

41. I: Swell. So long.

chapter 13

A Social-Work Interview:

Family and Job Adjustments
of a Discharged Psychiatric Patient

This is an exit interview with a man who is about to be released from the hospital after approximately one year, during which time he has been undergoing psychiatric treatment. The interview, conducted by a psychiatric social worker who is on the hospital staff, has several objectives. One is the administrative function of completing the records and paper work on a patient about to leave the hospital; another is to arrange for future therapy on an out-patient basis. The patient will continue therapy with the psychiatrist who has been primarily responsible for his treatment in the hospital. An additional purpose of this interview is to assess the attitudes and adjustment of the patient as he anticipates his return to his family and to his job.

There are, of course, many kinds of social-work interviews. In fact, the range covered by this kind of interview is so extensive that it is difficult to select any single interview as representative of the work done by the profession. Social workers sometimes interview in situations in which the discovery of objective facts is the entire purpose. For example, a social worker may interview a potential client to determine the amount of money needed to assist a destitute family. On the other hand, much of the interviewing done by social workers has a therapeutic purpose, and in this respect it resembles the psychiatric therapeutic interview.

The example we have chosen is somewhere in the middle of this range. The psychiatric social worker in this case is attempting to elicit patient attitudes that are deeper and more difficult to obtain than more objective kinds of information. But the social worker's purpose is clearly not to administer therapy. In the course of the interview, the interviewer shows a good deal of sensitivity in restricting himself to the information-getting function and avoiding topics which are more appropriately those of the therapist.

The interview takes place in the psychiatric ward of the hospital where the patient has been receiving treatment. The interview has been initiated by the social worker, and takes place in his office.

The patient reveals himself as an intelligent person. In listening to the recordings, one is struck with his fluency, the rapidity with which he begins to respond, and the rush of words that characterizes many of his responses. The social worker, experienced in his profession, is generally at ease in the course of the interview. There is some ambiguity in the social worker's role, primarily because of the patient's continuing relationship with the psychiatrist. The social worker clearly wants to avoid encroaching upon the functions of the psychiatrist, but at the same time wants to ascertain the respondent's reactions and feelings as he looks forward to re-entering society, family, and his job.

Interview

1. I: I wanted to have a chance to talk with you a little while today before you did leave town, to get some ideas of your plans following discharge, and also we are sort of interested in how you feel about leaving the hospital. I guess you have been here for a while. If you have, it isn't easy always to just take off and start in working again, particularly with the responsibilities at home.

> [I-1. Here we have the interviewer giving the structure or the introduction to the interview. Two objectives are stated: first, the interviewer is interested in the patient's feelings about his hospitalization; second, he is interested in the particular problems which the patient may visualize as he goes back into the world to re-enter his work and home life.]

R: Well, I do think that, uh, having been here for some time, within the shelter of the hospital, uh, it was a certain amount of reluctance, about going, but I feel it is quite natural. As I say, from having enjoyed the shelter of the hospital, uh, presently I feel confident that I can do it, whereas a few months ago I had much more qualms of conscience about it, actually a matter of a few weeks ago, but uh, I have become quite confident that no matter how difficult it may be, that I can overcome it. I think it especially important that I return to work immediately, and, uh, for that reason I have made arrangements, I have contacted my employer, and I will be going to work Monday morning.

[R-1. We notice immediately that we have a highly verbal respondent. Also, this response indicates that he is somewhat defensive and somewhat concerned about his ability to cope with the realities of the outside world.]

2. I: This coming Monday?
   R: That's right. I'll be released Friday, and I'll be going to work the following Monday morning. I, uh, plan on returning to the hospital for out-patient treatment—
3. I: Uh-huh.
   R: —and I'll see Dr. Jones in the out-patient clinic.
4. I: You're coming in in the evening?
   R: Yes.
5. I: Have you, uh, had any of these feelings about—well—ah, difficulties arising around your leaving the hospital? For instance, when you've been home on pass, have you felt at times, uh, maybe a little uncomfortable?

[I-5. The interviewer is responding to the statement which the respondent has just made, in which he indicates that things seem to be in good shape, that he has no particular problems. The interviewer is again bringing up the possibility of difficulties in leaving the hospital, at home, on the job, and so forth, to keep the respondent's attention focused on this kind of problem.]

   R: Well, I've felt stress at certain times at home. Uh, I have been aware of the added responsibilities of four children.
6. I: Uh-huh.
   R: And, uh, I perhaps have been more conscious of them because of the rarity in which I have encountered it. I mean the fact that I have just been conscious of them on week ends, perhaps, and actually in the hospital I am not aware of these responsibilities, which has perhaps caused some alarm, but I do feel that once I take up the reins of providing a livelihood for my family again, that I won't be as aware of it in the sense of a liability.

[R-5 and R-6. The probe which the interviewer used was successful, in that the respondent begins to verbalize some of the problems which he foresees as he gets back home. He does, however, at the conclusion of this statement, reiterate feeling that he is able to cope with the problems as they arise.]

7. I: Uh, have you felt that you have been pushing yourself at times during week ends? Uh, do they get pretty long at times?

[I-7. The interviewer does an excellent job in picking up the thought which the respondent has expressed about his consciousness of some of the problems on week ends. He does, however, appear to push the respondent a little too hard. It might have been better if he had used a more neutral probe, such as "Well, tell me a little bit more about how it worked out on week ends."]

R: No, I wouldn't say they become long. There are periods of discomfort during the week end, but I wouldn't say that it has made it appear longer.

8. I: Uh-huh.

R: I have been most anxious to remain the entire week end, I mean without ever taking flight and coming back to the security of the hospital—

9. I: Uh-huh.

R: —to be sure that I could overcome any difficulties.

[R-7 to R-9. Note the immediate reaction of the respondent to having been pushed too hard. The entire statement appears to be a reaction to the probe which the interviewer has used.]

10. I: Uh-huh. You have battled it out each time.

[I-10. The interviewer is trying to get back on the track, and is trying to keep within the framework of the attitude of the respondent. Notice that his probe is a recognition of the attitude the respondent has been expressing in R-8 and R-9.]

R: Which has made me more comfortable—

11. I: Yuh. That isn't always easy to do.

R: —and confident that I can handle the situation.

12. I: Uh-hmm. I notice you have been taking longer week ends, for instance over Thanksgiving for about four or five days—

R: Uh-huh, and Armistice Day.

13. I: Armistice Day too, uh-huh.

R: I think I had three long week ends, and I had a leave, a five-day leave, and strangely enough I didn't seem to run into any more upsetting situations during the five days than I did in the two or three, that is, it seemed the longer I was home, the more able I was to cope with the situation.

14. I: Uh, did this influence your decision to leave now? In your talking it over with the doctor to consider the possibility of returning home and going back to work, and arranging for out-patient treatment, do you feel that these long week ends, as they became, uh, uh, call it more successful, and, uh, you found you were getting more enjoyment out of them, do you think this influenced your final decision?

[I-14. The interviewer appears to depart from his objectives somewhat. He asks the specific question at first; then, apparently recognizing the fact that this has been somewhat off the track, he tries to patch it up with two or three other questions, none of which really fulfills a very useful function.]

R: Well, to be perfectly honest, the biggest thing that prompted my decision to go presently is my awareness of my responsibilities at home, which I became more conscious of during the longer week ends, I think. Uh, this awareness of this responsibility caused

me to weigh the hospitalization against it and see if it justified or
merited my remaining here.

15. I: Uh-huh.

R: And though I do feel I could obtain something out of further hospitalization, I feel that weighed against my responsibilities at
home and the urgency with which I feel that I am needed there,
that I can compensate for that by returning to the out-patient
clinic once a week, which may be a *slower* form of complete re-
covery but which will be offset by my supplying the needs at
home.

[R-14 and R-15. The respondent continues his previous
statement almost as though the interviewer's probe had not occurred. Nevertheless, the interviewer's questions serve to lead
the respondent to discuss the basis for his decision in the final
part of this response.]

16. I: Uh-huh. You have been pretty concerned recently about these
things?

[I-16. This is an excellent probe, in which the interviewer
senses the conflict and attitude which the respondent is implying by his comments. Notice how effectively it hits home.]

R: I certainly have.

17. I: Uh-huh. Are there—

R: I have been aware of the fact at home, I mean constantly since
I have been hospitalized. More so with the approach of the
winter months—

18. I: Uh-huh.

R: —and the increased cares of my wife.

[R-16 to R-18. The respondent really starts to talk about his
concerns as he anticipates leaving the hospital.]

19. I: Uh-huh. Particularly with a lot of other bills coming up, coal
and everything else?

[I-19. This is a natural, human kind of statement. It serves
no particular purpose and does not advance the interview towards its objectives.]

R: Sure, and additional clothing, and the holidays approaching of
course.

20. I: Uh-huh. (Pause.) How do you feel about leaving? Do you
feel pretty confident?

R: I feel, uh, not as confident as I should *like* to feel about it—

21. I: Uh-humm.

R: —but I hope that the complete feeling of confidence will develop
with the act of accomplishment. That having left, and being
successful in my return to my work, and finding that I am able to
work, will heighten the feeling of confidence—

22. I: Uh-huh.

R: —and as I say, lessen this feeling of reluctance I have. After all,
there *is* a certain amount of pleasure, or relief, in being hospitalized. You are isolated from your problems—

23. I: Uh-huh.
    R: —and therefore—of course, being realistic about it, we know that isolation from your problems doesn't eliminate them.

    [R-20 to R-23. The interviewer reaps the rewards of patient probing. The respondent states for the first time the trepidation and lack of confidence which his previous assertiveness might have led us to suspect.]

24. I: Uh-huh. You have worked out, I see, difficult problems while you have been here, too. Isn't that so? While you have been here in the hospital.

    [I-24. This is a good probe, acknowledging the respondent's insight that hospitalization has its secondary gains. The probe, however, is not properly balanced, in that "Isn't that so?" makes it more difficult for the respondent to answer no.]

    R: Yes, I appreciate that fact.
25. I: Uh-huh.
    R: There was the problem of my commitment—
26. I: Uh-huh.
    R: And my feeling of (unintelligible) . . . to overcome.
27. I: And these things you have handled pretty well, at least we feel here at the hospital anyhow. You took the initiative and went and resolved these things without much assistance from anyone here in the hospital, and I think this is going to carry over, too, to your making arrangements at home. I think you mentioned the other day working things out with your old job, getting it back and getting straightened around there.

    [I-27. This statement marks the close of the first phase of the interview, in which the respondent has expressed some of his ambivalent feelings about hospitalization. The interviewer ends this phase with gentle reassurance, and praise for his performance. The second sentence represents a shift to the next objective, which is to get more information about the transition from the hospital to the job.]

    R: I'll tell you. I do think my job is my chief concern.
28. I: Uh-huh.
    R: I have been alarmed about the limitations that might be placed upon me because of having been hospitalized for something of this sort, and having talked it over to a certain degree with my employer, I think we've worked it out somewhat.
29. I: Uh-huh.
    R: At least I don't have the feeling that such limitations as may be placed on me, when returning immediately to work, will be permanent.
30. I: Uh-huh.
    R: And that within my own mind I have been able to justify these feelings that, uh—
31. I: You feel that there are any excessive demands they are making?
    R: No, I feel that—
32. I: Uh-huh.

R: —that these are reasonable doubts they have about it, and that
certainly they are not completely out of order in demanding a
certain period of time just to prove that my health has been sufficiently restored, as to be a dependable employee—

33. I: Uh-huh.

R: —and I'll grant that the six months which I regard as a proba-
tionary period are going to seem somewhat long—

34. I: Uh-huh.

R: —a long time.   Yet if I feel that there is a goal to be achieved
at the end of the six months, I'm certain that I'll be able to put
up with it.

35. I: Uh-huh.

R: It will be enough to go on.

36. I: Uh, you mentioned this letter yesterday—that you felt might be
required eventually by the—is it the chief of engineers?

[I-36. This introduces a new topic in the interview.   The
interviewer is apparently satisfied with the respondent's acceptance of his employer's wish to try him out on a simpler,
less stressful job before reinstating him to his own previous
position.   He now refers to a more specific topic, that is, the
question of a written statement from the hospital that the respondent is ready to resume the responsibilities of a job.]

R: Yes, the engineering manager.

37. I: How do you feel about that?   Would you rather hold off on having the hospital write anything to him at first?

R: Well, I hadn't cared about you addressing it to him directly, in-
asmuch as I hadn't had any conversation with the man at all.   I
would rather speak to him first about it, but presently my immediate supervisor had asked that I bring a letter from my doctor,
but he had specified that it be a "to whom it may concern" letter.

38. I: Uh-huh.

R: Whether he would forward it to the engineering manager or not,
that is to say I have not had any direct contact with the top
supervision about it.

39. I: Uh-huh.

R: And the manager, therefore, not having contacted him personally,
I wouldn't care to take a letter addressed to him.

40. I: Uh-huh.   This is a— I guess it is a pretty common practice, and
may be tied up with insurance and stuff like that.   Almost all
employers want some kind of a letter from patients who are out
of the hospital that they are ready to return to work, and I imagine they want to be covered in their insurance clauses.

R: Yeah, I mean there seems to be a great deal of importance placed
upon the testimony of a professional doctor.   That is, that the
testimony can give them some advice in the matter.   They feel
that he is much more qualified, and all, and then there is the suspicion that the patient might not be absolutely truthful with
them.

[R-37 to R-40.   We have the specific topic of the letter being
worked out in some detail, with minimal but appropriate en-

couragement from the interviewer. At the end of response R-40, however, the respondent introduces the idea that the requirement of a letter is prompted by distrust of the patient.]

41. I: Do you think that they question you there? Is there any feeling of that?

[I-41. The interviewer, with excellent sensitivity to this statement, focuses on the respondent himself and whether he feels a personal distrust in this situation. The interviewer's objectives deal with an effort to understand the respondent's emotional situation, and his reaction to the emotion or attitude of the previous response is sensitive and appropriate. The respondent seems to indicate (R-41) that his integrity is not being questioned, and the interviewer, satisfied on this score, returns to seeking out the previous topic.]

R: I don't feel that they really question me there. I feel that it is as much a matter of formality as anything.

42. I: Uh-huh.

R: And I feel that this is a bit more direct than that release, which is just a form—

43. I: Uh-huh.

R: —like the registrar's form, which is not specific in any way.

44. I: They want to have the letter brought in by you when you come to work, do you think?

R: Yes, to the effect that to drive, or operate equipment, that your doctor feels that I am competent to do so. That is to say, I presume, that you feel that I am not subject to blackouts or seizures.

45. I: Uh-huh. Have you made arrangements to take this with you? Is Dr. Jones going to have it?

R: Uh-huh.

46. I: Good deal, uh-huh.

R: He said Monday that he would write such a letter for me.

47. I: Well, you seem to have this deal pretty well squared away as far as returning Monday, and—

[I-47. The interviewer acknowledges the thoroughness of the respondent's arrangements, accepts the basis of his return to work.]

R: Yes. As far as returning Monday, I will—

48. I: You are going back to a full week, are you, right off the bat?

[I-48. This is a straight factual question introducing a new content area. It is interesting that this question has the effect of bringing the respondent face to face with reality, and produces more emotionally toned responses and brings forth more anxiety about the transition than we have previously encountered.]

R: I am going to start right in full time. In prior hospitalizations I *have* had a good deal more confidence about leaving.

49. I: Have you?

[I-49. Here we have evidence of excellent sensitivity on the part of the interviewer. Instead of pushing ahead with his factual line of questioning, he adapts his pace to the emotion which the respondent has expressed, and contents himself with a very general sort of probe.]

R: Uh, I have not been nearly as satisfied that I have received treatment that would compare with this—that is, that I have received as favorable treatment. However, the hospitalization has never been quite so long—and in prior hospitalizations I am certain that I *have* pressured the hospital staff to release me—

50. I: Uh-huh.

R: Sooner than they probably cared to do so, but I think that's why I think that largely this lack of confidence is from having been hospitalized so long.

51. I: Yeah. You feel that this has made a difference then, huh?

[I-50 and I-51. The interviewer continues to focus on and acknowledge the concern which the respondent is verbalizing.]

R: Yes, I feel that having been isolated from my job so long, I feel a bit of a stranger to it—

52. I: Uh-huh.

R: —a bit uncertain as to whether I can fit into it again. And having that feeling of reluctance has made me more anxious to plunge into it—

53. I: Uh-huh.

R: —before it becomes a—

54. I: You want to prove this to yourself?

[I-54. Here we might question whether the interviewer may not have overstated the respondent's attitudes.]

R: —before the feeling becomes more overpowering.

55. I: I'm sure the doctor here at the hospital, the whole staff, as far as that goes, feel that you are quite capable of doing this, and they think you'll work it out with the vocational counselor and the tests you took with him. And Stan was pretty well convinced that you are quite capable of managing this job you've had previously, as well as other things that might come along, in the event you are interested in moving into some other area.

[I-55. It appears that the interviewer may have questioned the appropriateness of his previous probe and is now attempting to reassure the respondent.]

R: Well, presently I am doubtful about moving into another job.

56. I: Uh-huh.

R: I do feel that there certainly might be jobs in which I could take a great deal more pride than I do in my present job, but—

[R-56. The respondent accepts the reassurance but rejects the implication that he might consider moving into another job. His expression of ambivalence is interesting.]

57. I: Do you like the people there?

[I-57. It is difficult to see why the interviewer felt called upon to use this probe. It appears that he has blocked off the respondent's interesting speculations on whether or not he would consider other jobs, and forced prematurely the topic of interpersonal relations on the present job.]

R: Yes, I enjoy them. I enjoy working with them to a large extent.

58. I: Uh-huh.

R: There have been times when I have had considerable pride in my job—

59. I: Uh-huh.

R: —and I suppose the job would be all that I could desire, but there also have been times when I suspicioned that there wasn't a sufficient amount of pride in the job, to think of it as a fitting occupation for my entire future.

[R-57 to R-59. The respondent acknowledges and replies to the interviewer's question, but then returns to the question of the job itself and his pride in it. At this point the telephone rings and interrupts the interview.]

60. I: One thing you can't control is the telephone, interruptions at any time. Would you feel more confident, do you think, if you return there and things do work out O.K.?

[I-60. The interviewer resumes with an appropriate apology for the telephone interruption. Unfortunately, however, he is not able to pick up the precise thread of the previous conversation, and retreats to a more general question about the respondent's confidence in his return to work. It is only in R-63 that the respondent again returns to the previous specific topic of his pride in the job.]

R: Yeah, that's the way I've felt about the job—

61. I: Uh-huh.

R: —that presently the challenge is to return to my present job.

62. I: Uh-huh. This is often harder to do than get a new job, you know.

R: Well, I'm not completely convinced that that's true in this case.

63. I: Uh-huh.

R: I don't have that feeling about it, but I do feel there is a challenge at the present job—

64. I: Uh-huh.

R: —and that if I can cope with that and come out satisfactorily, then 'I would certainly have more confidence. Were I to obtain another job and feel more favor to seek another job presently, and it doesn't seem that I would have very much to offer in the way of references, if I had not made a successful comeback in my previous job.

65. I: Uh-huh.

R: I don't feel that that would be a very good reference to take to a future employer.

66. I: Uh-huh. Sort of unfinished business, uh?

R: That's right. I feel I must face up to this present problem.

67. I: Uh-huh. How about financially? Will that work out O.K.? Will you be able to maintain the family all right?

[I-67. The interviewer apparently feels that he has enough information about the job and the respondent's attitudes toward going back to his previous work. Here he shifts the topic to family relations.]

R: Well, certainly. I mean I make good wages. I can certainly support my family.

68. I: Uh-huh.
R: I will be receiving help in this respect in that my wife plans to continue with her work.

69. I: Oh, does she?
R: Yes. She anticipates getting her hours changed to the day shift so that we can live a somewhat normal life.

70. I: (Interrupting.) You'll both be working days, huh?
R: Yes.

71. I: Well, that is a good deal.
R: Uh-huh.

72. I: You have talked this over with her, your plans for leaving now?
R: Yeah, a couple of weeks ago. She plans to be on days, which means we'll have every evening at home, which would be a normal situation. I presume that week ends of course she'd be working much of the time.

73. I: Uh-huh. Does she work a six-day week?
R: No, five days. But her two days are not necessarily week ends. In fact, they are apt to be any two days in the week.

74. I: Uh-huh.

[I-70 to I-74. The interviewer is following up his original question by collecting factual information about the family's work situation. The questions appear to be well formulated and adequate for the purpose.]

R: Either consecutive days or a week end.

75. I: You mentioned a little earlier this idea too of returning to responsibilities, and you also mentioned the fact that being in the hospital here it *is* different from a normal living situation, where you have a lot of responsibility. Uh, I wonder if you could tell me what this means to you. Returning and resuming so much responsibility all at once sounds like it is going to be quite a job.

[I-75. The interviewer now wishes to switch from factual to attitudinal information. He wants to know how the respondent feels about the situation. Notice that he returns to a theme which has occurred earlier in the interview. The main formulation of his question "I wonder if you could tell me what this means to you?" is an excellent type of probe to get the discussion on the affective level. Unfortunately, the interviewer did not leave it here but added the last sentence, which at least partially destroys the effectiveness of the probe. Why it was that the interviewer added this last sentence is not clear, but the respondent's reply does make it clear that it was ill-advised. Note that instead of responding, as the interviewer had hoped, with attitudinal information, he reacts specifically to this last sentence and denies that he is going to assume the responsibility all at once. The question has some of the elements of a double-barreled question. He asks for affect; he also asks for the respondent's reaction to assuming responsibility on the job. The respondent chooses to pick up only the latter for comment.]

R: Well, I am not sure that I am assuming so much responsibility at once, particularly in the job area. I don't feel that I would be assuming a great deal of responsibility.

76. I: Uh-huh.

R: And at home, I don't feel that I would be faced with an exorbitant amount of responsibility at one time.

77. I: Uh-huh.

R: That is to say even, as I mentioned, this financial area, my wife would be working, and it is not as if I am a complete stranger to my home because I have spent week-end passes almost continually—

78. I: Sure.

R: —since the latter part of July. And within the past month I have spent three long week ends at home. Out of the past month or five weeks, I have spent about fifteen or twenty days—

79. I: Uh-huh.

R: —at home altogether.

80. I: Uh-huh. That is a large part of the time, isn't it?

R: Yes, it is much of the time, as I say—

81. I: Uh-huh.

R: —that I've spent at home. I do think it well that they consider this fact that I do not feel that I am faced with an abnormal amount of responsibility—

82. I: Uh-huh.

R: —at the present time, that I consider the amount of help that I have had with it—

83. I: Uh-huh.

R: —and that I will have with it in the future, instead of regarding it as an insurmountable amount of responsibility.

84. I: Uh-huh. In other words, you have sort of been picking up your responsibilities and keeping in touch with your family all along—

R: Yes. Yes.

85. I: —week ends and passes, and so on.

R: And also the responsibility is not mine solely.

86. I: Uh-huh.

R: That I have a wife who is very competent to share the responsibility with me.

87. I: Uh-huh.

R: In fact, it appears from looking at the past summer that she could shoulder that responsibility alone much of the time, and knowing this, I should feel confident that together we can assume that quite capably.

[R-76 to R-86. The respondent is continuing the defensive reaction initiated by the interviewer's assertion that difficulties could be expected in reassuming the home responsibilities. Fortunately, in this series of responses, triggered by the interviewer's unnecessary last sentence (I-75), the interviewer shows a good deal of skill in accepting and encouraging the respondent to complete his statement of defense. Nevertheless, in assessing the information communicated by this series of responses, we are left with the feeling that a difficult problem of interpretation is involved in this apparently rich material. Specifically, we must decide to what extent this material accurately reflects the respondent's feelings about returning home, and to what extent it constitutes a defensively overoptimistic statement offered in retaliation to the interviewer's apparent skepticism. This ambiguity represents the major cost of the unfortunate question-wording.]

88. I: How about—
    R: (Interrupts.)   I—
89. I: Excuse me.
    R: I think that it was possibly being unaware of this fact that prompted my illness in the first place which has—
90. I: How do you mean?
    R: Well, all this anxiety and concern over problems with which I felt confronted that were just overwhelming.
91. I: They were just building up?
    R: Yeah.   That I wasn't capable of handling by myself.   In other words, perhaps I felt somewhat the indispensable man in the situation.
92. I: Uh-huh.   Trying to do all things?
    R: That's right.   Besides being somewhat shocked by the death of my father, the circumstances of the death, that is to say, the suffering—
93. I: Uh-huh.
    R: —which he endured, but suddenly I felt that perhaps my mother —she was making her home with us—of being responsible for her again.
94. I: Uh-huh.
    R: And it seemed as though—
95. I: That you were taking on more and more of a load, huh?
    R: Yeah, and that, uh, I was not sure that I was secure, that I could take care of any of the responsibilities that I was already faced with, and it seems that I regarded her as an additional responsibility, and the fact that surrounding the death of my father—
96. I: Uh-huh.
    R: —the enormous hospital bill, the funeral expense, and so on, which at that time I was not sure would be adequately covered by his insurance—
97. I: Uh-huh.
    R: —and there was no provision for any amount of insurance left to provide for my mother's future.

98. I: How do you feel she will get along now? How has she been making out while you have been here in the hospital?

R: Well, she is receiving a certain amount of compensation from an insurance policy, which will last her for about two years. There will be a period of almost a year, so far as I can ascertain, that she will have no income, until she becomes eligible for Social Security.

99. I: Uh-huh.

[I-88 to I-99. Several points in this sequence deserve comment. First, the interviewer is attempting to shift the discussion from emotionally loaded material toward more objective questions of the situation to which the respondent is returning. It seems likely that the interviewer is doing this because he feels that some of the respondent's deeper emotional problems are not within the objectives of this interview, but are more properly the business of the psychiatrist. Examples of the interviewer's attempts to switch the content of the interview in this way include I-88, I-89, and I-98, in which he ignores the respondent's discussion of his attitudes toward his mother and the death of his father, and concentrates upon the mother's present situation. During this sequence the interviewer's probe questions are on the whole insightful and well timed (I-90 through I-95). I-91 and I-92 are good examples of brief summarizing questions that serve to clarify what has gone before and encourage further exposition by the respondent. The interviewer's introductory questions for each new objective are on the whole less skillful, however, and less fortunately worded. I-75 is one example of this problem, I-98 is another. These examples emphasize the difficulty of formulating spontaneously the major questions of an interview such as this, and suggest that there might have been considerable advantage to the interviewer in thinking through and even in formulating in advance the language of the key questions in the interview. Beginning with I-98, the interviewer shifts the topic toward the situational factors in the home environment to which the respondent is returning. On the whole, this series of four or five responses goes smoothly.]

R: But during those two years I guess she will be able to earn something—

100. I: Uh-huh.

R: —and we, uh, she will be able to get along, and we should be able to contribute toward her support for this period.

101. I: Has she been working at all?

R: Well, she has been baby-sitting.

102. I: Oh, has she?

R: And things of that sort, yeah, but so far she has not earned a great deal, $10 a week or something like that, which I believe she has been able to save, though, and she does have something of a bank account.   But I do know that I do not have to regard my mother as a liability in this case.

103.   I: So actually it seems like there are less pressures than there were before?   Do you feel this is true?

> [I-103. Despite the generally good interaction in this series of questions and responses, a kind of disparity persists between the objectives of the interviewer and those of the respondent. The interviewer continues his attempt to focus the discussion on external situational factors.   The respondent is equally intent on wanting to talk about his own reactions and attitudes toward his situation.   Thus, in I-103 the interviewer asks a question which refers to reduced pressures in the environment, and the respondent answers (R-103) by denying a difference in the environment but asserting a difference in his own point of view.   In this case the interviewer shows good flexibility in going along with this line of response.]

   R: Yeah, at least that there are, if there are not less pressures, at last I have come to regard them in their true proportions.

104.   I: Uh-huh.

   R: Of course, when I was acutely ill and entered the hospital, I had a distorted view about the size of these liabilities.   They seemed to be tremendous burdens to me.

105.   I: Uh-huh.

   R: I think I saw them in a great deal different light than they actually existed.   I think I saw them as overpowering problems, which were actually *not* overpowering.   Had I been able to look at them with a more calculating eye, and seen them in their proper proportions, I wouldn't have been so alarmed by them.

106.   I: You think it was more your feelings about them?

> [I-106. This is a specific acceptance of the respondent's previous statement, and an effective one.]

   R: Yeah, I think it was the state of emotional upset in which I was in that made me regard my problems in such a light.

107.   I: So it looks like when you go home again this time you won't have so many pressures and the ones you do have, you feel you have a better view of, and—

   R: That is right.

108.   I: And so in control.

   R: I feel that perhaps I will see them in their proper categories, to a much greater extent.

109.   I: How about the children?   Will there be any children at home while you and your wife are working?

> [I-109. The interviewer again interrupts the respondent's discussion of his attitudes, to ask a question in a less emotionally loaded area.   The interviewer is clearly trying to lead the respondent away from introspective material and toward a realistic assessment of the situation which will shortly confront him.   I-109 initiates the topic of arrangements which will be made for the children.   This topic continues through R-125.]

R: Yes, there will be one at home, there will be the little girl.

110. I: Uh-huh. The other three will be in school all day?

R: Well, the younger boy will only be in school a half day—

111. I: Uh-huh.

R: —so that is half of the working day that will be two children at home, and then the younger child will be at home in the afternoon always, but I feel we will be able to hire someone competent to stay with him.

112. I: Uh-huh.

R: I mean I'm certain that my wife would not work if she couldn't find—

113. I: Uh-huh.

R: —someone competent.

114. I: Uh-huh.

R: That is the kind of situation that we have had in the past and will be true in the future.

115. I: Then you will be working toward getting somebody to come in during the day?

R: I believe she has been able to procure someone to do that.

116. I: Uh-huh.

R: Someone who will work days rather than the afternoon. I have been wondering if it was possibly too great a sacrifice, if we're sacrificing something in the upbringing of the children, to work, but I feel that presently the need for additional financial help, with my wife working—

117. I: Uh-huh.

R: —offsets the need of the children. I mean I don't think that is too great a sacrifice to make presently—

118. I: Uh-huh.

R: —and from what I have seen during the past several months, I can't see that the children have suffered any—

119. I: Uh-huh.

R: —because their mother is with them a great deal of the time. Also, that I will be home spending the evenings with them, and I have been gone almost the greater part of the summer.

120. I: Uh-huh.

R: I can't see that they have suffered any effects from it so far, and I have reason to believe that conditions will improve.

121. I: Uh-huh. They will have you home all the time, and your wife home every evening.

R: Every evening. Uh-huh. Which she has not been while they were going to school.

122. I: Well, in the summer too, they were out of school. Now that they are in school they are pretty well occupied.

R: I feel that way about it too.

123. I: Uh-huh.

R: As I say, the younger child, the one who is home all the time, certainly has not seemed to suffer any ill effects from it at all. She seems to be perfectly normal in every way.

124. I: Uh-huh.

R: I can't feel that she seems to be suffering from the parental care in any way—

125. I. Uh-huh.

R: —from the lack of parental care.

126. I: Now, about following your discharge this Friday, will you be coming in pretty regularly to see the doctor?

[With this question the interviewer closes the topic of the children, refusing gently to explore the matter of effects on the children, which seems to hold some interest for the respondent. With I-126 the interviewer introduces the topic of out-patient therapy. He offers the respondent a good deal of reassurance with regard to the physician's interest in his case. This topic is terminated by the interruption of the telephone, which occurs during R-140.]

R: I anticipate coming in one night a week.

127. I: Uh-huh.

R: Whatever night the doctor says it will be.

128. I: Uh-huh.

R: It is true that there will be a considerable amount of driving, but I feel that presently I can do that much cheaper than I can afford out-patient treatment privately.

129. I: Uh-huh.

R: That is, to go to a private psychiatrist, the minimum rate would be about $15 an hour—

130. I: Uh-huh.

R: —and I am certain I can make the trip over here for less than that.

131. I: Uh-huh.

R: As I say, I am already established with Dr. Jones here.

132. I: You feel pretty confident in what you are getting here.

R: Yeah. I feel confident that he has an understanding of the problem, which if you went to a—a different doctor the entire case history would have to be worked up again, including that part which Dr. Jones has already.

133. I: Yes, and I know that he is anxious to go on working with you, too.

R: I do feel that this time at the hospital, and especially a factor in my favor is that I won't be losing contact—

134. I: Uh-huh.

R: —completely, and should a problem come up that I can't cope with, I will always know that I can seek professional advice on it—

135. I: Uh-huh.

R: —and that the professional advice would be available—

136. I: Uh-huh.

R: —to me each week, and I feel that that should be very much a governing factor as far as keeping my emotions in check.

137. I: Uh-huh.

R: As I say, it seems certain that conditions are favorable under which I am leaving. I can't see anything especially hazardous about leaving at this time—

138. I: Uh-huh.
      R: —though there might be something gained by continuing the hospitalization, I feel that this is not justified compared with the urgency with which I feel that I am needed at home.
139. I: Uh-huh. Feel that you can accomplish, uh—
      R: Though out-patient treatment, or what may be derived from this type of therapy may be slower—
140. I: Uh-huh.
      R: —than hospitalization, I feel that ultimately it can reach the same end.

       [Telephone rings here and the interview is interrupted.]

      R: (Continues.)   —The point is that it will take a longer time.
141. I: Do you anticipate that things, uh—problems will evolve after you leave? You mentioned that, uh—

       [I-141. The interviewer now uses an open question to learn whether there are other problems which the respondent has in mind.]

      R: What I mostly anticipate—
142. I: Uh-huh.
      R: —is during the six months probationary period of my job, possibly a feeling of boredom developing.

       [R-141 and R-142. The respondent answers the open question by returning to the problem of the job, especially the trial or probationary period which his employer is imposing on him.]

143. I: Uh-huh. This happened before, hum?
      R: Yes. After being hospitalized last time, I felt that a similar probationary period, that I was working under—as I say, I worked as a laborer before, and I couldn't derive any satisfaction from my job. However, at that time I had not gone to my employer to find out if such limitations were permanent or not, and I was laboring then under the apprehension and under the feeling that such a condition was permanent; therefore, as I say, I felt absolutely no pride in my job, that there was no ultimate goal, and that such a condition could go on endlessly.
144. I: Sort of put a ceiling on you?
      R: That is right.
145. I: Uh-huh.
      R: And I didn't work with any anticipation of the future, the job became more boring to me. I gradually became more depressed, which made me quite ripe for a complete emotional upset, and then the shock and the tragedy of my father's death came about.

       [R-145. Here the respondent begins to wander from the discussion of the job to a discussion of his own reaction to his father's death.]

146. I: Sure.

R: I certainly was not stable emotionally to withstand such a shock.

147. I: Uh-huh. You sure weren't getting much satisfaction on the job, were you?

[I-147. The interviewer rather firmly directs the discussion back from the experience of the father's death to the question of job satisfaction. If we assume that this is a further example of the interviewer's wish to differentiate his role from that of the psychiatrist and to avoid material which is more properly the subject of discussion between therapist and patient, this directiveness becomes quite appropriate.]

R: That is right.

148. I: As far as building up your confidence.

R: I don't feel, although I know such a condition is not existent, now, that is, I feel that it isn't, I still anticipate that the suspicion of such a condition might materialize, during the six months that I am working on probation. I may become suspicious of my job future again.

149. I: Uh-huh.

R: As I say, I think that that is the greatest problem I face.

150. I: Uh-huh.

R: The problem of being bored with work while working in such a capacity without responsibility—

151. I: Uh-huh.

R: —without being able to take a great deal of pride in my work as I go along.

152. I: Uh-huh. I guess you are working towards other goals too with the doctor, as far as that goes, as far as treatment. How about something that you said earlier about not feeling this time as you have in previous discharges from hospitals?

[I-152. The interviewer appears to be following his previous open question (I-141) with a series of questions designed to follow up subjects which were opened but not pursued further.]

R: Well, in other hospitalizations it seems that I never quite—I mean the awareness of my responsibilities at home was much more acute during my hospitalization, which resulted in my pressurizing the staff to get out sooner.

153. I: Uh-huh.

R: I mean that the condition this time may have come about because of the fact that my wife went to work and I was not as aware of there being such a financial need at home.

154. I: Uh-huh.

R: That is, we weren't pressed so financially at home, so I reconciled myself to wanting to stay in the hospital, and having stayed this long and, as I say, having been isolated, I think it makes me a bit reluctant to take up my responsibilities again.

155. I: Uh-huh.

R: After all, it hasn't been a completely unpleasant situation.

156. I: I guess not.

R: Completely relieved of work and actually of all the chores—
157. I: Uh-huh.
R: —that go with maintaining a family.
158. I: Uh-huh. So you sort of leave with mixed feelings, huh?

[I-158. This is an excellent probe, aptly summarizing the emotions which the respondent has just expressed, and encouraging further exposition of his feelings. It is worth noting that the interviewer here is encouraging the communication of attitudinal material, whereas in several previous situations we have noted his attempts to move the respondent from attitudinal and introspective to more objective material. Apparently the respondent is here expressing attitudes on a subject which the interviewer regards as the major objective of the interview, that is, attitudes toward the situation to which he is returning. So long as the respondent continues to speak on this subject, the interviewer encourages him. The interviewer is not adverse to obtaining material of some depth on this topic, and shows considerable skill in eliciting it.]

R: Certainly.
159. I: Uh-huh.
R: There is a certain amount of reluctance to take those up. Realistically speaking, I know that even though I was isolated from my responsibilities, they were still existent—
160. I: Uh-huh.
R: —but I was not really as aware of them before.
161. I: Uh-huh.
R: As I say, I never let myself become so completely—
162. I: Uh-huh.
R: —unaware of my responsibilities, which may have had a great deal to do with the fact that I don't think that I derived as much out of hospitalization—
163. I: Uh-huh.
R: —previously as I have this time. I feel that I have come much farther during this hospitalization—
164. I: Uh-huh.
R: —and that I have received much more help here than I have in any previous hospitalization.
165. I: Uh-huh. You feel that your leaving in earlier instances was the result of these outside pressures rather than from your particularly feeling ready to leave?
R: That is right.
166. I: Uh-huh.
R: I don't think that in most of these instances that doctors who were caring for me felt that I had gotten the most out of treatment. I think they felt it would have been beneficial for me to stay in the hospital, but it seemed that I had been successful in convincing them of the urgency—
167. I: Uh-huh.
R: —so that their better judgment was overruled in those instances.

168. I: Uh-huh.
     R: I feel this also has been responsible for recurrent hospitalizations.
169. I: You left before you were quite ready?
     R: That's right, that I have left always before I was quite ready.
170. I: Uh-huh.
     R: And I am hopeful that such a situation is not going to evolve in the future.
171. I: Uh-huh.
     R: And I should like very much to think that this is my last hospitalization, yes, but I realize that thinking it does not necessarily make it so. But I do think that an optimistic outlook about it may have a good deal to do with whether or not such feelings of depression as may occur will necessitate being hospitalized again.

> [R-171. This is an interesting response. The respondent here is speaking rapidly, expressing fairly deep feeling and some doubts about himself.]

172. I: On these previous hospitalizations, did you arrange for out-patient treatment?

> [I-172. Again the interviewer responds to the emotional outburst by bringing the respondent back to the discussion of some objective arrangements.]

     R: No, I never did that.
173. I: You never did.
     R: I have never taken out-patient treatment before after I was released from the hospital. It was suggested last year when I left that I do so, but as I say, I couldn't afford it privately, and I couldn't return to the hospital at any time but during a work day—
174. I: Uh-huh.
     R: —and I went on a six day a week schedule immediately upon leaving the hospital—
175. I: Yeah.
     R: —and this just didn't leave any opportunity to return to the hospital without taking time off from work. And I realize this is a great deal of condescension on Dr. Jones to allow me to return in the evening.
176. I: Is this a mutual desire for you and him? Did you request to go on to continue contacts with him?
     R: Well, he suggested that I definitely go on with out-patient treatment, and I suggested that I return at night, so that it wouldn't interfere with my work, and he was completely favorable toward it.
177. I: Do you feel that you have put more into it this time, to your hospitalization, than you did before? You've made more of an investment?
     R: Well, that may be, but I feel if that was the case I have been prompted to do so by the method of treatment.
178. I: Uh-huh.

R: I feel that group therapy and individual conferences with doctors to the extent that we have them here, have been very much of a guiding influence, have been a guiding kind of treatment, so that I don't feel that the effort has been entirely on my part. I feel that it was constantly directed by the staff.

179. I: Uh-huh. At the same time, when you get right down to it, you are the one that has to make the initial effort to get things straightened out, and have to make the investment and treatment, I think.

R: Oh, I feel that I have—certainly I feel that I have made more of an effort this time, but I feel sure that there was the opportunity to make more of an effort.

180. I: Uh-huh.

R: In previous hospitals, hospitals like (name of hospital), it was not possible to see a doctor as frequently—

181. I: Uh-huh.

R: —and there was certainly nothing like the group therapy and nothing like the— The treatment there was more the physical medicine—

182. I: Uh-huh.

R: —that is to say hydrotherapy, or in the case of the private hospital I was in, electric shock treatment, and it was a process that was entirely different. I don't feel that it was something you could enter into or get as much out of as you can in conference where you can bring problems immediately to the fore and have them reckoned with—

183. I: Uh-huh.

R: —which you can do with Dr. Jones.

184. I: Uh-huh. There is this much that I can mention, in reference to continued treatment as an out-patient, and that is that at the present time, after talking with Dr. Jones, I think it would be advisable if we could continue to see your wife occasionally and, like we have in the past, just continue our contact, to see if we can be of any service in case anything comes up that we can be of any help with. I wonder how this is going to work out with her other schedules too, as far as her work goes, and being in the home, this is going to be a bit of an interruption there, I think.

> [I-184. Here the interviewer is assuming another role. He enters actively into the arrangements which are to be made for out-patient treatment, and suggests that these arrangements should include the respondent's wife. This discussion of arrangements continues through R-196.]

R: I don't know. I thought she had talked to you—

185. I: Uh-huh.

R: —about this to some extent, has she not?

186. I: Yeah.

R: She mentioned to me that she had talked to you. I don't know, uh—

187. I: Uh-huh. She talked about continuing to try to work out Friday so that we could get together, but unfortunately we are not here in the evenings. Otherwise you could both get together at once when you come in to see the doctor.

R: Yeah, that's too bad.

188. I: What time do you usually get off work at night? What time would that be?

R: At five o'clock. At four-thirty or quarter to five.

189. I: You'll probably be coming in about seven, or something like that, I guess?

R: Yeah, about six-thirty or seven.

190. I: Uh-huh. Well, uh, and this will be changing each week probably.

R: To a different day, yeah.

191. I: Uh-huh. Well, maybe when I get together with her on Friday, we could work out something that will make less demands on her, as far as coming in every week. I think if we got together every other week, or every two weeks, that would be frequent enough.

R: And you have been seeing her every two weeks during my hospitalization?

192. I: Yeah. And then as time goes on, this might be changed to three or four weeks, depending on how things go along. I can talk with her, and maybe we can work out a definite appointment time. She mentioned that she feels she could fit it into her schedule better if she had a definite day, because she does have to ask for time in advance—

R: Um-hmm.

193. I: —so that might be a little more to the point. (Pause.) Do you have any questions or anything that you would like to bring up about leaving the hospital, or anything about the paper work or one thing or another? Has that been taken care of, the letters?

R: Well, I think so. I have already asked for a letter from Dr. Jones—

194. I: Uh-huh.

R: —relative to my capabilities to operate machinery, et cetera.

195. I: Uh-huh.

R: And the other is taken care of from the registrar's office, isn't it, as a matter of form—

196. I: Uh-huh.

R: —in relation to the hospitalization.

197. I: Well, I think it is the feeling of everyone here at the hospital that you have really put a lot into getting back on your feet, and taking the initiative in planning and even to the point of making all your arrangements for returning to your job, things like that and, uh—

    [I-197. With this discussion the interviewer begins a final statement of professional confidence in the respondent's ability to make the adjustment. This is part of a theme of reassurance which has occurred earlier (for example I-179). It is clear in this instance, however, that the interviewer is making a farewell speech.]

R: Well, it certainly seems to me that making arrangements for returning to a job and so on is the individual's responsibility.

198. I: Uh-huh.

R: I mean he may require help with it, at least letters of recommendation and so on, but other than that it certainly seems that the initiative *should* be up to the individual concerned.

199. I: Uh-huh. This isn't always the possibility. Quite often the person won't feel capable of making these arrangements. I think the fact that you have been able to take this responsibility and go ahead and make all of your plans about your date of discharge and working out of plans for continued contact with the doctor, that all this is a real good indication that you are prepared to— that you are ready to do it, and we sure have a lot of confidence in the fact that you, uh—

R: I certainly appreciate the confidence that the staff *does* have, and I hope to prove worthy of such confidence. I hope that I, uh, don't snafu when I leave here, and I am not pessimistic about doing it, as I say, I feel confident that I can make it. I am not without some misgivings, but—

200. I: Uh-huh.

R: I feel confident that ultimately that everything will work out all right.

201. I: Uh-huh. Well, we sure feel the same, and we would like to keep in touch with you. I imagine I will see you again on Friday before you do leave.

R: Well, I imagine we will be leaving quite early.

202. I: Will you?

R: I want to see Dr. Jones today to be sure that I can be released by noon.

203. I: Uh-huh.

R: I have this appointment with him at eleven, so that we don't have to hurry home immediately.

204. I: Uh-huh.

R: That is, when we get home she has to return to work.

205. I: Uh-huh. She does that in the afternoon?

R: Yeah, about three.

206. I: Well, I hope to see you before then, and in the event I don't, I wish you a lot of luck.

R: O.K.

207. I: And keep in touch with us.

R: O.K. I'll see you.

Bibliography

American Jewish Committee, unpublished manuscript reporting analysis of errors in an interview experiment, Department of Scientific Research, New York.

Atkinson, J. W., "Explorations Using Imaginative Thought to Assess the Strength of Human Motives," in M. R. Jones, *Nebraska Symposium on Motivation,* University of Nebraska Press, Lincoln, 1954.

Bancroft, Gertrude, and Emmett H. Welch, "Recent Experience with Problems of Labor Force Measurement," *Journal of the American Statistical Association,* **41,** 303–312 (1946).

Barron, Margaret, "Role Practice in Interview Training," *Sociatry,* **1,** No. 2 (June 1947).

Bartemeier, L. A., "The Attitudes of the Physician," *Journal of the American Medical Association,* **145,** 1122–1125 (1951).

Bartlett, F. C., *Remembering,* Cambridge University Press, London, 1932.

Bavelas, Alex, "Role Playing and Management Training," *Sociatry,* **1,** No. 2 (June 1947).

Bellows, Roger M., and M. Frances Estep, *Employment Psychology: The Interview,* Rinehart, New York, 1954.

Bennet, E. A., "The Diagnostic Interview," in J. R. Rees, *Modern Practice in Psychological Medicine,* Paul B. Hoeber, New York, 1949.

Benney, Mark, David Riesman, and Shirley Star, "Group-Membership Effects in the Interview," unpublished manuscript.

Bingham, Walter, and Bruce V. Moore, *How to Interview* (3rd ed.), Harper and Brothers, New York, 1941.

Blankenship, Albert B., "Does the Question Form Influence Public Opinion Poll Results?", *Journal of Applied Psychology,* **24,** 27–30 (1940).

——— "Influence of the Question Form on the Response in a Public Opinion Poll," *Psychological Record,* **3,** 345–424 (1940).

——— "Pre-testing a Questionnaire for a Public Opinion Poll," *Sociometry*, **3**, 263–269 (1940).

——— "The Choice of Words in Poll Questions," *Sociological and Social Research*, **25**, 12–18 (1940).

——— "The Effect of the Interviewer upon the Response in a Public Opinion Poll," *Journal of Consulting Psychology*, **4**, 134–136 (1940).

Burtt, H. E., and H. V. Gaskill, "Suggestibility and the Form of the Question," *Journal of Applied Psychology*, **16**, 358–373 (1932).

Cady, H. M., "On the Psychology of Testimony," *American Journal of Psychology*, **35**, 110–112 (1924).

Cahalan, D., V. Tamulonis, and H. W. Verner, "Interviewer Bias Involved in Certain Types of Opinion Survey Questions," *International Journal of Opinion and Attitude Research*, **1**, No. 1, 63–77 (1947).

Campbell, Angus, "Attitude Stability and Change; a Reinterview Study of the National Population," *American Psychologist*, **3**, 272 (1948).

——— "Polling, Open Interviewing, and the Problem of Interpretation," *Journal of Social Issues*, November 1946.

——— "Two Problems in the Use of the Open Question," *Journal of Abnormal and Social Psychology*, **40**, No. 3, 340–343 (July 1945).

Cannell, Charles F., and Morris Axelrod, "The Respondent Reports on the Interview," *American Journal of Sociology*, **62**, No. 2, 177–181 (1956).

Canter, R., *et al.*, *Adult Leadership*, **2**, No. 2 (June 1953).

Cantril, Hadley A., "Experiments in Wording of Questions," *Public Opinion Quarterly*, **4**, 330–332 (1940).

——— *Gauging Public Opinion*, Princeton University Press, Princeton, 1944.

Clark, E., "Value of Student Interviewers," *Journal of Personnel Research*, **5**, 204–207 (1926).

Cobb, Stanley, "Technique of Interviewing a Patient with Psychosomatic Disorder," *Medical Clinics of North America*, **28**, 1210–1216 (1944).

Crissey, O. L., "Personnel Selection," in W. Dennis (ed.), *Current Trends in Industrial Psychology*, University of Pittsburgh Press, Pittsburgh, 1949, pp. 55–83.

Crutchfield, R. S., and D. A. Gordon, "Variations in Respondents' Interpretations of an Opinion-poll Question," *International Journal of Opinion and Attitude Research*, **1**, No. 3, 1–12 (1947).

Curtis, Alberta, "Reliability of a Report on Listening Habits," *Journal of Applied Psychology*, **23**, 127–130 (1939).

Daniels, Harry W., and Jay L. Otis, "A Method of Analyzing Employment Interviewers," *Personnel Psychology*, **3**, 425–444 (1950).

Dewey, John, *Democracy in Education*, Macmillan, New York, 1916.

Dinerman, Helen, "1948 Votes in the Making: A Preview," *Public Opinion Quarterly*, **12**, 585–598 (1948).

Drake, Frances, *Manual for Employment Interviewing*, American Management Association publication, Research Report No. 9, 1946.

Durbin, J., and A. Stuart, "Differences in Response Rates of Experienced and Inexperienced Interviewers," *Journal of the Royal Statistical Society*, Series A, **114** (1951).

Edwards, A. L., "Political Frames of Reference as a Factor Influencing Recognition," *Journal of Abnormal and Social Psychology*, **36**, 34–50 (1941).

Fearing, F., "The Appraisal Interview," in Q. MacNemar and M. Merrill, *Studies in Personality*, McGraw-Hill, New York, 1942.

Fearing, F., and F. M. Fearing, "Factors in the Appraisal Interview Considered with Particular Reference to the Selection of Public Personnel," *Journal of Psychology*, 14, 131–153 (1942).

Feldman, J., H. Hyman, and C. Hart, "A Field Study of Interviewer Effects on the Quality of Survey Data," *Public Opinion Quarterly*, 15, 734–763 (1951).

Fenlason, Anne F., *Essentials in Interviewing*, Harper and Brothers, New York, 1952.

Ferber, Robert, and Hugh Wales, "Detection and Correction of Interviewer Bias," *Public Opinion Quarterly*, 16, 107–127 (1952).

Festinger, L., and D. Katz, *Research Methods in the Behavioral Sciences*, Dryden Press, New York, 1953.

Festinger, L., S. Schachter, and K. W. Back, *Social Pressures in Informal Groups*, Harper and Brothers, New York, 1950.

Festinger, Leon, *et al.*, *Theory and Experiment in Social Communication*, Institute for Social Research, University of Michigan, Ann Arbor, 1950.

Flowerman, S., "Polls on Anti-Semitism: An Experiment in Validity," *American Psychologist*, 2, 328 (1947).

Freeman, G. L., *et al.*, "The Stress Interview," *Journal of Abnormal and Social Psychology*, 37, 427–447 (1942).

Friedman, P. A., "A Second Experiment of Interviewer Bias," *Sociometry*, 15, 378–381 (1942).

Freud, S., *Collected Papers*, Hogarth Press, London, 1924.

———— *The Problem of Lay Analysis*, Brentano's, New York, 1927.

Gallup, G., "Question Wording in Public Opinion Polls: Comments on Points Raised by Mr. Stagner," *Sociometry*, 4, 259–268 (1941).

Garrett, A., *Interviewing: Its Principles and Methods*, Family Welfare Association of America, New York, 1942.

Gilbert, G. M., "The New Status of Experimental Studies on the Relationship of Feeling to Memory," *Psychological Bulletin*, 35, 26–35 (1938).

Gill, M., R. Newman, and F. C. Redlich, *The Initial Interview in Psychiatric Practice*, International Universities Press, New York, 1954.

Guest, L. L., "A Study of Interviewer Competence," *International Journal of Opinion and Attitude Research*, 1, No. 4, 17–30 (1947).

Guest, L. L., and R. Nuckels, "A Laboratory Experiment in Recording in Public Opinion Interviewing," *International Journal of Opinion and Attitude Research*, 4, 336–352 (1950).

Haire, Mason, "Projective Techniques in Marketing Research," *Journal of Marketing*, 14, 649–656 (1950).

Hansen, Morris H., William N. Hurwitz, Eli S. Marks, and W. P. Mauldin, "Response Errors in Surveys," *Journal of the American Statistical Association*, 46, 147–190 (1951).

Harral, Stewart, *Keys to Successful Interviewing*, University of Oklahoma Press, Norman, 1954.

Harvey, S. M., "A Preliminary Investigation of the Interview," *British Journal of Psychology*, 28, 263–287 (1938).

Hayakawa, S. I., *Language In Action*, Harcourt, Brace and Company, New York, 1940.

Heath, Clark W., "An Interview Method for Obtaining Personal Histories," *New England Journal of Medicine,* **234,** 251–257 (1946).

Henderson, D. K., and R. D. Gillespie, *A Textbook in Psychiatry,* Oxford University Press, Oxford, 1946.

Horvitz, D., "Sampling and Field Procedures of the Pittsburgh Morbidity Survey," *Public Health Reports,* 67 (1952).

Hovland, C. I., and E. F. Wonderlic, "Prediction of Success from a Standardized Interview," *Journal of Applied Psychology,* **23,** 537–546 (1939).

Hyman, Herbert H., "Do They Tell the Truth?", *Public Opinion Quarterly,* **8,** 557–559, (1944).

Hyman, Herbert H., *Survey Design and Analysis,* Free Press, Glencoe, Illinois, 1955.

Hyman, Herbert H., *et al., Interviewing in Social Research,* University of Chicago Press, Chicago, 1954.

Jahoda, Marie, Morton Deutsch, and Stuart W. Cook, *Research Methods in Social Relations,* Dryden Press, New York, 1951.

Johnson, Wendell, *People in Quandaries,* Harper and Brothers, New York, 1946.

—— "Speech and Personality," in *The Communication of Ideas,* Institute for Religious and Social Studies, New York, 1948.

Katona, George, *Organizing and Memorizing,* Columbia University Press, New York, 1940.

—— *Psychological Analysis of Economic Behavior,* McGraw-Hill, New York, 1951.

Katz, Daniel, "Do Interviewers Bias Poll Results?", *Public Opinion Quarterly,* **6,** 248–268 (1942).

—— "Psychological Barriers to Communication," *Annals of the American Academy of Political and Social Science,* March 1947.

—— "The Interpretation of Survey Findings," *Journal of Social Issues,* **2,** No. 2, 33–44 (1946).

Kinsey, Alfred C., Wardell B. Pomeroy, and Clyde E. Martin, *Sexual Behavior in the Human Male,* W. B. Saunders, Philadelphia, 1948.

Koffka, Kurt, *Principles of Gestalt Psychology,* Harcourt, Brace and Company, New York, 1935.

Kohler, Wolfgang, *Gestalt Psychology,* Liveright, New York, 1947.

Krech, David, and R. S. Crutchfield, *Theory and Problems of Social Psychology,* McGraw-Hill, New York, 1948.

Lazarsfeld, Paul F., "The Art of Asking Why," *National Marketing Review,* **1,** 26–38 (1935).

—— "The Controversy Over Detailed Interviews—An Offer for Negotiation," *Public Opinion Quarterly,* **8,** 38–60 (1944).

Levit, Grace, and Helen Hall Jennings, "Learning Through Role Playing," *Adult Leadership,* **2,** No. 5, 10 (October 1953).

Lewin, Kurt, *A Dynamic Theory of Personality,* McGraw-Hill, New York, 1935.

—— *Field Theory in Social Science* (ed. by Dorwin Cartwright), Harper and Brothers, New York, 1951.

—— *Principles of Topological Psychology,* McGraw-Hill, New York, 1936.

—— *Resolving Social Conflicts,* Harper and Brothers, New York, 1948.

Lienau, C., "Selection, Training, and Performance of the National Health Survey Field Staff," *American Journal of Hygiene,* **34,** 110–132 (1941).

Lindzey, G., "A Note on Interviewer Bias," *Journal of Applied Psychology*, **35**, 182–184 (1951).

Main, T. F., "Industrial Stress and Psychiatric Illness," in J. R. Rees, *Modern Practice in Psychological Medicine*, Paul B. Hoeber, New York, 1949.

Marks, E. S., and W. P. Mauldin, "Response Errors in Census Research," *Journal of the American Statistical Association*, **45**, 424–438 (1950).

Marston, W. M., "Studies in Testimony," *Journal of Criminal Law and Criminology*, **15**, 5–31 (1924).

Mayer, N. A., "Non-directive Employment Interviewing," *Personnel*, **24**, 377–396 (1948).

Menefee, S. C., "The Effect of Stereotyped Words on Political Judgments," *American Sociological Review*, **1**, 614–621 (1936).

Merton, K., M. Fiske, and P. Kendall, *The Focussed Interview*, Bureau of Applied Social Research, Columbia University, New York, 1952.

Miller, S. M., "The Participant-Observer and 'Over-Rapport,'" *American Sociological Review*, **17**, 97–99 (1952).

Moreno, J. L., *Who Shall Survive?*, Beacon House, Beacon, N. Y., 1953.

Mowrer, O. Hobart, *et al.*, *Psychotherapy, Theory and Research*, Ronald Press Company, New York, 1953.

Myers, Robert J., "Errors and Bias in the Reporting of Ages in Census Data," *Transactions of the Actuarial Society of America*, **41**, 395–415 (1940).

Neely, Twila E., *A Study of Error in the Interview*, privately printed, 1937.

Newcomb, Theodore M., *Social Psychology*, Dryden Press, New York, 1950.

Oldfield, R. C., *The Psychology of the Interview*, Methuen and Company, Ltd., London, 1951.

Otis, J. L., "Improvement of Employment Interviewing," *Journal of Consulting Psychology*, **8**, 64–69 (1944).

Parry, Hugh, and Helen Crossley, "Validity of Responses to Survey Questions," *Public Opinion Quarterly*, **14**, 61–80 (1950).

Parten, Mildred B., *Surveys, Polls, and Samples*, Harper and Brothers, 1950.

Payne, Stanley L., "Interviewer Memory Faults," *Public Opinion Quarterly*, **13**, 684–685 (1949).

———— *The Art of Asking Questions*, Princeton University Press, Princeton, 1951.

Proshansky, H. M., "A Projective Method for the Study of Attitudes," *Journal of Abnormal and Social Psychology*, **38**, 393–395 (1943).

Psychological Corporation, "Further Contributions, 20th Anniversary of Psychological Corporation and to Honor Its Founder, James McKeen Cattell," *Journal of Applied Psychology*, **26**, 16–17 (1942).

Radke, M., H. G. Traeger, and H. Davis, "Social Perceptions in Attitudes of Children," *Genetic Psychology Monographs*, **40**, 327–447 (1949).

Rapaport, D., "Principles Underlying Projective Techniques," *Character and Personality*, **10**, 213–219 (1942).

Rice, Stuart A., "Contagious Bias in the Interview: A Methodological Note," *American Journal of Sociology*, **35**, 420–423 (1929).

Riesman, David, and Mark Benney, "The Sociology of the Interview," *Midwest Sociologist*, **18**, 3–15 (1956).

Robinson, D., and S. Rohde, "Two Experiments with an Anti-Semitism Poll," *Journal of Abnormal and Social Psychology*, **41**, 136–144 (1946).

Roethlisberger, F. J., and W. J. Dickson, *Management and the Worker*, Harvard University Press, Cambridge, 1939.

Rogers, Carl R., *Client-Centered Therapy,* Houghton Mifflin, Boston, 1951.
——— *Counseling and Psychotherapy,* Houghton Mifflin, Boston, 1942.
——— "The Non-Directive Method as a Technique in Social Research," *American Journal of Sociology,* **50,** 279–283 (1945).
Rogers, Carl R., and F. J. Roethlisberger, "Barriers and Gateways to Communication," *Harvard Business Review,* **30,** No. 4, 46–52 (July–August 1952).
Roslow, S., and A. B. Blankenship, "Phrasing the Question in Consumer Research," *Journal of Applied Psychology,* **23,** 612–622 (1939).
Rugg, Donald, "Experiments in Wording Questions, II," *Public Opinion Quarterly,* **5,** 91–92 (1941).
Rugg, Donald, and H. Cantril, "The Wording of Questions in Public Opinion Polls," *Journal of Abnormal and Social Psychology,* **37,** 469–495 (1942).
Sanford, Fillmore H., "The Use of a Projective Device in Attitude Surveying," *Public Opinion Quarterly,* **14,** 667–709 (1950–1951).
Schramm, Wilbur (ed.), *Mass Communications,* University of Illinois Press, Urbana, 1949.
Scott, William A., "The Avoidance of Threatening Material in Imaginative Behavior," *Journal of Abnormal and Social Psychology,* **52,** No. 3, 338–346 (1956).
Shapiro, S., and J. C. Eberhart, "Interviewer Differences in an Intensive Interview Survey," *International Journal of Opinion and Attitude Research,* **1,** No. 2, 1–17 (1947).
Smith, H. L., and H. Hyman, "The Biasing Effect of Interviewer Expectations on Survey Results," *Public Opinion Quarterly,* **14,** 491–506 (1950).
Stanton, F., and K. H. Baker, "Interviewer Bias and the Recall of Incompletely Learned Materials," *Sociometry,* **5,** 123–134 (1942).
Stember, Herbert, and Herbert Hyman, "Interviewer Effects in the Classification of Responses," *Public Opinion Quarterly,* **13,** 669–682 (1949).
Stern, W., "Lectures on the Psychology of Testimony and on the Study of Individuality," *American Journal of Psychology,* **21,** 270–282 (1910).
Stevenson, Ian, and Robert Matthews, "The Art of Interviewing," *General Practitioner,* **2,** No. 4, 59–69 (1950).
Stock, J. S., and J. Hochstim, "A Method of Measuring Interviewer Variability," *Public Opinion Quarterly,* **15,** 322–334 (1951).
Sullivan, H. S., "A Note on Implications of Psychiatry, The Study of Interpersonal Relations, For Investigations in Social Science," *American Journal of Sociology,* **42,** 848–861 (1936–1937).
——— *The Psychiatric Interview,* W. W. Norton, New York, 1954.
——— "The Psychiatric Interview, I," *Psychiatry,* **14,** 361–373 (1951).
Survey Research Center, *Manual for Interviewers,* University of Michigan, Ann Arbor, 1955.
Symonds, P. M., and D. H. Dietrich, "The Effect of Variations in the Time Interval Between an Interview and Its Recording," *Journal of Abnormal and Social Psychology,* **36,** 593–598 (1941).
Udow, A. B., "The 'Interviewer-Effect' in Public Opinion and Market Research Surveys," *Archives of Psychology,* No. 277, 1942.
Wagner, R., "The Employment Interview: A Critical Summary," *Personnel Psychology,* **2,** 17–46 (1949).
Wallen, R., "Ego Involvement as a Determinant of Selective Forgetting," *Journal of Abnormal and Social Psychology,* **37,** 20–39 (1942).

Whitehead, Alfred N., *Process and Reality*, Macmillan, New York, 1929.

Williams, F., and H. Cantril, "The Use of Interviewer Rapport as a Method of Detecting Differences Between 'Public' and 'Private' Opinion," *Journal of Social Psychology*, **22**, 171–175 (1945).

Wittkower, E. D., "Psychosomatic Medicine," in J. R. Rees, *Modern Practice in Psychological Medicine*, Paul B. Hoeber, New York, 1949.

Wyatt, Dale F., and Donald T. Campbell, "A Study of Interviewer Bias as Related to Interviewers' Expectations and Opinions," *International Journal of Opinion and Attitude Research*, **4**, 77–83 (1950).

Young, P. V., *Interviewing in Social Work: A Sociological Analysis*, McGraw-Hill, New York, 1935.

Young, Pauline, *Interviewing in Social Work*, McGraw-Hill, 1935.

Index

Acceptance in the therapeutic relationship, 72
Aggression, 42
Ambivalence in medical interview, 259
American Jewish Committee, Department of Scientific Research, 188
American Psychological Association, 89
Attitude change to eliminate bias, 200, 201
Attitude scales, 160
Attitudes, 39 ff.
  and closed questions, 136, 137
  and perceptions, 153
  as predispositions to behavior, 185
  as sources of bias, 185, 186
  conscious and unconscious, 152, 153
  definition of, 39
  true value of, 173, 175

Background characteristics, and perceptions, 182
  and psychological characteristics, 181, 182
  bias in, 180–183, 193–195
  control of, 197–199
  cues from, 182
  effects of, 197, 198

Baker, Kenneth H., 184
Bancroft, Gertrude, 120
Barriers to communication in supervisor-subordinate interview, 317
Barron, Margaret, 238
Bavelas, Alex, 235, 237
Behavior, as a resultant of forces, 30
  attitudinal basis of, 39
  duality of, 28, 29
  emotional aspects of, 26
  evaluative, 8
  field theoretical approach to, 30
  Freudian approach to, 28
  principles of, 35
  psychoanalytic approach to, 28
  rational aspects of, 24–26
Bender-Gestalt, 156
Bias, and behavioral factors, 186, 187–193
  and inappropriate motivation, 192
  and interaction, 195, 196
  and interview content, 185
  and interviewer attitudes, 183, 184
  and interviewer expectations, 184
  and lack of sensitivity to respondent, 192

Leading questions (*Continued*)
due to interviewer-respondent relationship, 128
Legal interview, example of, 78
probing method in, 226, 230
Level of information and type of question, 135, 136
Levit, Grace, 238
Lewin, Kurt, 30
Likert, Rensis, 160

Manifest content in personnel interview, 247
Marks, Eli, 178
Martin, Clyde, 178
Mauldin, W. Parker, 178
Measurement, assumptions of, 171
bias in, 169
error in, 168 ff.
in medicine, 169, 170
in the interview, 167, 168
in the questionnaire, 167
random error in, 168, 169
true value and, 171 ff.
Medical diagnostic interview, 257
Medical interview, ambivalence in, 259
biased questions in, 276
development of objectives for, 100
doctor's role in, 52
inhibiting forces in, 52, 283
introduction in, 88
measurement error in, 169, 170
motivational forces in, 57
positive forces in, 52
probing methods in, 206, 211, 225, 226, 261
psychological forces in, 52
Memory, 43–45
definition of, 44
failure of, 9
repression, 43
Moore, Bruce, 97
Moreno, J. L., 237
Motivating respondent, errors in, 191–193
Motivation, 32
and bias, 192
and closed questions, 138, 139
and inadequate response, 218, 219
and probing methods, 208
and social norms, 48

Motivation (*Continued*)
duality of, 28 ff.
emotional aspects of, 26
extrinsic, 45, 46
field theoretical approach to, 31
in medical interview, 57
inappropriate, 192
instability of, 53, 54
intrinsic, 46, 70
potential source of bias, 187
principles of, 34
problems of, 6
rational aspects of, 24–26
see also Respondent motivation
Motive, attitudinal components of, 39
definition of, 33
Mowrer, O. Hobart, 72, 73
Multiple questions, and objectives, 157
and open questions, 158
attitudes and beliefs, 157, 158
use of, 156–158
Myers, Robert J., 177

Need, definition of, 33
Needs and behavior, 32
Neely, Twila, 177
Nondirective techniques in client-centered therapy, 208–210
Nonresponse, 217

Objectives, and closed questions, 132
and open questions, 132
and true value, 175
formulation of, 92 ff.
sources of, 98
Observational interviews, 240, 241
Office of Strategic Services, 175
Open question, definition of, 131
Open questions, 108
and interview objectives, 132 ff.
and level of information, 135, 136
and respondent's attitudes, 136, 137
appropriate uses of, 134, 137, 138
motivating power of, 138, 139
strengths and weaknesses of, 133, 134
Opening questions, 162
Order of topics, and frame of reference, 162
criteria for, 162, 163